I WILL LEAD YOU ALONG

The Life of

Henry B. Eyring

I WILL LEAD YOU ALONG

The Life of

Henry B. Eyring

ROBERT I. EATON AND HENRY J. EYRING

DESERET
BOOK

Photo Credits

Page 49 Special Collections Dept., J. Willard Marriott Library, University of Utah

Page 66 U.S. Navy National Museum of Naval Aviation/Public Domain

Page 73 © Jorge Salcedo/Shutterstock.com

Page 77 © Romakoma/Shutterstock.com

Page 140 © Bettmann/Corbis /AP Images

Page 333 courtesy of John Gibby

Pages 351, 398 courtesy of Brigham Young University

Pages 176, 179, 186, 192, 196, 240, 264, 276, 279 courtesy of Brigham Young University–Idaho

Pages 42, 55, 139, 167, 198, 211, 220, 290, 293, 295, 306, 326, 356, 360, 367, 383, 415, 428, 444, 469, 474, 497 © Intellectual Reserve, Inc.

Page 450 by Jeffrey D. Allred/*Deseret News*

Page 463 by Jeffrey D. Allred/*Deseret News*

Artifacts and paintings photographed by John Luke

All other photos courtesy of the Eyring Family

Library of Congress Cataloging-in-Publication Data

(CIP data on file)

ISBN 978-1-60907-783-9

Printed in the United States of America
Publishers Printing, Salt Lake City, UT

10   9   8   7   6   5   4   3   2   1

CONTENTS

CONTENTS

INTRODUCTION

Ye are little children,
And ye have not as yet understood
How great blessings the Father hath in his own hands
And prepared for you;
And ye cannot bear all things now;
Nevertheless, be of good cheer,
For I will lead you along.
—DOCTRINE AND COVENANTS 78:17–18

When Hal Eyring was a small boy living in Princeton, New Jersey, he had a sweet, unforgettable dream. He found himself walking through a field of lush grass, bathed in sunshine. He didn't know where he was going, but he felt great peace and confidence. The feeling came from a light, silken rope around his neck and shoulders. He couldn't see the figure holding the other end of the rope, walking to his side and slightly behind him. But he sensed that it was the Savior.

> Behold, I will go before you and be your rearward; and I will be in your midst, and you shall not be confounded.
> —DOCTRINE AND COVENANTS 49:27

That feeling of being lovingly guided toward happiness has stayed with Hal, buoying him in the face of uncertainty and trials. For the past fifty years, the feeling has been embodied in his eternal companion, Kathleen Johnson Eyring. She has walked with him, hewing to the Savior's path. Both of them have looked to Him as their guide.

This book provides glimpses of Hal and Kathy's walk through life. Much of the story is told in Hal's own words, written as he went along. Beginning with an impression received in 1970, when he and Kathy were the parents of three young boys, he made a daily record of his activities. Most entries comprise just a paragraph. But some are much longer, and all are written in a succinct, candid style. He describes both what he and his family did and also how he felt about his personal performance. His journal is a window not only into his past but also into his struggle to be a better man.

Throughout this book, these journal entries are reproduced in a typeface similar to the one on the typewriter Hal used when he originally recorded the journals. Here's a sample entry, which describes a day devoted to sons Henry, Stuart, and Matthew, and their cousin Mark Johnson.

I hope a day spent with boys somehow matters more eternally than it seems to at the end of it. My bones and head ache. And as nearly as an outsider could tell the sum total of the day is Matthew's wooden steam engine, two pieces of wood he glued together and which he calls his airplane, an amphibian airplane model Henry and I built, a racing car I made with Stuart, and a speedboat created by Mark and me. That's it. No spiritual study. No physical recreation. No professional development. Just me and boys and scraps of wood. And I've got a feeling that's the best of days. Maybe that's what eternal life is about: Boys creating themselves by shaping some wood into a vision, and making a Dad happy while they do it. (July 15, 1972)

The discovery of such candidly introspective passages is both inspiring and encouraging. "Here's a fellow," you think, "destined for Churchwide leadership responsibilities, who is apparently being prepared by routine fatherhood. And sometimes it makes his head ache, just like it does mine." The journal shows how a good-but-imperfect man works each day to win divine approval.

Another aspect of the journal that features prominently in this book is an artistic one. From his childhood, Hal had an interest in—and a talent for—drawing. A sketchbook from those childhood years shows his fascination with the sort of things that were interesting to a young boy of his era: cowboys and soldiers and the like.

Hal rediscovered and honed the talent as an adult, when in the early 1970s he began to include sketches in his journal. As he explained in 1975: "I carry a sketch pad around and illustrate things that I see. My sketches are not lovely, but the work is interesting to my family. At

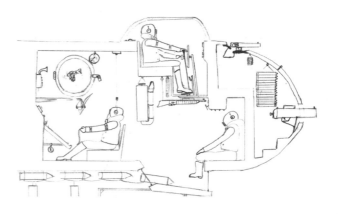

the end of the year, I paste these sketches in my daily journal, Xerox it, have it bound, and give copies to my children. I didn't put any sketches in the journal in 1973, and one of my little sons asked, 'Where are the pictures?' When I said there weren't any, just words, he said, 'Oh.' The disappointment was there. The pictures grab him now; later, I hope the words will."[1]

Just as they appeared in the margins of Hal's journals, a number of those sketches are reproduced in the margins of this book. The ghosted-back sketch that accompanies the chapter openings is typical, depicting the tennis facility where Hal and Kathy played during a business-sponsored trip to the exclusive (and out of his personal price range) Greenbrier resort in West Virginia.

Our walk with Hal generally proceeds chronologically, though each

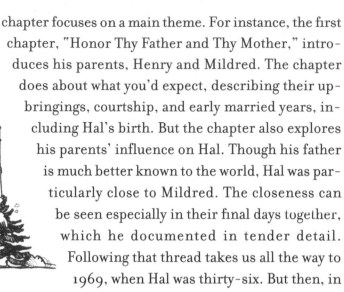

chapter focuses on a main theme. For instance, the first chapter, "Honor Thy Father and Thy Mother," introduces his parents, Henry and Mildred. The chapter does about what you'd expect, describing their upbringings, courtship, and early married years, including Hal's birth. But the chapter also explores his parents' influence on Hal. Though his father is much better known to the world, Hal was particularly close to Mildred. The closeness can be seen especially in their final days together, which he documented in tender detail. Following that thread takes us all the way to 1969, when Hal was thirty-six. But then, in the succeeding chapter, we go back to his youth and begin moving forward in time again.

Some chapters draw more heavily from certain sources than others. For example, Hal's journal features prominently in the middle chapters. That's because he kept the journal most consistently from 1970 to the early 1990s. After that, he shifted his focus to a family newsletter that his young daughters, Elizabeth and Mary, helped him publish and share with their older brothers, who had left home. Thus, earlier and later chapters draw personal reminisces more from Hal's talks.

> I never wore a ring before Kathy gave me my wedding ring. Its being on my finger still comes as a surprise. I always smile inwardly when I see it. It brings again the feeling of delight that I should ever know, let alone marry, Kathy for time and eternity.
>
> —JOURNAL, MARCH 15, 1974

In addition to Hal's writings, we encounter quotes from him and from others. Many of these appear as "call-outs" from the text. When a journal entry appears this way, the date is listed below the quote.

By contrast, when the quote comes from one of the interviews Hal gave for this book, or from one of his talks—as in a reference to an ornamental box he built for Kathy to symbolize their mutual dependence in qualifying for eternal life—the date of the talk or interview is given; the full citation for material quoted from talks appears in endnotes.

If the source of the quote is any other person interviewed for the book, his or her name appears. Usually it will be someone recognizable either as a public figure or a character already encountered in the text, such as Hal's fellow Harvard Business School graduate and close friend Roger Sant.

Now, with that bit of explanation out of the way, it's time to start our walk with Hal Eyring.

On the lid I carved our family monogram. On the front I placed two panels. On one panel I carved my initial, and my wife's initial on the other. The box can only be unlocked by using two different keys, one to open the lock by my initial and the other the lock by my wife's initial.
—TALK, DECEMBER 2, 2012[2]

Kathy may be more spiritual than Hal is.
—ROGER SANT[3]

nephew, Mark, sometime last week, forced her out of
our double's match this morning; within an hour she'd
sent a replacement, so I played six sets. Result: I
soaked my elbow in a tub of hot water propped on the
table in the breakfast room at grandpa's, while I watched
the boys with the boys. Annette served the whole

1

HONOR THY FATHER
AND THY MOTHER

Wherefore, worship the Lord thy God,
And honor thy father and thy mother,
That thy days may be long
In the land which the Lord thy God shall give thee.
—1 NEPHI 17:55

Henry Bennion Eyring was born on May 31, 1933, in Princeton,
New Jersey. Exactly five months earlier, his father, Henry, a
thirty-two-year-old chemist at Princeton University, had won a national "best-paper" award that would mark the beginning of his rise to
world renown. The $1,000 prize that came with the award amounted to
nearly two years' rent for their two-bedroom apartment, which comprised just the first floor of a small house. But Dr. Eyring and his wife,
Mildred Bennion Eyring, gave no thought to using this bounty to move
into a home of their own. It was the low point of the Great Depression,
and they were glad simply to have employment and two bedrooms, one
for themselves and another for newborn Henry Bennion and his older
brother, Ted.

The new baby's name was rich in heritage, the combination of a father's first name and a mother's family name. Yet from the start it was
doomed to get little use. The boy's mother didn't like the name *Henry*.
"I've never thought it was a pleasing-sounding word—nor beautiful to

look at," Mildred would confide in her autobiography thirty-five years later, recalling that she and her husband argued for several days over the matter. "But I finally had to compromise. I agreed the boy could be officially christened Henry—but he would be called Hal."[1] Mildred contended that a name should uniquely fit a child rather than be given in an attempt to honor a progenitor. "The family name is sufficient to tie him to the group," she reasoned.[2]

As this naming episode suggests, Mildred and her husband were equally matched in drive and intellect. Little Hal was born to two teachers, westerners who had happened to meet at the University of Wisconsin in 1927. Henry was teaching chemistry and performing post-doctoral research there, having completed his PhD the spring before at the University of California at Berkeley. Mildred was doing graduate studies, on leave from the women's physical education department at the University of Utah, where she had been serving as chair.

> My brothers and I thought Mother was smarter than Dad, and we knew that he was world famous.
> —2008 INTERVIEW[3]

In addition to being among the tiny fraction of Americans pursuing higher education beyond the bachelor's level at the time, Henry and Mildred had other things in common. Both had been raised on small farms, on which their families struggled to subsist. Henry was a refugee from the Mexican Revolution, driven from a prosperous ranch in the Mormon colonies as an eleven-year-old boy and resettled on a hardscrabble farm in the southeastern Arizona desert. The eldest son in a polygamous family of sixteen children, he was working nights as a janitor and sending money home to his father when he and Mildred met in Wisconsin; his financial contributions, made throughout eight years as a university student and well into his career as a professor, kept the family farming operation out of foreclosure.

Mildred's family, the Bennions, worked much more hospitable ground in the central Salt Lake Valley. Still, the Bennion operation was small and, like the Eyring farm, debt-laden. Mildred won her father Marcus's gratitude by working alongside her two brothers as though she were one of the boys; like her husband-to-be, she had a particular gift for handling horses and cattle. She also sang and played the piano for her father during his final year of life, when he was bedridden with diabetes. After Marcus's death, when Mildred was just seventeen, she supported her mother much as Henry did his parents, working first as a public school teacher and then at the University of Utah while her younger brother Lett shouldered responsibility for the farming operation.

The rigors of farm life taught both Henry and Mildred to prize education not only for the joy of learning but also for the more stable life it afforded. Even as Henry's professional success brought financial good fortune their parents could only dream of, the couple would remain rooted in their shared traditions of hard work, frugality, and taking nothing for granted.

DIFFERENT PERSONALITIES

Similarities of heritage and experience notwithstanding, Mildred's memories of their first meeting focused on their personality differences. The first time they met, Mildred and Henry squared off over a game that involved throwing rubber rings onto numbered pegs on a board. Henry, surprised by Mildred's athletic skill, failed to conceal his zeal for beating her. She, by contrast, couldn't have cared less about winning. When the party ended, Henry and a colleague offered to walk Mildred and a girlfriend of hers home. As they walked, Henry jockeyed to get Mildred by herself so he could inquire into her background. He

MILDRED AT HIGH SCHOOL GRADUATION

particularly probed for details of her family, education, and church activity. He was pleased to learn of her well-known relatives, including Samuel O. and Adam S. Bennion, both leaders in the Church (and the latter a Berkeley graduate). She could see his obvious disappointment when she admitted to having never heard of any Eyrings.

In addition to noting Henry's competitive drive, Mildred immediately recognized his gregariousness. In this they came from opposite poles. While Henry could make a friend of a stranger in minutes, Mildred was naturally reserved, inclined to share intimate feelings only among a few close girlfriends. He had grown up as the favored eldest son and ringleader of a giant family of academic overachievers. She had loved the relative isolation and solitude of her wooded girlhood home, with its mailbox a quarter-mile from the house and her elementary school another mile-and-a-half walk beyond that. Mildred's fondest memories were of strolling alone through her family's carefully cultivated fruit trees and flowers. Where Henry could enthusiastically recall the name and vital statistics of a passing acquaintance or the details of a mathematical equation encountered years before, her fondest recollections were reserved for the fragrance of a lilac, the taste of a succulent peach, and the personality of a favorite horse.

> She could have been anything she wanted, but instead she chose to be our mother.
>
> —1995 INTERVIEW[4]

Though Mildred differed in temperament from Henry, people mattered as much to her as they did to her husband. That can be seen in her recollection of the first day of school and her "very pretty young teacher, Lorilla Horne." More than sixty years later, she would recall: "Miss Horne was dressed in a flowered print, pink flowers on white, and wore a wide pink sash. I know now that it was her first day of teaching too, and she was probably more frightened than I was."[5]

Henry and Mildred differed perhaps most markedly in their ambitions and ambitiousness. Henry had always believed—and acted upon—his parents' assurances that he could achieve anything. There had never been a prize to which he aspired that he had not won (though the Nobel Prize, for which he was nominated more than once, ultimately eluded him). Mildred, by contrast, shunned the spotlight and was prone to underrate herself. For her, teaching was a source of financial income and the little personal satisfaction she allowed herself to feel, but never a profession. Ironically, educational leaders readily recognized the capabilities that Mildred doubted in herself—she resisted promotions and declined offers of employment at both Utah Agricultural College (now Utah State University) and Brigham Young University before taking temporary leave to study at Wisconsin.

DIFFERENT FAMILIES

Part of the difference between Henry's outsized ambitions and Mildred's more modest, family-centered ones may have been a function of parenting. Their fathers were similar in many respects. Both were soft-spoken, shy men who preferred the company of horses to people. Though both liked reading and enjoyed learning, each attended Brigham Young Academy for less than a year before returning to his respective family ranch. They also avoided the public eye. Henry's father, Edward Christian Eyring, served faithfully on a high council, but once told his son that he hoped that being a bishop, with its public speaking requirements, wasn't a condition of exaltation.

While Edward Christian Eyring preferred to keep a low public profile, Marcus Bennion, Mildred's father, did so at almost all costs. His uncle and boyhood bishop, Samuel O. Bennion, once made the mistake of telling Marcus that he planned to call on some of the young men in the ward to speak in a meeting that was about to start. Teenaged Marcus immediately ducked out of the building and never went to church again. He encouraged his family in their attendance, and he was generous in his financial contributions. When the members of the ward determined to buy an organ, Marcus urged that it be a good one and gave double the amount asked. "But," as Mildred later observed, "except for attending funerals and a very few ward 'plays' I think he never went inside the meetinghouse."[6]

A more significant difference between the two men than their church attendance was their attitude toward praise. Ed Eyring, though generally quiet, always had a word of encouragement for his eldest son, Henry. They had ridden the range and farmed together from the time Henry could walk, and as his son went away to college, won superlative academic marks, and sent money back home, Ed's admiration and appreciation only grew. While Henry was in Wisconsin, his mother wrote, "Papa says there is only one Henry in this whole wide world. I know he loves you just a little more than anyone else in this whole wide world, and I know father and son were never more devoted on this earth."[7]

Marcus Bennion, by contrast, was sparing in his compliments. Mildred adored him, and he appreciated how she, as the last of four daughters born before two sons finally arrived, willingly joined him in milking cows and other farm chores. But life was hard on Marcus. He developed diabetes in his early thirties, at a time—the turn of the twentieth century—when there was no effective treatment. The condition was worsened by stress attendant to business failure. Marcus and a brother, Edwin, ventured into sheep raising not long before Edwin accepted a call to serve a mission in Holland. While Edwin was away, the price of wool dropped precipitously, forcing the liquidation of the business. Marcus mortgaged his farm to satisfy the outstanding debts and bore the interest payments for the remainder of his life, which ended when he was just forty-two.

In the secluded Bennion home, both Marcus and his wife, soft-spoken Lucy Smith Bennion, had enjoyed reading. They encouraged Mildred in her studies. "It was always taken for granted that the children would go on to school as long as possible," Mildred would remember, "at least as long as they cared to, and they were encouraged to care."[8] But the encouragement to study and achieve was subtle, particularly as it came from Mildred's mother, Lucy. Mildred described her mother's modest ambitions and understated influence this way:

> She was much more concerned (and often worried) about her family than she appeared to be. Her children and home were her primary interest and I appreciate now, much more than I did as a youngster, her feelings about us. . . . Mother was not ambitious for wealth or position. She was content with simple things while making the most of the possibilities. Honor and integrity were her guides. She said very little about such things but somehow managed to let her children know what they could and could not do with her approval. We knew she was right.[9]

Among the Eyrings, meanwhile, education was not just a priority: it was a family cause. The chief proponent was Henry's mother, Caroline Romney Eyring. Caroline taught school for a time at the Juarez Academy in Mexico, and throughout her life she systematically urged her eight children to academic achievement. They rewarded her efforts with six bachelor's degrees, four master's degrees, and three PhDs among them. Henry led the way, with his parents celebrating every achievement. What Mildred saw in their first encounter, a drive to excel in everything from education to throwing rubber rings over wooden pegs, was in Henry's blood and upbringing. He was blessed to find a wife who would temper that competitive ambition—not only in him but in the three sons she would bear.

EDWARD AND CAROLINE EYRING AT THEIR WEDDING

COURTSHIP AND MARRIAGE

Henry was typically methodical about the process of courting Mildred. Learning of her love for the out-of-doors, he bought a canoe, and they spent the spring and early summer of 1928 paddling the waters and strolling the shores of Madison's picturesque Lake Mendota. It was an unusual time for Henry. With no classes to be taught and no major research project under way, he could give Mildred his full attention. But the romantic interlude didn't last. They were married by summer's end, at which time Henry sold the canoe and went back to his research with his typical unwavering focus.

Because of prior professional commitments—he to the University of Wisconsin and she to the University of Utah—they began their first year of married life apart. In addition to feeling an obligation to her university, Mildred wanted to help her widowed mother at home, and she rationalized the separation as being only temporary.

Yet it almost became permanent that winter, when Mildred contracted spinal meningitis. Henry, told by her doctors that she would likely die, came immediately from Wisconsin. He attended lovingly to her during three weeks of hospitalization, feeding her and spending every hour in her room that the hospital staff would allow. She appreciated his sacrifice. Still, even as he served in what he considered the most selfless manner possible, she found it necessary to educate him. She had to explain, for instance, her preference for alternating among the items on the plate, rather than eating one thing at a time, which was his method—all of the vegetable, then all of the meat, then the potato, and so on. She also resented his request for her help in drafting her will. He considered it a matter of simple prudence.

To her doctors' amazement, Mildred recovered. But the recovery process was slow and painful. Shortly after Mildred emerged from the hospital and Henry returned to Madison, they learned that he had won a National Research Foundation fellowship for a year's study in Berlin, then the capital of the scientific world. Mildred's reaction, recorded

May 31, 1984
Thursday

I wrote in the Atherton guest house of the Johnsons, looking down on the trees and drive of our first home. Elizabeth and Mary Kathleen watched me blow out candles on my birthday cake, after a dinner by Trudie. The Holy Ghost helped me teach a Sunday School work

June
Frida

Eliza
the
work
Gary
Los
to h
time
Alto

June
Satu

I to
infla
Mar
com
purple dress, a perfect
match to the beautiful
hair that marks her as
Stuart's and Matthew's
sister. Grandpa Johnson
and I watched Stephanie
dance in a musical.

June 3, 1984
Sunday

Kathy, Elizabeth, and Mary Kathleen were dressed and packed early for our drive from Atherton to the San Jose airport. On the flight home, a stewardess made a bullseye with a glass full of orange juice on my lap. It was so cold and complete a soaking that I laughed for the rest of the trip. I used bags to shield the results as I got us to the car.

View from the poo

MILDRED AND HENRY EYRING AT THE
TIME OF THEIR MARRIAGE

in her autobiography, reveals both her stoic support of her husband and her medical knowledge, the product of teaching women's health classes for many years and also closely monitoring her own treatment in the hospital:

> The doctors had decided that the pain in my back and legs when sitting or standing was due to adhesions that had formed in the spine around the sciatic nerves and that there was nothing to be done but wait for time to allow the scar tissue to soften and stretch. I had tried heat, massage and exercise with no beneficial results. We decided that I could pass the time on the bed in Berlin as well as anywhere and Henry could work as he wanted to do. The doctors predicted it would be a year before I was comfortable, and they were right.[10]

In Germany, Henry made discoveries and established relationships that served as the foundation for a storied scientific career. With the crash of the stock market and the onset of the Great Depression, they were fortunate after the year in Berlin to receive an invitation to return to Berkeley on a one-year appointment. Their first son, Edward Marcus, or "Ted," was born in California. The Eyrings ultimately settled on the other side of the country in Princeton, where Hal arrived two years later.

LITTLE HAL

In addition to provoking debate between his parents about a name, newborn Hal Eyring presented parenting challenges that his older brother, Ted, had not. In Mildred's words:

> Hal was about as different in disposition from Ted as two babies could be. He was a restless, howling wiggler. Ted was still using the crib, so we put Hal in a basket. No matter what position he was placed in, he would kick himself to the end in two thrusts and yell there because his head hit it. . . . I had to fashion a sleeping bag of thin muslin to sort of tie him down so he would not kick the covers off. He never learned to lie quietly. His bed has

always had to be made up each day "from scratch." His wiggling was the chief bone of contention between him and Ted when they slept on a double-deck bed for about three years. It was a great relief to both of them when we finally were able to give them separate rooms—which was not until they were ten and eight years old.[11]

BABY HAL WITH HIS AUNT IVY

For the first two months of Hal's life, Mildred's older sister Ivy, visiting from Utah, cared for him day and night. As in the case of Henry's feeding her at the hospital, Mildred appreciated the help but disapproved of the methods. "It seemed to me that Ivy was really spoiling him terribly," she later recalled, "and I was very pleasantly surprised when it took only about three days after she had gone for him to learn to go to sleep when he was put down without being rocked to sleep as she had done it."[12]

Mildred applied this discovery about baby discipline with her third and last child, Harden, who was born in Princeton when Hal was six. By that time, Mildred, five years her husband's senior, was forty-three. Ivy couldn't be there to help as she had with Hal, but Henry attempted to provide a similarly high level of coddling, again to Mildred's disdain:

> Harden was a bonus baby and always a joy. Henry was a bit daffy over our good fortune and did his best to spoil the baby. Henry would not let the baby cry himself to sleep at 6 p.m. and so would hold him from 6 to 10 p.m. while I slept. That lasted only until I felt strong and fit again, and then I became the

disciplinarian for father and son, and, as with Hal, it took only a few days for the baby to learn what was expected of him.[13]

TWO PARENTING STYLES

Henry and Mildred's personality differences came out strongly in their approaches to parenting. Though both held high expectations for their three sons, the word *expectation* had a literal meaning for Henry: he naturally expected his sons to succeed, as though their success were already assured.

Henry knew from experience that success had a price, and he taught his boys to work hard. When his second son was a college student majoring in physics, Henry warned, "Hal, you'll never amount to anything unless you learn to work until your ears ring." But Henry taught the importance of work and other character traits more by example than by exhortation. He was forgiving and inclined to encourage through praise, as his own parents had been. His motto in giving feedback was, "Life will knock them down; I try to build them up."

> **My father thought I was perfect.**
> —2008 INTERVIEW[14]

Consistent with this motto, Henry took his sons' academic and athletic successes as validation of the boys' greatness, while largely overlooking their failures. When teenaged Ted and Hal used a home painting kit to improve the appearance of the family's old '37 Ford, Henry made no complaint about the swirls and streaks their mitts made in the blue paint they had chosen. He drove the car until it stopped running years later, unconcerned for its appearance and without any sign of chagrin for his sons' failed beautification efforts.

Youngest son Harden appreciated his father's generous reaction to another auto-related incident. As a thirteen-year-old, he and two friends took the family car (a new one) joyriding while his mother was out of the house and his father was traveling on scientific business.

Returning home after a successful tour of the neighborhood, Harden drove the vehicle into the corner of the family's living room, damaging both the car and the house's brick exterior. Mildred responded by garnishing his paper-route wages until the cost of the damage, $100, had been covered. She also made Harden call his father.

Henry's response pleasantly surprised his shaken son. Rather than lecturing, Henry told Harden a story of one of his own childhood mistakes. At thirteen, Henry and a friend had taken a giant buffalo gun from the fireplace mantel in the Eyring family home in Arizona. Waving it in jest at a neighborhood boy walking by the house, Henry had inadvertently pulled the trigger. He had narrowly missed killing the terrified fellow. Young Harden recognized that the telling of this story signaled his father's empathy and recognition that the necessary lesson had already been learned.

Hal felt that empathy many times, including once after a sacrament meeting he had struggled to enjoy. In 1988, at a fireside at Brigham Young University, he told the story of that tedious meeting and his father's understanding response:

> Years ago I was sitting in a sacrament meeting with my father. He seemed to be enjoying what I thought was a terrible talk. I watched my father, and to my amazement, his face was beaming as the speaker droned on. I kept stealing looks back at him, and sure enough, through the whole thing he had this beatific smile.
>
> Our home was near enough to the ward that we walked home. I remember walking with my father on the shoulder of the road that wasn't paved. I kicked a stone ahead of me as I plotted what I would do next. I finally got up enough courage to ask him what he thought of the meeting. He said it was wonderful.
>
> Now I really had a problem. My father had a wonderful sense of humor, but you didn't want to push it too far. I was puzzled. I was

trying to summon up enough courage to ask him how I could have such a different opinion of that meeting and that speaker.

Like all good fathers, he must have read my mind, because he started to laugh. He said: "Hal, let me tell you something. Since I was a very young man, I have taught myself to do something in a church meeting. When the speaker begins, I listen carefully and ask myself what it is he is trying to say. Then once I think I know what he is trying to accomplish, I give myself a sermon on that subject." He let that sink in for a moment as we walked along. Then, with that special self-deprecating chuckle of his, he said, "Hal, since then I have never been to a bad meeting."[15]

"GETTING HER APPROVAL WAS A RARE THING"

Mildred's philosophy of nurturing was dramatically different from her husband's, almost the polar opposite. She summarized it in a talk given to the women of the Church in 1961. Speaking as a member of the Relief Society general board, she said:

> There is an old Chinese proverb which reads, "He who tells me of my faults is my teacher; he who tells me of my virtues does me harm." Perhaps that is drastic, but it is true. We must recognize our faults if we are to correct them, and praise can be harmful. Today I shall not praise our virtues, but rather I shall ask that we all appraise ourselves and perhaps recognize some of our weaknesses. I am speaking of myself as I speak to you.[16]

Mildred was, in fact, as hard on herself as she was on anyone else, including her sons. Reflecting on her own life at a time when all three boys had completed doctoral degrees and were soon to be called as bishops, she wrote, "My only occupations have been teaching and housekeeping, and I'm not sure I've been really successful in either one. It is hard to measure success in these fields."[17]

Mildred's stoicism could be seen especially in the final years of life, as her health failed. Cancer and fibrosis required one surgery after another. Though suffering horribly, she wrote about her ordeal in truly clinical terms:

The operation I was waiting for when I last wrote was a dilly—lasted eight hours. There seems to be no record of a similar one anywhere, so I can claim to be unique in one thing. Dr. Russell Nelson has had a ten-minute movie in color made of the procedure—cut from the films taken during the surgery. . . . It is really very interesting to see one's heart and lungs working and the surgeons' hands working to get the fibrosis out. . . . Now I'm taking different drugs in addition to old ones. So far we have failed to find the magic formula. It is an interesting mystery story to study (but not to be the chief character in).[19]

> Mildred was a powerful Latter-day Saint. A powerful Latter-day Saint is a thinking Latter-day Saint, one who reasons well, one who synthesizes data well.
>
> —ELDER RUSSELL M. NELSON[18]

Throughout their lives, Henry and the boys got similarly clinical feedback from Mildred. She referred to her husband's award-winning work at Princeton as "very satisfactory."[20] Belle Spafford, the general Relief Society president who called Mildred to what became an eighteen-year term on her board, remembered the difficulty of complimenting Mildred on Henry's success:

At one time when I called to the attention of the Board, as I did from time to time, a special recognition he had been given, she dropped her eyes in modesty. Then I said to her, "How many honorary doctorates and national and international citations has he received?" She answered simply, "Quite a few." I persisted, "You must be very proud of him." In a soft-toned voice; almost as if speaking to herself, she replied with genuine sincerity: "Of course, I am."[21]

One of the greatest compliments Hal ever received from his mother involved no words. It was on the day of his graduation with an

MBA degree from the Harvard Business School in 1959. Mildred attended the graduation ceremony in Boston and had her arm in his as he was handed his diploma on the lawn of the school's stately quad. The dean, Stanley Poole, remarked, "Congratulations, Mr. Eyring. It is always a pleasure to award a degree with distinction." Mildred said nothing, but she squeezed her son's elbow.

> She had very high standards for herself, and she communicated that in the way she treated you. She was not cruel, but you knew that getting her approval was a rare thing.
>
> —2008 INTERVIEW[22]

Hal and his brothers recognized their mother's general approval of them, and they understood her reason for not showing it much. Like her mother, Lucy Smith Bennion, Mildred found her guides in honor and integrity, and she worried that Henry's unreserved praise might be bad for the boys, tempting them to pride.

A FRANK TEACHER

Throughout her life, Mildred taught her loved ones and associates according to her own maxim, "He who tells me of my faults is my teacher." Belle Spafford was one of many associates who appreciated Mildred's unwavering candor. "In all the years that I have been associated with her," Belle would say at Mildred's funeral, "I have never seen one shred of pretense." She went on:

> Personally, I have liked her straightforwardness. I have liked her viewpoints and the original thinking which she brought to matters coming before the board. I have appreciated the wisdom of her judgments. Often, in presenting matters of particular importance to the board, I would look at Mildred, in her place in the circle, to ascertain her reaction. I have been greatly strengthened when her expression indicated agreement or support. Thus, I valued her opinion. She was a smart woman.
>
> From time to time she would write me a personal letter, in which she would analyze a program or procedure that was under

consideration and offer suggestions. These, invariably, revealed insight and independent thinking, and they were stimulating and valued. The last time I called at her home she said, "I'm going to write you another letter."

"Fine," I said, "what is it to be about?"

"Just an idea that I want to try out on you," she replied.[23]

President Spafford never received the promised letter. Mildred died in the summer of 1969 before it could be written. In her final days she was occupied with another missive, one for Elder Mark E. Petersen of the Church's Quorum of the Twelve. The subject was sex education. Mildred wrote to tell Elder Petersen she agreed with the Church's position that "sex education should be carried on in the home by parents." "However," she argued, "I see a very real problem in this situation. How can parents teach their children facts which they do not know how to teach?" She urged the creation of a kind of textbook, with questions and problems to engage the reader, to be used under the direction of parents in the home. "Much of my concern," she concluded, "has been aroused by my conversations with my three bishop sons, all of whom are troubled by the problems in their wards which point up the need for more help in this field."[24]

MILDRED'S LAST LESSONS

Hal was with his mother in those final days, when she was still more concerned about the needs of the Church than about her own imminent passing. Sensing that the end was near, he had come from California, where he was a professor at Stanford University and bishop of the Stanford single student ward. She had just completed a major project, the editing and publication of the journal of her paternal grandfather, John Bennion. Mother and son spent two days together in her bedroom, talking privately as they had done when Hal was a student at the nearby University of Utah. After dates he would come to that room and, while his father slumbered, chat with his mother into the early morning hours.

During this visit, Hal had the responsibility of administering medication through a tube placed in his mother's stomach. She was, as he
recorded in his journal, "fairly patient" with his clumsiness:

> I say fairly because Mother never could tolerate ineptitude,
> and at the start I was clearly inept. She had the effect on me
> that she always had of making me proud when I got better.
> In fact, at the end of my stay, I told her with some pride how
> much I felt I'd improved, and she congratulated me mildly.
> (June 16, 1969)

In addition to discussing the letter to Elder Petersen, they talked
about the presiding authorities of the Church, among whom they had
several relatives. Those included Henry's brother-in-law Spencer W.
Kimball and cousin Marion G. Romney, both of whom would serve in
the Church's First Presidency. There was also Mildred's cousin Adam
S. Bennion, a deceased Apostle. Mildred stated her opinion that the
Brethren had for years been a little slow in adopting some of the ideas
that she and other members of the general board of the Relief Society
had offered up. She surprised Hal with her understanding and empathy, suggesting that, successful and great as these men were, they
were sincerely humble about their abilities and prone to worry about
not being up to the tasks that the Lord had given them. She expressed
confidence that the Lord was running the Church, notwithstanding the
human side of the prophets through whom He worked. She also expressed implicit approval of her sons, whose success seemed to be a
source of confidence for her as she prepared to enter the next life, as
Hal recorded in his journal:

> Although she never said so, it was clear from the way she
> talked that she had great satisfaction in the fact that all of her
> sons were active bishops. We talked some about how it was that
> she had been so successful. In my case, she indicated by patting
> on the side of the bed she was lying on how important she
> thought the talks that we had had at two in the morning or

one in the morning had been. She said one of the reasons was that we could always talk, and said, "I always knew you'd come in to see me when you came home." She had a note of warmth in her voice that indicated that those had been special times to her, and had given her great confidence. (June 16, 1969)

In typical fashion, Mildred took charge as their two-day visit came to a close. Though they both sensed that it would be their final opportunity to talk in this life, she prevailed upon him to take an earlier flight home so as to be well-rested for a professional presentation he would make the next day. Hal held her hand and knelt beside the bed with the intent to pray, but he felt his throat swelling and feared that his voice might break. She matter-of-factly suggested that he not kiss her, as she had self-diagnosed an infection that she didn't want him to catch. The moment for prayer passed.

> You may have been blessed by a mother as I was for whom the plan of salvation was reality. More than once I complained about some difficulty in my school days. Her answer, given in a matter-of-fact tone, was, "Hal, what else did you expect? Life is a test." She knew that because I understood the plan, her statement of the obvious would give me hope, not discouragement.
> —TALK, OCTOBER 21, 1997[25]

As he was leaving, Hal paused in the doorway. "Mother," he asked, smiling, "don't you have any more criticism for me?"

"No, Hal," she replied with a smile of her own. "You're not that bad."

"I'll see you soon," he said.

"Yes, dear."

Mildred slipped into a coma two days later and was gone in a little over a week. The quiet dignity with which she endured her final trial left no question in Hal's mind that for his mother "the plan of salvation was reality." As he would explain in a BYU devotional address:

> She knew and I knew that the greater the test the greater the compliment from a loving Heavenly Father. She died after a decade of suffering with cancer. At her funeral, President Kimball said something like this, "Some of you may wonder what great

sins Mildred committed to explain her having to endure such suffering. It had nothing to do with sin. It was that her Heavenly Father wanted to polish her a little more."

I remember as I sat there at the time wondering what trials might lie ahead for me if a woman that good could be blessed by that much hard polishing.[26]

LASTING INFLUENCES

Throughout Hal's life, the expectations of his parents would motivate him, each in their unique way. From the pulpit he would tend to speak more of his well-known father. He admired Henry's childlike faith and willingness to testify of the truth in any setting, including scientific conferences where few people shared his faith. In his father Hal saw the effects of "a humility which is energizing, not innervating." That would allow him to explain the apparent paradox of the divine injunctions to be both wise and humble:

> You are to pursue educational excellence while avoiding pride, the great spiritual destroyer. Most people would question whether it is possible to pursue excellence in anything without feeling some measure of pride. . . . I will tell you that not only can you pursue educational excellence and humility at the same time to avoid spiritual danger but that the way to humility is also the doorway to educational excellence.[27]

Hal admired and learned vital lessons from both of his parents. But if he leaned by temperament toward one or the other, it may have been Mildred. The first reminiscence Hal shared with the Church at large was not about his famous father, but about his mother. A year after her death, in 1970, he was asked to write an article describing her parental influence for *The Instructor*, the magazine of the Sunday School organization. He recounted his last discussion with her in an article titled, "Faith in Mother's Discipline." The article began, "The

May 31, 1984
Thursday

I wrote in the Atherton guest house of the Johnsons, looking down on the trees and drive of our first home. Elizabeth and Mary Kathleen watched me blow out candles on my birthday ca... dinner by ... Holy Ghost ... teach a Su... workshop in ...

June 1, 1984
Friday

Elizabeth an... the pool ... worked on a ... Gary came ... Los Angeles ... to hear me ... time to y... Altos.

June 2, 198...
Saturday

I towed Eli... inflated, ... Mary Ka... complime... purple dres... match to ... hair that ... Stuart's an... sister. Gra... and I watched Stephanie dance in a musical.

June 3, 1984
Sunday

MILDRED AND HENRY SHORTLY
BEFORE MILDRED'S DEATH

Kathy, Elizabeth, and Mary Kathleen were dressed and packed early for our drive from Atherton to the San Jose airport. On the flight home, a stewardess made a bullseye with a glass full of orange juice on my lap. It was so cold and complete a soaking that I laughed for the rest of the trip. I used bags to shield the results as I got us to the car.

last time I talked with my mother I asked for her disapproval. I felt let down," he said, "not to get her criticism." He explained:

Why should anyone want to be corrected? Like most people I feel a hot flush come up my neck, right behind the ears, whenever someone tries to straighten me out, be it a priesthood leader or my son. And yet Mother's discipline, dealt out in terms as firm as I've ever heard, seldom brought that flash of rebellion I still feel when someone else corrects me. Why?

This is my Mother's birthday today. I thought of her. In my mind she is tall and strong, yet kind. The thought of her makes me sit taller, reach a little higher. She always did that for me. A great woman, and my friend.

—JOURNAL, MAY 23, 1972

In answering his own question, Hal cited two of his mother's outstanding qualities. "First, she knew what she was talking about. I was just sure she knew what would make me unhappy. Second, I knew that Mother put my welfare ahead of her own."

Mother wasn't perfect, but she seemed perfect to me in one thing. You could believe in her discipline. That fact made you accept it—in fact, almost seek it. When she said you were wrong it had a special meaning. It was not just that you had broken her rules or disappointed her. You knew that you had done something that would hurt you unless you repented. Any discipline that works must rest squarely on that faith. Discipline without that faith creates rebellion, and then the need for more discipline, in a never-ending cycle.

Children do not expect perfection. But they must believe that discipline comes from real understanding and real unselfishness, at least most of the time. A child can count on that best when he knows his parents accept discipline themselves.

By coincidence, Hal was up from California, visiting his father in Salt Lake City, when he wrote the *Instructor* article. He stayed in his boyhood room, down in the basement of the family home. He ended the article with these lines:

HAL AND MILDRED DURING HER LAST VISIT TO HIS HOME IN CALIFORNIA

I have just looked into that room where Mother and I had our last talk. There are three pictures grouped on the wall, all of Jesus. Mother never talked much about the Savior. But I felt she knew Him. That made it easier to give her the benefit of the doubt. Maybe she did not always know what was best, and maybe she did not always put me ahead of herself. But I do not remember a time when I was willing to take a chance on it. I knew too well where she got both her understanding and her compassion.

I wish she had corrected me one more time.[28]

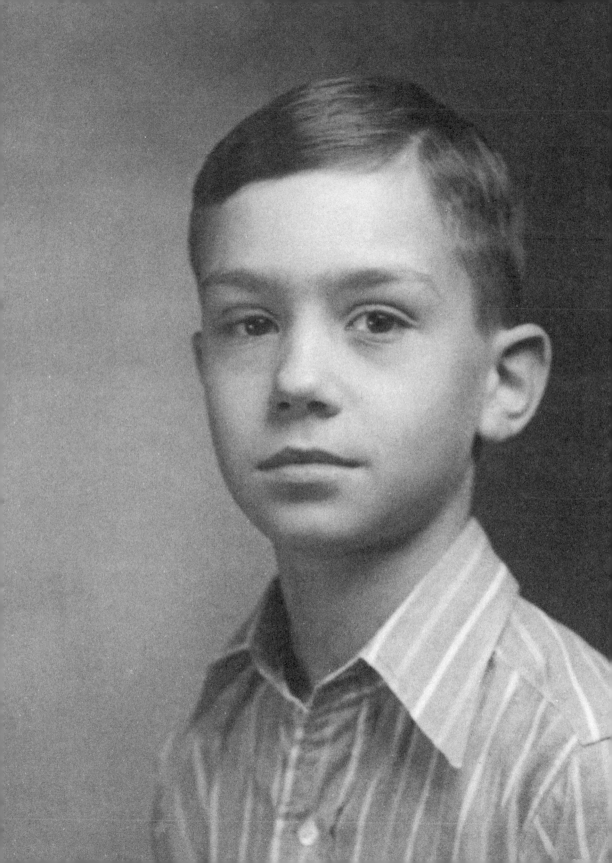

nephew, Mark, sometime last week, forced her out of
our double's match this morning; within an hour she'd
sent a replacement, so I played six sets. Result: I
soaked my elbow in a tub of hot water propped on the
table   the breakfast room at grandpa's, while I watched
the b   with the boys. Annette served the whole

2

ASK GOD IF THESE THINGS ARE NOT TRUE

And when ye shall receive
  these things,
I would exhort you that ye would
  ask God, the Eternal Father,
In the name of Christ,
If these things are not true;

And if ye shall ask with a sincere
  heart, with real intent,
Having faith in Christ,
He will manifest the truth of it
  unto you,
By the power of the Holy Ghost.

—MORONI 10:4

Young Hal Eyring was blessed by a family legacy of testimony. His parents never wavered in their conviction that The Church of Jesus Christ of Latter-day Saints was established through Joseph Smith in exactly the way he testified. Hal's father, Henry, had believed the testimony of Joseph Smith shared by *his* father, Ed, on the day before he left for college. Henry told the story this way:

It was a Friday evening in September, 1919. I had been hauling hay all day in Pima, Arizona. It had been very hot, and we'd been drinking lots of water. On Monday I was going to start classes at the University of Arizona, where I was to study Mining Engineering. In the evening my father, as fathers often do, felt that he'd like to have a last talk with his son. He wanted to be sure I'd stay on the straight and narrow. He said, "Henry, won't you come and sit down? I want to talk to you."

Well, I'd rather do that than pitch hay any time. So, I went over and sat down with him.

"We're pretty good friends, aren't we?"

"Yes," I said, "I think we are."

"Henry we've ridden on the range, and we've farmed together. I think we understand each other. Well, I want to say this to you: I'm convinced that the Lord used the Prophet Joseph Smith to restore His Church. For me that is a reality. I haven't any doubt about it. Now, there are a lot of other matters which are much less clear to me. But in this Church you don't have to believe anything that isn't true. You go over to the University of Arizona and learn everything you can, and whatever is true is part of the gospel. The Lord is actually running this universe. I'm convinced that he inspired the Prophet Joseph Smith. And I want to tell you something else: If you go to the University and are not profane, if you'll live in such a way that you'll feel comfortable in the company of good people, and if you go to church and do the other things that we've always done, I don't worry about your getting away from the Lord.'"[1]

"THE BEST EXPLANATION"

Henry built on this testimony of Joseph Smith throughout his life. In addition to trusting his father implicitly, he could see the logic in Joseph Smith's story of meeting God the Father and Jesus Christ, and of all that happened to him after that First Vision. He often likened Joseph's experience to that of Paul, who saw the Savior on the road to Damascus. In Henry's mind, it simply made sense to believe the stories that Paul and Joseph Smith told, based on what they accomplished in their lives. He was convinced that they had been divinely instructed. He wanted to follow such men because of what they could teach him about his Heavenly Father, with whom he wanted to communicate.

With typical enthusiasm and wit, he explained his view to a group gathered at Brigham Young University:

> What kind of man was Paul? I would say that there are two things about him that are certain. First, he was extremely able. You couldn't do the missionary work and write all those epistles that he did and do all the work that he did without being a first-rate mind. Secondly, the man was himself absolutely convinced of this experience. He may have been wrong. He may have had epilepsy. He may have been crazy as a loon, but I'd like to be crazy the same way.
>
> The Prophet Joseph Smith, I would say, is almost exactly like Paul. I mean, there isn't any other question in my mind about whether he was able—the kind of men that gathered around him and listened to him, and were impressed, and built their whole lives around him; the way the Gospel got on; the tremendous concepts that he had of eternal life and of a pre-existence and a continuing on through the eternities, and this being just a tremendous journey. And he's tremendous. But he also was convinced. Whether you say Joseph Smith saw somebody or he didn't, as far as he was concerned, everything indicates that he was absolutely convinced, just like Paul was convinced. Well, maybe both of them were epileptics. But I don't believe it, and I don't think that's the best explanation. I have to decide for me, but I'm convinced that the best explanation is their explanation.[2]

As a chemist, Henry was a model builder. The atoms he loved to think about are impossible to see at the level that really matters in chemical reactions, that of the electron. In keeping with something called the Heisenberg uncertainty principle, the best a chemist can do is to build models that approximate the behavior of atomic particles. Henry, a gifted mathematician, created a widely used equation, or mathematical model, for predicting that behavior. The model, which he tested in laboratory experiments, ultimately allowed him to "see" atoms and electrons in his mind's eye. Thanks to mathematical calculations and observations of experiments, he could imagine the invisible reality hidden to his natural eyes. The model proved useful not only in his science but in all sorts of practical applications, from

DR. HENRY EYRING DEMONSTRATING
MOLECULAR ENERGY

the production of industrial chemicals to the treating of disease. Henry and those who used the "Eyring equation" could operate confidently in the day-to-day world because of his model of the unseen world.

Henry seems to have taken a similar approach to understanding spiritual realities. Like his father, Ed, he trusted the reports that Paul and Joseph Smith gave of their visions, two great spiritual "experiments" that revealed the nature of Heavenly Father and the Savior. In particular, Henry concluded from the testimonies of Paul and Joseph Smith that he could expect ongoing revelation, including answers to his own prayers. In fact, he had

run his own spiritual experiments and found satisfying evidence that his Heavenly Father was as concerned and close as his earthly father:

> I have actually tried what the Savior said and prayed, and, as far as I'm concerned, have had answers to prayers. And so then that is the same kind of feeling that I would have knowing that I have an earthly father. I've associated with Him and known things about Him. I've gotten things from Him, prayed and had answers to prayers that I am convinced were not just chance. And so then the whole thing, as far as I am concerned, is reality.[3]

Henry concluded that Joseph Smith had not only seen Heavenly Father and the Savior but also received priesthood power. Thus, he felt no concern about the human frailties of either Joseph or his priesthood successors. If they were good enough for God, he reasoned, they were good enough for him. In fact, Henry saw in the imperfections of even the best Church members reason to hope that he could be a contributor in the Lord's kingdom. It was a vision of God's ability to work through imperfect men and women that would later give Hal hope in his ministry. Henry articulated the theory this way:

> I like contradictions. I like a little bit of a mess, and I am glad when one of the brethren says something that I think is little bit foolish, because I think if the Lord can stand him, maybe he can stand me. So that's it, and I think that maybe there's a certain stumbling block that some of us have: we expect other people to be a kind of perfection that we don't even attempt to approach ourselves. We expect the brethren or the bishop or the stake president or the General Authorities to be not human, even. We expect the Lord to just open and shut their mouths, but He doesn't do that—they are human beings; but they're wonderful, and they do better than they would if it weren't for the Lord helping them.[4]

> Clearly, my problem and your problem is to hear the word of God from and through imperfect teachers and leaders. That is your test and mine. And it is our opportunity. . . . God has said that if we are going to make it home again, we must not only hear his voice privately by our own effort, but also through the voice of his servants who, when they speak by the power of the Spirit, speak as if it were his voice.
>
> —TALK, SEPTEMBER 4, 1998[5]

MILDRED'S TESTIMONY OF MORMONISM

Like her husband, Mildred Bennion Eyring gained at an early age an unshakable testimony of the restored gospel of Jesus Christ. It was rooted in memories of her upbringing. Late in her life, she observed:

> Religion has always been more to me than just a "philosophy of life," as many like to term it. It is much warmer, more personal, more deeply motivating than any intellectual philosophy could be. In my early childhood our home was not one that could be called very religious. My parents were not very active in the

Church—but I cannot recall a time when I didn't "say my prayers" before going to bed, and we always asked a blessing on the food. And we children were always expected to attend Sunday School and the other auxiliary meetings. There was no scripture reading or discussions of the scriptures by our parents—but the rules contained in the Ten Commandments were understood and followed. The only work that was done on Sunday was the necessary irrigating when our "water turn" came on that day, and the "chores" which had to be done, so that as we grew up and were drawn into activity in the Church there was no need for any revolutionary changes in our way of living. My "conversion" has been so gradual that I could not pinpoint when it happened. There hasn't been a time in my life when I have doubted the truth of the "Mormon" gospel.[6]

Also like Henry, Mildred seems to have strengthened her childhood faith with study and reasoning in adulthood:

History has always interested me, and the early Church history, Joseph Smith's life, and the Book of Mormon have always intrigued me and satisfied my matter-of-fact mind. To those who say they can accept anything except the miracles, I may not seem to be very matter-of-fact, but when something exists as the Church and the Book of Mormon do and there is only one way to explain their existence, then that explanation is logical even though it appears to be miraculous. The explanation that Joseph Smith gave is the best one that has been given so far, and there have been many attempts to give better ones—none of them, except Joseph's, holds up against the facts.

Mildred likewise shared her husband's view of the leaders of the Church—that their inevitable frailties were no cause for alarm or disbelief:

I'm glad that I'm not required to believe in the infallibility of any human being. My faith in the gospel has never depended on the behavior of people. I know my own weaknesses too well, and observe similar tendencies in others too often to believe that anyone is perfect. But since I believe in a God who is a wise and concerned Father, I'm willing to trust him to guide his sons to whom he has given the responsibilities of leadership as he sees fit. Sometimes they may do things I can't understand, but that doesn't change my relationship to God nor my faith in Him, nor my obligation to behave as I know I should. Free agency is a wonderful gift and a very great responsibility.[7]

HAL'S FEELINGS OF TESTIMONY

In his adulthood, Hal Eyring would often speak of the seeds of his testimony of the gospel. He gave the initial credit to his mother. Writing to her in 1955, while he was serving in the Air Force, he paid her this loving tribute:

> In some subtle way I don't understand, I learned at my Mother's knee that the gospel of Jesus Christ is true, that it had been restored to the earth, and that only serving our Father, through the Church, would bring any sort of happiness. I learned that the most wonderful thing in the world was a home where the gospel was the common bond of love and the way of life.[8]

Though Hal's earliest testimony came from his mother and father, it was a subtly different variety from theirs. Whereas they often expressed their faith in terms of reason, he more typically spoke of feelings. In fact, his parents' greatest contribution to his testimony came not from their words or their reasoning but from the way he felt when he observed them living the gospel.

> I don't remember much of what my parents said about the Holy Ghost, but I remember what I felt when I saw them do the things which brought the Holy Ghost into our home.
>
> —TALK, OCTOBER 5, 2003[9]

Hal's feelings of testimony also grew through reading the scriptures, especially a favorite one written by the Apostle Paul. In 1989, as a member of the Presiding Bishopric, he described his love for a well-known passage from Paul's letter to the Corinthian Saints.

One of my early memories is reading the scriptures in a school room. The law of the land did not yet forbid it, so the Princeton, New Jersey, public schools began each school day with a standard ritual. I can't remember the sequence, but I remember the content. In our classroom, we pledged allegiance to the flag—in unison, standing hand over heart. One student, a different one each school day, read verses he or she had chosen from the Bible, and then we recited aloud together the Lord's Prayer.

So about every twenty-five school days, my turn came to choose the scripture. I always chose the same one, so my classmates must have known what was coming when it was my day. I don't remember when I first heard the words; that is lost in the mists of childhood. But I can recite them to you now, and with them the feelings come back. It happened every time, and it still does:

"Though I speak with the tongues of men and of angels, and have not charity, I am become as sounding brass, or a tinkling cymbal.

"And though I have the gift of prophecy, and understand all mysteries, and all knowledge; and though I have all faith, so that I could remove mountains, and have not charity, I am nothing."
[1 Corinthians 13:1–2]

You remember the rest, through that thirteenth chapter of 1 Corinthians. By the time I read the first few words, the feeling would come back. The feeling was not just that the words were true, but that they were about some better world I wanted with all my heart to live in. For me, the feeling was even more specific, and I knew it did not come from within me. It was that there would or could be some better life, and that it would be in a family I would someday have. In that then-distant future, I would be able to live with people in some better, kinder way, beyond even the best and the kindest world I had known as a boy.

Now, little boys don't talk about such things, not to anyone. You might confide in someone that you wanted to play big league baseball someday. But you wouldn't say that you knew someday you'd have a home where you would feel the way you felt when you heard the thirteenth chapter of 1 Corinthians. So I never talked with anyone about those feelings.[10]

A TESTIMONY OF COVENANTS AND PRIESTHOOD POWER

Though Hal kept his feelings of testimony and faith in the future to himself, they steadily increased. A dramatic change came on the day of his baptism. His parents drove him the forty-five miles from their home in Princeton to Philadelphia, where the Church had completed a beautiful red-brick chapel just three years earlier. The chapel had a baptismal font, as well as a mural portraying Lehi's dream of the tree of life. Hal was impressed by the vivid images of the iron rod and the mists of darkness.

After the simple baptismal service, the Eyrings returned immediately to Princeton. Hal rode in the rear of the car but stood, leaning over the front seat and peering between his parents at the road ahead. A feeling of heavy responsibility settled on him. For several years he had been taught that baptism would make him accountable for his actions. At times, he had twisted that principle, rationalizing that mild indiscretions such as taking a dime from his mother's purse to buy ice cream might be all right for a boy under age eight. Even then

> Baptism is not a way into the Church; it is not a way to join the Church that loves families; it's not a way to join the Church of nice people. It is the thing one seeks when one has a broken heart and a contrite spirit, and enough understanding of the broken law to say, "I need the blessings of baptism. I need to be cleansed."
>
> —TALK, JANUARY 25, 1997[11]

he had felt the weight of that falsehood. But baptism brought the truth home with full force. "Now I'm really responsible," he thought.

Even before his baptism, Hal's appreciation for covenants and priesthood power had been growing. The memory of one youthful experience stayed with him throughout his life. He shared it publicly in his first address as a General Authority, given on Sunday, April 7, 1985. He had been sustained the afternoon before as first counselor to newly called Presiding Bishop Robert D. Hales. On that Sunday in the Salt Lake Tabernacle, he described the uneasiness he had felt since being called as a General Authority, two days before, by President Gordon B. Hinckley:

> Something happened to me yesterday afternoon that I found of great help to me, and it may be of help to you. Since that moment, the fear has gone. It was when Bishop Hales was speaking in conference. He mentioned that we had known each other since boyhood, and as he did a memory was replayed in my mind. It was of a hotel ballroom in New Brunswick, New Jersey. Bishop Hales was likely not there, since he lived in what seemed to us the well-established stake in New York. We were in the New Jersey District, a single district that covered the whole state. The Princeton Branch met in my parents' dining room. Dad was the branch president. Mother was both the pianist and chorister (which is hard to do if you think about it). There was not another family in the branch with children, so my brother Ted was the Aaronic Priesthood, and my brother, Harden, and I were all there were of Primary and junior Sunday School. The congregations were young students who happened to be there . . . and a few older converts—none with spouses that were members.
>
> There was no building, no gym, no stake center, and so we traveled to a hotel ballroom for what must have been a district conference. I was sitting on a folding chair somewhere near the back, next to my mother. I must have been very young because I can remember putting my legs through the back of the chair and sitting aft instead of forward. But then I remember hearing

something—a man's voice from the pulpit. I turned around and looked. I still remember that the speaker was at a rostrum set on wooden risers. There was a tall window behind him. He was the priesthood visitor. I don't know who he was, but he was tall and bald, and he seemed very old to me.

He must have been talking about the Savior or the Prophet Joseph, or both, because that was all that I remember much of hearing in those days. But as he spoke, I knew that what he said came from God and that it was true, and it burned in my heart. That was before scholars told me how hard it was to know. I just knew of certainty—I knew it was true. And when I listened to Bishop Hales yesterday, I knew that what he was saying was from God and that it was true, and then the fear left.[12]

Hal enjoyed a similar testimony-building experience a few years later when, during a summertime visit from New Jersey to Utah, his parents arranged for him to receive his patriarchal blessing. The patriarch, a distant relative, expressed ideas meaningful to Hal in ways that he could not have appreciated no matter how close his relationship.

When I was eleven, my parents dropped me off at the Salt Lake City home of my great-uncle Gaskell Romney. He was a patriarch and, because he was my father's uncle, he could give me, a boy from the mission field, a patriarchal blessing. I don't think he even sat down to visit with me. He didn't know me except as my father's son. He just led me through the house to a room where a recording device was on a table. He sat me down facing a fireplace, put his hands on my head, and began to give first my lineage and then a blessing.

He began to tell me about the home in which I would someday be the father. That's when I opened my eyes. I know the stones in the fireplace were there because I began to stare at them. I wondered, "How can this man know what is only in my heart?" He described in concrete detail what had been only a yearning; but I could recognize it. It was the desire of my heart, that future home and family that I thought was secret. But it was not secret, because God knew.[13]

These early experiences set a pattern in Hal's life: his testimony stemmed from feelings more than reason, and the feelings came from observing the actions and hearing the words of God's servants. That was true as he sat at his mother's knee and as he watched his parents in their Church service. It was also true in a New Brunswick hotel ballroom, where the priesthood visitor might have been tall, bald, and "very old" President Heber J. Grant—or he may have been a less-senior Church authority whose influence was nonetheless powerful on Hal. It was true as he sat before the fireplace of patriarch Gaskell Romney, who miraculously knew the secret desires of Hal's heart. In all of these cases, his testimony of the Church came from the assurance, borne to him by the Holy Ghost, that God's servants were speaking. He saw the Lord's anointed as standing not only on His authority but in His stead.

If you will wait upon the Lord the next time you listen to the General Authorities of the Church, if you will forget about them as human personalities and listen for the Lord's voice, I promise you that you will recognize it in the words spoken by his servants. You will have a quiet assurance that those human beings are called of God and that God honors their calls.

—TALK, SEPTEMBER 30, 1990[14]

TESTIMONY TESTED AND STRENGTHENED

Hal's testimony of the Church and its leaders was tested and strengthened in his teenage years. Growing up so far from the center of the Church brought unique trials but also invaluable blessings. With World War II gas rationing, the Eyrings couldn't travel beyond Princeton for Sunday meetings. Being the only well-established LDS family there, they opened their home for worship services. Mildred became, in her words, "the janitor, organist, class leader, and clerk, besides feeding visitors almost every week."[15] These modest meeting conditions taught Hal a valuable lesson: "I learned then that the

Church is not a building; the Church isn't even a lot of people. I felt close to Heavenly Father and knew that The Church of Jesus Christ of Latter-day Saints is His church; it didn't matter that our little branch met in our dining room."[16]

Among the most regular of the visitors Mildred fed were the full-time missionaries. Particularly during the war, the missionaries who gathered at the Eyring home felt deep gratitude for the love and support they received there. Nearly all of these elders had medical conditions that exempted them from military service but made missionary work difficult; many would have preferred to be healthy and fighting for their country. Hal felt drawn to and inspired by these unusually humble missionaries. At Mildred's funeral, her cousin Howard S. Bennion noted the beneficial effect on Hal and his brothers: "For years the Eyring home in Princeton was the scene of Sunday dinners for happy, hungry missionaries. A by-product of all this devoted Church service and association with missionary life was the making of three good Latter-day Saints out of their three sons."[17]

Princeton, where Hal and his older brother, Ted, were the only Church members in their school, gave Hal ample opportunity to be a kind of missionary himself. Mildred noted how he sought "friendship with the wrong type of boys at Township School, prompted by his feeling that he could help them."[18] In fact, Hal was simply being kind to the boys in their diverse, working-class neighborhood. Mildred and Henry had deliberately avoided "faculty row," the more upscale part of Princeton, where they feared not only the cost of living but also attitudes of privilege. The trade-off, though, was having the boys grow up with playmates whose home lives were gritty. Hal's closest friend was the son of an abusive alcoholic; notwithstanding Hal's friendship, the boy would later serve prison time for murder. Hal's effect on another close friend may have been greater. That boy grew up to be a minister.

As a college town in an otherwise industrial state, Princeton comprised divergent demographic groups. At one pole were the relatively wealthy families of local university professors and stockbrokers who commuted by train to New York City. At the other pole were Italian- and African-Americans, ethnic minorities who experienced much more limited educational and economic opportunities. From these two minority groups arose two large gangs, the Jokers and the Hawks. The Hawks wore black leather jackets, the Jokers dark maroon "slick" jackets. Both gangs had zip guns—homemade contraptions with a wooden handle, a small pipe serving as a gun barrel, a nail wrapped in a rubber band for the hammer, and a real 22-caliber bullet.

Mildred and Henry's decision not to live on faculty row meant that their sons were in the minority in their school. Older, stockier Ted held his own in the fights they inevitably faced, but tall, skinny Hal needed protection. It came not only from Ted but also from an unexpected source. Ten-year-old Hal was befriended by one of the African-American Hawks, a teenager named Tommy Holmes who was one of the gang's biggest, toughest members. Tommy first came to Hal's rescue when several young Hawks had him cornered. "He's my friend," Tommy declared in a voice that instantly ended the confrontation.

> In the middle of that world he was living in, Tommy was good. We always say that you'll be judged by how well you acted with what you had. Tommy was acting awfully well considering the challenges he faced.
>
> —2012 INTERVIEW

From then on, Hal enjoyed Tommy's protection, which was provided with no strings attached. Tommy's inexplicable appearance as a guardian fit a pattern that Hal would recognize throughout his life. He could see the divine power behind Tommy's protection. Hal drew another important lesson from Tommy's friendship: the Lord apparently wasn't limited to using members of the Church to accomplish His purposes.

May 31, 1984
Thursday

I wrote in the Atherton
guest house of the
Johnsons, looking down
on the trees and drive
of our first home.
E l i z a b
Kathleen
blow out
birthday
dinner b
Holy Gh
teach a
workshop

June 1,
Friday

Elizabeth
the poo
worked
Gary ca
Los Ang
to hear
time to
Altos.

June 2,
Saturday

I towed
inflated,
M a r y
compli
purple
match t
hair tha
Stuart's
sister.
and I w
dance in a musical.

June 3, 1984
Sunday

THE EYRING FAMILY IN PRINCETON

Kathy, Elizabeth, and Mary Kathleen were dressed and
packed early for our drive from Atherton to the San Jose
airport. On the flight home, a stewardess made a bullseye
with a glass full of orange juice on my lap. It was so cold
and complete a soaking that I laughed for the rest of the
trip. I used bags to shield the results as I got us to the car.

A DIFFICULT MOVE

Ironically, the family's move to Utah when Hal was thirteen provided tests of his faith as stern as Princeton had. Hal initially found life in Utah unpleasant. He was mocked for his accent, made no close friends, and longed to return to New Jersey. He took little satisfaction from his studies or even from basketball, for which he had a growing talent. In a moment of self-pity, he had an impression come to him. A spiritual voice spoke a warning in his mind:

I felt, not heard, a voice. It was an impression, which I knew then was from God. It was this thought, and close to these words: "Someday, when you know who you really are, you will be sorry you didn't use your time better." I thought then that the impression was odd, since I thought I was using my time pretty well, and I thought I knew who I was. Now, years later, I am beginning to know who I am, and who you are, and why we will be so sorry if we do not invest our time well.[19]

In my teen years, for the first time I felt the power of priesthood quorums and of a loving bishop. I still remember and can feel the assurances that came when I sat in a priests quorum next to a bishop and knew that he had the keys of a true judge in Israel.

—TALK, APRIL 6, 2008[20]

That impression marked a turning point in Hal's life. He threw his energy into study, especially of the Book of Mormon, which he read many times over. He also found a book by Church President David O. McKay called *Gospel Ideals*; it would become, in his words, "one of the lodestars of my life." One chapter in particular explored the way that men should view and treat women. Hal adopted it as a personal standard, though his commitment would be tested by opinions of associates who ought to have known better.

His lofty words more than touched my heart: I felt a confirmation that they were true. Without telling anyone, I took David O. McKay's words as one of my standards of goodness. Five or six years later, I was playing basketball with a very fine team in a league in a city. Our team was composed of returned missionaries, plus me, the kid. Up to that point, I had never had a date. And I had no sisters, so what I thought I knew about girls and how to treat them came mostly from the visions I got from *Gospel Ideals.* I remember riding home one night from a game with those returned missionaries. I sat in the back seat of the car. They talked about girls. I can still remember a moment, even where the car was, on which street, with the street lights flashing into the car as we passed under them. I can remember, as I listened to them, the thought coming into my mind: "I have been wrong. Those ideals about girls and how you should feel about them, how you should treat them, they are unrealistic."

Luckily, in a few years I learned that they were wrong and President McKay was right. Or perhaps, in fairness to those young men, I learned that what I *thought* they had said, what I thought they had felt, what I thought they actually did, were not the true standard of goodness.[21]

HAL AS A YOUNG SCOUT

The move to Utah caught Hal by surprise. He had expected that he was going to "Zion." He assumed that a large ward meeting in an elegant chapel and a high school with Church members in the majority would be easier places to live the gospel. But he discovered unrighteousness in Salt Lake City, just as in Princeton. He learned that immorality cut across economic and social status and even Church membership status. He also found, though, that the same was true of goodness.

As he grew older, Hal observed that the admixture of good and evil persisted not only from place to place but also through time. "The good old days" were a combination of both good and bad, like the present.

He became wary of classifying the Church as stronger in one place than another or one time as more wicked than another. He could see the forces of both good and evil at work, broadly and steadily. The key in all times and places, he decided, is to trust God's promises and the help that He sends to those who seek Him. He also concluded that Zion was in the house his mother made, whether that was in New Jersey or Utah.

Hal's decision to use his time better as a high school student included working harder on his basketball game, shooting at a hoop mounted over the family garage hour after hour until his fingers bled.

EAST HIGH SCHOOL'S "SIXTH MAN"

He made the basketball team at Salt Lake City's East High School, and though he never won a starting spot, merely being on the team gave him enough social standing that going to school no longer brought feelings of fear. He also enjoyed the tutelage of an outstanding bishop, Alvin R. Dyer, who would later serve as a counselor to David O. McKay in the First Presidency, and whom Hal would serve as an assistant in the ward's priests quorum. Bishop Dyer's example further strengthened his testimony of priesthood leadership.

Hal never felt that he fit in at high school. He attended seminary in the early morning rather than taking "released time" classes during the school day. That allowed him to graduate at the end of the basketball season in his senior year and move on to college in March, rather than staying with his classmates until May. Yet without knowing it at the time, Hal was becoming an example and a comfort to fellow youths who shared his feelings of social uncertainty and desires to be better spiritually. One of his East High School classmates expressed thanks thirty-five years later.

Dear Dr. Eyring:

You won't remember me, but that doesn't matter. I remember you.

This letter is a long overdue thank you. In high school, I was a non-entity. You were a popular athlete. Yet you always said hello to me in the halls. I realize that you said hello to everybody, but to this person, it made a difference.

You were not bounded by conceit or a flattering group. Everyone seemed to matter to you. I have tried to raise my family to reflect these same ideals.

Thank you for the smiles when I really needed them. Thank you for remaining true and faithful to the principles of the gospel.[22]

nephew, Mark, sometime last week, forced her out of
our double's match this morning; within an hour she'd
sent a replacement, so I played six sets. Result: I
soaked my elbow in a tub of hot water propped on the
table   breakfast room at grandpa's, while I watched

3

SEEK LEARNING

And as all have not faith,
Seek ye diligently
And teach one another words of wisdom;
Yea, seek ye out of the best books words of wisdom;
Seek learning,
Even by study
And also by faith.

—DOCTRINE AND COVENANTS 88:118

Hal played basketball well enough in high school to earn college scholarships, including one from Dartmouth. But the glamour of that offer faded in the light of a personal finance lesson from his father. Henry pointed out the reality that free tuition from Dartmouth couldn't compete with his offer of free room and board at home plus tuition at the nearby University of Utah, where Henry worked. Hal did the financial math and enrolled there. He soon became a happily overextended college student. Much of the blame lay with a case of late blooming, both as an athlete and as a popular man-about-campus.

At Salt Lake City's East High School, Hal had been a solid basketball player, sixth man on a perennially strong squad. But his full height and weight—six feet, three inches and 163 pounds—didn't come until after high school. By then it was too late to hope for a spot on the University of Utah's intercollegiate basketball team. However, Hal became an avid intramural and pickup-game player; throughout the academic school year he made weeknight games and practices a priority.

He also joined the university's intercollegiate track team as a high jumper. The team already boasted two All-Americans in the event, and so Hal wasn't invited to compete on road trips. However, he could clear nearly his own height, the competitive standard for collegians of the day. Often, at Utah's home track meets, he rounded out a 1-2-3 finish for the Utes.

In addition to maturing athletically in college, Hal blossomed socially. He was not only the son of the university's most famous professor but also tall, lean, and handsome. At the time, he had both hair and good eyesight. The hair was dark and thick, parted on the left. Instead of the trademark tortoiseshell glasses he would later wear, his most prominent facial features were his mother's strong, Roman nose and high forehead. Athletic and articulate, the Hal Eyring who had feared junior high school and never dated in high school found the tables turned in college.

> **He's not another stamped-out piece of common man.**
> —ELDER RICHARD G. SCOTT[1]

His one social liability stemmed from the condition his mother placed on joining a campus fraternity: he could do so only if he maintained an A average in his classes. Mildred rightly judged that Hal's athletic commitments and newfound social interests would make this bar hard to clear. But lack of a fraternity sweater proved to be no real disadvantage, and Hal was glad not to have to conform to anyone else's social "mold." As his mother recalled:

> Hal didn't meet the A-grade standard but had a marvelous time at all the rush affairs and became acquainted with all the fraternity men and the sorority girls. After a year of B averages he decided he didn't want to be a fraternity man. He had all the advantages and none of the disadvantages.[2]

SEEING THE CURL OF A VECTOR

Getting A's would have been easier for Hal had it not been for the condition his father put on paying tuition for his sons: that they major in physics. Henry, a chemist, believed that physics offered the best possible undergraduate training because of its emphasis on math and its relevance to technological innovation. In his lifetime Henry had seen manned flight move from the beaches of Kitty Hawk to the lower reaches of space. He personally associated with the scientists who harnessed the power of the atom and with others who created the earliest electronic computers. He knew that rockets would soon fly higher and computers run much faster, and he wanted his sons to be prepared for success in such a world.

Though Hal had ample intellectual capacity for physics, he wasn't drawn to it. Part of the problem lay in feelings of relative inadequacy. Ted, a returned missionary with disciplined work habits, consistently mastered the material. While Hal often went to their physics and math classes without finishing the homework problems, Ted always arrived fully prepared. His stellar performance was just what the physics professors expected of a son of the university's most distinguished scientist.

Hal, by contrast, became increasingly self-conscious of failing to live up the family reputation. "My life," he would later say, "was marginal, as I viewed it, in the Physics Department of the University of Utah. Some of those professors had a way of emphasizing to me my inadequacies."[3] He recalled a conversation with a physics professor who expressed amazement at Hal's inability to visualize a complex mathematical equation. "Do you mean to tell me, Mr. Eyring, that you cannot *see* the curl of a vector?" When Hal glumly shook his head, the professor sighed. "You may not have a future in physics," he said. Assuming that even a less-than-stellar son of Dr. Henry Eyring would be expected to stay in a scientific discipline, the professor suggested one that he apparently held in low regard: "Perhaps," he offered, "you should try organic chemistry."

Hal was wrong to conclude at the time that Ted had inherent capacities he lacked, or that he would never amount to much as a scientist. The real problem was that he hadn't yet found the field of study that would naturally draw his attention. Fortunately, his father correctly diagnosed the problem. It happened one evening in the basement of the Eyring home, in front of a chalkboard.

> **When Hal is focused, he can accomplish anything.**
> —TED EYRING[4]

FIRST PRINCIPLES AND SHOWER TIME

Hal often sought his father's assistance with difficult physics problems. Henry was a master mathematician, capable of solving complex equations in his head. The window of time to get his help, though, was narrow. Henry invariably stayed at the university until dinnertime, six o'clock. And Hal had a time constraint on the back end—his goal was to have the physics homework done before pickup basketball games at the university started at seven. To hit this narrow window, he tried to solve all but the knottiest problems in the late afternoon, leaving only a few to take to his father after they had finished dinner.

The strategy would have worked well were it not for Henry's belief in the importance of understanding what he called the "first principles" of physics. When Hal asked for help with a particularly complex equation, one needed to solve an unworked homework problem, his father typically replied, "Hal, let's not worry about what the textbook says; we can derive this equation ourselves, from first principles."

That would lead to a time-consuming trip downstairs, where a chalkboard hung on an unfinished basement wall. There Henry would begin to write the most fundamental equations of physics. From these he would lead Hal through an exercise of deriving for himself

HENRY AT THE BLACKBOARD

the complex formulae in his textbook. Working from first principles was, Henry knew, the best way to teach Hal not only physics but also the broader life lesson of paying the price to really understand a problem before trying to solve it. His willingness to spend time with Hal in front of the chalkboard reflected his belief that Hal had the capacity to be a good problem solver.

The rub, though, was that this deep dive into mathematical fundamentals nearly always took longer than Hal hoped, making him late for basketball games that were already under way by the time he arrived. It was at one of these tense moments, with precious court time slipping away, that Henry suddenly stopped. "Hal," he said, "we did this same kind of problem a week ago. You don't seem to know

I can't remember the gifts my dad wrapped and helped put under a tree, but I remember the chalkboard and his quiet voice and even his not-so-quiet voice as he built up my mathematics, and me.

—TALK, DECEMBER 9, 1980[5]

it any better now than you did then. Haven't you been working on it?" Embarrassed, Hal admitted that he hadn't been studying the problem.

Henry stepped back from the board and looked into his son's eyes. "You don't understand, Hal," he said. "When you walk down the street, when you're in the shower, when you don't have to be thinking about anything else, isn't this what you think about?" Again, the answer was no. It was a poignant moment for Henry, who had hoped that all of his sons would become scientists. After a pause, he said, "Hal, I think you'd better get out of physics. You ought to find something you love so much that when you don't have to think about anything, that's what you think about."[6]

> Educational behaviors, like reading books and writing and thinking, are totally different when your goal is blessing mankind rather than material gain.
>
> —TALK, AUGUST 24, 1971[7]

Though that counsel would later prove invaluable to Hal, he didn't find his passion-inspiring subject as a college student. He went ahead and finished in physics, without academic distinction but well-grounded in mathematics and science. He learned most by teaching physics in his final two years at the university, as an assistant instructor in introductory courses for non-science majors. In teaching he not only gained a deeper understanding of the first principles of physics but also discovered the joy of helping others learn. That discovery would guide him a few years later as he chose a profession.

Hal gained other benefits from studying physics. One was the experience of being stretched to his limits. Surviving this difficult major, even with a B average, prepared him to face the hardest analytical problems in other fields. Being pushed to the limits of his natural ability also produced spiritual benefits. One of his last physics exams taught him that revelatory insight can come even when the problems one faces appear to be purely temporal.

Preparing for this exam, like many others, required more study than Hal had time for. He prioritized by making his best guesses about what material was most likely to be tested. To his horror, sitting down to the exam he found that one of the central problems involved a type of math, a Hamiltonian equation, that he'd never heard of. Knowing that earning even a passing grade would require some success with this problem, he prayed for help, all too conscious that he didn't deserve it. Miraculously, insight came, and he worked enough of the problem to receive a passing grade. He would never forget the feeling of gratitude or the lesson he learned about revelation.

> I remember to this day the feeling of insight. . . . It is a sure thing that the process of insight into patterns is one that the Spirit of God can illuminate and lead.
> —TALK, JULY 6, 1971[8]

LEARNING BEYOND THE CLASSROOM

Perhaps as much as his classroom studies, work experiences played a critical role in Hal's college education. Majoring in physics wasn't the only condition Henry put on his providing room, board, and tuition for his sons. They also had to work part-time during the school year and full-time each summer. Henry arranged for Hal to work first on the university grounds crew and then as a janitor.

These university jobs provided important learning experiences. His supervisors in particular taught him more than he expected. They, he would later say, "may have given me more lasting lessons than I got from the physics department. And the physics department did a lot for me."[9]

Three experiences as a student employee proved particularly instructive for Hal. One was reporting for work on his first day to the university's head of physical facilities. Upon learning that he and a group of fellow workers would be digging trenches, Hal literally jumped to pick up a shovel and get started. The supervisor barked, "Slow down, Eyring, we don't run here." Hal soon realized the meaning behind that comment. The supervisor wasn't implying a slack attitude toward productivity; on the contrary, he proved to be a stern taskmaster. But he had correctly identified Hal's jump-to-it display as just that—an attempt to look better than the other fellows. Just ten minutes on the job, Hal had been taught the importance of working hard without seeking to impress.

Hal learned another memorable lesson a year later, when he moved inside to work as janitor of the university's Mines and Mineral Industries Building. He took pride in being trusted with sole responsibility for the cleaning of the building, and he put his all into it. After two weeks, though, he was approached by an agitated female secretary. "You can't possibly have failed to notice the deplorable condition of the women's restrooms," she chided. In fact, it was the first time Hal had been told that cleaning the whole building meant going into the women's restrooms. He checked with his supervisor, who said, "Of course. I didn't expect to have to tell you that."

A third lesson came when Hal learned to complete his janitorial tasks more quickly. As he grew more efficient, he could finish the daily cleaning—including the women's restrooms—before his shift ended. Rather than slow down, however, he looked for opportunities to do more. One of the large laboratories in the building was the site of coal and petroleum research that involved burning those materials. Over the years, the resulting smoke had left the windows caked with oily soot. Though it wasn't on his list of standard duties, Hal spent several days using time left at the end of his shift to wash those windows. The outcome proved even better than he had hoped: the clean windows allowed light through, illuminating the laboratory and delighting the scientists and students who labored there. Hal was surprised by the effusiveness of their praise and that of his supervisor, who said, "I would never have asked you to do that; we didn't think those windows had clear glass." These simple lessons benefited Hal throughout his life. They proved especially valuable as he served in the presiding councils of the Church. From that vantage point he would say:

Physics taught me to understand the changes occurring in the world at large. But the things I learned as a groundskeeper and a janitor were worth more in working with the Brethren. Among those is the expectation that you know your duty thoroughly, you do more than you're asked, and you do it in a way that doesn't stand out. President Monson is the supreme example of that.[10]

SPIRITUAL MENTORING AT HOME

Hal's college education also included special learning and mentoring in his home. In addition to the informal schooling Mildred and Henry provided via late-night talks and problem-solving exercises at the chalkboard, they engaged him in stimulating discussion at dinner every night. The subjects ranged from politics to religion to the events of that day.

Hal's parents treated him as their intellectual peer, even in matters beyond the ken of a college student. He was surprised, for instance, to have his father seek guidance regarding a letter drafted for Elder Adam S. Bennion of the Quorum of the Twelve. Elder Bennion, Mildred Eyring's cousin, had written to Henry seeking his opinion of a book called *Man, His Origin and Destiny,* authored by fellow Quorum member Joseph Fielding Smith. This book challenged scientific theories about the age of the earth and the organic evolution of man.

> I grew up in a family where you didn't spend very much time wondering why your parents didn't get it. . . . It was always just, "I hope I got it."
> —2008 INTERVIEW[11]

Henry drafted a reply to Elder Bennion in which he noted the book's inconsistency with broadly accepted research findings and with the opinions of two deceased members of the Quorum of the Twelve, James Talmage and John Widtsoe, both accomplished scientists. Henry knew that the letter was likely to create a stir in the Church's leading councils. Seeking guidance in this delicate task, he gave a draft of the

letter to Hal, saying, "You'll know if this is any good." Hal felt unquali-
fied to comment, but he appreciated his father's trust, as he later noted
in a fireside address to the Church's seminary and institute teachers:

> He was treating me then, as he did other times, the way Jared
> treated his brother. You remember the words Jared said to his
> brother: "Go and inquire of the Lord whether he will drive us out
> of the land" (Ether 1:38). He expected with perfect confidence
> that his brother would do it and that God would answer.
>
> A father was kind and wise enough to have that expectation
> for his immature son. He made me feel that he knew I would get
> the revelation that he needed about something that really mat-
> tered and was beyond human power. . . . I can still feel what it
> meant to be trusted to be able to hear the voice of the Spirit.[12]

Several weeks later, Hal learned that the letter had in fact done
some good. He picked up the phone at home one evening and heard a
voice say, "Hello, this is David McKay. Is your father there?" President
McKay had called to ask Henry to represent the Church at a national
conference in which the relationship between science and religion
would be discussed. That invitation was followed by many others, allowing Henry to play a conciliatory role among those who argued that
rational analysis and faith were inherently incompatible.

BISHOP ALVIN DYER

Though Hal's mother and father were his leading mentors in his
youth, there were others then and throughout his life. Notable among
them was his bishop, Alvin R. Dyer, who showed deep interest in Hal
from the time they sat together in the priests quorum. In a 2011 talk
given to the priesthood bearers of the Church, Hal reflected on the respect that he and his fellow quorum members felt from their bishop.

> As near as I could tell, he treated the opinions of young
> priests as if we were the wisest men in the world. He waited un-
> til all who would speak had spoken. He listened. And when he

decided what should be done, it seemed to me that the Spirit confirmed the decisions to us and to him. . . . I realize now I had felt what the scripture means when it says that the president is to sit in council with the members of his quorum.[13]

One Sunday during Hal's years as a college student, Bishop Dyer telephoned and said, "Hal, I need your help. I want you to join me in a visit to a needy member of the ward." The request caught Hal off guard. It surprised him that Bishop Dyer was calling on a young elder rather than one of his counselors or a high priest. He was also surprised to learn that there was a needy member in their Monument Park Ward, which appeared to him to be the most affluent in the Church.

ALVIN R. DYER

Bishop Dyer picked Hal up at home and they drove east, toward the mountains. They passed the university, and the paved road turned to dirt and dropped down into a tree-lined gully. Were it not for the road, Hal would have thought they were in a backwoods wilderness. They parked in front of a lone dwelling that looked more like a shack or cabin than a house.

In response to Bishop Dyer's knock, a voice called, "Come in!" Bishop Dyer opened the door and ushered Hal into a front room with no furniture other than a wooden table and a few straight-backed chairs. A woman wearing a housedress entered and joined them at the table. After greeting the woman, Bishop Dyer said, "Where is it? Where's the list?" The woman got up and grumbled as she walked into the kitchen. Hal could see its bare cupboards. She returned from the kitchen with a piece of paper. It listed household expenses, such as groceries and gas, but there were no figures next to any of the expense items.

To Hal's surprise, Bishop Dyer pushed, "Here is the list, but you haven't done anything with it. Where's your plan? I gave you the outline, but where is the budget?" Bishop Dyer then helped the woman estimate some but not all of her monthly expenses. Hal watched quietly as his bishop, a successful entrepreneur, taught this needy ward member to develop a budget. Before they left, Bishop Dyer said to the woman, "Now you get that done, and I'll be back."

On the drive home, Hal sat in stunned silence. He had never seen the Church's welfare system at work. His mother and father had occasionally provided food and some clothing to members of their branch—mostly missionaries—but this kind of formal welfare process was entirely new to him. "This is the way it works?" he thought.

> Those in abundance are to voluntarily sacrifice some of their comfort, time, skills, and resources to relieve the suffering of those in need. And the help is to be given in a way that increases the power of the recipients to care for themselves.
>
> —TALK, JUNE 8, 2011[14]

As they pulled up in front of Hal's house, Bishop Dyer looked at him with a smile, seeming to read his mind. "Hal, what do you think?" the bishop asked. "I'll bet that was quite an experience for you." Hal admitted his surprise at their having left an apparently needy member with no help other than a lesson in budgeting.

Bishop Dyer opened his scriptures and patiently began to teach the doctrines not only of succoring the poor but also of personal stewardship. He explained that the woman they had visited was not only able to work but had pension benefits sufficient to live on. "She could not only take care of herself," Bishop Dyer said, "she could take care of others. We just have to convince her to rise up, and that's what the budget is for."

A MISSION CALL

On a Sunday several years later, when Hal was nearing the end of his physics studies at the University of Utah, Bishop Dyer invited him to his office at the church. He announced that he would soon be released as bishop to serve as president of the Church's Central States Mission. "I've been called as the mission president in Independence," Bishop Dyer said excitedly, "and I want to take you with me."

Bishop Dyer's declaration surprised Hal. The Korean War was in full swing, and missionary service opportunities were severely limited. In fact, for the preceding two years, 1951 and 1952, the Church had been unable to call any draft-eligible U.S. male into missionary service. It was only by special agreement with the United States government, reached by Brother Gordon Hinckley, a Church employee, that each ward could begin to send one missionary per year into the field.[15] "I just got this permission," Bishop Dyer exultantly told Hal. "I can send one person."

Hal felt mixed emotions. His father, Henry, had been unable to serve a full-time mission because of his family's indebtedness during a post–World War I economic depression. But with that immediate exception, Hal descended from some of the Church's most faithful missionaries. His great-grandfather Henry Eyring served three full-time missions. Another great-grandfather, Miles Park Romney, twice left his family in response to mission calls. Like Mildred's grandfather John Bennion, both of these men essentially worked as missionaries at the direction of the Brethren all their lives. The tradition of full-time mission service ran deeply in the Eyring family.

[John Bennion's short journal] entries don't have much preaching in them. He doesn't testify that he knew Brigham Young was a prophet. He just records having answered "yes" every time the prophet called him on a mission from "over Jordan" to the Muddy mission, then on to a mission back to Wales. . . . There is even a family legend that the reason he died so close to the day when Brigham Young was buried was to follow the prophet one more time.

—TALK, APRIL 7, 1996[16]

On the other hand, at age twenty-one, Hal assumed that the time for a mission of his own had passed. He was dating and looked forward to marrying and starting a family. Also, his

ROTC commitment meant that he would have to spend two years in the Air Force, probably in Korea or Japan, immediately after graduating from college. With dozens of mission-eligible young men in Bishop Dyer's large ward, including some exempt from military service because of physical limitations, Hal hadn't anticipated a mission call.

Moreover, in those days mission service was admired but not expected in the Church. It would be another twenty years before President Spencer W. Kimball declared, "Certainly every male member of the Church should serve a mission."[17] In light of his age and military obligation, Hal felt justified in asking a fateful question. "Bishop," he said, "I need to know something: Is it the Lord asking or just you?" Bishop Dyer paused a moment before replying, "It's just me, Hal."

Hal left the bishop's office without giving a final answer. Back at home, his parents made their position clear. With a brutal land war raging on the Korean Peninsula, Mildred in particular didn't like the thought of Hal's dropping out of ROTC and potentially being drafted as an enlisted man after his mission; she had seen one of her friends welcome home a returned missionary son only to lose him as a casualty to the fighting in Korea. In addition, Hal's older brother, Ted, had recently returned from an unusually difficult mission to France, where his struggles with unreceptive listeners and disobedient companions had taken a significant toll on his physical and emotional health. Mildred left the decision to Hal, but she shared her recommendation, citing an impression based on prayer: "You're better off telling him no."

Hal took that answer back to Bishop Dyer. "I'm sorry," he said, "I can't go. Give the opportunity to someone else; it's a wonderful thing." Bishop Dyer accepted Hal's decision without argument.

Leaving the church building, Hal was surprised to find his uncle, Spencer Kimball of the Quorum of the Twelve, outside. Elder Kimball and his wife, Camilla, Henry's older sister, lived just a few blocks from the Eyrings. Elder Kimball loved Henry and Mildred and their sons, whom he saw often at family gatherings. He took enough personal interest in Hal and his brothers that they felt comfortable calling him "Uncle Spencer."

"What were you and the bishop talking about, Hal?" Uncle Spencer asked. Hal briefly related his discussion of mission service with Bishop Dyer.

"What did you tell him?"

"I said no, because my mother prayed and had a feeling that I shouldn't go."

"Well, Hal," Uncle Spencer asked, "did you pray?"

"No," Hal replied honestly, "but my mother's a spiritual person, and I respect her feelings."

"I see," said Uncle Spencer, letting Hal go on his way without further comment.

In the end, the decision had to be Hal's. As he sought the guidance of the Lord, he determined to stay the course with his military commitment. He didn't know at the time that missionary experiences would soon be coming to him in ways he hadn't expected.

He didn't say a word. He knew it was the most tragic mistake, tragic. The idea of serving a mission was everything, and he liked me. He never said a word; he just walked away. . . . Here this great man knew my heart and the way I would feel badly, but he didn't try to turn me around that day. He could have turned me around. But he was a believer that you let people make their choice and then try to help.

—2012 INTERVIEW

nephew, Mark, sometime last week, forced her out of
our double's match this morning; within an hour she'd
sent a replacement, so I played six sets. Result: I
soaked my elbow in a tub of hot water propped on the
table in the breakfast room at grandpa's, while I watched

4

LIFT UP YOUR HEART AND REJOICE

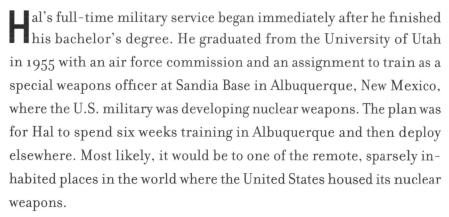

Lift up your heart and rejoice,
For the hour of your mission is come;
And your tongue shall be loosed,
And you shall declare glad tidings of great joy
Unto this generation.
　　　　　—DOCTRINE AND COVENANTS 31:3

Hal's full-time military service began immediately after he finished his bachelor's degree. He graduated from the University of Utah in 1955 with an air force commission and an assignment to train as a special weapons officer at Sandia Base in Albuquerque, New Mexico, where the U.S. military was developing nuclear weapons. The plan was for Hal to spend six weeks training in Albuquerque and then deploy elsewhere. Most likely, it would be to one of the remote, sparsely in-habited places in the world where the United States housed its nuclear weapons.

On his second Sunday in New Mexico, Hal was asked to meet with President Clement Hilton of the Church's Albuquerque District.[1] President Hilton called him to serve as a district missionary. Hal had mixed feelings about the call. It fulfilled a promise made in a bless-ing given before he left home. In that blessing his new bishop, Weldon Moore, had said that Hal's military service would be his mission. Yet his military orders were clear. "I'm happy to serve," he told President Hilton, "but I'll be leaving in four weeks."

"I don't know about that," replied President Hilton, "but we are to call you to serve."

Suppressing his doubts, Hal accepted the call and went to work, spending the recommended ten hours each week meeting and teaching investigators.

Toward the end of his six weeks of military training, Hal was summoned by a senior military officer. Rather than being transferred, he learned, he would be staying in Albuquerque. A staff officer had unexpectedly passed away, and Hal's physics education and performance during training had led to his being recommended to fill the open staff position. He would not only stay in Albuquerque but also work with a team of senior officers including colonels and generals from the air force, army, navy, and marines.

The most immediate benefit of this unexpected assignment was the continuation of his missionary labors. The Church in Albuquerque was small, but its district missionaries were well organized. They worked under the direction of President A. Lewis Elggren of the Western States Mission, which was headquartered in Denver. Hal ultimately received responsibility from President Elggren for a group of ten missionaries in the Albuquerque area.

JOYFUL MISSIONARY SERVICE

Hal's companions included young servicemen such as himself as well as older male members of the district. The weeknights and weekends that they spent teaching the gospel produced sweet fruit. Thanks in large part to U.S. military and scientific operations, Albuquerque was growing. Many of the newcomers were open to change, increasing their receptivity to the gospel message. Missionary referrals were common, and Hal participated in many conversions. He would later describe one of those experiences:

Years ago I took a young man, 20 years of age, into the waters of baptism. My companion and I had taught him the gospel. He was the first in his family to hear the message of the restored gospel. He asked to be baptized. The testimony of the Spirit made him want to follow the example of the Savior, who was baptized by John the Baptist even though He was without sin.

As I brought that young man up out of the waters of baptism, he surprised me by throwing his arms around my neck and whispering in my ear, tears streaming down his face, "I'm clean, I'm clean." That same young man, after we laid our hands on his head with the authority of the Melchizedek Priesthood and conferred on him the Holy Ghost, said to me, "When you spoke those words, I felt something like fire go down from the top of my head through my body, all the way to my feet."[2]

HAL AS A DISTRICT MISSIONARY

The companion with whom Hal served the longest, more than one year, was Jim Geddes. A hardworking farm boy from tiny Banida, Idaho, Jim piloted reconnaissance aircraft. He and his wife, Sylvia, were the parents of an infant daughter. The Geddeses often had Hal to dinner and made him feel like a member of the family. He felt great admiration for both Jim and Sylvia. He viewed their marriage as a model for the one he hoped to have.

Hal and Jim shared a common zeal for their labors. Each felt blessed by the unexpected mission-service opportunity, and each was thrilled to have a companion ready to work hard. As they drove to and from appointments, which consumed most evenings and weekends, they counseled together and sought divine guidance regarding what they should teach. The resulting inspiration bonded them to one another and to those they taught.

Among their most memorable labors was a request to administer to a critically injured young girl. The phone call came during a weekday, while both Hal and Jim were at work on the military base. The girl and her parents were at the base hospital, allowing the two missionary companions to get there in a matter of minutes.

At the hospital, the parents described their daughter's situation. She had been hit by a speeding car while crossing the road. The force of the impact had thrown her into a curb, crushing her skull. The doctors had told them that she was very unlikely to live.

The parents asked Elder Eyring and Elder Geddes to administer to their daughter. But before the pair entered the hospital's intensive care unit, the father asked them to pray with him and his wife. In the prayer, he expressed confidence that the doctors were wrong, that through the power of the priesthood his daughter would be healed. Elder Eyring and Elder Geddes, he made it clear, would invoke a miracle.

Even those called may well have felt some apprehension. And yet when they see through the eyes of faith the challenge as it really is, confidence replaces fear because they turn to God.

—TALK, APRIL 2, 2000[3]

Entering the girl's room, the elders found her lying in an oxygen tent, surrounded by doctors and nurses. Bandages covered her head and face. The attending medical professionals had apparently been told that the elders were coming. They gave way, but not without conveying their contempt for the two young intruders, who lacked the traditional trappings of clergy. The lead doctor growled, "I don't know what you plan to do, but you'd better do it quickly."

Elder Geddes deferred to Elder Eyring to act as voice in the blessing. To his surprise, Hal felt impressed to promise the critically injured girl that she would live. When he spoke those words, the medical team murmured their disapproval. But after several tense days, it appeared that the promise would be fulfilled. The doctors conceded that the girl would in fact not die. Still, they stood firm in a prognosis of paralysis. "Your daughter," they told her parents, "will never walk."

Again the distraught but confident couple called on the missionaries. And again Hal's blessing contradicted the medical prognosis. The girl continued to improve, slowly but surely. Before Hal's military and missionary service ended, she was walking, attending Church meetings in a beautiful yellow dress bought to celebrate the miracle of her recovery.

SPECIAL WEAPONS OFFICER

Along with the joy of missionary labor, Hal found his air force assignment unexpectedly rewarding. It drew significantly on his physics training and came with a top-secret military clearance and real decision-making responsibility. He served as liaison between senior military officers and scientists, including some at the nearby Los Alamos National Laboratory, where the first atomic bomb had been created a decade before. Though he never saw active duty in the Korean War, which was being waged at the time, his work exposed him to military training operations. In addition to inspecting nuclear arsenals around the world, he flew with air force pilots and boarded navy aircraft carriers.

There was danger in this top-secret work, but Hal's understanding of the physics of nuclear explosions precluded any sense of adventure. The magnitude of the danger struck him with particular force one day on the deck of an aircraft carrier, out on the high seas. As skittish young seamen attempted to mount a nuclear weapon under the wing of a jet, the pitching of the huge vessel caused the bomb to fall to the deck. The seamen scattered and took cover. After some nervous consultation, Hal finally joined one of them in surveying the damage. As they walked toward the bomb, this young man held a hand in front of his face, as though to deflect a blast. Hal thought of the irony—a hand would provide no protection against even a conventional weapon,

AIRCRAFT CARRIER ON THE HIGH SEAS

let alone a nuclear bomb capable of incinerating the whole aircraft carrier.

As his primary responsibility, Hal analyzed data from scientific tests of nuclear weapons to determine which ones should be added to or subtracted from the global arsenal of each of the four military branches. To each weapon type, he applied the test, "Is this bomb very likely to detonate as expected in the field but very unlikely to detonate in storage?" What he found disappointed him. It turned out that a weapon more likely to explode on cue was also more likely to explode accidentally. He characterized the problem with a domestic analogy: the watchdog bred and trained to bite a burglar is inevitably a threat to bite his master. Simply stated, you could get more of what you wanted, but only at a price. His experience in analyzing this apparently unavoidable tradeoff provided a valuable life lesson, leaving him wary of any proposition, temporal or moral, that seemed to partake of the spirit of having one's cake and eating it too.

As his two-year assignment drew to a close, Hal's superiors ordered him to summarize and report what he had learned. He hadn't expected such an assignment, and he wrestled long in choosing the right message. On the one hand, he knew that his superiors wouldn't like his finding that they couldn't have everything, that even the best weapon design would involve a trade-off between effectiveness and safety. He had gained a reputation for intelligence and dependability in his work, and he would have liked to offer at least some hope for a breakthrough.

In fact, the bomb-triggering mechanisms were becoming steadily more reliable, and the physicists and engineers often seemed to be on the edge of a true breakthrough. Hal saw several tempting arguments for emphasizing the future possibilities. In so doing, he could not only give his superiors hope but also impress them with his knowledge of the underlying science. This kind of focus on the future also would make for a longer, more interesting discussion, one supported by statistics and charts.

But Hal feared the possible consequences of focusing on making everyone, himself included, look and feel good. Though a technical breakthrough was possible, he couldn't warrant one. Over the preceding two years he had learned that the risks of an accidental nuclear explosion were real and, given existing technologies, irreducible. His best efforts had left him more humble than confident. If he didn't attempt to inspire that kind of humility in his superior officers, the consequences could be dire. Others, he decided, could take credit for announcing a breakthrough if and when it came. He determined to report things the way he saw them, regardless of the likely negative reaction.

When the day of reckoning came, Hal found himself in a larger room than expected. His surprise turned to worry as the room began to fill with more senior military personnel than he had ever seen in one place. The majority of attendees literally wore their rank on their sleeves or shoulders. Amazed at the size of the group, he made the mistake of beginning to count stars—one star for brigadier general or rear admiral, two for major general, and so on. The tally quickly exceeded a dozen collective stars, with the room still filling. He stopped counting, his stomach in a knot.

The surprising size of the gathering made Hal's planned presentation strategy seem all the more foolhardy. Having expected to lead an informal discussion among a relatively small group, he had come with no printed information or visual aids of any kind. Now he faced a crowd that would be hard to engage effectively, with a greater risk that at least someone would challenge his cautionary counsel.

> Those officers in that headquarters were sound, brilliant and good as any group of executives I've ever seen in my life.
>
> —2012 INTERVIEW

But the group surprised Hal. After he made his brief planned statement, men half a dozen ranks and thirty years senior to him asked questions calmly and even deferentially. The questions were thoughtful, reflective of sound understanding of the issues at hand and wisdom born of experience. These senior officers seemed not only to agree with Hal's conclusions but to have reached similar conclusions themselves. They were wise realists, so much so that Hal began to wonder how they might have reacted had he made the rosy forecast he had thought they wanted. After an hour of productive discussion, they thanked Hal for his work.

AN HONORABLE RELEASE AND A PROVIDENTIAL RECOMMENDATION

Hal served exactly two years as an air force officer and district missionary, deeply grateful for both opportunities. He returned home to Salt Lake City in the summer of 1957, expecting no fanfare, and was surprised to receive both a certificate of honorable release from his mission and an invitation to speak in the semiannual conference of his parents' Bonneville Stake.

The day after the stake conference, Uncle Spencer called Hal and invited him to come to his home. They met in the little study that was famous among the neighbors for typically having a light on late at night. It was the room where Elder Kimball wrote *The Miracle of*

Forgiveness and where he gave counsel to the spiritually and emotionally distressed.

The discussion with Uncle Spencer was a very different mission debrief from the one Hal had experienced as he left Albuquerque. Then, he had been confronted by a visiting General Authority assigned to create the first stake in New Mexico. In a special meeting with the full-time and district missionaries, this visiting authority asked each of them to provide a tally of the baptisms with which they had been associated: "your converts," he called them. Hal couldn't produce a number. When his turn to report came, he said, "I don't know." Surprised by Hal's coolness, the visitor sent him out of the room until he could come back with a count.

By contrast, Hal's interview with his uncle was intimate and quiet. Elder Kimball was suffering from throat cancer; within a month he would go under the knife to have the malignancy removed, along with all of one vocal cord and part of another. Uncle and nephew sat knee to knee. "Hal," Uncle Spencer whispered, "I want you to tell me about your experience in the military." As Hal described what he had been doing for the past two years, Uncle Spencer expressed greatest interest in his missionary labors. He asked his nephew to relate stories of investigators and missionary companions. He wanted to learn the details of each person and the work that Hal did with him or her. They talked for an hour. Finally, Uncle Spencer seemed satisfied. "Hal," he said solemnly, "as long as you live, when you're asked if you've served a mission, you say 'yes.'"

Hal returned to Utah knowing that he wouldn't be there long. Toward the end of his time in Albuquerque, he had decided to apply to

> You [mission presidents] will tend to praise your missionaries more for what they are becoming than for what they have done. You will help them recognize their growth in character. You will note how what they have done has helped you discern in them what God has helped them to become.
>
> —TALK, JUNE 24, 2010[4]

the Harvard Business School (HBS). His knowledge of HBS was limited to a dinner meeting with the school's dean, Stanley Poole, who had passed through Salt Lake when Hal was a senior in college. His uncle Grant Calder, an HBS graduate, had invited Hal to the dinner, and the memory of that night remained as he completed his two-year commitment of service to the air force.

Though he didn't know it at the time, Hal's chances of being admitted to Harvard were poor. His service as an officer satisfied the HBS requirement of managerial work experience, but his academic marks were marginal: a 3.1 (or "B") grade-point average and an 86th percentile score on the Graduate Management Admission Test (GMAT).[5] Nonetheless, Hal was one of 630 students admitted from an applicant pool of 1,980.[6] He later learned that the decisive factor in his admission was a letter of recommendation from one of his military commanders, a man present during his final report on nuclear weapons, who cited him as having extraordinary leadership potential.

Hal's father may have sensed the competitive reality into which his son was headed. A meeting of the American Chemical Society took Dr. Henry Eyring to New York as Hal was on his way to Boston. They bade farewell to one another on a New York street corner. Hal was confidently dressed in a new suit from Salt Lake City's finest men's tailor. Looking back more than forty years later, he recalled the parting:

> It was a sunny day, around noontime, the streets crowded with cars and pedestrians. On that particular corner there was a traffic light which stopped the cars and the people in all directions for a few minutes. The light changed to red; the cars stopped. The crowd of pedestrians hurried off the curbs, moving every way, including diagonally, across the intersection.
>
> The time had come for parting, and I started across the street. I stopped almost in the center, with people rushing by me. I turned to look back. Instead of moving off in the crowd, my father was still standing on the corner looking at me. To me he seemed

lonely and perhaps a little sad. I wanted to go back to him, but I realized the light would change and so I turned and hurried on.

Years later I talked to him about that moment. He told me that I had misread his face. He said he was not sad; he was concerned. He had seen me look back, as if I were a little boy, uncertain and looking for assurance. He told me in those later years that the thought in his mind had been: *Will he be all right? Have I taught him enough? Is he prepared for whatever may lie ahead?*[7]

Hal's initial reception at Harvard was personal in an almost magical way. He arrived several days early and found the HBS campus still largely empty. Striding across the quad in front of the school's iconic Baker Library, he was greeted by the only other person in sight, dean of admissions Chaffee Hall. Dean Hall, who each year took the trouble to memorize the name and face of every one of HBS's incoming students, thrust out his hand and, smiling broadly, said, "Welcome to the Harvard Business School, Mr. Eyring." It was a timely gesture that foreshadowed the many warm experiences Hal would enjoy during the ensuing five years. But getting used to HBS would take time.

WELL-HEELED ROOMMATES

From the moment his roommates arrived, Hal knew that he wasn't the best-educated man on campus. The three fellow students with whom he lived in the first year exemplified Harvard's rarefied student body. All were the product of boarding schools. One, George Montgomery, was the son of a prominent California real-estate developer; he came to HBS via Yale. Another, Harvard College graduate Powell Cabot, was a scion of one of Boston's "first families," a wealthy Brahmin clan described in the comic verse "Boston Toast":

> *And this is good old Boston,*
> *The home of the bean and the cod,*
> *Where the Lowells talk only to Cabots,*
> *And the Cabots talk only to God.*[8]

The student with whom Hal shared a bedroom, Englishman John Abel Smith, bore educational credentials that Hal could only dimly conceive. John was the namesake of a renowned merchant banker and British Member of Parliament. He had attended Eton, one of the world's most famous preparatory schools, before entering Cambridge, where he had "read" under the personal tutelage of English schol-ars. Hal began to understand the dif-ference between his public-school education and the background of his roommates when he surveyed them relative to a reading list he came across. It was titled, "One Hundred Books Every Educated Person Ought to Have Read." George Montgomery and Powell Cabot had read approx-imately seventy and eighty, respectively. John Abel Smith had read all but four. Hal had read (though not necessarily finished) six.

> The only thing we had in common was that we'd all asked for a single room.
>
> —GEORGE MONTGOMERY[9]

Hal also felt his social inferiority. He had long known that his par-ents weren't fashionable. His mother never had her hair done in a beauty parlor. His father owned only one pair of dress shoes at a time and frequently took long trips abroad with nothing but his briefcase and a single change of underwear, washing his clothes—including a "wash-and-wear" suit—in hotel sinks at night.

That was part of the reason why Hal took an expensive tailored suit—a broad-shouldered pinstripe—and a new fedora hat to Boston. He knew that he needed to rise to a new level, fashion-wise. But he re-alized that his fashion statement had failed when Powell Cabot asked, late in October, to borrow his suit and hat. Hal's swell of pride turned to chagrin when Powell explained his purpose—he had been invited to a Halloween costume party, and he wanted to go as a gangster.

"ONE OF THE THREE OF YOU WILL LIKELY FAIL"

Social differences notwithstanding, Hal soon made fast friends of his roommates, and he experienced unexpected success as a Master of

May 31, 1984
Thursday

I wrote in the Atherton
guest house of the
Johnsons,
on the tr
of our
E l i z a b e
Kathleen
blow out
birthday
dinner by
Holy Ghos
teach a
workshop i

June 1, 19
Friday

Elizabeth
the pool
worked on
Gary cam
Los Angel
to hear
time to
Altos.

June 2, 19
Saturday

I towed E
inflated,
M a r y K
c o m p l i n
purple dr
match to
hair that
Stuart's
sister. G
and I wat
dance in

HARVARD BUSINESS SCHOOL BAKER LIBRARY

June 3, 1984
Sunday

Kathy, Elizabeth, and Mary Kathleen were dressed and
packed early for our drive from Atherton to the San Jose
airport. On the flight home, a stewardess made a bullseye
with a glass full of orange juice on my lap. It was so cold
and complete a soaking that I laughed for the rest of the
trip. I used bags to shield the results as I got us to the car.

Business Administration (MBA) student at Harvard. He also received a wonderful opportunity to serve in the Church when Wilbur Cox, president of the Church's Boston District, called him as a counselor. The district was large, encompassing all of eastern Massachusetts and Rhode Island. President Cox and his counselors visited at least one branch every Sunday, traveling winding, tree-lined roads from dawn to dusk.

Hal was grateful for this calling, recognizing it as an extension of the missionary service he had enjoyed so much in Albuquerque. But at Harvard the cost of such service seemed greater than it had in the air force. As a military officer with heavy responsibilities, he had often worked evenings and Saturdays. But he hadn't faced the kind of competition that pervaded the world's most prestigious MBA program. He was grateful to find divine compensation for the time he spent in the district presidency, as he later recalled:

> Years ago I was admitted to a graduate program for which I was poorly prepared. The course was arduous. The competition was fierce. On the first day the professor said, "Look at the person on your left and on your right. One of the three of you will not be here at the end. One of the three of you will likely fail." The schedule of classes filled the five weekdays from early until late. Preparations for the next day's classes lasted until nearly midnight, often beyond. And then late on Friday a major paper was assigned, with no way to prepare until the assignment was given and with the paper due at nine o'clock on Saturday night.
>
> I can still remember the hours of frantic study and writing on those Saturdays. And as the nine o'clock deadline approached, crowds of students would stand around the slot in the wall of the library to cheer as the last desperate student would dash up to throw in his completed paper, just before the box inside the building was pulled away from beneath the slot to let the late papers fall into the oblivion of failure. Then the students would go back to their homes and to their rooms for a few hours of

celebration before starting preparations for Monday classes. And most of them would study all day on Sunday and late into the night.

For me, there was no party on Saturday and no studying on Sunday. The Lord gave me an opportunity to test His promise. Early in that year He called me, through a humble district president, to a Church service that took me across the hills of New England from the early hours of Sunday to late in the evening. I visited the tiny branches and the scattered Latter-day Saints from Newport and Cape Cod on the south to Worcester and Fort Devens on the west and Lynn and Georgetown on the north. I realize that those names mean more to me than they do to you. For me the words bring back the joy of going to those places, loving the Lord, and trusting that somehow He would keep His promise. He always did. In the few minutes I could give to preparation on Monday morning before classes, ideas and understanding came to more than match what others gained from a Sunday of study.[10]

In addition to seeing how heaven could magnify his time, Hal learned that academic success depended on having the right motives. Years later he would describe this lesson to one of his sons, Stuart. Following in his father's footsteps, Stuart was applying to business school. In 1991, Stuart called from the distant city in which he then lived to ask his father's advice on writing the required personal essays, in which applicants try to distinguish their capabilities, credentials, and connections. Hal responded by letter, referencing the papers that were due on Saturday nights:

I got to thinking over your question about applications. Even more important than getting the right name and title on anything you write is its tone. Admissions directors and admissions committees must get tired reading pompous prose. If you just imagine yourself talking to someone who likes you, who has a sense of humor, and who is relieved to visit for a moment with anyone as much fun as Stuart Eyring, you will write what you really are.

I've never told you how I learned that. In the first year of the MBA program, I turned in a written analysis of a case every Saturday night, or nearly every Saturday. I was told later, by Professor Tom Raymond, who ran the program, that each week as he prepared the readers to grade the 650 papers, he would read a few to calibrate their criticism. He said that mine were read regularly, as examples of work well done. He said to me, "But something happened. You lost your touch. You lost your flair." That wasn't what happened: I lost my reader. The girl reading my papers had a baby and was replaced by a grader who began writing hostile things on my papers. That tightened me up. I just had to get back to my string of A-grades, and so I began to be impressive. Kaput—end of good writing.[11]

A DISAPPOINTING SUMMER

Hal learned another hard but valuable lesson during the summer following his first year of business school. It was customary for Harvard MBA students to spend that summer in a professional internship, working for a prestigious company, bank, or consulting firm. The purpose of the internship was twofold. One was to apply the classroom learning of the preceding year in the "real world." The other was to secure an offer of a full-time job upon graduation. Only a small fraction of interns would return to campus without the comfort of an employment safety net as they sought additional job offers during their second year of study.

Hal's first-year performance helped him land an internship with Boston-based Arthur D. Little (ADL), the first business consulting firm and, at the time, one of the most prestigious. Hal's main assignment for the summer was to answer a question posed by a leading ADL client, Canada's Abitibi Power and Paper Company. Abitibi operated one of the world's largest logging operations. Founded in 1912, the company maintained a tradition of transporting logs from Canada's vast interior to sawmills on the Great Lakes via tributary rivers. Annual "log drives" still employed fearless men, self-proclaimed "river pigs,"

LOGS SUCCESSFULLY DELIVERED TO THE MILL

who followed and sometimes rode the logs down flooded, turbulent rivers to the mills.

Abitibi's question was straightforward: "How can we minimize the loss of logs on the rivers?" With a bit of study, Hal quickly grasped the problem. River logging operations had remained essentially the same since the early 1800s. In the fall, teams of loggers established camps in remote forests. They spent the winter building roads to nearby rivers, felling trees, and dragging logs to the riverbanks. Then, when the early-summer runoff swelled the rivers, they rolled the logs in and followed them downstream.

Hal learned that logs could be lost in a number of ways. The floodwaters that buoyed and sped the logs along also grabbed up boulders and fallen trees. If one of those obstructions caught a log, a jam could quickly build. The log drivers tried to spot these jams and break them up using peaveys—long wooden spears with a metal spike and hook on the end. In severe cases, when the jam became too impacted and large, they resorted to dynamite.

Though logs could be lost to these jams, the more common problem was drought. If the spring runoff was too light, logs could be left high and dry for a year or more on the riverbank, where they were prone to rot or to be damaged by insects or fire. The resulting financial loss went beyond the value of the wood itself—without logs to process, the sawmills and their workers sat idle.

That was the original reason for Abitibi's getting into the power business. The company had built dams initially not for power production but to store water for release in dry years, when log driving would otherwise have been impossible or unprofitable. Only later, with the invention of efficient hydroelectric generators and transmission lines, had Abitibi become a power producer.

The more deeply Hal looked into the problem of lost logs, the more strongly he felt that his client had posed the wrong question. Even if its current operations could be enhanced, Abitibi was playing a losing game. River logging was inherently inefficient and dangerous, and it would only become more costly. The prime stands of timber near the company's waterways had been tapped out, requiring more road-building into interior forests. And lawsuits were becoming more prevalent relating to the loss of a river logger's leg or life.

Hal also foresaw a separation of the power and paper operations. Both of these industries were consolidating, with the winning players becoming bigger and more focused. Abitibi's dams were more valuable as power generators than as backup systems for transporting logs. Ultimately, they would need to be deployed exclusively against their highest and best use, probably by a company focusing solely on hydroelectricity.

Having reached this conclusion, Hal decided to reframe the question that ADL's client had asked. Rather than just identifying improvements to Abitibi's river-logging system, he also studied a new alternative: transporting logs by truck, direct from forest to sawmill. His analysis, which included detailed mathematical modeling, showed that this was far and away the better option.

Impressed by Hal's ingenuity and the apparent sophistication of his analytical approach, his ADL supervisor let him run with it. At the end of the summer, he packed up his presentation and boarded a train for Toronto, home to Abitibi's headquarters. He'd been there once before, at the beginning of the summer, to gather data. This time, though, he would be meeting the CEO, to whom he'd make his recommendation to close the river-logging operation in favor of a trucking system. He expected the man to be pleased, as his analysis showed that the new roads and trucks would be so much more efficient that they would pay for themselves in only a few years.

> I don't have confidence that I can see everything or calculate everything. But I try to get a feeling of where things ought to go. And I probably get more revelation that way than I would if I thought I knew.
>
> —2012 INTERVIEW

Hal's first glimmer of the trouble ahead came as he entered the CEO's office. Rather than the expected business suit, this burly man wore a plaid woolen logger shirt, complete with button-down pockets to keep contents from spilling out in case a logger fell into the water. On the wall behind his desk hung a well-worn peavey. Hal gulped. It hadn't occurred to him that Abitibi's CEO might have a personal connection to river logging. He was unprepared to handle the potential emotional resistance to his analysis-based proposal.

To the CEO's credit, none came. It was clear from his furrowed brow and silence that Hal's proposal troubled him. But the man kept his cool. Not until Hal was deep into the presentation of his mathematical model did the first sign of real trouble appear. In fact, the trouble was initially apparent only to Hal. As he answered questions about his model, he realized that he had made a computational error. Though he wasn't sure how much it would affect his recommendation, he admitted the mistake and apologized, promising to go back to Boston and redo his calculations. But the feeling in the room had changed. The tension was gone, as though a batter with runners in scoring position had just struck out. The meeting ended without discussion of the long-term trends that had led Hal to recommend such a major change in the way Abitibi did business. He wasn't invited back for a follow-up meeting.

Hal was disappointed but not surprised when the summer ended with no offer of full-time employment from ADL. It was a blow to his confidence to return to HBS as one of the few "failed" interns. But the long-term learning proved valuable. Hal's feeling that he'd been right was vindicated five years later when Abitibi abandoned river logging; a few years after that, it sold its dams and hydroelectric operations, becoming simply Abitibi Paper Company.

In the years to come, Hal would forgive himself for the computational error that had seemed to mean the difference between failure and success that summer. The real mistake, he would realize, was in giving insufficient thought to his audience—not only their analytical needs but the emotional ones as well. It was one thing to give bad news to a roomful of generals with whom you'd worked closely for two years. It was another to surprise a stranger without considering what made him tick.

The experience in Toronto was the first of many that would temper Hal's zeal for purely quantitative analysis, and even for rational thinking generally. He would always be glad for his ability to understand equations and run calculations, first learned at the chalkboard with his father. But he would become increasingly wary of decisions based mainly on "the numbers." He had built his quantitative model for Abitibi pursuant to a feeling, gained as he studied the broader context and history of river logging, that change was coming. Probably, the CEO had felt the same thing. Numbers, Hal would come to believe, could shape inspired feelings, but they shouldn't be allowed to trump them.

A CHERISHED MENTOR

Hal's appreciation for feelings and common sense grew in his second year of business school, particularly under the tutelage of a great mentor, Georges Doriot. Called "General Doriot" because of the brigadier general rank he had attained while leading the United States Army's Military Planning Division during World War II, Doriot was one of the Harvard Business School's most influential professors. He taught a tremendously popular second-year MBA course titled *Manufacturing*.

The course was far more interesting than that name implied. In 1959, when Hal enrolled, General Doriot was a largely self-educated man already recognized as the father of American venture capital, having founded one of the first companies that raised money to invest in entrepreneurial ventures. Relative to most business-school professors, he possessed an unusually broad, commonsensical view of management and leadership. The curriculum of the time was divided into relatively narrow functional areas, such as finance and marketing; it was in that spirit that Doriot's course was called *Manufacturing*. The courses also tended to focus on theory rather than practice, the assumption being that graduates would make their own application in the workplace.

General Doriot ignored those conventions. He transcended academic subject-matter boundaries, constantly challenging his students to obtain a broad "sense of operation" and to set ambitious goals for themselves and others. He taught that ideas were more important than products, but that people were most important of all.

General Doriot's curriculum actually

I shall never forget his plea, "Oh, give me one man who says, I can make it work." The difference between the critic and the suggester of a better way may seem slight in words, but it looms large in life. What a leap between, "I see your error" to "I see a way that might make it better." Both point out the error. But one pushes down, the other lifts. The lifting takes the tougher mind.

—TALK, AUGUST 18, 1972[12]

amounted to a series of practical maxims. "Read the *New York Times* every day," he taught, so as to stay abreast of leading-edge developments, and the local newspaper to understand the ideas influencing one's customers. "Always remember," he would caution, "that someone somewhere is making a product that will make your product obsolete." He was a prescient contrarian. At a time when American companies ruled supreme, he predicted globalization. To his analytically minded and achievement-oriented students, he preached creativity, teamwork, and compassion.

Like many of his classmates, Hal appreciated General Doriot most for his personal example and love. Hal was one of many students who felt that "The General" treated him like a son. During Doriot's forty-year teaching career, more than seven thousand students passed through his classroom.[13] It was his practice to obtain copies of the HBS admissions applications of all of his ninety students each year and study their backgrounds and college grades. Then, during the first third of the semester, he would meet with each individually at least twice in his office, establishing a personal relationship that often lasted a lifetime.

That proved true for Hal. As his graduation from the MBA program approached, General Doriot asked Hal to join him as a personal assistant in his venture capital company. Doriot went so far as to introduce Hal to Ken Olsen, the founder of Digital Equipment Company (DEC), who had a dream of building small, user-friendly computers to compete with IBM's larger, more complex machines. Doriot's venture capital company had bought 70 percent of DEC for $70,000, a large investment at the time, and he wanted someone like Hal to help him oversee this and similar investments.

The offer, which almost any of his classmates would have jumped at, made Hal wonder why his heart wasn't drawn to this kind of business opportunity. General Doriot and Ken Olsen were both brilliant and likable, and they had great business sense (the $70,000 investment in DEC became worth $355 million just ten years later, in 1968, when the company went public). Yet Hal realized that what he loved about business wasn't making products or "doing deals." It was thinking critically about complex problems. For the first time he thought, *Maybe I should stay in school and become a professor.* General Doriot, who would remain Hal's lifelong friend and mentor, took graciously Hal's decision to decline.

A DOCTORAL STUDENT'S TESTIMONY OF DIVINE ASSISTANCE

Hal performed well enough in the MBA program to graduate with distinction, meaning he finished in the top 15 to 20 percent of his class in both the first and second years. Based on this performance and the recommendation of General Doriot, he readily won acceptance to Harvard's Doctor of Business Administration (DBA) program, which was expanding rapidly, from forty students the year before to fifty as Hal sought admission.[14] The DBA curriculum was related to but significantly different from what Hal had experienced as an MBA student. Rather than preparing far into the night for two or three classes each day as he had in the MBA program, Hal as a doctoral candidate took few formal courses. He spent most of his time performing research and writing the kind of discussion cases that had kept him up late as an MBA student. He also took seminars in leading case-based classroom discussions, developing teaching skills that would serve him throughout his life.

The moment of truth in Hal's doctoral program came in the second year, when he took his qualifying examination. The exam was based on a hypothetical business problem that he received the weekend before meeting with a committee of professorial judges. As usual, Hal's service in the district presidency consumed half of the weekend, which other candidates would have spent wholly in preparation. But a miracle occurred as he explored the problem with President Cox, an accomplished business executive and MIT-trained engineer, on their long Sunday drive to a distant branch. "I see the key issue!" Hal declared. The next day, what would have been a three-hour decision-making process by the examination committee took less than ninety minutes, though they kept Hal for the full three hours to explore the ideas that had come to him.

Hal's best experiences as a graduate student reinforced those he enjoyed in Harvard's MBA program and in the physics department at the University of Utah. Through nine years of higher education, he found that Heavenly Father cares about all types of learning, and that He can help all of His children learn. Hal would share that testimony with Latter-day Saint students in a 2001 talk called "Education for Real Life."

A SERIOUS HARVARD STUDENT

Your life is carefully watched over, as was mine. The Lord knows both what He will need you to do and what you will need to know. He is kind and He is all-knowing. So you can with confidence expect that He has prepared opportunities for you to learn in preparation for the service you will give. You will not recognize those opportunities perfectly, as I did not. But when you put the spiritual things first in your life, you will be blessed to feel directed toward certain learning, and you will be motivated to work harder. You will recognize later that your power to serve was increased, and you will be grateful. . . .

The Lord loves you and watches over you. He is all-powerful, and He promised you this: "But seek ye first the kingdom of God, and his righteousness; and all these things shall be added unto you" (Matthew 6:33).

That is a true promise. When we put God's purposes first, He will give us miracles. If we pray to know what He would have us do next, He will multiply the effects of what we do in such a way that time seems to be expanded. He may do it in different ways for each individual, but I know from long experience that He is faithful to His word. . . .

I cannot promise academic success. . . . Nor can I tell you the way in which He will honor His promise of adding blessings upon you. But I can promise you that if you will go to Him in prayer and ask what He would have you do next, promising that you will put His kingdom first, He will answer your prayer and He will keep His promise to add upon your head blessings, enough and to spare. Those apparent prison walls of "not enough time" will begin to recede, even as you are called to do more.

The real life we're preparing for is eternal life. Secular knowledge has for us eternal significance. Our conviction is that God, our Heavenly Father, wants us to live the life that He does. We learn both the spiritual things and the secular things "so we may one day create worlds [and] people and govern them."[15] All we can learn that is true while we are in this life will rise with us in the Resurrection. And all that we can learn will enhance our capacity to serve. That is a destiny reserved not alone for the brilliant, those who learn the most quickly, or those who enter the most respected professions. It will be given to those who are humbly good, who love God, and who serve Him with all their capacities, however limited those capacities are—as are all our capacities, compared with the capacities of God.[16]

Hal had experienced miracles throughout his educational experience. Blessedly, by the time he graduated from the DBA program in 1962, he had received another miracle in his life. He had finally found his long-sought eternal companion.

Kathy's sore elbow, developed arm-wrestling with her
nephew, Mark, sometime last week, forced her out of
our double's match this morning; within an hour she'd
sent a replacement, so I played six sets. Result: I
soaked my elbow in a tub of hot water propped on the
table the breakfast room at grandpa's, while I watched
the games with the boys. Annette served the whole

5

LOVE THY WIFE

Thou shalt love thy wife
With all thy heart,
And shalt cleave unto her
And none else.
—DOCTRINE AND COVENANTS 42:22

Though Hal enjoyed his studies and Church service while at Harvard, it was a lonely time. His worry went beyond his being single in his late twenties. It included not having the family of which he had dreamed since he was a little boy, even before receiving his Uncle Gaskell Romney's patriarchal promise of a home full of children and peace. He had felt angst over the fulfillment of this promise for years, as evidenced by a letter he wrote to his mother, Mildred, from Albuquerque when he was only twenty-two.

My Dearest Mother,

I've just opened your first jar of applesauce, and although I meant to eat it slowly as I wrote, I've already finished half of it. There's only one food like applesauce and only one applesauce like Mother's. There goes some more. I just can't leave it alone.

I wanted to talk a little with you tonight, Mother, the way we'd do if you'd been here when I came home from tracting or if I were with you. I know how much my Mother loves me, but sometimes I wonder if you understand how much I love you.

From you I learned that the most wonderful thing in the world was a home where the gospel was the common bond of love and the way of life. I don't think you could have dreamed about my home or your grandchildren any more than I have over the years, Mother. I've lost fifteen pounds in the last four months, and to a large extent over concern for your grandchildren. If I thought much more about it, perhaps neither of us would live to know them.[1]

Hal's longing for children was neither idle nor new. From his teenage years he had not only thought of his future children but imagined them. In his mind's eye they had red hair like his mother's; he even called them "the Redheads." When he faced temptation, he would remind himself, "I can't do that—the Redheads are counting on me."

STILL SINGLE IN BOSTON

Hal was still single as an HBS doctoral student in the spring of 1960, at age twenty-seven. Over the preceding half-dozen years he had courted young women of great character and faith. In several cases, the relationship had deepened to the point that he sought divine direction in proceeding. Yet to his sorrow both for himself and for these lovely women, no spiritual confirmation to marry had come. Though he was grateful for dinner and other social invitations from his married Harvard classmates, including Bob Hales and his wife, Mary, he became increasingly conscious of the differences between their homes and his. Thirty-five years later, in a Church Educational System fireside, he would describe his feelings about the boardinghouse in which he lived during those Harvard years. It belonged to a kindly couple, the Sopers.

Costs have changed, so this will be hard for you to believe, but this was the deal the Sopers gave me: My own large room and bath, furniture and sheets provided, maid service, six big breakfasts and five wonderful dinners a week—all at the price of twenty-one dollars a week. More than that, the meals were ample and prepared with such skill that we called our landlady with some affection "Ma Soper." Just talking about it with you makes me realize that I didn't thank Mrs. Soper often enough, nor Mr. Soper and their daughter, since it must have been some burden to have twelve single men to dinner every weeknight.

Now, you aren't tempted by that description of a boarding-house, and neither am I. It could have the most spacious rooms, the best service, and the finest eleven men you could ever know as fellow boarders and we wouldn't want to live there more than a short while. If it were beautiful beyond our power to imagine, we wouldn't want to live there forever, single, if we have even the dimmest memory or the faintest vision of a family with beloved parents and children like the one from which we came to this earth and the one that is our destiny to form and to live in forever. There is only one place where there will be families—the highest degree of the celestial kingdom. That is where we will want to be.[2]

The realization of Hal's lifelong dream of a family of his own finally began on an early summer morning in Rindge, New Hampshire, a two-hour drive to the west and north from Boston. Hal was assigned by President Cox to represent the district presidency at a single-adult "morningside" held at the Cathedral of the Pines, a natural amphitheater atop a wooded hill near Mount Monadnock. After the event Hal walked through the trees surrounding the amphitheater toward the parking lot where he had left his red Volkswagen Beetle, an MBA graduation gift from his father.

Entering the lot, Hal sighted an auburn-haired young woman in a red and white seersucker dress. He had never seen her before and knew nothing about her. But he was immediately impressed by the goodness she radiated. The thought came, "That's the best person I've ever seen. If I could be with her, I could be every good thing I ever wanted to be."[3]

The next day the Boston District presidency attended sacrament meeting at the Church's historic Longfellow Park chapel in Cambridge, near Harvard Yard. Seated on the stand next to President Cox, Hal saw the young woman again, sitting with a friend in the congregation. He leaned over to President Cox and said, "That's the girl I would give anything to marry."

The girl, Kathleen Johnson, was from Palo Alto, California, as far from Boston as one can get in the continental United States. She was a twenty-year-old student from the University of California at Berkeley who hadn't intended to be in Massachusetts that summer. Early in the spring, one of her sorority sisters had described a plan to attend summer school at Harvard. "That sounds like fun," Kathy replied good-naturedly. Several weeks later this friend reported that she had enrolled and bought her plane ticket. "Won't we have fun?" she asked. Caught off guard, Kathy casually replied that she'd never had any intention of going. Her friend was equally surprised and vehement in her response: "I'm counting on you to be my roommate. You *have* to go!"

Whatever valid excuses Kathy could have made, lack of financial means wasn't one of them. The year before, her parents had paid for a semester of French language study at the Sorbonne, home to the University of Paris; the year before that she had studied at the University of Vienna. Though Kathy wasn't eager to go to Boston, she didn't have uneasy feelings about it. In the spirit of friendship, and with her parents' blessing, she went along. A good student at Cal, she faced no difficulty in getting into the Harvard summer program, which was run precisely for well-to-do students such as Kathy from other schools.

Pulling rank with the ward clerk after seeing her in sacrament meeting, Hal got Kathy's phone number. He called for a first date several days later. Knowing neither his name nor his face, she nonchalantly hedged: "If you're in church on Sunday, we'll talk then." Hal made sure that he was there, asking President Cox to excuse him from the usual visit to a distant branch for the sake of this greater personal cause.

The next Sunday at Longfellow Park, Hal was thrilled by Kathy's reply to his question about her interests: "I like to play tennis," she said. The words were music to Hal's ears. With his doctoral qualifying examination behind him and the business school all but deserted for the summer, he had more time on his hands than he had enjoyed for years. He'd been playing tennis several times a week with a former collegiate tennis player; his game was at an all-time high. It would be the perfect first date.

> **I found out that when the game gets tough, she gets better.**
> —2012 INTERVIEW

The initial set of tennis, played several days later on Harvard's clay courts, went just as Hal had planned: he won six games to three. As they switched sides for the next set, he airily complimented Kathy's play, in a manner intended to be charming. She stared straight ahead and said nothing. While he prepared to serve from his baseline, she crouched low behind hers, gently but firmly hitting the clay court with her wooden racquet.

Hal wouldn't recall the final score of that second set, but in later years he freely admitted, "She cleaned me out." In the discussion of their first date, Kathy hadn't mentioned that she had captained the tennis team at her private girls' high school. As they took the court, she may have underrated her balding, bespectacled date from Utah. In any case, one set was all Prince Charming would win from this stoic, determined young woman.

A PRIVILEGED UPBRINGING

As Hal and Kathy continued to date during the few weeks she would spend in Boston before returning to California, he began to appreciate the paradox of her privileged upbringing and her unaffected personality. Kathy was the second of three children born to J. Cyril ("Sid") and La Prele Lindsay Johnson. Sid and La Prele had both grown up in

Utah, but under vastly different circumstances. While the Johnsons struggled to eke out a living in the sparsely populated and unforgiving Uintah Basin, near Roosevelt, the Lindsays were among Utah's wealthiest ranching families. In 1922, when La Prele was twelve, the Lindsay Land and Livestock Company controlled more than 175,000 acres in northern Utah and had an appraised value of $1.5 million, or nearly $20 million today. Raised in an elegant new home built the year before her birth, La Prele developed refined tastes. She loved poetry, drama, music, and shopping. Her older brother Clyde called her "the aristocrat."

La Prele's father, Walter John ("W. J.") Lindsay, had been born in poverty. He built his empire through a combination of hard work, shrewd management, and risk taking. Fortune turned against him in 1922, when a financial downturn led to foreclosure of the entire Lindsay operation. But in typical fashion, W. J. found new opportunities. Flat broke at age fifty-nine, he rallied his grown sons and sons-in-law and moved to northern California, where they sensed potential in home building and real-estate development. Within a year, the Lindsay clan had built and sold eight houses. Though the family would never return to the heights of affluence they had known in Utah, La Prele moved from Utah to San Francisco with little sense of economic hardship. In the process, her father found more time for gospel study and worship. Largely inactive in the Church until the move to California, W. J. served as a stake patriarch during the final two decades of his life. The testimony he bore of heaven's kindness to the Lindsays was a statement of gratitude and a warning to his family. "Losing our wealth was a blessing in disguise," he told them before he died. "That money would have spoiled you all. Now you have made your own way and have remained good Church members."[4]

Even in humbler circumstances, La Prele retained an air of aristocracy. She became a prominent performer in amateur speech festivals and plays. San Francisco also offered new opportunities to refine her social graces and fashion sense. Throughout her life she would

May 31, 1984
Thursday

I wrote in the Atherton
guest house of the
Johnsons, looking down
on the
of
Eliza
Kathle
blow
birthda
dinner
Holy
teach
works

June
Friday

Elizab
the
worke
Gary
Los A
to he
time
Altos.

June
Satur

I tow
inflat
M a r y
c o m p
purple
match
hair
Stuar
sister
and I
dance

June 3, 1984
Sunday

J. CYRIL ("SID") AND LA PRELE LINDSAY JOHNSON,
KATHY'S PARENTS.

Kathy, Elizabeth, and Mary Kathleen were dressed and
packed early for our drive from Atherton to the San Jose
airport. On the flight home, a stewardess made a bullseye
with a glass full of orange juice on my lap. It was so cold
and complete a soaking that I laughed for the rest of the
trip. I used bags to shield the results as I got us to the car.

> As a young girl, I can remember her driving week after week to pick up handicapped children to take them to a special school at the Children's Health Council, so that the children could have education they would not have otherwise received, and taking them home afterwards, so that their mothers would have a break that they would not otherwise receive.
>
> —KATHLEEN JOHNSON EYRING[5]

make unstinting contributions of time in the Church and local community, serving several times as a ward Relief Society president and leader of her children's school associations.

Yet La Prele also served a term as president of the Town and Country Club, an elite women's group headquartered in Union Square, San Francisco's shopping district. She became a member of the opera's informal "first-nighter" club, displaying her fashion sense via elegant gowns and jewelry and occasionally appearing in the society pages of the newspaper. As a Relief Society president, La Prele was known by the sisters of the ward both for her Christian service and for timely warnings against fashion faux pas, such as wearing white after Labor Day.

Sid Johnson, whose day-laborer's penury had driven him to San Francisco just as bankruptcy had the wealthy Lindsays, keenly sensed their social differences as he courted La Prele. He gamely joined her in Church plays, in which his limited talent for acting and singing showed painfully. He was glad to have just enough rhythm to lead La Prele on the dance floor and happy to own a car to drive her to the church. Chauffeuring La Prele to dances allowed him to sign his name on at least two lines of her dance card, which always filled soon after they arrived.

At the time Sid began to court La Prele, he was a construction worker moving from one temporary job to another and renting an apartment with three other fellows. What little he could save, he sent home to his struggling family in Utah. The car was his lone tangible asset, and the gloom of the Great Depression gripped his otherwise optimistic heart. Though he loved La Prele, doubts about his ability to meet her expectations plagued him. They dated for two years, falling gradually but deeply in love. Finally, La Prele informed Sid that a decision had to be made. As he well knew, there were other suitors.

Sid's breakthrough came as he passed through Salt Lake City on a trip to visit his parents in Utah. Stopping to see Church Patriarch Eldred G. Smith, he received a blessing that gave him the courage to ask for La Prele's hand. He later recalled, "Emphasizing that every blessing is predicated on obedience, it gave me the assurance that I would be able to provide for La Prele and our family, and that together, with help from the Lord, we would be able to work out our problems."[6]

A dogged, resourceful entrepreneur in the spirit of his father-in-law, W. J. Lindsay, Sid more than succeeded in providing for La Prele and their three children. Kathy grew up in San Francisco and then Palo Alto in homes built by her father. A maid named Trudy Lucas, hired at the time of Kathy's birth, served the family for forty-five years. While their father developed real estate in the booming Bay Area, Kathy and her siblings—older sister, Annette, and younger brother, Craig—spent summers with their mother and Trudy, along with their Lindsay aunts and cousins, at Lake Tahoe; Sid made the four-hour drive to join them each weekend. Kathy spent sixteen consecutive summers enjoying the beauty of Tahoe's beaches and forests, where she developed a deep love for nature and its generous Creator.

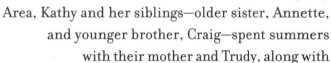

To La Prele's chagrin, Kathy resisted efforts to prepare her for induction into San Francisco's social aristocracy. Though elegant and refined in her own way, Kathy was outgoing and fun-loving, a

KATHY AS A HIGH SCHOOL SENIOR

natural athlete like her golf-playing and fly-fishing father. On shopping trips she preferred baseball gloves to party dresses. She excelled in sports but took less interest in voice and elocution lessons.

At Castilleja, the elite girls' school she attended, Kathy was an outgoing, generous friend to all. In sophomore biology class she enjoyed chatting with "Gracie" Wing, who would later marry a guitarist by the last name of Slick and become an icon of the psychedelic rock-and-roll era. Kathy drove the few blocks to school each day in a sporty black Ford convertible, a gift from her parents that sat wrapped with a giant red bow in the driveway on her fifteenth Christmas (more than four months before she turned sixteen). Having served as student-body president and won valedictorian honors in her senior year, she left this yearbook "last will and testament" to her Castilleja classmates: "[I bequeath] the ability to drive from my house to school in two minutes flat, to anyone who wishes to appear in traffic court as often as I have."

AN UNAFFECTED YOUNG WOMAN

Kathy's parents trusted her with the car and the study-abroad trips to Europe because they knew her incorruptibility, though even they were surprised on that Christmas morning of the convertible. "They got much less of a rise from her than they expected when she saw the car," her younger brother, Craig, would recall. Craig and others recognized in his sister a rare paradox. Though she was talented and could appear carefree, she was spiritually centered, fiercely so. Financial wealth meant little to her. And as she grew older and began to realize the potentially harmful effects of worldliness, she increasingly guarded herself against them.

The year after graduating from Castilleja, Kathy went off to Berkeley, where she followed the lead of her older sister, Annette, and successfully rushed the Kappa Kappa Gamma sorority. She moved into the Kappa house, a stately gray mansion with a traditional Greek portico. She hadn't realized how the Kappas, one of the most elite sororities, were viewed by the ordinary students at Berkeley; they called the Kappa house "The Big Gray Money Bin." Noting that her sporty black convertible stood out in the parking lots of public Berkeley in a way it hadn't at private Castilleja, Kathy came home one weekend and swapped cars with Trudy, the maid. Trudy got the convertible for trips to the market, while Kathy took a battleship-gray station wagon back to Berkeley.

> **Kathy was a free spirit who always chose well.**
> —CRAIG JOHNSON[7]

Kathy found a way to distance herself from the luxuries of her upbringing without distancing herself from her parents, who provided the luxuries only out of love. The key was to celebrate their common commitment to the gospel, something she did all her life. For example, in a 1992 Christmas letter to her mother, Kathy shared a copy of a talk given by Elder Mark E. Petersen, a member of the Quorum of the Twelve Apostles. The site of Elder Petersen's remarks, the Paris Mission home, had reminded Kathy of a visit La Prele made to France when her daughter was studying at the University of Paris. Kathy wrote:

> As I read this talk given at the mission home in Paris 24 years ago, I thought of the wonderful time you and I spent together in Paris at the museums, the restaurants, the shops, and the Hotel de Crillon. But even more, as I read Elder Petersen's remarks, I had an overwhelming feeling for gratitude that I was chosen to come into your home, to be your daughter. Every good thing in my life has come because you and Daddy not only taught me, but showed me the way to live.[8]

TESTS OF FAITH

Though still a decade from the violent protests that would paralyze the campus in the late 1960s, the University of California at Berkeley was already a place of radical ideology when Kathy arrived. Some of her professors took delight in challenging the simple faith of this bright, earnest political science major. Fortunately, her father was a self-taught gospel scholar and experienced stake missionary. On weekends, she drove across the San Francisco Bay from Berkeley to huddle with Sid in the study of the Johnsons' Palo Alto home. Together they buttressed her natural faith with deeper understanding of gospel principles. With her father's help, Kathy learned to transcend the sophistries of her university environment while making the most of the truths to be learned there.

In fact, the spiritual pressures of Berkeley crystallized Kathy's testimony of the gospel. From as far back as she could remember, she had felt that The Church of Jesus Christ of Latter-day Saints was true. Each week without fail, Sid and La Prele took their children to Sunday services, both morning and evening. Young Kathy felt the Spirit especially in the evening sacrament meetings.

She was grateful to renew that feeling weekly as a college student, in her parents' Palo Alto Ward. But the spiritual lift of the weekend at home was hard to maintain as she returned to Berkeley for Monday classes. One Sunday evening, back in her room at the Kappa house, she prayed fervently to feel the Spirit always, wherever she went. She received a strong reconfirmation of her testimony that The Church of Jesus Christ of Latter-day Saints was true and was really the Savior's Church.

With that feeling came a related thought. Kathy realized that her testimony was tied inextricably to Church services, to worshipping with other Saints. She was asking that the warm feelings of Sunday services carry over to the rest of the week, to all times and places. Of course, that couldn't happen unless she made those meetings, and all others sponsored by the Church, a top priority. That night, in the Kappa house at Berkeley, she committed to do that. The effect was life-changing not only for her but also for Hal, as she would recall decades later:

> That experience changed my life. From that time on, when I moved to a new city I tried to find out where the nearest Latter-day Saint branch of the Church met. In Massachusetts, I found the Cambridge branch of the Church on my first Sunday. Soon after I arrived they announced an early-morning meeting to be held outdoors in New Hampshire, at the Cathedral of the Pines. I went there because of the feeling I had that it was where the Lord would have me be.[9]

LONG-DISTANCE COURTSHIP

As Hal got to know Kathy, he was taken not only by her lack of airs or pretense but also by her spiritual maturity. She reminded him of one of the purest and most devoted of his missionary companions, Elder Geddes. She seemed unimpressed by Hal's educational and family background. Yet she was eager to join him in his Church work, traveling with him on Sundays to remote branches. While driving they shared testimonies and spiritual feelings as he had done with President Cox, Elder Geddes, and his parents. In the presence of this unaffected twenty-year-old girl Hal felt impelled to be a better man, to be worthy of her companionship. Though he couldn't be sure at the time, his efforts were working.

> One of the things that impressed me most about him was that he loved the Lord. And he loved Him enough to show this love by great service at the expense of worldly honors. He didn't seek the honors of men as he sought the love of the Lord.
> —KATHLEEN JOHNSON EYRING[10]

Throughout that idyllic summer, they saw one another regularly, playing tennis and taking a sailing trip with friends to Cape Cod.

They even visited Hal's boyhood home, Princeton. But the summer ended too soon, leaving the couple to correspond by letter and telephone when Kathy returned to California. She could afford to fly back to Boston for several visits, the first made with a college friend as chaperone. Hal reciprocated once, meeting Kathy's family on a trip to interview for a faculty position at Stanford; he stayed at the home of his MBA roommate George Montgomery, who lived in nearby Hillsborough. The Stanford interview produced a job offer, in addition to offers already received from Harvard and UCLA.

In early 1961, eight months after their first meeting, Kathy made a final visit to see Hal in Boston. By this time they were deeply in love. But Kathy agreed with her father, who knew from personal experience the feeling of "cold feet," that unchaperoned cross-country dating was inappropriate. On the final evening of this late-winter trip, Kathy told Hal that she would not be returning to see him again.

Hal shared Kathy's feeling that their dating relationship could not continue as it had been. For months he had been seeking heaven's blessing to marry Kathy, but no clear confirmation had come. The thought of losing her and the family they might have together—"the Redheads"—made his heart ache. But he was determined to receive divine confirmation. That night he prayed with greater fervency than ever, telling his Heavenly Father that he would not proceed without approval. Initially, his only answer was an enigmatic impression: "If you never saw her again, you'd have known more of love than most people do in a lifetime."

Hal continued to pray through the night. Finally the hoped-for confirmation came, in the form of a voice heard in his mind: "Go!" The next morning, before dawn, he prayed again to

I have had prayers answered. Those answers were most clear when what I wanted was silenced by an overpowering need to know what God wanted. It is then that the answer from a loving Heavenly Father can be spoken to the mind by the still, small voice and can be written on the heart.

—TALK, OCTOBER 1, 2000[11]

be sure that he had heard correctly. A feeling of reconfirmation enveloped him, triggering tears of joy.

Leaving the Sopers' place in his Volkswagen, Hal drove quickly to the well-known Longfellow's Wayside Inn, where Kathy was staying. Her bags were packed for the flight home. On the drive to the airport, still in the countryside, Hal stopped the car on a deserted road next to a stone wall. Turning to Kathy, he said, "I've been told to ask you to marry me." Kathy replied only with tears. Though in later years Hal would sometimes joke about never getting a verbal confirmation, he knew that her answer was as sure as heaven's.

nephew, Mark, sometime last week, forced her out of
our double's match this morning; within an hour she'd
sent a replacement, so I played six sets. Result: I
soaked my elbow in a tub of hot water propped on the
table

6

BE FRUITFUL

And God blessed Noah and his sons,
And said unto them,
Be fruitful,
And multiply,
And replenish the earth.
—GENESIS 9:1

Hal and Kathy were married on July 27, 1962, in the Logan Temple,
the more readily accessible Salt Lake Temple being closed at the
time for renovation. The marriage was performed by Elder Spencer
W. Kimball, Hal's uncle, who was then a member of the Quorum of
the Twelve Apostles. Hal was encouraged by Uncle Spencer's assess-
ment of Kathy: "There isn't a phony bone in her body," he privately
remarked. Hal was much less certain, though, about a piece of counsel
that Uncle Spencer gave the newlyweds. He admonished them, "Live in
such a way that when the call comes, you can walk away easily."

By then Hal knew what he would be doing, at least in the near
term—working as a professor at Stanford's Graduate School of
Business. He had accepted Stanford's offer over Harvard's for several
reasons. One, of course, was its location in Kathy's hometown, Palo
Alto. Another was counsel he received from General Doriot, his beloved professor and would-be employer. General Doriot urged Hal to
go to the West, where innovation was brewing, especially in what would

CUTTING THE CAKE IN PALO ALTO

become the "Silicon Valley" in which Stanford is centered.

The first year of marriage was busy for both Hal and Kathy. Within six months she was pregnant with their first child. While he worked long days at Stanford, she decorated and kept house in a series of temporarily vacant apartments owned by her father. Her parents' maid, Trudy, helped her learn to cook, a skill she hadn't developed during her busy years at Castilleja and Berkeley.

In those early years, Kathy also made a weekly drive across the San Francisco Bay to the Oakland Temple, where she sought to find the peace that Hal had discovered in the Salt Lake Temple as a young serviceman on his way to Albuquerque. On Hal's first visit to the temple, he had immediately felt at home. Kathy's initial temple experience, by contrast, had been disorienting. Everything was new, and it had all come at once. She and her parents had arrived in Utah the day before the wedding. They had met her in-laws for the first time at the airport and then had driven directly to the temple in Logan. The new people, places, and wedding events, on top of the temple experience itself, had left her unsettled. It was nearly a year before she found the peaceful feeling she sought, but she came to it in the Oakland Temple. The price was worth paying: throughout her life the temple was her second home, the one on which she modeled her family's home.

Hal's first year at Stanford proved similarly challenging but productive. He finished and defended his dissertation while simultaneously teaching a full load of courses, each one of which required first-time preparation. The dissertation was well received by the members of his committee, who approved it in the summer of 1963.

Nonetheless, Hal had mixed feelings about what he learned from his research. His topic of study was a mathematical model for managing complex, one-of-a-kind projects. The model, best known by its acronym, PERT (Program Evaluation Review Technique), had been developed several years earlier by the U.S. Navy; it was a planning tool for building nuclear submarines. Hal brought natural advantages to the study of this model's effectiveness, including strong quantitative skills and familiarity with both the military and nuclear technology.

What he found, though, was that even the most complex mathematics cannot account for uncertainties, such as unexpected difficulty in manufacturing a novel submarine component or the failure of a supplier to deliver a key part on time. When unforeseen things happen—as they often do in projects as complicated as the building of submarines—planning models designed to guide and control workers' activities can produce undesirable outcomes. Hal observed problems at both ends of the spectrum of compliance to planning-model prescriptions. Workers who failed to adjust the schedule prescribed by the model when necessary found their hands tied by it. Conversely, those who ignored or "gamed" the model for the sake of expediency lost the benefit of its coordinating power.

In short, Hal learned that even the most rational planner can't dictate and control the activities of a large organization and still get things done effectively. That insight would prove helpful to him later, when he led large organizations. However, for the time being it further blunted his enthusiasm for the kinds of quantitative research that Stanford had hired him to do.

A LESSON IN BEING MENTORED

Having done her best to decorate two temporary apartments during their first fall and winter, Kathy packed everything up again and put most of it into storage at the beginning of the summer of 1963. She and Hal felt grateful to have won a research fellowship from RAND Corporation, a renowned policy think tank headquartered in Santa Monica, California, with offices overlooking the Pacific Ocean. RAND attracted some of the world's leading thinkers, with whom Hal was eager to rub shoulders. After a year spent focused on teaching and completing a dissertation that seemed to be an analytical dead end, he hoped that a summer at RAND would jump-start the research he needed to win tenure at Stanford.

To his disappointment, the summer got off to a slow start. Notwithstanding the opportunity to focus all his time and attention on research in an intellectually rarefied environment, there were no eureka moments. It was just as hard to find and develop an intriguing line of inquiry at RAND as it had been at Stanford and Harvard. Sensing Hal's malaise, the man to whom Hal reported provided a unique opportunity: he would arrange a private meeting for Hal with the institute's most renowned researcher. More than thirty years later, Hal described to a group of BYU faculty members the once-in-a-lifetime learning experience. The most profound lesson wasn't about the way to produce business research, but about the way to mentor and to be mentored.

A kind department head offered me the chance to talk with Herbert Simon. Professor Simon was another of the people there that summer. You would have had to have worked in that field in that faraway time to know what such an invitation meant. No one had done more than he had to change the way all of us thought about how decisions are shaped in organizations. He had not yet won the Nobel Prize in economics. In fact, I'm not sure there was such a prize yet.[1] But I knew what an opportunity I was being offered. I could scarcely believe my good fortune.

I found that he had read my work, carefully and critically. It was clear at the outset that he had been pondering my problem. The few questions he asked cut deep, revealing the weaknesses in what I had done. He obviously felt that helping me with my problem was going to be more important than making me comfortable. He seemed to assume that I cared more about my work than my ego.

And yet, forthright and candid as he was, he was not my adversary nor my rival. He listened with great kindness, with what felt almost like sympathy. He listened with complete absorption. It was as if there were no other person alive but me and no ideas in the world but mine. It is not too extreme, at least for me, to say that only my mother, my wife, and my other mentors have ever listened to me with such compassion. After what seemed an hour, he began to do the talking, quietly. I recognized the continuity, the steadiness in his counsel because it reflected what I had read of his publications. But he talked about my work, not his. He corrected not so much by pointing out mistakes as by showing me where to find opportunities to add value to my work.

He had obviously no intention of doing the work for me, or even telling me how to do it. He instead described where it might lead and what value it might have. He spent hours with me. And, at the end, he said words that gave the impression to me that he would continue to care about me and my work.[2]

Professor Simon's example of outstanding mentoring would prove invaluable throughout Hal's life, particularly as he raised his children. Those children would be the beneficiaries of a father who treated them as peers, correcting constructively and with sensitivity to their willingness to receive instruction. But his own doubts betrayed him in the mentoring relationship he might have enjoyed with Professor Simon not only that summer but throughout his academic career.

The decision was an incremental and not entirely conscious one. It began with a failure to follow up quickly after that first meeting. Hal rationalized that he needed to be fully prepared for a second meeting

You decide to grant the mentor authority by your trust. You choose to try to prolong the relationship. And you hold the power to end it.

If you want praise more than instruction, you may get neither.

—TALK, AUGUST 23, 1993[3]

so as not to disappoint Professor Simon (or embarrass himself). Before long, he began to drift from the initially suggested direction; that made him less eager to follow up at all. The summer ended without another conversation with this potentially invaluable mentor. It was a painful lesson that Hal remembered and would be careful not to repeat when heaven provided other mentors later in life.

THE HOUSE ON THE HILL

Returning to Palo Alto at the end of the summer, Hal and Kathy didn't stay settled long. She was due to deliver their first child in September. Coincidentally, Sid had his eye on a special piece of property with two houses on it, one for Hal and the mother-to-be. The larger house could hardly be called by that name. Built by a Virginia railroad baron in 1917, it was modeled on the Grand and Petit Trianons at Versailles, residences for French royalty. It sat on a twelve-acre hilltop estate in Atherton, one of the most exclusive communities in the United States, with views of the San Francisco Bay to the east and California's Coast Ranges to the west. The estate included formal gardens, an oversized swimming pool with bathhouses, a tennis court, riding stables, and—significantly for Hal and Kathy—a four-bedroom guest house designed in the style of a European hunting lodge.

The Atherton property was a bold reach for Sid, notwithstanding the success of his real-estate investment company, which by then owned a major shopping center. But he smelled a deal in the making. The hilltop estate, owned by an aging daughter of one of San Francisco's leading families, had fallen into disrepair. For all its elegance of design, the estate had the look of a fixer-upper. Sid-the-handyman saw in the crumbling pavement of the quarter-mile-long driveway and the main house's leaky slate roof an opportunity to buy

THE COLONNADE OF THE MAIN HOUSE

a palace fit for his queen, at a price he could afford. In fact, he already had a plan for subdividing and selling the stable and its pasture. Sid-the-real-estate-speculator saw two building lots that might pay for the whole deal.

He took Hal and Kathy to see the property when they returned from Santa Monica. After driving the length of Atherton's Walsh Road, they passed through a towering, wrought-iron gate and beyond the gardener's house at the foot of the hill. The oak-lined driveway rose via two switchbacks cut into the sandstone. As they climbed, Hal had a sense of familiarity. Rounding the second turn, where the corner of the main house became visible, he recognized the place. He turned to Kathy and said, "I saw this spot in my mind as Uncle Spencer told us to be ready to walk away easily when the call comes."

A NEW HOME

Hal and Kathy's first child, christened Henry Johnson, arrived on September 19, 1963, at Stanford Hospital. They brought him home to

THE GUEST HOUSE

the guest house at the hilltop estate in Atherton, which Sid had purchased for $250,000—cash. It was an idyllic place to start a family. The guest house was spacious. Hal and Kathy's bedroom, which offered a beautiful view of the Coast Ranges, adjoined a large bathroom that also served a second bedroom, where they put the baby. Hal, an early riser, took an upstairs bathroom as his own, allowing Kathy and the baby to sleep as he showered and dressed for work.

The guest house was far enough from the main house (about a hundred feet) to offer a feeling of privacy, thanks to the huge oak and fir trees separating them. However, Trudy's car, which she parked by the manicured boxwood hedge in front of the guest house, symbolized the strength of the homemaking and child-care resources Kathy had near at hand. Not much farther away than the main house was the tennis court, where Kathy and Hal often played in the evenings after he returned from work. Atherton was close enough to the Stanford campus that he rode his bike in good weather, which was the norm in mild

Northern California. Years later, Kathy would fondly recall the family's days living in the Atherton guest house:

> I was blessed to live with my husband and three of our six children in my parents' guest cottage. I'm sure we outwore our welcome as guests—we lived there ten years—but Mother was always wonderful to us. She was the best neighbor I've ever had. Not long ago, my young daughter looked at me and thoughtfully said, "When you lived next door to Grandma, did you go to the store to buy groceries, or did you just go over to Grandma's and borrow?"
>
> It was a perceptive question, but a rather painful one for me to answer, for I had to admit that on more than one occasion I went over to Grandma's to borrow more than a cup of sugar. But Mother was always very kind and gracious, and as my husband is fond of saying, we lived next to Mother for ten years without a cross word or an unkind feeling passing between us.[4]

Though Hal still faced the pressure of winning tenure in Stanford's highly competitive scholarly environment, he had the advantage in that second year of being familiar with at least some of the courses he taught. Still, he often worked through the night preparing for classes that he was developing on the fly. He was self-conscious about his lack of published research, the key determinant of tenure, which made it all the more important for him to succeed in the classroom.

Fortunately, Hal was recognized by his colleagues as an unusually skillful teacher, and he was generally well liked. Among his close friends at Stanford was Roger Sant, a part-time lecturer in finance whom Hal had known at HBS as a fellow student in the MBA program. Another friend was a statistics wizard named Ed Zschau (pronounced "shout," without the "t"). Both men were young but brimming with talent. Sant, a member of the Church, was an entrepreneur with a strong social conscience. He would leave Palo Alto to work in the Nixon and Ford administrations and then would go on to found an environment-friendly global energy company that made him a billionaire. Upon retirement, he would publicly commit to give nearly all of his fortune to charity.

Ed Zschau was a lighthearted Renaissance man still in his twenties, a philosophy undergraduate from Princeton who earned two master's degrees and a PhD in statistics at Stanford. With Hal's help he would found one of the early Silicon Valley computer companies, System Industries, make a small fortune, and run for Congress, where he served two terms. A ukulele player who became known as "the singing Congressman," he delighted Stanford students in the classroom and party guests on the Hill with original, tongue-in-cheek compositions, including a witty company song for System Industries.

Both great teachers themselves, Sant and Zschau admired Hal's skill in the classroom. Roger considered Hal "a commanding presence" who could draw students from the sidelines into the heart of a discussion with "wonderful sensitivity."[5] Ed credited Hal with being "just inspirational, almost tears in your eyes: it was sort of like preaching but in a classroom or auditorium."[6]

Hal was blessed to have been well trained as a teacher at Harvard, where his professors were masters of the case method of instruction, the approach that Stanford also adopted. Rather than lecturing, case-method instructors work from stories about real situations, such as a money-losing business. Students read the case and discuss it in small groups before coming to class, where they are invited to share their ideas for solving the problem sketched out in the case.

Hal's dissertation committee chair and personal mentor, C. Roland ("Chris") Christensen, was recognized as the world's leading practitioner of case-method teaching. Unlike the Harvard Business School professor who had terrified Hal and his first-year MBA classmates with the warning, "One

> Those of you who think of yourselves as the weakest intellectually have incredible powers of thought. Your problem—my problem—is not the poverty of my intellectual equipment. Your problem is having far more intellectual capacity than you have any ability to harness.
>
> —TALK, JANUARY 1, 1977[7]

of the three of you will likely fail," Professor Christensen preached a teaching philosophy of hope and love for his students, based on his belief that "teaching is a moral act":

> I believe in the unlimited potential of every student. At first glance they range, like instructors, from mediocre to magnificent. But potential is invisible to the superficial gaze. It takes faith to discern it, but I have witnessed too many academic miracles to doubt its existence. I now view each student as "material for a work of art." If I have faith, deep faith, in students' capacities for creativity and growth, how very much we can accomplish together.[8]

Thanks to Professor Christensen and other professors committed to their craft, Hal and his fellow HBS doctoral students learned how to see and bring out the best in their students. That skill won Hal the respect of both his students and his faculty colleagues, relieving some of the pressure he felt at having no clear research agenda.

A YEAR AT MIT

Much to Hal's surprise, in 1964 his Stanford colleagues nominated him for a prestigious Alfred P. Sloan faculty fellowship.[9] The award meant that he and Kathy could take a year, at full salary, to study at MIT, just down the Charles River from Harvard. It would prove to be not only a great honor but a providential fork in the intellectual road Hal was traveling. It would also shape his views of leadership, especially in his own family.

In the early 1960s, MIT was the site of cutting-edge research in the field of "systems analysis," the kind of work that Hal had done for his dissertation and continued to pursue during his summer at RAND. MIT's stars in this mathematical field included Jay Forrester, a pioneering developer of modern computers. By the time Hal arrived, Forrester had begun to use computers to model the complex decisions that organizational leaders face. Applying computer power to the kinds of equations Hal had tackled with only a slide rule, Forrester could make sophisticated predictions about the future. For example, he advised his former MIT student Ken Olsen, the Digital Equipment Corporation founder with whom Hal might have worked had he taken General Doriot's job offer in 1959, to expand his manufacturing capacity in advance of the customer demand for computers that his model said was coming. Olsen took the advice, built new factories, and made a fortune. Forrester's work, embodied in a celebrated book titled *Industrial Dynamics*, was hailed as opening a new era in management science.

Though it would have been natural—and consistent with the expectations of his Stanford colleagues—for Hal to work with Forrester and other quantitatively inclined researchers at MIT, he went in a different direction. He felt drawn to a group of scholars creating a new field called organizational behavior, which was addressing questions raised by the work of Herbert Simon, Hal's mentor for that afternoon at RAND. Among MIT's pioneers of organizational behavior was Harvard-trained psychologist Douglas McGregor, who had written a path-breaking book, *The Human Side of Enterprise.* In this book, McGregor identified a fundamental choice that leaders face. He asserted that leaders must choose the degree to which they will view workers as inherently motivated and capable of self-direction. McGregor noted that the design of most organizations reflects the assumption that workers need motivation and direction to be given and even imposed on them by others. McGregor called this view Theory X. He cited it as the rationale behind the procedures, rules, and incentive systems of nearly all large organizations.

McGregor contrasted Theory X with what he called Theory Y. Leaders subscribing to Theory Y—who by McGregor's admission are rare—presume that people perform best when allowed to find their own motivation and to direct themselves. These leaders are willing to give up a degree of organizational control to get something potentially more valuable: individual inspiration and innovation. Though

McGregor didn't advocate Theory Y to the exclusion of Theory X, his identification of the tension between the two represented a ground-breaking challenge to decades of management thinking.

Douglas McGregor's Theory Y Assumptions

The expenditure of physical and mental effort in work is as natural as play or rest.

Control and punishment are not the only ways to make people work; man will direct himself if he is committed to the aims of the organization.

If a job is satisfying, then the result will be commitment to the organization.

The average man learns, under proper conditions, not only to accept but to seek responsibility.[10]

Hal spent the year at MIT sampling the courses required for a PhD in organizational behavior. Douglas McGregor died suddenly that fall of a heart attack, but Hal studied with two of his key collaborators, Ed Schein and Warren Bennis. Schein was a psychologist known for his study of the brainwashing of U.S. prisoners of war captured by the Chinese military in the Korean conflict. During Hal's year at MIT, Schein was researching, writing, and teaching about the use of what he called "persuasive coercion" in corporations.

Budding leadership guru Warren Bennis, Schein's collaborator, was predicting the end of such persuasive coercion. A few months before Hal's arrival he had published a *Harvard Business Review* article titled "Democracy Is Inevitable," in which he predicted the demise of Communism, a bold position to take at a time when the Soviet Union seemed so commandingly ahead of the West in the arms and space races. Bennis predicted a similar decline in organizational bureaucracy, which he foresaw as giving way to the widespread application of the more humane principles of Theory Y.

Hal enjoyed a year of exploring this new management field with its founders. In addition to sampling the core organization courses, he traveled with Warren Bennis to the U.S. National Training Laboratories in Bethel, Maine, home to experiments in "sensitivity training." He observed T-groups, in which participants expressed emotions in an environment free from constraint or judgment, the goal being to better understand themselves and one another. The T-groups were becoming fashionable among organizational theorists and consultants, who advocated them to government and industry as tools for team building and corporate culture enhancement.

Hal sensed the benefits as well as the potential costs of the highly emotional, unstructured T-group discussions, much as he had recognized the limits of rational planning and managerial control in his dissertation research. An overreliance on Theory Y's celebration of individual liberty, he concluded, could be as dangerous as Theory X's doctrine of behavioral control. By the same token, he saw the need to temper the distinction, for which Warren Bennis would become famous, between the tasks of management and leadership.

> The manager does things right; the leader does the right thing.
> —WARREN BENNIS[11]

It was tempting to think that leaders could be not only more valuable to an organization but also more popular than mere managers, by granting their subordinates free rein to innovate. But Hal had enough respect for his mother, who could be both an inspiring leader and a tough manager, to recognize the need for both. In fact, the same was true of his father. Superficially, Henry could have been characterized as a good-natured subscriber to Theory Y and Mildred a stern practitioner of Theory X. But although Henry and Mildred often played complementary roles as parents, each could be either authoritative or laissez-faire according to the needs of a given son in a given situation. Hal recognized that kind of generally balanced, customized treatment from his other mentors. Bishop Dyer, his Uncle Spencer, General Doriot, and C. Roland Christensen were all task-oriented thinkers with generous hearts and the wisdom to apply those gifts contingently to the benefit of those around them.

Hal determined that, when given the opportunity, he would try to lead by establishing high expectations rather than tight management systems. He realized that this would require an associated state of mind and heart. He would have to consider himself no wiser or more well-intentioned than his subordinates. He would need to see his job as building them up. The earliest beneficiaries of this enlightened view of leadership would be the "Redheads."

GROWING SONS

Hal and Kathy marked the midpoint of the year in Massachusetts with the birth of their second son—and the first true redhead—Stuart Johnson, on January 19, 1965. Kathy was grateful for Hal's learning experiences at MIT, but she was glad to return that spring to warmer Atherton to care for her two sons, an energetic infant and a curious toddler who had found the small rented house in Lexington confining.

Hal was surprised to come home to the Hill and see no sign of his red VW Beetle, an MBA graduation gift from his father. To Hal's astonishment and mild consternation, Sid had given the car to a nephew as a wedding present. Before Hal and Kathy left for Massachusetts, Sid had turned over to Hal his late-model Ford Thunderbird, a classic American gas-guzzler with rear "suicide doors," hinged at the back rather than the front. (In automobile lore, suicide doors were favored by 1930s-era gangsters, who supposedly found it easier to throw victims out and fire machine guns with the wind holding the door open rather than pushing it closed.) In addition to being expensive at the pump, the T-Bird was the only vehicle of its kind in the Stanford faculty parking lot. Hal preferred driving the Beetle to work.

Though he never said anything, Hal suspected that his mother-in-law, La Prele, had encouraged Sid to give the Beetle away. It had been the most run-down vehicle on the Hill, with the possible exception of the old pickup truck driven by gardener Harry Ogami, which Harry

HAL'S RED BEETLE, BEING WASHED BY HENRY (FOREGROUND) AND STUART

carefully parked out of sight of visitors. As Sid and La Prele methodically spruced up the Hill, the Beetle was a sitting duck.

Overall, though, Hal couldn't have asked more of his in-laws. They gave Kathy and the boys free run of the main house and the property, especially the swimming pool. Hal got not only a rent-free home but the tennis court to enjoy with Kathy, as well as a personal "office" in one of the bathhouses near the swimming pool, where he could write without interruption.

By contrast, the Johnsons never invited themselves to the guest house. And they were clearly proud of their hardworking, accomplished son-in-law. They admired not only Hal's career success but also his attentiveness to the needs of Kathy and the boys. They often came by invitation to family home evening, which became a favorite event as the Eyring family grew.

GROWING PROFESSIONAL RESPONSIBILITIES

Hal's professional responsibilities continued to multiply. His study of organizational behavior and leadership led to new courses that he developed and taught to Stanford's increasingly demanding MBA students. When he had first come to Palo Alto in 1962, the difference between Stanford MBAs and their Harvard counterparts that had most impressed him was their casual attire. While students at the Harvard Business School were still wearing dress shirts and neckties to class, Stanford had no discernible dress code. A few students dressed up, but others sported T-shirts, shorts, and sandals. Hal was particularly intrigued by one casually dressed fellow who seemed to writhe in his seat by the window, turning first one way and then another. Hal initially thought that the student must be dealing with pain, but finally realized that he was adjusting position in the sunlight to ensure an even suntan.

By the end of the 1960s, the violent campus protests that seized the University of California at Berkeley, on the other side of San Francisco Bay, began to make their way into more-conservative Stanford. When Hal's office window was broken by rocks thrown during a demonstration, the university's maintenance staff declined to fix it, noting that the window faced the demonstrators' favorite sidewalk and would undoubtedly be broken again. There were protests even in Hal's classrooms. One unruly class of students, who had complained from the beginning of the semester about the course workload, finally staged a walkout. Hal spent two restless nights fearing that they might not return for the next class session and wondering whether his faculty bosses would blame them or him. He thanked heaven when the students showed up as though nothing had happened, their revolutionary zeal tempered by the prospect of a bad grade.

Hal's professional time was taken up not only by teaching and research but also by professional consulting and the founding of several companies. He helped Ed Zschau found System Industries and took a seat on the board. Though Hal's stake was small relative to Ed's, he invested time and effort as though they were equal owners. Ed would credit Hal with many of the strategic insights that got the company off the ground. Together they also developed a consulting business that took them around the world making presentations to major corporations, often inventing new ideas literally on the fly, having planned to prepare on the airplane. Kathy called the venture the "Flying Carpet."

> On a scale of likeability and capability and commitment, he was a 10— and fun. We had a great time, and I stole his stuff.
>
> —ED ZSCHAU[12]

Hal likewise cofounded and became an investor with Roger Sant in a company called Finnigan Instrument Corporation, which made diagnostic equipment for measuring levels of toxins in the environment and illegal drugs in the blood of athletes. All the while, he kept his eye on the tenure bar, slipping down to his office in the bathhouse to prepare for classes and write research papers— most of which came back rejected by the good academic journals—after spending evenings and Saturday mornings with Kathy and the boys.

CHALLENGING TEACHING ASSIGNMENTS

Hal's skill in the classroom and his broad, applied view of management caught the eye of Stanford's business school dean, Ernest C. "Ernie" Arbuckle, who had hired Hal and arranged for his sabbatical year at MIT. Arbuckle, a war hero and former corporate executive with no academic experience other than earning a Stanford MBA, had embarked on an aggressive campaign to make the business school one of the best in the world. Hiring Hal and Roger Sant and others from Harvard was part of that campaign. So was making the Stanford curriculum more cross-disciplinary and practical, in the spirit of the courses taught by Georges Doriot and C. Roland Christensen.

Dean Arbuckle tapped Hal to develop and teach a capstone course for the Stanford MBA program. It would bear the imposing name "Management of the Total Enterprise." From a traditional academic perspective, the task seemed preposterous. It ran counter to the discipline-focused structure of the other courses in the MBA. Pulling all of those disciplines together in a single course would be virtually impossible, yet failing do so would result in undisciplined, incomplete analysis. The course would devolve into fuzzy discussions and unsupported conclusions.

Then there was the challenge of inculcating real managerial skills, rather than just studying the techniques of a particular discipline such as finance or marketing. The case method of instruction, by which students and instructor explore actual business problems, was gaining ground, but these cases focused on a single discipline, or perhaps a combination of two. Developing a course such as "Management of the Total Enterprise" would require developing both theories and cases broader than any Hal or his colleagues had encountered.

Yet Hal soon discovered that his circuitous, seemingly random path through school and professional assignments had prepared him well for this unique challenge. General Doriot's practical maxims and homilies, which proved of greater worth than anything else Hal had learned at Harvard, pointed the direction for this new course. His operations research and consulting experiences gave him the quantitative background needed—as well as an appreciation of the practical limits of such numerical analysis. And at MIT he had grounded himself in the leading theories of human behavior, a missing ingredient in most plans to manage organizations effectively.

Hal appreciated heaven's hand in helping him in this special assignment from Dean Arbuckle, which would win the admiration of his peers. Decades later, he would look back and see how creating the course had prepared him well for professional assignments in the coming decades—assignments that would require him to manage large, complex enterprises of notably different types. But at the time, he was painfully conscious not only of the late nights and weekends required but also of the way the work pulled him off a viable tenure track. The publication of original research necessitated focus on one academic discipline. As he invested the vast majority of his professional time in teaching cross-disciplinary courses and advising students, he could hear the tenure clock ticking away. He felt a growing sense of helplessness and even doom.

In addition to late nights, Hal was also working early mornings, as a volunteer seminary teacher. His class of a dozen students met at Palo Alto's Cubberley High School. Though they attended faithfully, not all seemed to understand Hal's popularity with Stanford's MBA students or his sterling reputation with his faculty colleagues. Two young men appeared particularly uninterested in the class. Each morning they trudged to the back of the room, took their seats, and sat stone-faced, sometimes sleeping.

Hal found himself increasingly troubled by these two students in particular. He began to pray for help in engaging them, to no apparent effect. He gained new appreciation for the teachers, all volunteers, who had taught him in the early mornings at East High School. They had brought great experience to the job. One, Wallace Toronto, was the current president of the Czech Mission, temporarily (he hoped) expelled with his missionaries by a Communist revolution and teaching seminary while waiting to return to Prague. Another, Blanche Stoddard, served with Mildred on the Relief Society general board.

More than experience, though, these teachers had brought something intangible to their teaching. Hal hadn't fully appreciated it at the time, but as he struggled to connect with the two boys in his class, he realized that Sister Stoddard and Brother Toronto had reached him in ways that went beyond curriculum, teaching style, or even personal testimony. He decided to step back and assess the situation coolly, the way he would a case of ineffective business management. In doing so, he opened his mind and heart to an important discovery: he had been praying for success in teaching the boys, but not for the boys themselves. Chastened by that realization, he took a new tack, one he would describe nearly fifty years later in an address to the seminary and institute teachers of the Church:

> I learned all I could about them. I prayed for them individually and by name. I prayed for their parents, whom I came to know. As I look back now, I realize that the Spirit answered my

prayers by increasing my love for those two boys and my desire to reach them.

But more than that, my concern for them ignited a personal concern for their classmates. I began to teach them and pray for them as individuals. The Spirit came into the classroom.[13]

Hal's tenure as an early-morning seminary teacher was brief, just one year. Yet the experience would prove preparatory in many ways. One of the primary responsibilities it prepared him for was the raising of six children, including four sons who would at times remind him of the two sleepy young men in the back of his seminary classroom.

Faith is what those you help will need and what you will need to find the patience and the persistence it takes to make a difference in someone else's life.

—TALK, MAY 9, 2002 [14]

kathy's sore elbow, developed arm wrestling with her
nephew, Mark, sometime last week, forced her out of
our double's match this morning; within an hour she'd
sent a replacement, so I played six sets. Result: I
soaked   elbow in a tub of hot water propped on the
table   e breakfast room at grandpa's, while I watched
the b   es with the boys. Annette served the whole

7

FATHERS ARE
TO PRESIDE

By divine design,
Fathers are to preside over their families
In love and righteousness
And are responsible to provide the necessities of life
And protection for their families.
— THE FAMILY: A PROCLAMATION TO THE WORLD

Hal and Kathy's third son, Matthew, was born on July 19, 1969.
Family and friends couldn't resist commenting on Kathy's consistency. She had delivered three sons, all on the 19th day of the month
(Henry and Stuart were born on September 19 and January 19, respectively). These observers wondered at the burdens Kathy gracefully
bore. Just twenty-seven years old, she managed a lively home while
supporting a husband who seemed to be everywhere at once—teaching,
traveling, doing research, and, for the past two years, serving as bishop
of the Stanford single adult ward.

Those closest to the Eyrings, though, knew that Hal was also a
faithful father, presiding over his family in the spirit of the Savior's
injunction to the Twelve: "If any man desire to be first, the same shall
be last of all, and servant of all."[1] It was true that Hal worked the equivalent of a career and a half, or even two. But outside of his professional
and Church work, every waking moment, including hours that might
reasonably have been spent sleeping, belonged to Kathy and the boys.

Wise and selfless, Kathy requested that Hal give the vast bulk of that time to their children.

SATURDAY PROJECTS

Knowing that his professional life was driven by regularly scheduled obligations, such as teaching classes and conducting Church meetings, Hal sought to create similar periodic commitments to the boys. One of those was something they called Saturday projects. Each Saturday morning, the boys could expect to be enlisted in some form of work on the Hill.

The aging estate offered ample fixer-upper projects. They repaired leaky faucets, changed lightbulbs, and cleaned decades of accumulated debris from tantalizingly spooky places such as the crawl space under the old chauffeur's quarters. An all-time favorite project involved donning Hal's old dress shirts, buying green paint and brushes at the hardware store, and painting a wooden greenhouse, having spent the preceding Saturday replacing many of its broken slats. Hal recorded these projects in a journal that he felt inspired to write as the boys grew.

Henry, Stuart, and I began the day putting green paint on the roof of the slat-house. Midway through, Henry thought of putting a roller on the end of a pole. Up to that point the boys had been working on the roof from a press-board, about three feet by six, which spread their weight. We wanted to be sure they wouldn't crash through the roof, the way they almost did before. With the pole, Stuart worked from a ladder next to the slat-house to get the lower part, and Henry stood on the pressboard to get at the top. We were done in twenty minutes after

Henry

we got the pole. The boys were really rolling it on at the end. (Saturday, October 3, 1971)

Hal kept the boys engaged with a mix of projects and "fun," though the fun often had an element of creating and learning. Driving over the Coast Range to Half Moon Bay, home to world-class tidal pools teeming with marine life, was a favorite activity for Kathy as well as the boys. So was building toy ships and airplanes from scrap wood gathered from Grandpa Sid Johnson's construction sites. Particularly in the summer, when the boys were out of school, "fun" projects begun on a Saturday took on a life of their own, carrying over into the following week.

 From eight-thirty until one, we built a submarine from paper boxes. The materials-gathering took the first two hours. I learned that Macy's is the place to get boxes big enough for boys. You go to the storeroom between men's clothing and men's shoes. They have both a range of products that come in large boxes and a friendly attitude toward customers. The boys painted the boxes black while I made two periscopes from 39-cent mirrors and kitchen-wrap boxes. (Saturday, October 24, 1970)

***

The boys are ever-deeper in secret agent work. Henry asked for another "case" to work on. Kathy gave him the "cat caper": Why doesn't the cat eat at night anymore? Henry's working theory is that the cat eats birds instead. His solution is to feed the cat during the day. Stuart is deeply in the intrigue. He has one "fort" in the ornamental well in Grandma's flower garden and another under the house. His disguise is a yarn mustache, dark glasses, and a blue uniform. These are exciting times. (Tuesday, July 28, 1970)

THE JOURNAL

The Eyring children, who ultimately included a fourth son, John, and daughters Elizabeth and Mary Kathleen, would grow up assuming that their father had always conscientiously kept a journal, in which they played the leading roles. Each night, they expected to hear the sound of Hal's typing before bed on a small portable typewriter, manual keys striking onionskin pages with the sound of a small firecracker. They never read what he wrote, though each year he would pay one of them a penny a page to hand-feed his work onto a photocopier so that his personal journal could be reproduced, bound, and given to each child as a gift for the future.

In fact, the journal didn't exist until 1970, when Hal was instructed to begin writing. The instruction came as a mild rebuke, as he would explain by letter a decade later to Henry, who was then serving a mission in Japan.

Dear Henry,

When you were still a little boy, I came home one night, late, from my bishop's work. It was dark. As I walked up to the front door of the guest house on Walsh Road, I was startled to see a figure coming up from the side porch next to your bedroom. It was Grandpa Johnson, carrying a 15-foot length of white plastic pipe. He smiled at me and said he'd been working late installing the sprinkler system he had ingeniously constructed using run-off water from the Sharon Heights golf course below us. He had already put the pump in the creek and installed two huge storage tanks out by the compost bin on top of our hill.

I was struck at that moment, as I always have been, by his pioneer style. As he passed me, almost on a run, I heard a voice in my mind say clearly, "I'm not giving you these experiences just for yourself. Write them down." I never knew whether the prompting was about the spiritual experiences of being a bishop or of the inspiration of Grandpa's example, but from that night to this, for more than 10 years, I've done as I was told.

And I knew this: I was doing it for you to read someday, because you and your brothers and sisters would be the most important people I would ever serve. And I knew that I was to make a record of how God watched over you and helped me be your father. When I was ordained a bishop, Elder Henry D. Taylor[2] said, "Your family will be your most important work." That's still true, and will be forever.

I love you,

Dad[3]

Hal's journal entries recorded not only his patient teaching and mentoring of the children, but also what he learned from them. That can be seen in his entries describing a July 4th celebration hosted by the Eyrings' Menlo Park Ward. Hal was invited to give an Independence Day talk by ward activities committee chairman Julian Smith.

Just finished my July 4 talk. Saw for the first time the opportunity to help boys believe in elective process by meeting some candidates, judicial process by seeing honest judges and a Dad who respects them, and the efficacy of magnanimity in public disagreements by listening to people I know are wrong. (July 4, 1970, 1:49 a.m., so this is really for July 3)

***

My talk provided my real learning today. But the learning came before and after. Before the talk Henry kidded me by hiding my notebook. We laughed, but after about ten minutes my nerves jangled. I said, "Henry, I feel just like you do on the starting platform before a swimming race. I'm nervous." He looked very serious, said "Oh," and was completely quiet. He understood, and so did I. Swimming must be a nightmare

After the talk, Henry said: "Golly, Dad, your talk was long and boring." He said, "I hate the talks in church. And the songs. I don't know them, and I don't understand what the talks are about. Could you understand your Dad when you were a little boy hearing his talks?"

When a boy as bright and spiritual as Henry says that, we've got a problem. He's very honest and intelligent, and he knows he doesn't feel anything in the meetings. I understand better why I remember the Oscar Kirkhams.[4] They told stories. I'll bet the children understood Christ's stories. Maybe better than the adults. (July 4, 1970, 10:55 p.m.)

***

Julian Smith knocked at the door around 4:00 p.m. He handed me an Uncle Sam hat. A cassette tape of my talk was Scotch-taped to the crown. He gave it to me with gracious compliments. As he got into his car with his wife and son, he said Henry had told him—in response to Julian's question—that my talk was a little long and boring. We all laughed. I got both the compliment and the idea for improvement. (July 5, 1970, 11:38 p.m.)

MENTAL MODELS OF GROWING CHILDREN

As the boys grew, Hal increasingly saw them not as children but as adults in the making. By now he was a teacher by habit as well as by vocation. Working with his Stanford students, in the classroom or on research projects, he developed mental models of their learning needs. He began by identifying the relative strengths and weaknesses of each individual. Often, he found, the two were connected. An unusually gifted thinker, for example, could be more likely to discount others' views or to jump to unsupported conclusions. With this working model, Hal could give instruction and counsel designed to ameliorate the weaknesses while building on the strengths.

Hal had also learned to test his own blind spots as he did this analysis of his students. He drew upon a principle learned from one of his Harvard professors, Ray Bauer. Professor Bauer had arrived at HBS in 1957, the year Hal had started in the MBA program. Bauer was one of three social psychologists hired to create an organizational behavior curriculum of the type that Hal would later study during his Sloan fellowship year at MIT.

Hal got to know Professor Bauer personally during his doctoral coursework and research efforts. Bauer liked Hal, but he could see the tendency of the bright young MBA graduate to dismiss ideas different from his own—along with the people who held those ideas. One day, when Hal called one of their colleagues' views "irrational," Professor Bauer offered a gentle challenge: "Hal, you'll understand people better if you assume that their behavior is rational *from their point of view.*"

Hal took that challenge to heart as he worked with students, especially the lifelong students, his children. With the birth of each child, he was blessed to sense that child's inherent goodness. Armed with that conviction, and with Professor Bauer's great behavioral insight, he learned to see any weakness in his children as the product of a mistaken perception of reality made by an inherently good person. In helping them see those misperceptions, he worked not from their apparent personal weaknesses but from their potential strengths. He sensed that the weaknesses were rooted largely in fear and self-doubt, and so he took every opportunity to build faith and self-confidence.

Hal designed family activities, such as Saturday projects, with these mental models of his sons and daughters in mind. He also created tangible images of their potential. In a 2012 general conference, when all of the children were grown and married, he explained the process to the priesthood bearers of the Church.

Almost everything that I've been able to accomplish as a priesthood bearer is because individuals who knew me saw things in me that I couldn't see. As a young father I prayed to know what contributions my children might make in the Lord's kingdom. For the boys, I knew they could have priesthood opportunities. For the girls, I knew they would give service representing the Lord. All

Henry

would be doing His work. I knew each
was an individual, and therefore the
Lord would have given them specific gifts for each to use in His
service.

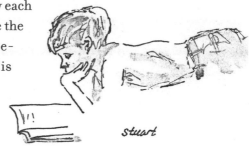

stuart

Now, I cannot tell every
father and every leader of
youth the details of what is
best for you to do. But I can promise you that you will bless them
to help them recognize the spiritual gifts with which they were
born. Every person is different and has a different contribution
to make. No one is destined to fail. As you seek revelation to see
gifts God sees in those you lead in the priesthood—particularly
the young—you will be blessed to lift their sights to the service
they can perform. With your guidance, those you lead will be able
to see, want, and believe they can achieve their full potential for
service in God's kingdom.

With my own children, I prayed for revelation to know how
I could help each of them individually prepare for specific opportunities to serve God. And then I tried to help them visualize,
hope, and work for this future. I carved a board for each son with
a quotation from scripture that described his special gifts and
an image that represented this gift. Beneath the picture and the
legend, I carved the dates of each boy's baptism and ordination
into priesthood offices, with his height marked at the date of each
milestone.[5]

Matthew

For Henry, the six-year-old who
cowered on the starting blocks at swimming meets, Hal would carve an eagle. He
took the inscription above it, "On Eagles'
Wings," from Isaiah's promise that "they
that wait upon the Lord shall renew their
strength; they shall mount up with wings
as eagles."[6] For another son, whose

shyness seemed extreme, Hal carved a lion and the words "Bold as a Lion," taken from Proverbs 28:1. It declares, "The wicked flee when no man pursueth: but the righteous are bold as a lion."

John

FAMILY HOME EVENINGS

Along with Saturday projects, Hal made family home evening a weekly tradition. In fact, in those days before President Joseph Fielding Smith's 1970 declaration that Monday should be set aside for that purpose, the Eyring boys begged for family home evening on most nights.

For Henry, Stuart, and infant son Matthew, family home evening was an adventure. It began with a trip to Harry Ogami's giant firewood pile, made of limbs trimmed from the Hill's oak, fir, and fruit trees. Filling a red wagon and their arms to overflowing, Hal and the boys came back and built a virtual bonfire. The living room of the guest house had a fireplace sized to heat the entire two-story space, in the spirit of the hunting lodge it was designed to resemble; the boys could actually step inside the fireplace to put their logs on the giant grate. The mostly hardwood fuel would blaze for hours, making it necessary to open windows to cool the room, especially on hot summer days (when fire building was, for the boys, nonetheless de rigueur).

The Eyring family home evenings were full of music and mirth. Kathy accompanied the boys' singing with a zither, a kind of horizontal harp with buttons she could press to make chords while strumming the strings with a guitar pick. They laughed delightedly at the comical faces she made while trying to read from her special zither hymnbook and often running late with the chord changes.

Hal made scriptures the focal point of family home evening lessons. He learned that the lessons worked best when he involved the boys, with assignments and parts devised in the spirit of the business school case method of instruction. They particularly enjoyed dressing

HENRY AND STUART IN THEIR PAGEANT COSTUMES

up as prophets and angels, making year-round use of their Christmas pageant costumes and props. Even with that kind of audience participation, though, Hal learned to keep the lessons focused and well paced. He accepted the mixed compliment the boys offered as their highest praise: "Great lesson, Dad: short!"

The bulk of family home evening was reserved for games, into which Hal and Kathy tried to weave a modicum of learning and social development. For example, they sold the boys on the idea that the guest house's large, formal entryway, which could be closed off from the living room by a door usually left open, was a giant elevator. The boys enjoyed taking turns serving as elevator operators, greeting passengers such as Sid and La Prele with a personal introduction and bidding them farewell at their desired "floors." The real fun came, though, when Hal and Kathy led everyone down into a large, open basement filled with toys and games, including a tetherball hanging from the ceiling.

Family night was high jumping and pole vaulting in Grandpa's backyard. Both Henry and Stuart cleared about two feet, six inches. Then, Kathy, the boys, and I went to the Menlo Park Library to return and get books. Everyone enjoyed the evening.

—JOURNAL, JULY 30, 1970

As the boys grew older, family home evening at the Eyring home became more emotionally complex and sometimes contentious. Hal's professional and ecclesiastical workload only increased, making it harder to prepare lessons and activities capable of capturing the boys' attention. The challenge increasingly appeared in the journal.

 During the day I settled down to churn out letters and interview students. My motivation was my determination to be relaxed and loving at family night. I knew from experience that guilt from not getting things done—and the subsequent need to take an impossible amount of work home—makes me impatient with the family. Sure enough, we had a marvelous family night, a pleasant discussion with Grandpa afterward, and a great hour by the fire after putting the boys down. All without a cross word. (April 19, 1971)

Like most fathers, Hal would learn to celebrate the smallest successes of family home evening and overlook the failures. Looking back, he would urge parents to do the same, offering hope that the steady effort would pay off:

> I have a memory of watching my little boys kick each other as they lay before me on the floor during our family night as I taught a lesson on peace in the family. In fact, that topic would bring it on. They heard me, they understood me, and yet they had been kicking for a long time before I started preaching. Now, years later, they reach across the world to help each other. But the change takes time. So be patient and persistent.[7]

READING THE SCRIPTURES WITH LOVE

Kathy appreciated Hal's steady effort and general good humor. She fully supported him in his professional grind, though she would occasionally ask whether he wouldn't be happier and do more good in the world as a full-time seminary teacher. While he slaved at his desk in the bathhouse office, she developed a bedtime routine for the boys. They gathered in bed to read a large simplified and illustrated version of the Book of Mormon. As with family home evening, the time spent each night in the scriptures wasn't long. The boys were easily diverted by distractions such as a family of skunks that often came to eat from a bowl of food left by the

> After a quick dinner, I went down to the bathhouse to work for an hour. . . . Coming out the door, I met a young skunk: range, five feet. Luckily, we passed without speaking.
>
> —JOURNAL, OCTOBER 15, 1970

HENRY AND STUART ON THE HEARTH OF
THE GUEST HOUSE FIREPLACE

front door for their cat. But they read the Book of Mormon through more than once, and the stories stuck.

Over the years, the Eyrings' scripture-study patterns would shift to best meet the needs of the time. With six children—the last of whom, Mary Kathleen, wouldn't arrive until after Henry returned from his mission—satisfying everyone would prove difficult. Morning reading worked well until the older boys became high-school swimmers with practices before school. Then it became necessary to read in two shifts, one at the breakfast table and another in the evening. But even that often proved inadequate, as school and Church activities, part-time jobs, and social events atomized the group. Hal learned to take a pragmatic, optimistic view, one he would share in 2005, the year that Mary Kathleen married, emptying the Eyring family nest.

For me at least, and I think my six children would agree, scripture study works well only if your children know you love the scriptures and they also know as individuals that you love them. . . .

It's important to read the scriptures together in a way that lets your children know you include them because you love them. However, reading together may break down during the teenage years. Teens may say, "I'd rather read on my own." My encouragement to families in that situation is to see that as victory, not defeat. Your child may be saying, "I'm getting something when I'm alone that I don't get when we're all here together." Take that as a wonderful sign that scripture study is beginning to take hold in your teen's heart. The main purpose is to fall in love with the scriptures and feast upon them, whether we are alone or together.[8]

Hal's teenage children would be grateful for his generous pragmatism in scripture reading and other family traditions. They wouldn't realize it until they had children of their own, but even as a young father he presided with maturity beyond his years. For that they could thank Hal's parents and priesthood leaders for their example and Kathy for her gentle nudges. But they were also the beneficiaries of Hal's experience in another presiding role: that of bishop in a single student ward.

8

A BISHOP TO BE APPOINTED UNTO YOU

For verily thus saith the Lord,
It is expedient in me
For a bishop to be appointed unto you,
Or of you,
Unto the church
In this part of the Lord's vineyard.
—DOCTRINE AND COVENANTS 72:2

Hal's call to serve as a bishop came in 1967, the year before Stanford University would decide whether to grant him tenure. The tenure decision loomed large. Dean Arbuckle and his administrative colleagues had hired aggressively six years before, but the business school wasn't growing commensurately; staying relatively small while increasing the quality of the student body and faculty was the linchpin of their strategy for boosting Stanford's prestige. Consequently, only one of the seven new hires in Hal's cohort would receive tenure.

In addition to bearing the uncertainty and pressure of his professional world, young Bishop Eyring undertook his new assignment during a time of unusual political and social unrest. In the 1960s, the San Francisco Bay Area led the Western world in a cultural revolution. Students at the University of California at Berkeley, across the bay from Stanford, organized some of the earliest protests against U.S. military involvement in Vietnam. In the beginning, they sought only freedom of political speech, but soon they had seized control of parts of their campus. By the end of the decade, their protests would trigger the mobilization of National Guard troops by California Governor Ronald Reagan and result in deadly violence.

Before the violence, however, came San Francisco's 1967 "Summer of Love." Lured by the prospect of free food and rock-and-roll concerts, tens of thousands of young people from across the country streamed into the city's Haight-Ashbury district. They experimented with mind-altering drugs and illicit sexual relationships, believing that they had found a new and enduring source of freedom. Like the political protests, the Summer of Love ended in disappointment and heartache, yet many who participated remained convinced that happiness lay in unfettered social and moral freedom.

The spirit of moral experimentation and political rebelliousness made its way south to Stanford. The university's most popular course, Human Sexuality, drew so much interest that it had to be moved to the

SIXTIES-ERA STUDENT PROTESTORS

1,700-seat Memorial Auditorium. "No one registered but everyone went," recalled Stanford student and native Utahn Scott Cameron.[1] Small-scale but disturbing violence racked the campus. The windows in Hal's office were broken by demonstrators on their way to do more serious damage, such as setting fire to the Navy ROTC building and the university president's office.

The Church was also a target of protest on the campus. Citing racism, Stanford had severed athletic ties with Brigham Young University, refusing to engage in any sporting contests. For a time, members of Hal's ward took turns at night guarding the LDS institute building, where the ward met. Having begun the decade in Harvard Business School classrooms where neckties were still required and crew cuts common, by the late 1960s Bishop Eyring would be serving young people surrounded by a "hippie" culture that celebrated long hair, rejection of authority, and violent protest.

OPTIMISM UNDER FIRE

Like all bishops, Hal experienced new personal pressures when he was called to preside over the Stanford First Ward. With both his home and office near the Stanford Institute of Religion building, where the ward met, he was easily accessible seven days a week. It was an unusual day at the office when at least one ward member didn't stop in for personal counseling, and the porch light was typically on late at the guest house. Once the boys were in bed, the house served as a secondary bishop's office.

> He was immensely popular. The Stanford Ward members were so drawn to him. And his interview schedule was just horrendous.
>
> —DALE E. MILLER, STANFORD WARD BISHOPRIC COUNSELOR AND LATER A MEMBER OF THE SECOND QUORUM OF THE SEVENTY[2]

Hal's journal entry for Monday, January 25, 1971, portrays the juggling act required to keep all of these balls in the air. He had hoped to spend most of the day and some of the evening finishing a case study of the Hawaiian conglomerate Castle &

Cooke, owner of Dole Food Company. Castle & Cooke was an unusually well-run company, and when he finally finished the case it would become a staple of classroom discussion at business schools for more than a decade. That day, though, he was thinking not about the case's future but about its publication deadline, already past.

Things looked good until noon, when he was interrupted by Harper Boyd, a Stanford marketing professor who ran the school's education programs for business executives. These executives demanded both first-rate thinking and outstanding classroom skills, putting Hal high on Harper's list of teachers. Hal liked Harper, a gregarious marketing genius and tennis champion who sometimes came to the Hill to play with him and Kathy. But conversations with Harper were rarely short. Neither were the Eyrings' Monday night activities. After an unplanned visit from a Stanford Ward member, the day ended late, with little progress made on his most pressing professional obligation.

 Worked on the Castle and Cooke case today with three interruptions: Stanford obligations, family joys, and Stanford Ward counseling. From noon until two I met with Harper Boyd on the continuing education program for Stanford. From six until nine I worked with the family, starting with Matthew in the bathhouse and ending with a music-and-arts family night. A ward member called and came right up for an appointment from nine-thirty until eleven. (January 25, 1971)

> The best interviews I ever had were more like conversations. A real conversation means that two people listen to each other and express honest feelings.
>
> —1986 INTERVIEW[3]

Such evenings of impromptu counseling were common, and they often yielded sweet fruit. A young student who came to the guest house after eleven o'clock on a Sunday night recorded his gratitude for counsel and a priesthood blessing received:

I don't think I have had a blessing that I could roughly compare to this one—my patriarchal blessing, perhaps. I was enveloped with a feeling of love and confidence and faith. I really knew I had been forgiven and that God desired that my life would change and that I had been given special talents that had been unused.

The Bishop walked with me out to my car and I realized that our meeting was a blessing to him as well as to me—that together we were closer to God than we had been before.[4]

Hal's journal record of a late-night interview with a different young man confirms that the work was indeed blessing him as well as the members of the ward:

After dinner Stuart roller skated, and then we read from the story of King Laman. Spent from 8:15 to 10:30 with a member of the ward. He had felt impressed to confess a transgression. It was marvelous to see his submission to the Lord. The Spirit was there, teaching him. He walked home, and I went with him to the top of the Hill. The stars sparkled, and I felt the glow of the Spirit. It's a good work. (June 22, 1970)

Still, the ward was an island in a spiritually stormy sea. Many of its members, mostly students from smaller cities and towns, had never encountered intellectual and moral challenges as strong as those they faced in the San Francisco Bay Area. Most rose to the challenges, but some faltered seriously. At times, the ward seemed inundated with temptation and transgression. Yet Hal was blessed with energy and optimism, as this journal entry from 1970 reveals:

> Just as God called you and will guide you, He will magnify you. You will need that magnification. Your calling will surely bring opposition. You are in the Master's service. You are His representative. Eternal lives depend on you. He faced opposition, and He said that facing opposition would be the lot of those He called.
>
> —TALK, OCTOBER 6, 2002[5]

Saturday night, after ward General Priesthood meeting, I sat talking with my counselors and Dan Johnson, our executive secretary, for more than an hour. I shared my feeling, growing for more than a month, that the Lord knew of something seriously wrong in the Stanford Ward. We vowed to show the Lord that we would change anything we were doing as a bishopric. To get the spirit of openness to change, we spent Sunday morning discussing twenty customs of operating we've developed over the years. We will change at least ten of them, from when we hold bishopric meetings to starting early-morning scripture study classes as a bishopric.

I feel both that we have a challenge but that the Lord has prepared the people and given us the warning we need to overcome: There's great growth coming to the Stanford Ward. (November 24, 1970)

SEEING DIVINE POTENTIAL

Hal's optimism was a gift, a blessing attendant to his bishop's mantle. It enabled him to see the divine potential of his ward members, even at their weakest moments. A particularly powerful manifestation of that gift came early in his service, on a day when he was called from his Stanford University office to the Palo Alto police station. The officer on the other end of the phone line asked, "Are you Bishop Eyring? We have a fellow here who says he's a member of your congregation."

At the police station Hal learned that a newly baptized member of the ward, driving while intoxicated, had crashed his car through the plate glass window and into the lobby of the Palo Alto branch of the Bank of America. As the bank guard brandished his revolver, the dazed ward member behind the wheel of the car cried, "Don't shoot! I'm a Mormon."

Hal waited in an interview room while the officers retrieved the young man from his cell. His stomach churning with anger, Hal outlined a sermon in his mind. When he prepared a talk or a teaching plan for the classroom, he began with a statement of objective, followed by an outline of key doctrines. In this case, his objective was to inspire fear and remorse. This young man had failed to honor his baptismal covenants, and he had besmirched the reputation of the Church. This was the worst such offense, but it was not the first. Hal determined to rebuke the boy sternly and perhaps even threaten him with loss of Church membership.

In the midst of these fierce, angry feelings, and as the young offender was led into the room, Hal heard a calm voice in his mind. The voice said, "I'm going to let you see him as I see him." For just a moment, the disheveled, dazed youth before Hal appeared in his mind's eye in an otherworldly light: clean, strong, and faithful, a valiant son of his Heavenly Father. The vision, though fleeting, was indelible. The conversation that ensued wasn't easy, but Bishop Eyring was filled with love and hope for this Stanford Ward member.

> The place to start is with our own hearts. . . . We can begin today to try to see those we are to nourish as our Heavenly Father sees them and so feel some of what He feels for them.
> —TALK, OCTOBER 5, 1997[6]

The gift of seeing divine potential blessed Hal in serving other members of the ward. Newcomers were often surprised to see people in church who didn't seem to belong there. Some of those misfits, such as a long-haired young man passing the sacrament, appeared to have the bishop's approval. But those who knew the history of the ward and the love of its bishop understood. They remembered when the young man had been less active in the Church. They guessed that the woven-hemp headband he wore was an implicit compromise with the bishop—a way to keep his hair out of his face until he worked up the courage to cut it, an act that would mean abandonment by his current friends. The headband wouldn't last, but the gratitude of the returning prodigal would.

SPARSE, DOCTRINE-BASED COUNSEL

In his love for ward members, Bishop Eyring tended to counsel them lightly. Many interviews ran past their allotted time, as supplicants shared and explored poignant feelings and complex concerns. But though Bishop Eyring listened long, he usually said little. Many years later, he explained this reasoning to a son newly called as a bishop. "Your goal in giving counsel," hc taught, "is to increase the likelihood that the listener will seek counsel directly from the Lord. That will mean giving less advice than either the listener or you might like at the time." Hal's own adherence to this principle can be seen in many journal entries, particularly this one, written late at the end of a busy Saturday. Earlier in the day, he had washed windows with the boys, written a talk with their help on the typewriter, and attended the wedding of a Stanford Ward member.

At five I baptized a twenty-seven-year-old fellow. His wife and child were there. A year ago she had called, asking that I come to see her. When I got there she said she was pregnant, was sure she should not marry the father, and was going to have an abortion. After praying with her, I felt clearly that she should marry the father. Seconds later, still on my knees, I felt I should not tell her. She said she was willing to pray.

Two days later she telephoned. She said she felt that she should marry the fellow. After that she didn't call for months.

When she called again it was to say that she had married, that the baby was due in a few days, and that she wanted a blessing. She and her husband, the father of the child, came to my bishop's office. My counselor Bob Todd was there. We talked for three minutes, knelt and prayed, and then gave her a blessing. They left. She called to say that the baby had been born and that she and he were well.

Her husband called two weeks ago to ask that I baptize him. Today I did, and confirmed him, with his wife and the beautiful baby sitting on the second row. (April 17, 1971)

Hal's strategy of inviting ward members seeking counsel to pray, evident in this case, was his standard procedure. So was listening patiently and inviting them to listen for the Lord's answers to their prayers.

Yesterday I talked with a young fellow. I felt impressed to keep talking, even after an hour-and-a-half. Finally, he confessed a youthful transgression, the first time he had told anyone. It had weighed on his mind, shaping and hurting his life for years. I'm sure Heavenly Father helped me keep quiet during the long minute or two he was deciding to tell me. He was overwhelmed by the magnitude of the job of repentance ahead of him, but I was elated that he was on the way.

Today he called. He had a marvelous spiritual experience. He went up on Skyline Boulevard,[7] fasting in prayer, and reading the scriptures. He felt a sorrow that almost made him physically ill. Finally, he wept for minutes and then felt a sense of peace. He asked my opinion. I told him I felt it was Heavenly Father reassuring him that he is loved. That certainly is not the end of the sorrow nor of the learning of repentance, but it is an assurance that Heavenly Father will be with him, loving him all the way. (August 11, 1970)

Even when the stakes were high and he felt personal uneasiness about a ward member's situation, Bishop Eyring often suppressed his opinions, preaching instead the universally applicable doctrines of righteousness and prayer, as recorded at the end of a summer day in 1970:

After lunch I met with a non-LDS graduate student. He is deeply involved with a member of the Church, loves her, but can't live with real pressure he will feel to join the Church. He seemed either very nice and morally blind or very cunning. Despite my liking for him I felt uneasy, as if I'd seen a picture with something out of place but couldn't tell what. I'm going to call the girl. She's expecting advice on what to do about him. I'll only advise her to straighten her own life out. It's not clear to me where she should head after that. But I'm sure she'll not be able to handle this fellow until she can handle herself. (July 22, 1970)

LEARNING TO RECOGNIZE REPENTANCE

Counseling with ward members, especially those struggling with sin and sorrow, required Hal to deepen his understanding of the Atonement. Serving as what Section 107 of the Doctrine and Covenants calls a common judge, he learned not just to have faith in the infinite power of the Atonement but also to judge the success of ward members' efforts to apply that power in their lives. One particularly helpful lesson came from his uncle Spencer W. Kimball, as Hal later recalled before a group of BYU students:

> I learned a long time ago that it is hard to know how you are doing in being born again and why it is not easy. Once, as a bishop of a ward, I worked with a young man not much older than many of you. He'd made great mistakes and had been moved by faith in the Lord Jesus Christ to make long and painful repentance. We were down to the weeks before he was to be married in the temple. I had long before forgiven him in the name of the Church and had given him his temple recommend. Yet he remembered that I had said, "The Lord will forgive you in his own time and in his own way." But now he was deeply concerned. He came to my office and he said: "You told me that the Lord would someday let me know that I was forgiven. But I am going to the temple to marry a wonderful girl. I want to be the best I can be for her. I need to know that I am forgiven. And I need to know now. Tell me how to find out." I said I would try.
>
> He gave me a deadline. My memory is that it was within less than two weeks. Fortunately, I already had a trip scheduled. During that period of time I went to Salt Lake City, and there I found myself seeing Elder Spencer W. Kimball, then a member of the Quorum of the Twelve, at a social function. It was crowded, and yet he somehow found me. He walked up to me in that crowd

and said, "Hal, I understand that you are now a bishop. Do you have anything you would like to ask me?"

I said that I did, but I didn't think that was the place to talk about it. He thought it was. It was an outdoor party. My memory is that we went behind a shrub and there had our interview. Without breaking confidences, as I have not with you, I outlined the concerns and the question of this young man in my ward. Then I asked Elder Kimball, "How can he get that revelation? How can he know whether his sins are remitted?"

I thought Elder Kimball would talk to me about fasting or prayer or listening for the still small voice. But he surprised me. Instead he said, "Tell me something about the young man."

I said, "What would you like to know?"

And then he began a series of the most simple questions. Some of the ones I remember were:

"Does he come to his priesthood meetings?"

I said, after a moment of thought, "Yes."

"Does he come early?"

"Yes."

"Does he sit down front?"

I thought for a moment and then realized, to my amazement, that he did.

"Does he home teach?"

"Yes."

"Does he go early in the month?"

"Yes, he does."

"Does he go more than once?"

"Yes."

I can't remember the other questions. But they were all like that—little things, simple acts of obedience, of submission. And for each question I was surprised that my answer was always yes. Yes, he wasn't just at all his meetings: he was early; he was smiling; he was there not only with his whole heart, but with the broken heart of a little child, as he was every time the Lord asked anything of him. And after I had said yes to each of his questions, Elder Kimball looked at me, paused, and then very quietly said, "There is your revelation." . . .

When I went back to the young man and told him what I then knew, he accepted it. . . . He went forward with his marriage. I've seen him since. To me he still looks as he did on the front bench before a priesthood meeting.[8]

> I bear you my testimony that the broken heart and contrite spirit that are the requirements for forgiveness are also its fruits. The very humility that is the sign of having been forgiven is protection against future sin.
>
> —TALK, OCTOBER 29, 1989[9]

This lesson learned from his wise uncle guided and comforted Hal in ministering to Stanford Ward members, some of whom fell into serious transgression and lost hope of finding forgiveness. Even he had such moments of doubt. But notes he wrote for a sacrament meeting address on Easter Sunday of 1971 show that he gained a firm conviction of the Atonement's power to blot out the most serious stains:

I recall being in the temple with a couple whom I had given recommends. Just as the ceremony was being performed, I had a pang of doubt. How could anyone who had done what one of them had be there? How could it be fair to the other? And I felt absolute assurance that the couple were as pure and clean as little children. (April 1971)[10]

FAITH IN PRIESTHOOD DIRECTION

As a bishop Hal gained increased faith in priesthood direction, not only as it came from his Uncle Spencer of the Twelve but also as received from his stake president, Richard Sonne. President Sonne was a well-educated, successful business executive, an MBA graduate from Stanford and the vice president of finance at Del Monte Foods.

Notwithstanding his deep leadership experience, including service as a bishop, President Sonne provided Hal little formal training. In their regular interviews, he mostly praised the young bishop of the Stanford Ward. He taught by example, speaking lovingly of the people with whom he had worked as a priesthood leader, a style of teaching Hal would later recognize in President Thomas S. Monson.

Paradoxically, Hal had the opportunity to influence the formal training of the Church's bishops, through his friend and fellow missionary Hugh Pinnock. They had labored together in the Western States Mission, when Hal had led a district of servicemen missionaries in Albuquerque and Hugh had served as an assistant to President Lewis Elggren. After the mission, Hugh remained a faithful friend. He surprised Hal by driving from Salt Lake City to Logan to attend his wedding, one of few non-family members who made that effort.

Prior to his call as a General Authority in 1977, Hugh served on several Churchwide committees, one of which developed a training program for bishops. Knowing that Hal was then serving as a bishop, and appreciating his skills as an educator, Hugh invited Hal to contribute to the work. When the new manual came out in fall 1970, Hal found modest evidence of that contribution.

On Sunday morning I started typing my genealogy family group sheets at six. By seven I had them done, and by eight I was in my bishopric meeting. During that meeting we opened a package that contained the new bishop's training program. Hugh Pinnock sent me the copy because of the writing I did for it last fall. It was fun to find my stuff buried here and there in new material, at least as good as my own. (October 12, 1970)

Though he appreciated and emulated the light hand of priesthood leaders such as President Sonne and his Uncle Spencer, Hal felt great confidence in the leadership of those in priesthood authority over him, especially the Brethren. He often expressed that faith to his fellow bishopric members. His journal records one special instance, as he prepared to leave California for a family reunion in Utah and then for a three-week stint teaching business executives for Stanford in Europe. Before this extended absence, he and the other leaders of the Stanford Ward convened an impromptu testimony meeting in the bishop's office. Hal testified last:

> I felt strongly to urge us all to use the instructions, in detail, we already have from the Lord through the prophets. I suggested we could have great success if we just obtained and followed all the instructions, even apparently trivial, from the Brethren. I said, "I'm sure some instructions must be in error. But in more than three years, I can't remember trying anything I was told that wasn't a source of great blessings." We left with love for each other and optimism. (August 11, 1970)

LIFTING AND GROWING

Hal's testimony and commitment to righteousness grew as he succored others in their afflictions. Most of those afflictions were of the spiritual, self-inflicted sort. But the greatest single trial in the Stanford Ward came with the news that four stalwart members had lost their lives together. In the late summer of 1969, Hal received word that Bruce Lindorf, Pamela Howell, and brothers Jesse and Carl Pearson had died in a private airplane crash. The four were on their way to attend the marriage of a fellow Stanford Ward member in the Salt Lake Temple. The civil authorities who notified Hal asked that he inform several of the parents, who did not yet know of the tragic accident.

Hal marveled at the strength of the parents of these valiant ward members, each of whom he had recently interviewed for temple

There will be times when you will feel overwhelmed. One of the ways you will be attacked is with the feeling that you are inadequate. Well, you are inadequate to answer a call to represent God with only your own powers. But you have access to more than your natural capacities, and you do not work alone.

—TALK, OCTOBER 6, 2002[11]

recommends. The reaction of each parent was an expression of faith in eternity, along with a desire to reach out to the other parents. At a memorial service held one week after the accident, Hal told friends gathered in the Stanford Institute chapel, including many not members of the Church, that their departed colleagues would have a similar desire to minister to and teach them.

> I think one of the greatest tributes that you could pay, honestly, to these four young people is that they could have, with what they knew to be true, comforted you tonight and helped you learn. And I think that it's important, if we are to really honor them and take comfort and learn from this experience, to understand not just what they hoped death was, but what they had absolute confidence death was.[12]

Inspired by the goodness of Bruce, Pamela, Jesse, and Carl, Hal taught the doctrines of paradise and the missionary work among the spirits in prison. He noted that that work would be a continuation of what these four had been doing in mortality. Having ascertained their spiritual worthiness just weeks before, he was able to attest not only to their missionary efforts but also to their testimonies of the Resurrection and their worthiness to come forth in the morning of the First Resurrection.

> These young people believed that if they lived righteously, if they had accepted the covenants of the gospel of Jesus Christ and lived them, that at the time of the coming of the Savior, they might come forth in the morning of the First Resurrection. Now to them that meant literally,

> We knew that Bruce and Pamela and Jesse and Carl were well; we saw this as a test for us.
>
> —BOB TODD, FIRST COUNSELOR IN THE STANFORD WARD BISHOPRIC[13]

not just that their spirits would endure but that bodies would be prepared for them that would be reunited with their spirits, for them to live eternally. That was their belief to the point of knowledge; they were sure of it. They were sure of it.

Therefore, their problem is not really a problem at all. They had none: they lived well. They lived briefly but well. We know, as they knew, that life is not here simply that we might live it long and joyously—although often it can be long and joyous—but that it is given to us as an opportunity to be tested, to grow, to have experience, and above all to prove that we will live the gospel of Jesus Christ. They met that test. They were released from this experience early, but they had passed the test, and they can have perfect assurance that they will rise in the morning of the First Resurrection.

Therefore, the only problem is really ours, and I think they would have me say that. They would, I think, say to you if they were here that the only real tragedy is sin, for sin might keep us from being rejoined with them again, as we can be if we will live the gospel of Jesus Christ as we know it to be true.[14]

The members of the ward took Hal's sermon to heart. Many in need of repentance sought out Bishop Eyring, and even the most faithful reflected and committed to live better. The tragedy galvanized and lifted the ward.

"GOD MAGNIFIES THOSE HE CALLS"

Hal sensed the value and the privilege of serving as bishop of the Stanford Ward throughout a term that ultimately ran to four years. He was a bit surprised when a release didn't come in 1970, after what he thought was the standard three-year term for bishops of young single adult wards. His uncle Spencer Kimball, however, disabused him of that expectation. During a conversation at a family gathering in Utah, Hal casually mentioned his mixed feelings about coming to the end of his time. Elder Kimball dismissively replied, "Who told you there was a time limit?" A few months later, President Sonne asked Hal if he would be willing to serve for a fourth year; he happily agreed to do so.

When the release finally came, in the late winter of 1971, Hal was grateful to return to the Menlo Park Ward, where he could help Kathy with their three boys, now ages seven, six, and two. He took his turn wrestling them on the bench in sacrament meeting and occasionally in the chapel's large "cry room." He also enjoyed spending more time with them at home on Sundays, and he even caught an occasional Sabbath nap.

Non-bishop Sundays have their charms. I arrived for Priesthood meeting at nine, with an hour more sleep than usual under my calm exterior.

After Sunday School I brought the boys home, had lunch, and then prepared my talk for the sacrament meeting of the new Stanford Third Ward with Henry and Stuart. We made a list of topics—many at their suggestion—and then prayed together. It seemed clear afterward that I should speak on "Good and Evil," one of their topics. I prepared and snoozed on the couch by my typewriter until time to go. The boys went with me to Bishop Dale Miller's[15] office for prayer before the meeting. Many members of the Stanford First Ward were there, in addition to some alumni from both Dale's ward and mine. The Spirit was there. (Sunday, March 21, 1971)

Though Hal enjoyed the newfound time with Kathy and the boys, he was caught off guard by the feeling of loss attendant to his release. That feeling brought a bit of sorrow. It also came with a great insight into the power of callings to serve in the Lord's kingdom. He summarized that insight more than thirty years later in a general conference talk titled "Rise to Your Call." He began with a warning that an experienced bishop may mistakenly take for granted the divine power that allows him to minister effectively.

The Lord will magnify what you say and what you do in the eyes of the people you serve. He will send the Holy Ghost to manifest to them that what you spoke was true. What you say and do will carry hope and give direction to people far beyond your natural abilities and your own understanding. That miracle has been a mark of the Lord's Church in every dispensation. It is so much a part of your call that you may begin to take it for granted.

Hal then illustrated this potential mistake with a personal story:

The day of your release will teach you a great lesson. On the day I was released as a bishop, one of the ward members came to my home afterwards and said: "I know you are no longer my bishop, but could we talk just one more time? You have always spoken words I needed and given me such good counsel. The new bishop doesn't know me the way you do. Could we just talk one more time?"

Reluctantly I agreed. The member sat down in a chair opposite mine. It seemed to be just as it had been in the hundreds of times I had interviewed members of the ward as a judge in Israel. The conversation began. There came the moment when counsel was needed. I waited for the ideas, the words, and the feelings to flow into my mind, as they always had.

Nothing came. In my heart and mind there was only silence. After a few moments, I said: "I'm sorry. I appreciate your kindness and your trust. But I'm afraid I can't help you."

When you are released from your calling, you will learn what I learned then. God magnifies those He calls, even in what may seem to you a small or inconspicuous service. You will have the gift of seeing your service magnified. Give thanks while that gift is yours. You will appreciate its worth more than you can imagine when it is gone.[16]

Hal retained this insight into priesthood callings throughout his life. But his opportunity to rest and ponder after the release from the Stanford Ward bishopric was brief. He already had another kind of call to serve in the Church, one that required leaving the beautiful house on the Hill in Atherton.

nephew, Mark, sometime last week, forced her out of
our double's match this morning; within an hour she'd
sent a replacement, so I played six sets. Result: I
soaked my elbow in a tub of hot water propped on the
table in the breakfast room at grandpa's, while I watched
the boys with the boys. Annette served the whole

COME, FOLLOW ME

Jesus said unto him,
If thou wilt be perfect,
Go and sell that thou hast,
And give to the poor,
And thou shalt have treasure in heaven:
And come and follow me.

—MATTHEW 19:21

O n Saturday, December 19, 1970, a few months before his release
as Stanford Ward bishop, Hal made an unusual journal entry. The
day was typically packed. He woke before five a.m. so as to be at the
Stanford Institute at six, where he met two students. Just after seven,
they were at the Oakland Temple, joined by half a dozen other Stanford
Ward members for a temple session.

After returning from the temple, Hal helped his two older sons,
Henry and Stuart, write Christmas notes to include in a box with a stool
they had hand-painted for their grandpa Henry Eyring, who lived in
Utah. Hal took eighteen-month-old Matthew to the post office to mail
it. He stayed with all three of the boys in the late afternoon while Kathy
attended an open house at the home of fellow Menlo Park Ward members. Somehow he found time to do other things along the way. His
account of the day's activities ends with this line: "Today I've graded
about twenty final exams, dictated a letter, run around the driveway,
and talked on the phone to three Stanford Ward members."

CLOCKWISE FROM LEFT: KATHY, HENRY, STUART,
HAL, AND MATTHEW

The unusual part of the journal entry was an attached page with the heading *Things Every House Should Have.* The list ran to twenty-eight items. Many addressed the physical needs of growing children, including "a mud and snow porch for boys, easily accessible" and "a large, rough basement or other playroom with a bath." Hal envisioned even grander projects than the ones that they had undertaken to that point, as evidenced by this feature: "a room for projects, large enough and rough enough to work on and store a kayak, or a miniature racer."

The boys' spiritual needs were also on his mind, as reflected in detailed provisions for family home evening. They included "a storage closet for films, cameras, and screens near the room where family night is held," and a piano in that room "situated so that the pianist can see a song leader standing by the fireplace."

The list of features reflected Hal's desire to facilitate Kathy's homemaking. He specified "at least five electrical outlets by the kitchen table," "a large kitchen pantry," "a dirty clothes chute from bathroom to laundry," and "an ironing room." He also wanted the house to accentuate the romance of marriage while giving Kathy increased privacy and protection from his early-morning routine. There was to be "room for two chairs in the bedroom," in which they could sit to talk, but also "one bathroom far enough from the sleepers that you can shave before dawn without being heard," and "dressing rooms so that husband and wife can dress and undress with the light on while the other is trying to sleep."

The list also suggests that Hal expected to continue his life as a scholar. The house was to have both "a paneled study with a glass door" and "a shed or bathhouse retreat for writing." Of course the house would be beautiful and light, with "a big entry hall" and "a kitchen table bay window with a beautiful view and light." It also needed to be warm, as slender Kathy disliked the cold. Thus, there would be "large fireplaces in several rooms" and "a porch with a corner facing southwest to catch the sun in winter . . . you can sit, shielded in the corner."[1]

It made sense for Hal to be thinking about a home of their own.

They had been living, rent-free, in the guest house for more than seven years. Though everyone loved the amenities of the Hill, including being so close to Grandma and Grandpa Johnson, the guest house wasn't built with a large family in mind. Matthew's room was directly above Hal and Kathy's, accessible only by traversing two hallways, four small flights of stairs, and the grand entryway.

Hal also felt self-conscious about his freeloader status. Of course, Sid never said a word about it. In Sid Johnson's mind, anything that he owned belonged equally to every member of his family, especially when an asset, such as the guest house, would otherwise have gone unused. (Hal had learned that the hard way with his old Volkswagen Beetle.) But Hal was now a tenured professor at one of the world's leading universities, as well as a founder and part owner of two successful companies, to say nothing of the additional income he earned from business consulting and participation in Stanford's executive education programs. Moving to a home of their own was inevitable, and they would soon be able to afford it.

"ARE YOU SURE?"

Hal got to bed late that night; his journal entry shows that he began typing at 10:10 p.m. After finishing that entry and offering his usual kneeling prayer, he climbed into bed carefully, assuming that Kathy was asleep. To his surprise, he felt a finger poke him in the back. The poke was followed by an even more surprising question from Kathy: "Hal, are you sure you're doing what you ought to be doing with your career?"

Hal was more than surprised. Given that he'd just completed eighteen hours of service as a bishop, Saturday project organizer, professor, babysitter, and house planner, the question didn't just catch him off guard; it irked him a bit. "What do you mean?" he asked grumpily.

Kathy calmly replied, "Couldn't you do studies for Neal Maxwell?"

At this suggestion, Hal's grumpiness turned to amazement and exasperation. Brother Neal Maxwell had recently been appointed as the Church's new Commissioner of Education, but Hal couldn't imagine how Kathy would know that. Hal had met Neal only once, when the two of them had spoken at a Saturday morning conference for youth in Oakland nearly a year before. Kathy hadn't been with him at the time.

Hal was also offended by his wife's apparent underestimation of his current professional position. He knew that Kathy wasn't starstruck by Stanford, as evidenced by her repeated intimations that he could be happier teaching seminary for a living. But to suggest that he give up a tenure-track position to do some kind of vaguely defined "studies" seemed outlandish, the abandonment of everything he had been working for, including his newly specified home of their dreams.

> God is never hidden, yet sometimes we are, covered by a pavilion of motivations that draw us away from God and make Him seem distant and inaccessible. Our own desires, rather than a feeling of "Thy will be done," create the feeling of a pavilion blocking God.
>
> —TALK, OCTOBER 7, 2012[2]

"You don't understand," he replied. "It would be inappropriate for me to do that kind of work. Brother Maxwell could have a graduate student perform research for him."

"Will you pray about it?" she asked.

"Yes, I will," he said, and immediately rolled back out of bed and onto his knees. He offered a short prayer and waited for an answer. None came. He returned to bed, satisfied at having taken Kathy's challenge and apparently settled the matter. They talked briefly, and she let him sleep.

The next morning, during bishopric meeting at the Stanford Institute, Hal got the answer that hadn't come the night before. He recorded it that evening in the journal.

The remarkable feature of the morning for me was an-swer to prayer. Last night Kathy and I prayed to know what to do with my career. We expressed openness to be taught af-ter I had pronounced certain jobs as "inappropriate" given my station professionally. Today, during the morning, I felt two clear impressions: "Don't use your human judgment to eliminate opportunities presented to you: pray about them all with an open mind." And, second, "Do the tasks you are assigned in the Church and your profession as well as you can; they are prepa-ration." I was delighted to see Kathy in the Menlo Park Ward when I was there for tithing settlement. I told her what I had learned. (December 21, 1970)

Hal would later recall his first impression, the one about job of-fers, as coming in the form of a voice to his mind, which said, "Don't you ever make that mistake again. You don't know which end is up in your career." The mistake, he realized, was partly in having declined three offers that had come in the preceding year.

All three offers had both a military and a political connection, and Hal assumed that he had been recommended in each case by General Doriot, his Harvard Business School mentor. General Doriot had hoped that Hal would parlay his Air Force experience and busi-ness education into a high government position, perhaps in the U.S. Departments of Defense or State. When Hal was choosing among his initial academic offers from Harvard, Stanford, and UCLA, General Doriot advocated Stanford for its technological strength and for being in the entrepreneurial West. "When you go to Washington," he said, "you will come from the West."

Though none of the jobs would have made Hal a chief executive, each involved a position of authority and high profile. The first offer came from a newly elected U.S. senator, Henry Bellmon of Oklahoma, who wanted Hal to be his chief of staff. Bellmon was a war hero, a Marine tank platoon leader who had participated in four amphibious landings in the Pacific, including Iwo Jima. Bellmon had been gov-ernor of Oklahoma and was national chairman of Richard Nixon's presidential election campaign when he successfully ran for the U.S. Senate in 1968.

Another chief-of-staff offer came from Werner Von Braun, head of NASA and the world's most renowned rocket engineer. Von Braun made the offer through Edwin Teller, the physicist credited with inventing the hydrogen bomb. Teller, then a professor at Berkeley, personally drove across the Bay and came to the guest house in Atherton to make the offer.

Hal received a third offer from Governor Nelson Rockefeller of New York, a three-time Republican candidate for president who would later become vice president to Gerald Ford. Rockefeller wanted Hal to serve as his chief science officer.

Hal declined all three offers. Each seemed to fit General Doriot's plan for a move into government, and each had career stepping-stone potential. However, none intrigued him enough to give up the good job and life he was enjoying. He didn't bother to pray about any of the offers. That, he realized when he heard the voice in his mind, had been a mistake. The rebuke, "Don't you ever make that mistake again," applied not only to his initial dismissal of Kathy's suggestion about doing studies for Neal Maxwell, but also to his failure to take the other job possibilities to the Lord in prayer.

AN INVITATION TO COME TO SALT LAKE CITY

The Christmas and New Year's holidays were typically pleasant, but they brought no new insights into Hal's professional future. Kathy organized the traditional family Christmas pageant, complete with dress rehearsal on December 23. That night's journal entry noted the complexity of the production, which portrayed sacred Christmas stories from both the Holy Land and the

It's not even a cast of tens, let alone thousands, but Kathy will need the marshalling skills of Cecil B. DeMille.

—JOURNAL, DECEMBER 23, 1970

Americas, drawing on the limited acting talent and attention span of the boys and their cousins.

In fact, if anything the holidays reinforced the importance of Hal's service in the Stanford Ward and at the university, as well as the joy of living on the Hill. Hal spent each day engaged with Kathy and the boys, doing projects and taking two trips to the tide pools at Half Moon Bay, one of Kathy's favorite places. He missed the family while working in Hawaii on the Castle & Cooke case. His discussions with the senior executives there went well at both the professional and the personal level. In addition to conducting three full days of productive meetings, he celebrated Hanukkah in the home of the company's chief executive, Harry Flagg, with whom he was staying. A cab ride across Honolulu suggested that he was on heaven's errand. The cab driver, Joseph R. TeNgaio, introduced himself as a Church member from New Zealand whose parents had often hosted Elder Matthew Cowley and who knew and loved Hal's father from a visit he had made to New Zealand. Brother TeNgaio's son managed the Dole Pineapple pavilion. In his journal, Hal recognized heaven's hand in the meeting:

> My cab driver this morning began our conversation by saying he was working to support his graduate studies at the University of Hawaii. He then said he taught in New Zealand. I asked, "Were your parents born there?
>
> "Yes."
>
> "Are you Maori?"
>
> "Yes, full-blooded."
>
> "Well, I feel a kinship to your people. I'm a Mormon."
>
> At that, he turned around and said, "I'm a Mormon, born in the Church. Let me shake your hand."
>
> We didn't crash, and I found tears coming to my eyes as we talked. (December 28, 1970)

Labor in the Stanford Ward also filled the holidays. Ward member Rinard Sewell died in an auto accident the day after Christmas, on his way to visit Kathy's brother, Craig, in Utah. Rinard was a recent convert to the Church, set to receive the Melchizedek Priesthood the next week. Hal had begun that day fasting for another ward member in need, and so was spiritually prepared for the news of Rinard's death.

The Sundays before Stanford's winter semester began in January were full of ministration. On Sunday, January 3, Hal conducted meetings and interviews from 7:30 a.m. to 9:30 p.m., seeing more than twenty ward members privately. The night before, he and Kathy had taken in a young woman whose parents had expelled her from their home. The first and second days of the new semester brought two memorial services, one for Rinard Sewell and one for the father of Marilyn Miller, another member of the Stanford Ward. After the second service, on Wednesday, January 6, Hal conducted interviews in his bishop's office in the Institute until 10:30.

That January 6 entry also included an addendum. After recounting the other events of the day, Hal wrote this:

 An unusual thing happened during the day. On the way to my office in the morning, I stopped to pick up suits at the dry cleaner. Just as I drove out onto El Camino Real, I felt great doubts about the reality of the gospel run through my mind. They persisted for about five minutes, the only such experience I have had in my recollection. I thought, "This must be the fear people who doubt feel." Within an hour after reaching my office, I got a phone call from Neal Maxwell, the Church's Commissioner of Education. He asked to see me in Salt Lake immediately. After juggling my schedule I called back to confirm my arrival tomorrow evening. (January 6, 1971)

The next day Hal's plane to Salt Lake was delayed, getting him into Salt Lake close to nine o'clock at night. Neal Maxwell wanted to keep the appointment notwithstanding the late hour. He offered to come to Hal's boyhood home, where he was overnighting with his father. Neal arrived in snow boots and parka and got right to the point: "I'd like to ask you to be the president of Ricks College." Neal made it clear that the job offer was not a call and that it would last only "two or three years."

Hal replied, "I'll have to pray about it." He then explained his bedtime prayer with Kathy and the rebuke that had come the next day in his bishop's office. Neal agreed that the experience had been preparatory, and he encouraged Hal to confer with his family and make the decision a matter of prayer. But he also encouraged Hal to be expeditious. "We meet with the First Presidency," Neal announced as he prepared to leave, "at eight thirty tomorrow morning."

NEAL A. MAXWELL

Hal spent that night in the unfinished basement room that had been his as a high school student. He slept soundly for six hours and then rose early to seek the confirmation that had not come as he prayed before retiring. Of course he wanted to have an answer for the First Presidency. Given his careful attention to the rebuke received just a few weeks before, he naturally expected one. He was willing to go to a place he had never set eyes on and, in the process, sacrifice the prestige of Stanford and the comforts of the Hill. But there was no reply to his question about taking the Ricks College job. The only impression that came to his mind was an enigmatic statement: "It's my school."

A MEETING WITH THE FIRST PRESIDENCY

Hal arrived early at the Church Administration Building, in spite of stopping with his younger brother, Harden, to help a girl push her car out of a snowbank—an ironic reminder of the difference in the weather to be expected if he accepted the job in Rexburg. Neal arrived at 8:25, and they sat in a large waiting room until the counselors in the First Presidency, Harold B. Lee and N. Eldon Tanner, walked in at 8:30. President Lee remarked that he had watched Hal grow up. President Tanner introduced himself without comment.

They moved together into a large, exquisitely paneled conference room at the back of the building. Neal directed Hal to sit at one end of a large table, in a chair immediately to President Lee's right. President Tanner sat to President Lee's left, with an empty chair between them. The journal records the ensuing discussion in detail.

President Lee asked all or most of the questions. He began by asking what my feelings were. In this question, as in the entire conversation, neither the name of Ricks College nor the job of a university president was ever mentioned. I responded that I had prayed and felt assurance that what I had been asked to do was the Lord's business, but that I had been told no more. Neal suggested that I recount the incident of being told in answer to prayer to bring career choices to God after consideration, eliminating none. President Lee said essentially, "That's the pattern . . ." and suggested that my parents had influenced me to behave that way.

He then asked a series of questions which, in retrospect, are a personal interview, yet it is impossible for me to recreate on paper the tone. Personal questions were asked with a kindness that seemed to give total assurance to me, and the questions of judgment seemed to be asked not to test me but as if the Brethren sincerely valued my opinions. At no point, throughout the entire process, was there the least indication of lack of time or hurrying. The sense of peace was remarkable. (January 8, 1971)

The questions put to Hal revealed that Presidents Lee and Tanner knew much about his work. They asked, for example, about Stanford University's decision, made a year before, to suspend athletic competition with BYU because of the Church's policy of denying the priesthood to black men. Stanford's president, Kenneth Pitzer, had invited Hal to his office to discuss the matter before announcing the university's decision.

Presidents Lee and Tanner also explored Hal's views of the

Church's institute program and of higher education in general. President Lee asked what could be done to make the institutes more effective. "Some have said that the Church schools are for the orthodox and the institutes for the others," he remarked. "Do you agree?" He also asked about the challenges to education in the coming decade, specifically for the Church. The conversation was more dialogue than interrogation. Presidents Lee and Tanner commented on most of Hal's replies, and President Lee in particular told stories to illustrate the issues and principles they discussed.

At exactly nine o'clock, President Lee turned to President Tanner and said, "The light is on under the President's door." He was looking at a closed door at the far end of the room, which apparently led to the office of President Joseph Fielding Smith. President Tanner went to the door, entered President Smith's office, and closed the door behind him. He returned a minute later. Not long after that, President Smith, joined by two aides, entered the room. He walked to Hal's side of the table, and Hal rose to greet this renowned man he had never met. President Smith, then ninety-four years of age, moved slowly, with his head slightly bowed. He took Hal's hand, said hello with a smile, and passed by without coming to a full stop.

President Smith took the chair between his two counselors. President Lee reported to the prophet that they were talking with Hal about a key job in the Church Educational System. He asked President Smith whether he would like to conduct the interview. President Smith paused, looked down, and then said with a smile, "I think you're quite able to do it." The three men smiled at each other, and President Lee continued to pose questions, with only slightly greater formality than he had been employing for the past thirty minutes.

The questions included, "Do you have any reservations about the doctrines of the Church," and "Do you have any trouble with any of the Brethren, accepting them?" Hal answered that he had never had real disagreements in the Church and worried about taking a position that might produce them. President Tanner replied, "If you take this job, you'll have some." Yet this comment, like the others before, led to pleasant discussion.

At one point President Lee approvingly ascribed some of Hal's responses to his father's influence. President Tanner interjected, "I knew his mother." President Lee agreed and paid tribute to Mildred. Both men referred to Hal's parents repeatedly.

The most memorable and moving interview question came from President Lee. He began by noting that Hal had earlier borne a "strong testimony." He then put his hand on President Smith's arm and asked, "Do you think that such a great man as this is the prophet of God?"

Hal could have confidently answered that question at any time, but he was particularly well prepared to do so that day. Earlier in the week, at the memorial service for Stanford Ward member Rinard Sewell, he had shared reminiscences of their personal interviews. A recent convert to the Church, Rinard developed childlike faith in the face of heavy trials. Diabetes was taking his eyesight even as he struggled to make a living with little formal education, crushing financial debts, and a former spouse and children to support. He trusted a priesthood blessing that promised him the ability to see as long as he lived, but he still learned Braille.

As Hal told those gathered at the memorial service, he had counseled with Rinard frequently, especially in preparation for his receiving the Melchizedek Priesthood. Rinard always came to their interviews fasting. In the weeks leading up to what was to have been their final interview, on January 6, the day Neal Maxwell phoned Hal at his Stanford office, each discussion included a review of the priesthood worthiness questions. In answering the questions about testimony, including belief that the current President of the Church was God's prophet on the earth, Rinard would reply with not just a "yes" but an emphatic "yes, *sir.*"

> To keep ourselves grounded in the Lord's Church, we can and must train our eyes to recognize the power of the Lord in the service of those He has called.
> —TALK, OCTOBER 2, 2004[3]

Having reflected so recently on Rinard's enthusiastic faith in a man he had never met, it was easier than ever before to respond confidently to President Lee's question, "Do you think that such a great man as this is the prophet of God?" The answer came to Hal like fire in his chest: "I'm sure of it," he said. President Smith simply looked up at Hal and then looked down again.

DECIDING TO GO

As Neal and Hal exited the conference room, they encountered the members of the Presiding Bishopric, John H. Vandenburg, Robert L. Simpson, and Victor L. Brown, seated in the waiting area that the two of them had occupied an hour before. Only fifteen years later, when he was called into the Presiding Bishopric himself, would Hal learn that the bishopric's weekly meeting with the First Presidency was scheduled for nine o'clock, and that he had been given twice the time allotted for his interview, keeping these men waiting.

As they walked down the large granite front steps of the Church Administration Building, Neal said, "I'm sure you have the job if you want it." They turned west toward the Hotel Utah, where a cab was waiting. Hal said, "I'll have to wait for God's direction, and I won't give Him a deadline." Neal replied, "He  doesn't wear our wristwatch, does He?" As Hal got into the cab and asked the driver to take him to the airport, Neal added, "Thanks for a great experience."

Neal's wristwatch comment proved prophetic. The letdown from their remarkable meeting with the First Presidency came almost immediately, as Hal arrived at the Salt Lake City airport to find his flight canceled. That meant missing a class he was scheduled to teach in Palo Alto. When he finally got to San Francisco, his Thunderbird's massive engine blew a hose on the drive home. After dinner and an evening in the park with the boys and their cousins, there was less time than he wanted to talk with Kathy and her parents about the Ricks College offer.

For his wife and in-laws, the course was clear. Sid wanted to get to work on the move immediately. Kathy and the boys would need a house in Rexburg, and he was ready to dispatch one of his construction foremen to buy a piece of property and draft up building plans. As Hal noted in the journal, "He's not against prayer, but is urging lots of action in addition to and after prayer."[4]

Kathy felt less hurried but was equally resolved to go forward. Her impression that Hal should be working for Neal Maxwell had been literally fulfilled. She had known for some time that they needed to leave the Hill. The boys were too young to understand or be affected by the opulence in which they lived, but that wouldn't last. She knew that the Eden they had roamed as innocent youngsters was no place to grow up.

Moreover, Hal's schedule wasn't sustainable for any of them. That could be seen as early as the next day, Saturday, when he taught a class on business strategy to the employees of System Industries in the morning, attended a wedding reception in the afternoon, and performed a wedding that night.

But Kathy had recognized the handwriting on the wall for more than a year. Hal's success at Stanford brought more invitations to teach and speak and consult than he could possibly fulfill, and for whatever reason—some will-weakening mix of obligation and pride, perhaps— he had a hard time saying no. The writing of the Castle & Cooke case, which had taken him to Hawaii during the holidays and consumed every spare moment since, was only the latest example. Much harder for her and the boys had been a recent three-week trip to Denmark and Belgium to teach in a Stanford program for European executives. The plan had been for her to join him during the middle of the trip, toward the end of August. While he taught for just a few hours each day, she would shop and see the sights; he would then join her for afternoons on the beaches adjoining the luxury hotels Stanford had booked for their high-flying executive customers.

Of course, it didn't play out as planned. The idea had sounded good the winter before, when Hal made the commitment. But by July, Matthew was one year old and every bit as difficult to corral as his older brothers. Kathy couldn't bring herself to leave the boys. As it turned out, Hal wouldn't have been a pleasant travel companion. The European executives, who were sacrificing their summer vacations, proved to be hard-to-please students who demanded more of their instructors than they did of themselves. Hal worked all day and into the night, just as at home, to avoid disaster in the classroom. From the moment he arrived in Europe, he longed to be back on the Hill, as recorded in the first of seventeen full-page typed letters he sent.

Dearest Kathy:

I more than miss you. I find myself, in the midst of reading or even writing, picturing you walking down the hall to my door. Sometimes I see the boys' faces, always about six inches from mine, in full color. It's not good to write about it, since that just runs the pictures past me again. The end of three weeks looks like a tunnel opening, so far away there is just a spot of light. But I've got my eye fixed on that spot. It will get bigger every day. Ah, that's the picture![5]

Kathy had less time to write, but she managed to send three handwritten notes in her elegant penmanship and witty style. The first one included a reminder that they needed to find a better balance between Hal's professional and personal responsibilities.

Dear Hal:

I was reading *The Art of Being a Member Missionary* tonight and read a quote from your Instructor article several years ago. It's still a great article, and I'm looking forward to your next one. The book is a very inspiring one (even without your quote), and I am determined to ask the milkman the Golden Questions.

Craig and I took the kids to the beach on Saturday. Matthew was covered from head to foot with sand and looked like a giant sand crab crawling along with his hands and feet.

We're going to the beach again tomorrow. This must be some great subconscious urge I have to be with you on the beach in Aarhus.[6] Three weeks is an incredibly long time. Let's remember that the next time this comes up.[7]

In fact, Hal's own writings reflected the need for change, as evident in this journal entry:

I've noticed a slight misrepresentation in this journal. At the same time, I detect an unpleasant revelation. The misrepresentation comes from the act of writing: I enjoy it enough that an exuberance tends to come over me at the typewriter, and that tends to color my descriptions. In honesty, I'm dragging through many of the things I seem to zip through on these pages.

The revelation is a certain sense of awe over my own busy schedule. The reader may get the unpleasant but true impression that I may take too much stock in trying hard rather than getting results that matter. In fact, my lifestyle in the past few years has been like a wildcat oil driller who lacks faith in any one location to put one deep well down but spreads lots of shallow holes all over the countryside. Quite a few—like Finnigan Instruments—have turned out to be dry holes, perhaps at least partially because I didn't move in on them and take charge. (October 21, 1970)

Hal wasn't satisfied, though, with going to Ricks simply for the focus it would bring to his life; he would need to develop the ability to prioritize in Rexburg just as in Palo Alto. He also wasn't willing to default to treating the job offer as a Church call. Neal had drawn that distinction carefully in their first conversation, and the members of the First Presidency hadn't so much as spoken of the job offer, let alone couched it in the language of a call. He felt ready to do as Uncle Spencer had counseled—to walk away from the Hill and his Stanford career. But the decision he faced now required more than just trusting the Brethren's judgment. The voice in his mind had said, "Don't you ever make that mistake again," and the implication was clear: even this job offer from the First Presidency needed divine ratification.

After a week of prayer, though, Hal received only a reconfirmation of the message that had come as he prayed in the basement of his father's home: "It's my school." The experience reminded him of one that Oliver Cowdery had had when he asked for confirmation of the Prophet Joseph's testimony of the gold plates. In Hal's case, it would have been nice to receive something more definitive, especially as pertaining to his future. Neal had said that the job would be for only two or three years. In that time his ties to Stanford and the business community would be severed. It was hard to imagine ever being able to go back, at least not without significant professional cost.

> Verily, verily, I say unto you, if you desire a further witness, cast your mind upon the night that you cried unto me in your heart, that you might know concerning the truth of these things. Did I not speak peace to your mind concerning the matter? What greater witness can you have than from God?
>
> —DOCTRINE AND COVENANTS 6:22–23

On Tuesday, February 2, 1971, the news media in Salt Lake City and southeast Idaho announced that Hal would be the next president of Ricks College. Hal's Stanford colleagues, none of whom had heard of Ricks, were dumbstruck. Peers such as Roger Sant had expected him to become dean of the business school and perhaps president of the university.[8] But Dean Arjay Miller, who knew Hal's heart, saw the logic of the new assignment. "Professor Eyring is now going to have his own university," he wryly commented at Hal's last faculty meeting. "And now he can give *all* of his attention to his church."[9]

Hal's journal records his sons' reaction: "The boys seemed genuinely pleased at dinner when we told them we were going to Idaho. Henry said, with a smile and enthusiasm, 'I wish we could carry you on our shoulders.'"[10] None of the Eyrings, though, could really envision where they were going. During show-and-tell the next morning in his second-grade class, seven-year-old Henry stood and proudly announced, "My family is moving to Rexburg, Iowa."

A SCHOOL IN ZION

Behold, I say unto you,
Concerning the school in Zion,
I, the Lord, am well pleased
That there should be a school in Zion.
—DOCTRINE AND COVENANTS 97:3

On March 2, 1971, before ever setting foot on the campus of Ricks College, Hal had his first meeting with the college's board of trustees in Salt Lake City. At the time, that group included every member of the First Presidency and the Quorum of the Twelve. Hal was caught off guard when President Harold B. Lee asked him to make a statement. He stood and said simply, "I have never been the president of a university or a college. I don't know what's needed or what's to be done. But I'll pray, and I'll find out what the Lord wants. I'll align myself with His will, and I won't fail."[1]

Hal first saw the Ricks College campus eight weeks later, at the end of April. His journal doesn't mention wind, but at that time of year it was almost certainly gusting. Whereas the Hill in Atherton was in full bloom, the Ricks grounds crew wouldn't be planting flowers for another month, knowing that killing frost could come as late as Memorial Day and that even June would see at least one good snowfall.

Hal flew into Idaho Falls on Monday and spent the night at the

Ramada Inn, where he worked until one a.m. on his talk for the next day's devotional, to which all of the college's students and employees were invited. He based his talk on Psalm 40, having found the hotel Bible in his room open to that page. The first three verses in particular caught his eye:

> I waited patiently for the Lord; and he inclined unto me, and heard my cry.
>
> He brought me up also out of an horrible pit, out of the miry clay, and set my feet upon a rock, and established my goings.
>
> And he hath put a new song in my mouth, even praise unto our God: many shall see it, and fear, and shall trust in the Lord.[2]

This theme, of being lifted and established by the Lord, had been the focus of his thoughts for several weeks. He had pondered the critical difference between choosing righteousness in response to instruction versus being impelled to change by the bitterness of sin, as David was. Hal hoped to make proactive change in his life and to inspire it in others as he assumed leadership of Ricks College. His learning objective read:

> Listeners consciously and effectively trying to hear the Spirit teach them of the Savior, and thus to change or continue changing their lives.

The next morning, Hal continued to work on the talk before driving the thirty minutes to Rexburg, where he was greeted warmly by outgoing president John L. Clarke and several of his administrative colleagues. At noon, they and representatives of the faculty and students lunched with Spencer W. Kimball, then President of the Quorum of the Twelve. President Kimball and his wife, Camilla, had flown up from Salt Lake City that morning.

Today alternated between sunny clear skies, gray overcast, and a wind around five that would pass in some parts for a hurricane. When I first came people made that old joke: "If you don't like the weather, just wait a minute." Today that was so.

—JOURNAL, JUNE 2, 1972

Hal was pensive during lunch, and he didn't eat. Noticing this, President Kimball said—loudly enough for everyone in the room to hear—"Why aren't you eating, Hal?" Hal answered, "I'm fasting." Without smiling, President Kimball retorted, "What's the matter? Aren't you prepared to give your talk?" Later, when the talk had been delivered, President Kimball took him aside and said, "That was a fine Sunday School talk, Hal. But you didn't tell them what you're going to *do*."

HARD SHOES TO FILL

Hal was surprised by President Kimball's comment. He had assumed that a devotional was no place to lay out a vision for Ricks College, particularly not in the presence of the still-sitting president. He had also determined to reserve judgment, let alone strategic decision making, until he got to know the college and its people better. But he of course took President Kimball's rebuke seriously. He determined to quickly learn enough about the school to qualify for revelation about what to do for it.

His knowledge of Ricks at that point comprised only a combination of high-level statistics and personal anecdotes. The college was small relative to Stanford or BYU, but it was growing at a break-neck pace. The student body of five thousand represented an increase in size of 50 percent over the preceding four years, and the building space on the campus had more than doubled during that time.

SPORI ADMINISTRATION BUILDING, ERECTED 1903

At the individual level, Hal learned that Ricks operated with the spirit and customs of an extended family. President Clarke, who had served for twenty-seven years at the college and also presided over the Rexburg

Stake, was a beloved champion of the school. When he took the helm in 1944, Ricks had just two stone buildings and a wartime-draft-depleted student body of roughly a hundred women and exactly eight men. President Clarke had not only overseen a fifty-fold increase in students but had also won, briefly, four-year status for the school. Ricks offered bachelor's degrees in the 1950s, until the Church Board of Education directed a return to junior college status, preferring to concentrate the Church's university-level activities and investments at BYU.

President Clarke had championed not just the institution but also its people. Hugh C. Bennion, dean of the faculty and a distant cousin to Hal's mother, Mildred, told the *New Era*, "President Clarke is an eternal optimist. He refuses to see faults in others and, consequently, others are anxious to improve their efforts." And in the same article, the student editor of the college newspaper, the *Viking Scroll*, paid this tribute: "As is true of other Church schools, we have had no riots or demonstrations against the administration and no burning of buildings. Yet there is an atmosphere of awareness and academic freedom that has thrived under the confident leadership of this great man."[3] For Hal, it was hard to imagine matching his predecessor's personal embodiment of the college community's cherished "Spirit of Ricks."

President
John L.
Clarke

The few impressions Hal had felt pertained to the students. After his release as bishop of the Stanford Ward in mid-March, his thoughts had begun to turn to Ricks, notwithstanding a workload at the university made greater by his impending departure. In a journal entry, he reasoned that the best way to determine Ricks's role in the Church Educational System was to study the needs of its students, and that the best way to do that was to teach them. "The president-elect of Harvard, Bok," he noted, "intends to teach a seminar for freshmen."

If Bok has the time, I should be able to organize to do it. He wisely said he wanted discussion, not his lecturing. I might offer a non-credit course or seminar, once a week for the first six weeks. I might share the course with a perceptive person, both to get his input to the seminar and to use his judgments of what the students seek as a check on my perceptions. (March 17, 1971)

After Hal's visit to Rexburg in late April, his thoughts also turned to the students' observance of the school's standards of spiritual worthiness and dress and grooming, as recorded in a May journal entry. His thinking reflects the combination of confidence and tough love he learned from Mildred and Henry, as well as his insights into psychology and the workings of the Spirit.

After reflection, I've decided two things about standards: (1) to communicate love and confidence to the young people and my testimony that the standards are inspired, and (2) that the people who police the standards must communicate love and a sincere desire to deal with the motivations behind the misbehaviors.

By prayer, most young people can get the same feeling of acceptance I have for standards, if not total explanations. My feeling is that the purpose of the standards may largely be to develop humble acceptance and to allow those feeling rebellion to signal the need to talk with someone. (May 5, 1971)

Hal also had impressions about relative priorities. The consistent theme was putting eternal, spiritual matters ahead of temporal

It is clear that our first priority should go to spiritual learning. For us, reading the scriptures would come before reading history books. Prayer would come before memorizing those Spanish verbs. A temple recommend would be worth more to us than standing first in our graduating class. But it is also clear that spiritual learning would not replace our drive for secular learning. . . . On the contrary, it gives our secular learning purpose and motivates us to work harder at it.

—TALK, MAY 6, 2001 [4]

ones. During a visit to the Oakland Temple, he was reminded of the need to place family ahead of all other duties:

> I felt impressed with my obligations first to Kathy and our boys, and with the critical need to have the peace of the gospel in my heart to be effective at home and in my Ricks College service. (May 22, 1971)

The next day, he recorded an impression that spiritual considerations at the college should take precedence over finances, even when significant sums of money might be at stake, as in the case of a proposed facility for the visual and performing arts.

> How critical is a decision, say, about the arts building, in terms of producing young people at peace and able to live the gospel in this troubled world? Will a design change later be a disaster? (May 23, 1971)

LEAVING STANFORD AND THE HILL

Hal pushed hard to hit the June 13 departure date that would allow him to arrive in Rexburg to assume his duties on June 15. Events, though, seemed to conspire against him. Sid needed help with a shopping center that was teetering on the edge of bankruptcy. Hal pitched in, proposing deal structures for selling half of the center and creating the financial projections necessary to entice prospective partners. The effort ultimately proved successful but was time-consuming for Hal.

Simultaneously, he and Kathy had a real-estate problem of their own. With the help of one of Sid's construction foremen, they had purchased a building lot a few blocks west of the Ricks College campus, on Yale Avenue (only Hal's colleagues from Harvard, Yale's traditional rival, could fully appreciate the irony of his new street address). Sid's foreman had gotten the new house started but was pulled off the job to tackle pressing projects back in California. Because the change in leadership would further delay the already behind-schedule house project, that meant finding not only a new contractor but also temporary quarters in Rexburg. Fortunately, the college had just constructed a small trailer park for married students, and one of the trailers was available for the Eyrings.

This harried, uncertain time, though, also brought unexpected comforts. One was the graciousness of Hal's Stanford colleagues, especially the dean of the Graduate School of Business, Arjay Miller. As Hal's final semester at Stanford was winding down, Dean Miller invited him to lunch.

At noon I lunched with Arjay Miller. In addition to a pleasant chat about business schools, auto companies, and the Mormon Church, he invited me to contact him should I for any reason leave Ricks College. He seemed to genuinely want me back and at the same time respect my decision to go. (May 24, 1971)

As my Palo Alto dentist drilled and filled a tooth this morning, he mused about the idyllic life he could have in Rexburg.

—JOURNAL, MAY 18, 1971

Hal was also surprised by the desire of a handful of current and former Stanford Ward members to join him as faculty members at Ricks. They included one of his counselors, Bob Todd, as well as Michelle Howell, Jim Jacobs, and Scott Cameron. Each of these young scholars was a Stanford graduate, and the decision to go to work at a junior college with no research activities and at salaries far below what any university was offering represented a major sacrifice, as Hal noted:

Bob Todd called today. He and his wife, Janell, have felt impressed to accept the offer to teach at Ricks College. He will be the first Ph.D. in mechanical engineering to teach there. He had offers from the General Motors Institute and a large tractor company. He expects an offer to be an assistant professor at the University of Utah. The news brought a happy note to his voice and a tear to my eye. (June 4, 1971)

When the day for departure came, Hal was ready for a new chapter, and he had his family firmly behind him. Sadly, in the near term that would be true in the literal sense. Kathy would stay in Atherton with the boys for the time being, waiting to join Hal in Rexburg when the new house was ready. But everyone looked forward to the new experience, confident that the path ahead was divinely marked.

> The boys saw me off today, with Stuart putting cold applesauce in a thermos for me. After we had prayers, Henry dropped a tear or two. I miss them, too. Matthew was up all night, perhaps sensing my going.
>
> The drive to Elko was easy and lovely. The spaces in Nevada give me feelings of expanding. The smell is lovely, and unique. When I went through the low parts of the Humboldt River valley in the evening I blasted through a horde of bugs. As I turned the washers and windshield wipers on to clear them I remembered the same experience, going the other way to marry Kathy nine years ago. My Volkswagen lacked the fancy washers then. I've come up in the world, I guess. But the charm was greater going to Kathy, not away. (June 13, 1971)

A DIFFERENT WORLD

In the afternoon of Monday, June 14, Hal was met in Rexburg by Iris Hathaway, secretary to President John Clarke, and her husband, Elmo. The Hathaways took Hal to his temporary home, a new single-wide trailer on which workmen were installing an air-conditioning unit. Looking over the other forty or so trailers in the park and seeing no other air conditioner, he felt grateful for the special treatment.

On his way to meet President Clarke, Hal stopped at the college's new athletic field house, where he received a locker in the faculty locker room. His meeting with President Clarke, in the college's historic Spori Building, was pleasant but not long. President Clarke was just two weeks from reporting with his wife, LaRae, as the new president of the New England Mission, headquartered in Boston. Their conversation was akin to the one that President Clarke would have with the outgoing mission president, Elder Paul Dunn—brief and more tactical than strategic.

The Hart Fieldhouse

After his visit with President Clarke, Hal stopped by the home site on Yale Avenue. He also went grocery shopping. The husband-and-wife proprietors of Brown's grocery store had closed for the day, but they reopened just for him. A bachelor's portion of provisions loaded into the trunk of the Thunderbird, he found a pay phone ("apparently the only one in town," he wrote) and called Kathy to report a great start in Rexburg.

Hal began the next day, his first as the college's president, with morning scripture study of Mormon's wartime correspondence with his son Moroni; he also planned for one-on-one interviews with senior members of the Ricks administrative team. In the first interview, he followed an impression to begin with kneeling prayer. Pleased with the result, he did the same in the meetings that followed. At noon he went for a run on the college's outdoor track. Later in the day, Neal Maxwell called to express his love and his willingness to pay for Kathy and the boys to visit Rexburg. That night, Hal's journal entry began, "This was an exhilarating day for me." Succeeding entries expressed similar enthusiasm.

This was a beautiful day for me. The watershed was my 10 a.m. meeting with the mathematics and physical sciences faculty group. Dr. Hugh Bennion and I met them in the Classroom Office Building.[5] I asked Brother Gordon Dixon to lead us in prayer. We knelt around the conference table. What followed was an informative, free-wheeling discussion of the curriculum, in which I clearly felt the Spirit of the Lord. I closed by observing what a joy it was for me to combine my two loves, the gospel and education, and how fortunate those men were to be having that rare experience. It was a remarkable experience for me, and it colored my entire day. (June 16, 1971)

Soon, though, a thorny issue emerged. In discussions with the college's Counseling Services group and Dean of Students office, Hal heard concerns about many students' resistance to Ricks's dress and grooming standards. The style of the times was long hair and beards for men; for women, it was short skirts or tight jeans and tops. The dress code for all of the Church schools forbade these styles.

Incoming Ricks students knew of this code, but many were surprised and even outraged to find that it was strictly enforced, beginning with registration day. As the students came to pick up their class schedules, representatives of the Dean of Students office informed the

SEVENTIES STYLES AT RICKS

noncompliant that they would need to change clothes, cut their hair, or sometimes both. For the shaggy men, there was an on-site barber, brought in for the day from his shop on Main Street. Those who refused his services weren't allowed to enroll in classes. Some left town immediately, deprecating the college and its officers as they went.

The inspection effort was hard on the frontline enforcers. A member of the Dean of Students office described for Hal the emotional unpleasantness he had experienced judging hair length the year before. He attributed the subsequent "egging" of his house to retribution by an offended student. Members of the Counseling Services office confirmed that many Ricks students, as well as some employees, resented the apparent divide between the rules and justice of the college and those of the gospel. "That perceived split," Hal wrote in the evening, "must be reduced."[6]

SETTLING IN

Though it seemed much longer, Kathy and the boys arrived in Rexburg just ten days after bidding Hal farewell in Atherton. The boys immediately declared the trailer "cool." Even cooler was the agenda for their first full day: a private airplane flight over the Tetons and Yellowstone Park; a show in the college planetarium, followed by physics demonstrations that included huge magnets and a bed of nails; lunch with their friend Scott Cameron from Stanford; and a trip to the giant sand dunes north of town.

Activities such as these, each sponsored by a generous Ricks employee, continued for the next three days. The boys enjoyed the college pool, Elmo and Iris Hathaway's power boat and camper, a farm with ponies and motorcycles, and the ground-level beauties of Yellowstone. They returned to California convinced that there was no place more fun than Idaho. Hal, though, immediately missed them.

Kathy and the boys left today. After my afternoon appointments, I met our architect and rearranged the house. Lonely. (June 28, 1971)

***

I left the office at 6:30 and drove to our house. It seemed lovely to me, so much like Kathy I could feel her there. I talked to her tonight after a fine dinner. The dinner was spiced with fresh bread, handed to me by one of our neighbors as I left our new home this evening. Somehow that catches Rexburg: a fine young man, daughter in hand, taking fresh home-baked bread to a neighbor on the street. (July 12, 1971)

Hal was grateful for the kindness of neighbors, and for the temporary companionship of Scott Cameron, one of the Stanford Ward students who had hired on as Ricks faculty members. Hal shared the trailer with Scott while he found his own lodgings. They stayed up late each night for a week, processing Hal's experiences as a new president and pondering the future of the college. They also talked about Scott's future. Still single at the time, Scott was comforted by stories of Hal's finding and marrying Kathy relatively late in life.

In his loneliness, Hal frequented the Idaho Falls Temple. He also took several long drives to Jackson Hole and Yellowstone. During those temple trips and drives, he thought of the college. The challenge of preserving and even raising its standards of worthiness occupied his mind as he traveled. As a result, he gained special insights from things he saw and heard. After his first trip to Jackson since he and Kathy had honeymooned there, he observed:

A week at Ricks College has already softened me. Jackson Hole has that special worldliness I will always associate with serious skiers in the 1950s. Even though the young people in Jackson now wear long hair and the new grubby uniform, and even though the shops are filled with too-expensive art crafts and the smell of incense from candles, that hard sophistication I remember so well tears at my insides. I think it tears because I fear it yet I feel its lure, the lure of being so serenely confident of who you are, of having no doubts. That confidence is probably largely attributed by me, rather than real. Yet I think it may be partly real, largely because it is possible to be pleased with yourself if you set lower goals for conduct. It's easier to be a pretty good mountain climber or candle seller in the right clothes than it is to be a real elder, one who can hear the Spirit. The man who is seriously after that goal has to give far more before he can walk through the day, sure that he will not fall. It's a tougher kind of skiing, and infinitely more rewarding. And a young person has to sense that it is more rewarding and that he can do it, or he'll settle for that easier feeling you might get in a few summers at Jackson. (June 19, 1971)

The journal records another standards-related insight gleaned in the Idaho Falls Temple one week before he was to speak at a campus devotional.

Just finished a bean, cheese, and tomato supper after returning from the temple. It was a lovely session. As I sat in the celestial room I listened to the talk being given to a couple being married in the adjoining room. The sealer referred to the fact that every blessing is predicated on a commandment. That gave me one of a series of insights I gained during the evening on teaching the keeping of standards: that I should try to understand and communicate the blessings that will come from living the college's standards. (June 29, 1971)

> Satan will expand the space that is not safe. He will try every way he can to persuade you that there is no danger in trying to come as close as you can to that dividing line. At the same time, he is trying to persuade people that there really is no line at all. Because he knows that you know it is there, he will say to you, "Come closer to the line."
>
> —TALK, SEPTEMBER 30, 1990[7]

"THE BEST EDUCATION IN THE WORLD"

Hal began to recognize one of the greatest blessings of Ricks's standards as he prepared for that devotional address, the first he would give as the college president. Though he knew that attendance would be light relative to a fall or winter devotional, he sought inspiration and prepared with his usual earnestness. During the afternoon and evening of the day before, the message he was to give became clear, as reflected in his notes for the address:

> The levels we set can and should be "unreasonably" high, if we are confident the goals are backed by God. Eighty percent of the results come from twenty percent of the people, not because they try a little harder but because they are going at it entirely differently.[8]

The talk he envisioned drew from his recent experiences in Jackson and Yellowstone. It also grew out of his months of thinking about the role of standards at Ricks College. He delivered it the next day, speaking without a written text. He began by establishing a premise that surprised even the most ardent supporters of the college—that a Ricks education could be the best in the world.

> I am grateful for this half hour in which I might explore with you the things that perhaps are most important to me and, I would think, to you, and that is the intertwining of the gospel of Jesus Christ and education. To even be here, each of you must have asked and answered the question, "Why should I get involved in education at a college sponsored by The Church of Jesus Christ of Latter-day Saints?" and then, I guess, the question, "Why Ricks College?"
>
> I suppose for some of us the answer might be, "Because it's the only college in town," and for others, "To meet Mormons," or perhaps, "To study in a religious atmosphere." I am not going to try to dissuade you from those good reasons, but to suggest and explain another reason you might have for being here. That is, to get the best education in the world.

Now, that reason takes a little explaining. A great many people, in and out of the Church, might not rank Ricks College as one of the great colleges of the world, with Harvard College and Reed College and Dartmouth College. And, to be honest, your own experience this summer might suggest that it is not equal to some other experiences you have had in other places. Nevertheless, I believe sincerely that a wise person could select Ricks College because he or she wanted the best education in the world, and I believe that whether or not they were members of The Church of Jesus Christ of Latter-day Saints.[9]

Hal sought to establish this claim of Ricks's offering the best higher education in the world by identifying what makes education valuable. The most valuable education, he suggested, confers the ability to see patterns in a changing world, where facts and theories become obsolete

> Education is what happens inside you, not around you. If the buildings are impressive, or the professors famous, or even the other students apparently learning at a great rate, that is essentially irrelevant to your education.
> —TALK, JULY 5, 1971[10]

but fundamental principles persist and can be used to make sense and create order. By way of illustration, Hal described his own college experience, which was just fifteen years in the past. The vacuum tubes he had studied then had already been replaced by several generations of solid-state devices. He would be unemployable, he conceded, as a frontline engineer in 1971.

However, his educational experiences at the University of Utah and the Harvard Business School had taught him to ask meaningful questions in new environments—such as the presidency of Ricks College—and to connect the answers received to unchanging principles. The fundamental principles of physics and finance and psychology he had learned as a student in the early 1950s remained valid in 1971. By asking questions of Ricks College employees and students with those principles in mind, he was already beginning to see similarities between the needs and opportunities of the college and those of the Air Force, of the companies he had studied as a business school professor and consultant, and of the Stanford Ward.

The process of questioning and learning how to question around patterns, how the world is put together and how people relate to each other, is, I believe, the essential skill of education. I believe that it is generalizable, and I believe that colleges have a special opportunity to teach that skill of questioning to acquire patterns and the use of patterns in questioning. [11]

STUDYING IN THE LIBRARY AT RICKS COLLEGE

This ability to see patterns, Hal taught, is largely a gift of the Spirit, given by revelation. Of course, he noted, pattern recognition capabilities are enhanced by formal education that teaches secular principles, such as Newton's laws of motion or the time value of money. But the discoverers, inventors, leaders, and teachers who are best at recognizing patterns also get heaven's help, whether they appreciate the help or not. All truth, secular and spiritual, is revealed by the Holy Ghost, as the Savior taught His disciples. [12] Hal testified that the strokes of insight he had received while working math problems or teaching business school cases were no different from those that had come to him as a missionary or bishop. "The process was the same," he told the students. "The feeling within me was the same . . . of joy and also the feeling of humility, of quietness, of prayer." [13]

This concept, that lasting patterns are best recognized by revelation, provides the link between high moral standards and outstanding educational experiences, as Hal went on to explain:

We know some things about revelation. We know some ways you have to be living in order to receive it. We know some things about being virtuous, about being humble, about being prayerful, about seeking God in order to have revelation. That tells us something about the school that would provide the world's best education, really. It says that the notion of standards, the notion of stakes and wards, the notion of a religious atmosphere are meant not simply to extend the lovely homes you have had or to replace them with a home perhaps more spiritual, more supportive than the one you have known. It isn't to show the world that we are good.

If we are to take advantage of the rare resource we have to be prompted by the Holy Spirit, it means that we need to do all we can to make this a place where, in all we do, in athletics, in dance, in our social lives, the possibility of revelation is not far away. Now, those of you who have taught the gospel of Jesus Christ, particularly the missionaries, know how hard it is to do. It's not simply to see how much you can take in the way of discipline. It is because by long experience we have learned that it is hard to have revelation unless you are living in certain ways that make it possible for the Holy Spirit to speak to you. I would suggest to you, if you believe what I have said about education, that that is essential to the spirit we have in gaining an education. And so, for Ricks College, that takes on an educational meaning far beyond custodianship of young people away from home.

> The standards we must meet in dress and conduct are unreasonable, unless you see that they come from the prophets and know that you can set a high target for achievement in important areas of real service, as well as high standards of modesty and kindness.
>
> —TALK, AUGUST 24, 1971[14]

Having explained the connection between living according to high moral standards and receiving revelation, especially in our ability to recognize the patterns that matter, Hal ended with a prayer that both high standards and the resulting revelation might be hallmarks of a Ricks College education.

My prayer is that that might be true in all we do and we might realize that, at Ricks College, as a blessing of God, we have been given the resources, literally, to provide the best education in the world.[15]

REACHING OUT

For Hal, the task of helping Ricks College provide such a quality education began in earnest in mid-August, after several weeks of vacation on the Hill in Atherton, during which he fulfilled a commitment to teach an executive program at Stanford. Back in Rexburg, he spent Saturday, August 14, with the student representatives who would officially welcome their colleagues to campus during the following week. On the next Monday, he spoke to all members of the faculty. The theme of his messages to both groups was consideration, which he identified as not only a feeling but also a skill. The skill of consideration, he taught, embraces altering one's communication and teaching approaches to meet an individual's needs. He had observed that skill in his most gifted teachers, especially his parents.

In advocating the skill of consideration, Hal built on the idea of pattern recognition that he had discussed in the July devotional. At that time, he had explained that effective teaching requires chastening with love, as described in the 121st section of the Doctrine and Covenants.

I will tell you that finding new patterns is, first of all, a humbling experience. It is one where you make mistakes. You can't find the way. You struggle. You fail from time to time. Therefore, the teacher must have a special quality. He must have the capacity to love you yet chasten you. He has to have the capacity to let you know he loves you, so that when you fail somehow that isn't a personal assault, a personal condemnation. And yet, at the same time, he must have the capacity to let you know you're failing. And those of you who have tried to do that with people—to chasten with love, to tell you you're wrong and not have it break you but lift you up—know that that is a rare skill in this world and one, again, that I would bear testimony is magnified by the gospel of Jesus Christ and living it well.[16]

> The notion that, "This is too much for me," is the key to learning.
>
> —2010 INTERVIEW

In his fall discussions with the faculty and student leaders, Hal applied these ideas to the tasks of welcoming new freshmen to campus and of helping all students learn in the classroom. To the faculty, he taught the importance of recognizing that a teacher's natural personal style requires expansion and variation according to an individual learner's needs. His teaching note for the student leaders included these remarks about the skill of consideration:

> Your task is not to present Ricks well, but to help people find in it what will be a blessing to them. You can have confidence that they will find something, for the school has some resources precious and rare to all people. The scarcest resource is consideration, shown in the time a teacher will spend with a student or a girl eating with a lonely and not very attractive boy. That is more than a nice attitude; it is at the heart of education because it allows the student to say, "I don't understand," and "I don't see," without fear.[17]

The next week, Hal joined the faculty and student leaders in greeting the Ricks student body. He took a personal approach. As the students came to pick up their class registration forms, he was there to shake hands. He also assumed the duty of judging compliance with the school's dress and grooming standards. Between seven thirty a.m. and four p.m. on Wednesday, August 18, he shook the hands of nearly two thousand students; during each of the two succeeding days he greeted a similar number.

May 31, 1984
Thursday

I wrote in the Atherton
guest house of the
Johnsons, looking down
on the trees and drive
of our first home.
Elizabeth and Mary
Kathleen watched me
blow out
birthday
dinner b
Holy Gh
teach a
workshop

June 1,
Friday

Elizabeth
the poo
worked
Gary ca
Los Ang
to hear
time to
Altos.

June 2,
Saturday

I towed
inflated,
M a r y
compli
purple
match t
hair tha
Stuart's
sister.
and I watched Stephanie
dance in a musical.

HAL WITH RICKS STUDENTS

June 3, 1984
Sunday

Kathy, Elizabeth, and Mary Kathleen were dressed and
packed early for our drive from Atherton to the San Jose
airport. On the flight home, a stewardess made a bullseye
with a glass full of orange juice on my lap. It was so cold
and complete a soaking that I laughed for the rest of the
trip. I used bags to shield the results as I got us to the car.

On Thursday evening, after the second day of hand shaking, Hal conducted a meeting for the new students. The journal records the sweetness of the experience:

> There is no set of notes for the talk I just gave in the orientation assembly. I prayed last night about several alternative ideas for that talk and others. I was impressed only that I should be humble. So I spoke tonight trying to forget being president, with my green freshman beanie on my head, and sharing the feelings of the most awed freshman. After the assembly, I sang "I Am a Child of God" on the stage with the student officers and with the audience. Then, the student cabinet knelt, and I knelt with them, behind the curtain, to thank God. I don't remember sharing a prayer of childlike thanks so totally when someone else—in this case student body president Mike Mulcady— was praying. (August 19, 1971)

From seven-thirty until four, Mike and I met students registering. We prayed together this morning and had our prayer answered that we might learn better how to talk to so many people.
—JOURNAL, AUGUST 19, 1971

During those three days of shaking hands, Hal was pleased but not fully satisfied by what he saw: "I was impressed at how childlike the girls seemed as I stared into those thousand-or-so eyes and how many fellows had obviously just hand-cut their shoulder-length hair. The hair was changed, but the hearts will have to come too."[18] Changing hearts, including his own, would become Hal's quest at Ricks College.

nephew, Mark, sometime last week, forced her out of
our double's match this morning; within an hour she'd
sent a replacement, so I played six sets. Result: I
soaked my elbow in a tub of hot water propped on the
table   e breakfast room at grandpa's, while I watched
the b   with the boys. Annette served the whole

11

PREPARE YE, PREPARE YE

Wherefore the voice of the Lord
Is unto the ends of the earth,
That all that will hear may hear:
Prepare ye, prepare ye
For that which is to come,
For the Lord is nigh.
—DOCTRINE AND COVENANTS 1:11–12

Hal scarcely had time to meet with the faculties of Ricks College's six academic "divisions" before receiving a major off-campus assignment from Neal Maxwell. In September 1971, Commissioner Maxwell asked Hal to chair a Select Committee on the future of higher education in the Church. The twenty-person committee included three of Hal's colleagues from Ricks: Bob Todd, religion professor Mel Hammond (later a member of the First Quorum of the Seventy), and Dean of Students Mack Shirley.

The seven BYU representatives included Academic Vice President Bob Thomas and faculty member David Merrill, a pioneer in the field of instructional science. Two future members of the First Quorum of the Seventy, Royden Derrick and James Mason, represented the Church's Sunday School and welfare organizations, respectively. LDS Business College President Ferris Kirkham and Church College of Hawaii Academic Dean Wayne Allison served as the sole representatives of their institutions.

PRESIDENT HAROLD B. LEE AND ELDER PAUL DUNN
WITH HAL AT HIS INAUGURATION

The members of the Select Committee met for the first time in October 1971 in Salt Lake City's McCune Mansion, a meeting place given to the Church in 1920 by railroad and mining tycoon Alfred McCune. The mansion, which overlooks Temple Square and offers a full view of the Salt Lake Valley, was a fitting place to consider the future of Church higher education. This first meeting went well, as Hal recorded in the journal:

The Select Committee meeting was an unusual blend of fresh, divergent thinking, sparked by disagreement, yet a feeling of the Spirit leading and shaping the discussion. That's amazing, with 20 strong men in the group. To my surprise, near the end of the three hours before lunch, we agreed that a reasonable question to pursue is: "If we looked at a 10-year planning horizon and assumed the Lord would come then, what behaviors, attitudes, and skills would the members of the Church and those around them need to have for the Lord to be able to come?" Here are just some of the answers:

1. The patriarchal order working well enough in most homes that the present auxiliary functions could be performed in the home.

2. Most families, worldwide, economically self-supporting with a surplus to support education and church service.

3. The solutions and people to implement them in place to produce social order and the health and nutrition environment for a peaceful, happy life. (Must be implemented soon after the Savior's coming.)

4. The members bilingual, with English as a first or second language.

5. Effective managers for the church in every country, many of them men now illiterate.

We developed numbers of others, each based on the teaching of prophets, and each having implications for higher education. We were unsure about one question of importance: "How much of the leadership must be members of the Church?" A second, related question we left unanswered was: "Whatever the numbers of Church leaders which must be produced, what part of their training is best done by the Church?"

What becomes clear is the magnitude of the efforts required and the unreality of hoping the Church can afford to use its tithing dollars duplicating the world's institutions unless they contribute directly to these needs for the Savior's coming. The Church system must be focused primarily at not only training but producing teachers. That might be done by allowing young people to teach as part of their education. (October 21, 1971)

SEEKING GUIDANCE

The members of the Select Committee were blessed by their clear focus on the kind of education necessary to prepare the Church and the world for the Savior's Second Coming. But the exact nature of that education, as well as the role each of the four CES institutions would play in providing it, was difficult to specify, as they found in subsequent meetings. Uncertainty about these matters led to differences of opinion and tensions that proved less productive than those inspired by the Spirit in their initial gathering. Committee members appreciated Hal's skill in directing the group's focus to the interests and concerns underlying the positions taken, rather than just battling over those positions.[1] Still, it was harder going than he had expected after the inspiring first meeting.

> Ted drove me to Harden's home after the Select Committee meeting. Ted said, "The Lord will give you the answers you need about the preparations needed in education for His coming."
> —JOURNAL, OCTOBER 21, 1971

In fulfilling his leadership role, Hal sought counsel from the senior Brethren, as well as from his file leaders in CES. Together they explored a vision of taking formal higher education beyond the traditional college campus and into the homes of Church members. With

Associate Commissioner Ken Beesley, Neal Maxwell's direct report and Hal's first contact in the Commissioner's office, Hal discussed "ideas about how the Church Educational System might be coordinated with and work through the regular priesthood organization, making their joint impact on the home. . . . It was clear," he observed in the journal, "We had been led to the same ideas, working apart."[2]

Spencer W. Kimball, then President of the Quorum of the Twelve Apostles, further expanded Hal's view of the future of Church education. In the course of a conversation about the Select Committee's work, Hal stated his assumption that though Church universities could help in preparations for the Millennium, they would not be part of it, that some more-advanced learning system would replace them. President Kimball gently corrected him, as Hal would recall to a group of BYU faculty members twenty-five years later:

> As we talked about the plans we should make for the future, I made what I thought was the logical suggestion that conditions during the Millennium would surely allow such educational innovation that we should assume our universities should be planned with the expectation that they would be replaced with some more effective institutions in that time when the Savior would be among us.
>
> There was what seemed to me a lengthy silence, and then he made the quiet statement that over the centuries universities had proved to be the most effective institutions we had developed to find, conserve, and transmit knowledge across numerous fields of inquiry, so why not expect that they would serve as well in the Millennium. That immediately seemed sensible to me.[3]

A meeting with President Harold B. Lee, at that time still first counselor to Joseph Fielding Smith, also proved seminal, not only relative to the work of the Select Committee but throughout Hal's life. After one Committee meeting, he and Bob Todd and Mack Shirley arranged to see President Lee in his office before driving back to Rexburg together. The Committee's meetings had begun to bog down in disagreements over the role and scope of each institution; in particular, the extent to which BYU would offer advanced degrees and perform scholarly research, both expensive activities, had become a divisive issue.

Hal and his colleagues from Ricks shared with President Lee the story of the first Committee meeting, when divergent opinions had produced surprising agreement about the role of Church education. Hal then described their current challenges and asked, "President Lee, how do you get revelation?" President Lee smiled. He began to tell stories about his involvement in the creation of new Church programs. Each story made the point that clarity and agreement had come only after careful, thorough study—sometimes repeated study. Hal recalled one of President Lee's stories in a 1990 fireside address:

> I bear you my testimony that the words *study it out* mean a degree of patience, of labor, of persistence commensurate with the value of what you seek.
> —TALK, SEPTEMBER 30, 1990[4]

> He said that during World War II he had been part of a group studying the question "What should the Church be doing for its members in the military service?" He said they conducted interviews at bases up and down the country. They had data gathered. They had the data analyzed. They went back for more interviews. But still, no plan emerged.
>
> Then he gave me the lesson, which I now give to you, in about these words: "Hal, when we had done all we knew how to do, when we had our backs to the wall, then God gave us the revelation. Hal, if you want to get revelation, do your homework."[5]

In his journal, Hal applied President Lee's story to the challenges that he and his Select Committee colleagues faced:

> He said that the Lord tells you the answer after you've done all you can, after you've worked into a brick wall. We could see we had jumped too quickly over the data gathering

and careful defining of where the Church Educational System really is now and what it has accomplished. (November 18, 1971)

THE SELECT COMMITTEE REPORT

The Committee continued to meet monthly, in daylong sessions, until May of the following year, 1972. Subcommittees also met, with an emphasis on the kind of data gathering that President Lee had recommended. As a June delivery deadline neared, Hal and the other Ricks Committee members began to write the first of what would prove to be more than a dozen full drafts of a final report. Along with Bob Todd and Mack Shirley, Stanford transplant Jim Jacobs, a professor of English, and student secretary Jo Ann Jolley joined Hal in a kind of writing, editing, and typing chain gang. The gang worked mostly nights, weekends, and holidays. Hal led, recording prose with a handheld dictation machine. Jo Ann produced rough drafts for Bob, Mack, and Jim, who marked them up and fed them back to Hal. The cycle continued hour after hour. For Hal the pressure was doubly great, as he faced a nearly simultaneous deadline to produce a report for Neal Maxwell on the role of Ricks College. It was also a stake conference weekend in the Rexburg Stake. The journal records the final push.

President Lee's prophecy, or really counsel, came true today. He said we'd get revelation when we'd done all we could and our backs were to the wall. Well, we backed into the wall today. On Monday I have my last chance to get reactions from the Select Committee members before the presentation to the Board on Wednesday. And the revelation seems to be coming. I dictated 17 pages today, largely what I expect to say to the Brethren. To my surprise, since I had not felt clear inspiration, Bob Todd, Mack Shirley, and Jim Jacobs all felt we came the closest to being right in this version. Time is running out, and we are getting help. (Thursday, June 1, 1972)

***

I left the house before anyone was stirring and had another
draft of the Select Committee
report done by noon. I worked
from then until three on the
Role of Ricks presentation.

After the 4:30 meeting with
Elder Ashton, as part of stake
conference, I met with the Ricks
members of the Select Committee
plus Jim Jacobs. By 7:30 we had
Jo Ann going on another draft,
and I went to another stake leadership meeting. It's eleven, I've

Window in my workroom

been home long enough to visit with each boy save Matthew,
and I've had some supper. (Saturday, June 3, 1972)

The final version of the Select Committee report began with a dis-
claimer, an admission that, "While we felt the blessings of the Spirit at
some point in each of our meetings, in only a few areas did our work
lead us to strong feelings of confidence and unanimity in our recommendations. Only those areas are treated in the report."[6]

The report proposed three ambitions, each in the form of a question: (1) "How can the Church use present CES facilities to serve more
students at approximately the same cost?" (2) "How can we make education available to those who cannot attend CES campuses?" and
(3) "How can the Church increase the practical impact of education
without materially increasing the cost per student?"[7] The report elab-
orated on the principle of practicality:

> The word "practical" was important. It seemed to us that
> for education to have value, it had to change the practical life of
> a student, both during his formal education and afterward. And
> "practical" meant becoming the leader of a family, both in teach-
> ing the family and in supporting it financially.[8]

In addition to suggesting limits on graduate programs and scholarly research at BYU and the other campuses, the report proposed that the reach of the Church Educational System be inexpensively extended in two main ways. One was to increase the number of institutes of religion, not only in North America but worldwide. The Committee members stated their belief that strong institute programs situated near well-regarded secular universities could provide many, though not all, of the benefits of a Church-owned institution, at a fraction of the cost to tithe payers.

The other recommendation was to explore technologies for teaching students without building physical campuses. The report ventured a bold view of the future:

> Some predict that most homes will have a television set within the next ten years that will allow the viewer to talk back to what he sees on the screen. If this happens, a technology-based program for delivering higher education would be both flexible and inexpensive. It would be low-investment simply because the individual would have already made the investment. The hardware would be sitting in his home waiting to be used. More students could be affected by the great teachers on our campuses.[9]

The report was ahead of its time, and some Committee members objected to the proposed limitations on graduate programs and scholarship. However, Hal's experience on the Select Committee shaped his thinking in ways that would prove valuable not only at Ricks but in subsequent Church assignments. Also, the report received a warm reception from the executive chairman of the Board of Education, Elder Gordon Hinckley.

> I know of a lot of reports that have been written by very able people, and I've been involved in some of them myself, that have had comparatively little value to persons who read them but immense value to those who wrote them, because of what they would later become.
> —ELDER DALLIN H. OAKS[10]

At 9:30 this morning I was in Salt Lake City and at 11:00 I was making the report of the Select Committee to the Board of Education. At the end, Elder Hinckley moved a vote of commendation and said, "This is the most significant thing that this group has heard." No one else joined in the praise, but several seemed interested. (June 7, 1972)

THE ROLE OF RICKS

As he labored to foresee the future of higher education in the Church at large, Hal undertook a similar study with the academic leaders of Ricks College, one focused just on their institution. They did so at the direction of Commissioner Neal Maxwell, who requested that each of the four CES schools of higher learning engage in a process of self-study and strategy development. In November 1971, Hal wrote a charge to the members of this "Role of Ricks" task force, comprising more than a dozen administrators and members of the faculty. He began with references to simultaneous growth in college costs and in the number of Church members who needed a college degree. He ended with a charge to do the kind of "homework," or data gathering, that President Lee had suggested to the Select Committee.

Our opportunities are shaped by changes in the world of education and in the development of the worldwide Church. Just at the time secular scholars are asking whether American higher education can afford to be all things to all people, the growth of the Church has presented more needs for educational services than we can meet with our present resources. Both events suggest two things: (1) that we identify needs and opportunities for higher education in the Church and the nation, and (2) that we identify which needs Ricks College can meet best. In the long run, the Lord may provide means that we may meet all needs for educational services. In the short run, it is clear that we must focus our limited resources on the education needs most important to the Church in a rapidly changing world.

Hal closed his charge to the task force members with a vision of what they might accomplish, based on sufficient effort:

> Your work could add to the Church and to the College. The Lord obviously has gone to great lengths to prepare Ricks College. He will reveal His intent for Ricks College only after we have studied the matter out carefully. It is your task to define the facts we should gather in that study.[11]

Hal had been thinking about the role of Ricks for nearly a year, ever since that early January night at his father's Salt Lake City home when Neal Maxwell had surprised him with the request to go to Rexburg. For several months before writing the formal charge to the Role of Ricks task force, he had been trying out ideas on unsuspecting audiences. One of those was the Rexburg Civic Club, a local women's group. In anticipation of speaking at their October luncheon, Hal outlined the following ideas, which began with a reference to a recently published national report by a Stanford colleague, Frank Newman:

> There are some important reasons why Ricks College must differentiate itself from other colleges, inside and outside of the Church Educational System:
>
> The Newman report[12] argued that part of the malaise of young people, of parents, of legislators (and we might say, Church governing boards) is the shared assumption of colleges that growth indicates progress and that Berkeley and Harvard are the models.
>
> As the Church becomes worldwide, the pressures on the tithing dollars for higher education will become greater.
>
> Taken together, these create an opportunity. We can differentiate ourselves by speaking to the emerging needs of the world and the Church.
>
> Why does anyone pay 500 or 5,000 dollars to go to a college for a year? It used to be that you did it largely to get status and a job. Neither will justify the cost now.
>
> The Oxford picture was a place for gentlemen to live the life of the mind. In Germany, at least in the late 1800s and 1900s, it

was to learn from research. In America it became both, with sort of a hope that the graduates and the research gave great lifts to the economy and the society. Our theology, our history, and our faculty suggest another philosophy for Ricks College: "[B]e ye doers of the word, and not hearers only . . ."[13]

What special advantages does Ricks College have in nurturing doers, not hearers only? The main challenge educationally is to convert young people from self-centeredness to consecration and to doing the work. We have a faculty who by skill and attitude are the best in the world at that.

Also, the region from which we have drawn many of our students is attuned in the homes both to education and to practicality. We have an area whose economy is well-suited to training young people in applying the theories they learn to practice, particularly in the developing parts of the world. Examples include biology, geology, agriculture, management, and simple manufacturing.

We have a tradition of training teachers, and a vision of a great oak whose branches reach out around the world.[14] We have only the vaguest visions, based on which we are now beginning to study, but we see enough to be excited by the outlines. We will need a special breed of young person, rare today, but becoming more common. Raise them and let us train them, not to save them, but to help them save the world. The College has a destiny, seen by its leader from the beginning, and it will fill that destiny.[15]

Hal was blessed to have read and discussed the Newman report with its author earlier in the year, while still in Palo Alto. The natural thing for a Harvard graduate and Stanford professor to do would have been to put Ricks College on a path to be more like those institutions. That was the course being urged by some at BYU, and it was certainly the national trend. Even Ricks College had been on that path when it had briefly attained four-year status in the 1950s. Since arriving in Rexburg, Hal had often heard the question, "When will Ricks be a four-year school again?"

But Newman and other policy specialists had documented the price of climbing the higher education "ladder." As institutions added bachelor's and graduate degree programs, and as faculty members spent more time performing research and less time teaching, the cost of a college education inevitably rose. That fact strengthened Hal's impression that Ricks needed to stay close to its roots. His ultimate recommendation regarding the Role of Ricks, made just two days before the final report of the Select Committee, proposed to do exactly that.

I was in the office just after four in the morning. By five I had the first glimmers of my presentation on the role of Ricks, and on the eight o'clock plane to Salt Lake City it became clear. I proposed that we serve the same mix of Idahoan, rural, and modest scholars. But that we do it with new programs in practical work experiences to aid in making educational choices, basic communicating skills, family teaching skills, and a more practical religion program aimed at transfer to everyday life. (June 5, 1972)

TEACHING RELIGION

Even without the challenge of leading two future-looking task forces, Hal would have been unusually busy during his first year at Ricks. While fulfilling the ordinary duties of the presidency, he made good on his promise to himself to teach a class. It wasn't the kind of wide-ranging seminar for freshman that Harvard's Derek Bok planned. Rather, Hal teamed with one of the most knowledgeable and dynamic members of the college's religion department, Keith Sellers. During Hal's first semester at Ricks, fall 1971, they taught a Doctrine and Covenants course together. Their class met on Tuesdays and Thursdays at one o'clock.

In addition to giving Hal intimate, sustained contact with students, teaching with Keith Sellers yielded great personal benefits. As they prepared together for each class, usually for an hour that morning,

Hal enjoyed the kind of missionary gospel study that his part-time mission hadn't afforded. In Spirit-aided give-and-take with Keith, his knowledge of the scriptures deepened. He also learned from Keith's freewheeling instructional style, a marked contrast to the relatively structured, note-driven approach to discussion leadership Hal had learned as a business school student and professor. In addition, he got instant feedback on his teaching performance, not only from Keith but also from Kathy, who attended class whenever she could find a babysitter for the boys.

HAL TEACHING FROM THE SCRIPTURES

The class was popular and large. Over the ensuing six years, between eighty and a hundred students enrolled each winter and fall semester. But, in each class session, Hal and Keith tried to identify at least one student with a special need or contribution to make.[16] Oftentimes, that student seemed an unlikely contributor. Hal recalled one such young man several years after leaving Ricks College.

I was teaching from section 25 of the Doctrine and Covenants. In that section Emma Smith is told that she should give her time to "writing and to learning much" (verse 8). About three rows back sat a blonde girl whose brow wrinkled as I urged the class to be diligent in developing writing skills. She raised her hand and said, "That doesn't seem reasonable to me. All I'll ever write are letters to my children." That brought laughter all around the class. I felt chagrined to have applied that scripture to her. Just looking at her I could imagine a full quiver of children around her, and I could even see the letters she'd write in purple ink, with handwriting slanting backwards; neat, round loops; and circles for the tops of the *i*'s. Maybe writing powerfully wouldn't matter to her.

Then a young man stood up, near the back. He'd said little during the term; I'm not sure he'd ever spoken before. He was older than the other students, and he was shy. He asked if he could speak. He told in a quiet voice of having been a soldier in Vietnam. One day, in what he thought would be a lull, he had left his rifle and walked across his fortified compound to mail call. Just as he got a letter in his hand, he heard a bugle blowing and shouts and mortar and rifle fire coming ahead of the swarming enemy. He fought his way back to his rifle, using his hands as weapons. With the men who survived, he drove the enemy out. The wounded were evacuated. Then he sat down among the living, and some of the dead, and he opened his letter. It was from his mother. She wrote that she'd had a spiritual experience that assured her that he would live to come home if he were righteous. In my class, the boy said quietly, "That letter was scripture to me. I kept it." And he sat down.[17]

In addition to being individual-focused, Hal and Keith agreed to avoid speculation and sensationalism. At the beginning of the first semester, they discussed the temptation for religion teachers to offer opinions in matters the scriptures and the Brethren hadn't specifically addressed. Hal particularly worried that his status as Ricks's president could lead students to assume that his opinion carried the weight of official Church doctrine. He took pains to avoid such mistakes. He was, by Keith's recollection, "very, very conservative in his approach of teaching the gospel."[18]

Hal and Keith soon developed an easy team-teaching rapport, as Hal noted in a 1973 journal entry:

Kathy said that in our New Testament class today, "I felt the spirit today, stronger than it has been. You could really feel it. I felt you were really speaking the truth." Brother Sellers and I remarked to each other afterwards that, in the last classes, we have felt a complete ease in teaching together, knowing just when to speak and never needing to back-track. It's been a remarkable growth in our teaching together. (November 1, 1973)

But even as the teaching became more natural, Hal found that it had a weighty effect on him, particularly as he and Keith undertook the Book of Mormon. After several weeks of waking with aching jaws, Hal self-diagnosed the pain as "an identity crisis that's been building since I taught the Book of Mormon for all of last year."

That experience raised an entirely new—and far more difficult—standard of what the Master expects. And I've not yet seen a change in behavior. So, the higher standard and the old behavior produce aching jaws. The key is hope: I need hope, faith mixed with love, that the standard is attainable for me. I've not prayed and worked for that hope specifically. I will. (November 29, 1973)

> We must teach the gospel in its simple purity. To do that we must pray in faith that the Spirit will warn us away from teaching false doctrine, from giving personal interpretation, and from all speculation as we teach the gospel. That restraint may become more difficult as we read more books and hear more talks with what seem to us to be novel or more profound expositions of the gospel.
>
> —TALK, FEBRUARY 26, 2010[19]

Preparing for and teaching religion, which he would do throughout his time at Ricks College, also helped Hal in his administrative work and parenting. A journal entry made in early October 1971, when he and Keith were teaching the Doctrine and Covenants course, records such an experience:

For some reason I began, at 7:30, reading the 7th and the 8th sections of the Doctrine and Covenants, which declare study to be a pre-condition to revelation. Taking the instructions literally, I puzzled out five major issues in my mind, made notes, and knelt down to ask if what I had thought was right. In each issue, one of my answers came clearly to mind. That didn't seem enough, so I asked for the burning in the bosom to confirm the guidance. That came slightly, but without the feeling of peace that has been my experience before. I went ahead, working on the answers in conferences and phone calls. As I worked, some of the decisions looked unreasonable for part of the morning, then seemed clearer as the day went along. I got more decisions made today than in any one day in weeks, yet I had to struggle to find the way. Revelation works. That's clear from my experience this morning. But it's also clear you must really work for it. (October 6, 1971)

RAISING STANDARDS FOR THE COLLEGE

During his first year at Ricks, Hal learned that he had to work hard not only for personal revelation but also for a strong institutional commitment to the school's standards of conduct and dress. Presiding over Ricks during a time of unprecedented moral and fashion decline, Hal found that reminding students of their commitment to the college honor code could be a full-time job.

Much of the appointment part of my day was spent with faculty and students, discussing dress standards. At the end of the day I told Kathy that I felt as if I'd been going off a high diving board all day—into very shallow water. Even with the Spirit guiding, when the stakes are the lives of slightly rebellious people, the day is a little wearing. (October 6, 1971)

In most cases the rebelliousness was truly slight, particularly given the general standards of the day. Like the Stanford Ward, the college was a small island in a vast cultural sea of immorality, drug use, and public protests. Though these ills afflicted a small percentage of Ricks students, the more common challenges on campus were long hair, immodest clothing, and curfew violation. Hal worked hard to help the students understand the spiritual implications of breaking seemingly small promises.

At seven-thirty this morning I met with a young student. He challenged the rules for having guests only at certain hours in our housing. I hope he felt and understood my message: the rules remind him of real danger, and the exact hours become important not because they are perfect boundaries but because we need to become perfect in exactly doing what we agree to do. (December 14, 1973)

From some quarters, Hal received unexpected help. He was approached by Val Dalling, head coach of the men's basketball team, with a stack of profiles of potential recruits. The profiles described not only athletic abilities but also marginal academic qualifications and, in some cases, criminal records. The coach had obviously selected recruits unlikely to abide by Church standards. "My question for you," the coach asked candidly, "is how much do you want to win?"

"To win, would I have to take those players?" Hal asked.

Coach Dalling nodded.

"I don't want to win that way," Hal said flatly.

To his amazement, the coach replied, "That's great."[20]

Met with the faculty of the department of physical education. I felt impressed to be firm in saying I supported education that would help the wide spectrum of students learn how to use and care for their bodies, but that I would not support expenditures or lowering standards to win in increasingly more-professional conference play. I said, "To me, the great value in competition is that it raises the boys' level of aspiration." Getting a new boy to get better won-lost records doesn't make sense. I bore my testimony with a tear I could not control, mentioning both of my parents' love of fitness.

—JOURNAL, JUNE 21, 1971

Hal was relieved to learn that his coach didn't intend to lose. In fact, that year the team enjoyed a strong season, captained by a gregarious Australian named Ed Palubinskas, who would go on to become the leading scorer in Olympic basketball history. Winning at Ricks, Hal was pleased to find, didn't have to mean cutting spiritual corners. Yet he was willing to pay whatever price necessary to qualify for the ministration of the Spirit on campus. "Mack," he told his dean of students, Mack Shirley, "I won't be the most popular president. A lot of people won't like what I'm doing."[21]

The nature of the issues that concerned Hal, and the degree to which he personally grappled with them, can be seen in his record of a request made by the school's student body leaders during the fall semester of 1971. In those days, even nationally known musical performers could be enticed to play in venues as small as Ricks's Hart Auditorium, the basketball arena with seating for fewer than five thousand (including chairs set up on the playing floor). The student body officers hoped to bring an up-and-coming rock-and-roll band, Bread, to perform during homecoming weekend in mid-October. With just two weeks to extend an invitation to the band and its mild-mannered leader, David Gates, the students appealed directly to President Eyring. Hal took the matter seriously.

 At nine I went to student leadership adviser Gary Olsen's to watch the group Bread perform on TV. Afterward we discussed with student leaders whether the group should be invited to play during homecoming. We saw the question as, "How would the Lord lift the students?" (September 28, 1971)

The next day, Hal and the students found an answer to that question:

 In a meeting at 9:30 we discussed the rock concert. At ten I felt that we should contact the group's leader, press for a commitment to our standards, and go ahead if Gary Olsen and counseling director Henry Isaksen felt the commitment was real.

Then, we should lift the students by assuring them of our trust that they would create with the group a better rock concert experience. (September 29, 1971)

This kind of personal attention by the college's president yielded dividends. Both Hal's fellow employees and the students rose to the challenge of living to a higher standard as they collectively focused on the spiritual benefits to be had. Within a year, Hal could see a marked difference at fall registration, where he once again greeted every student. At the end of the first day of hand shaking, he observed, "Our students this term not only are rising to the grooming standards, but more of the boys look you squarely in the eye, and the girls have a fresher look."[22] Two days and thousands of handshakes later, he was cautiously optimistic.

Another day of hand shaking. Again, I was struck with the forthrightness of the young people. Every boy had his hair cut, and every girl was dressed modestly. Perhaps it was self-selected, where only the good hearts would come to Ricks with the understanding they must really keep the standards. It almost certainly was also that the young people knew they were starting with their lives square. Whatever mixture of the two, I didn't find ten sets of eyes that wouldn't look into mine today. Out of almost two thousand students. (August 25, 1972)

Notwithstanding notable improvement in the general student body, Hal continued to worry about a few prominent rebels. Of particular concern were several young men who refused to cut their long hair, ignoring repeated warnings from the Dean of Students' office. By the end of the 1972–1973 school year, Hal felt the need to act, not only to counter the negative effects of the example being set but to help the young men themselves.

In mid-April, just two weeks before graduation, he published a letter to all students in the school newspaper, the *Viking Scroll.* His message offered sound spiritual reasoning, but it left no room for doubt about the practical consequences of disobedience:

The standards are approved by the Board of Trustees, and you committed to uphold them to a bishop or branch president. A commitment to a bishop or branch president is a commitment to a direct agent of the Lord. If we allowed you to remain on campus while breaking that commitment, we would teach you that commitments to the Master's representatives are not important. We cannot do that.

Violators may mistakenly assume that a commitment means less at the end of an academic year than it did on the first day. Can you imagine the harm we would do if, by not asking you to keep the standards now, we taught you that you need not keep commitments of performance in the last months of a mission, or in the last weeks before a temple marriage, or in the closing years of life? We cannot teach the false lesson that nearness to the end of term of a promise changes its reality.[23]

The *Scroll* letter raised some hackles. One young man who didn't identify himself called to berate Hal. "I don't want to get a haircut," he declared. He then called Hal "a lousy president" and accused him of being visible only at devotional assemblies.[24]

The following week, Hal authorized the Dean of Students' office to suspend two young men who had persistently ignored warnings of that outcome. Both asked to meet with him. One came in a spirit of contrition, as Hal recorded:

With tears in his eyes he said, "Last night, after I'd felt repentance from confessing and asking forgiveness, I prayed and for the first time in my life felt my prayer answered." All that came from our having confronted him with his failure to keep a promise to cut his hair. (April 27, 1973)

The other boy, who also came to see Hal, was civil but less contrite. When, several days later, a letter came from his mother, Hal feared the worst.

As I slit it open, I found myself bracing for the onslaught, determined not to become defensive and angry. I knew the parents could be justly incensed, with a son being sent home one week before the end of school. The letter began, "Thank God for men like you." She said that she and her husband were sure that her son being sent home was what the Savior wanted, that the Spirit had told her I loved the students, and that her son would grow from this. And she ended, "We love you."

Hal added this prayer to his record of that day:

I pray that the gospel will soften my heart even a tenth that much when someday I must accept rebuke for my family. The scriptures say, "Whom the Lord loveth, he chasteneth." (April 30, 1973)

The spiritual fruits of the College's attention to standards continued to be manifest as Hal shook hands at the beginning of each semester. "I greeted students today," he wrote the next fall.

Just under 1,600. That's below last year, and we're concerned. But the quality is not just a little better than last year but like another kingdom, another place. We're sending back a tenth as many students from registration for violation of the dress and grooming standards as we did last year. And not one student in a hundred is even cool to me as I greet them. We've had a miraculous change. (August 23, 1973)

nephew, Mark, sometime last week, forced her out of
our double's match this morning; within an hour she'd
sent a replacement, so I played six sets. Result: I
soaked my elbow in a tub of hot water propped on the
table in the breakfast room at grandpa's, while I watched
the ballgames with the boys. Annette served the whole

12

ORGANIZE YOURSELVES

And I give unto you,
Who are the first laborers in this last kingdom,
A commandment that you assemble yourselves together,
And organize yourselves,
And prepare yourselves,
And sanctify yourselves;
Yea, purify your hearts,
And cleanse your hands and your feet before me,
That I may make you clean.
—DOCTRINE AND COVENANTS 88:74

The concern that Hal felt over the fewer hands to be shaken in the fall of 1973 was well founded. In fact, his associates in the office of the Commissioner of the Church Educational System had seen the student shortfall coming. It was a simple matter of population trends. The post–World War II baby boom had produced a flood of college students in the 1960s. That had required both Ricks and its sister institutions, especially BYU, to dramatically expand their campus facilities and faculties. But as the 1970s dawned, the boom naturally subsided.

The Church, which already covered more than half of the cost of educating each college student in its higher education system, couldn't bear the full cost of declining enrollments. The only alternative to making up the lost tuition revenue was to cut operating budgets, a surprising reversal of fortune that happened to coincide with the arrival of the new Ricks College president.

BUDGET CUTS AND ORGANIZATIONAL UPHEAVAL

Hal got the bad news several days after Christmas 1971, when he presented his proposed budget for the coming year to Ken Beesley and Dee Andersen, the associate commissioners responsible for Ricks College and CES finances, respectively. The journal records his dismay but resolve to respond appropriately.

> At six this morning I was at the typewriter, preparing the discussion notes and three numeric exhibits for my discussion with Ken Beesley and Dee Anderson. The discussions went on from 9 until 3, with 45 minutes for lunch at the Lion House. The discussions were tough. Essentially, my budget proposal for next year was $600,000 high. To get in the range they require and yet launch some new programs, I've got to cut several departments. That, and the human havoc I'll cause when I reorganize the administration and faculty, will make a sadder but better man of me and many others. I must do the study which convinces me I'm doing the best thing, not proving my strength to the Commissioners. (December 29, 1971)

Hal's levelheaded, do-the-right-thing response belied the full gravity of the situation. The $600,000 in question was more than 10 percent of the total amount Hal had been seeking to run Ricks that year. Moreover, a significant fraction of the budget couldn't be cut. For example, the cost of heating buildings and clearing snow would remain the same regardless of student enrollment. As a result, Hal faced the need to cut more than 10 percent from the budget for other activities. The task would be all the more difficult if he proceeded with plans to grow certain academic programs he deemed vital to keeping Ricks "close to its roots," such as agriculture and animal husbandry.

Politically, it was a terrible way to begin a college presidency. Getting the budget into line required cutting cherished programs and administrative positions. Hal eliminated nearly a dozen athletic programs, including swimming, tennis, skiing, and rodeo. He also economized by consolidating ten academic divisions into five. He felt inspiration in the work, but the decisions were hard for those affected, and implementing them revealed, at times, the personal limitations of the college's young leader.

Today I did things I have always dreaded, yet I feel peace tonight. In the Administrative Advisory Committee I gave my carefully prepared presentation of the need to economize in order to have funds for new programs. I worked happily with the boys tonight, knowing both that the Lord had guided me today and that I acted with love, not malice. (January 4, 1972)

***

Today was a taste of New York's Wall Street on a panic day. I began my first appointment at 7:30 and dealt with a tough decision every thirty minutes until five, including lunch. To add spice, a number of decisions involved telling people some very bad news about themselves on the spot. My voice was a little high, my manner a little too driving, and my spirit not yet quite what it must be. I will be better. (February 7, 1972)

The painful, potentially divisive work of budget cutting and organizational consolidation continued through a long summer and into the fall. The saving grace was the guidance of the Spirit. Though Hal recognized his personal weaknesses and the travails of his Ricks colleagues, he felt confirmed in the difficult decisions and changes being made, as he noted on a Wednesday in late October:

At six, seven, and eight this morning, we met with three new divisions. Again, hearts were softened by the Spirit so that the possibilities for better service through the new organization were discerned by some of the people. I began to see better why we had been led as we were. I felt an assurance, again, that the people we called and the groupings of old departments were as they were to be. As nearly as I can tell, we made no change, no release, no call except where we were prompted. And we did it even when it was hard. There may be mistakes in what we did, but they are not from moving without promptings or failing to move when the promptings urged hard things to do. (October 25, 1972)

Inspired guidance notwithstanding, the upheaval took its toll. The news of budget cuts, just six months into Hal's administration, had come on top of the Role of Ricks study, which had undertaken an analysis of nearly everything being done on the campus. More than a dozen committees had been formed to identify ways to "focus our limited resources on the educational needs most important to the Church in a rapidly changing world."[1] Though Hal wasn't responsible for the budget cuts, it was natural for college employees, especially the faculty, to identify him with the ruin of the cherished "Spirit of Ricks." Hal's time became consumed with outreach and encouragement.

These days have been feeling long, perhaps because they have been. I was in my office at seven this morning and at ten-thirty tonight. We are discovering and having to deal with the inevitable resentment in some of our faculty at the massive changes in organization. I am seeing faculty members individually and will meet with the entire faculty next Monday. (November 15, 1972)

There seemed no end to the bad news. Late in November of that long year, Neal Maxwell warned Hal that Ricks would have to delay four major building projects that he and his faculty colleagues had been planning on. Still, the pain of waiting for new buildings was slight compared to the human toll of the ongoing budget cuts. Hal tried to be optimistic, but his heart went out to his colleagues. He knew that several faculty members who were required to retire would face destitution.

Hal spent a tortured Christmas holiday making hard budget decisions. In a meeting of the Board just before the end of the year, he received a bit of good news: the budget cut for the coming year would be less than the one he had offered up. Nonetheless, he returned to

Rexburg wishing that he could have done more for his colleagues, who couldn't help but express their disappointment.

 A tough, tough day. The uneasiness of the faculty is still evident. They feel much has been asked and little given. (January 10, 1973)

***

I heard rumblings of discontent today about my straight talk in the faculty meeting yesterday. I was honest with them about the financial realities of new program funding, their salaries, and the use of funds. (January 11, 1973)

FORCE REDUCTION

Things grew even more difficult the following year, when the expected student-enrollment drop materialized. By then Hal and his administrative team had cut expenses to the bone. Among the frugality measures implemented was a faculty salary schedule based solely on academic degree and years of experience, independent of discipline, gender, or any personal achievement. In a move that would prove of lasting benefit to Ricks and its successor, BYU–Idaho, everyone on the faculty was paid essentially the same way, regardless of whether they specialized in relatively high-priced academic fields such as business and accounting or the less-remunerative humanities and arts. The elimination of discipline-based pay differentials, a chronic source of envy and ill will on many campuses, further unified the Ricks faculty.

By late 1973, though, there was no alternative but to eliminate faculty positions in proportion to the reduced number of students to be taught. One week before Christmas, Ken Beesley challenged Hal to identify for layoff between 20 and 25 members of the faculty, the number likely to be required for a balanced operating budget. In his heavyheartedness, Hal sought spiritual guidance and was reminded of President Harold B. Lee's charge to "do your homework."

I walked to my office fasting this morning. I had many, many needs for guidance, and so my prayers were fervent. Some answers came so clearly, by a burning in the bosom, that I wrote them down afterwards. But no answer came to my request to know how to handle Ricks College's over-staffing. And the reason for the silence was given: I've not done enough work yet. (December 22, 1973)

> The day was budgets and hard interviews. I confirmed retirements with two men today. One of them served the college almost longer than I've lived and the other shared spiritual and touching stories of his long, hard life.
>
> —JOURNAL, DECEMBER 15, 1972

Hal determined to engage the college's academic leaders in the difficult analysis of which faculty members to lay off. At seven thirty a.m. on January 2, 1974, the first working day of the year, he met with the department heads and announced the charge to "bring faculty numbers into line with declining student enrollments." Thirty minutes later he made the same announcement to all members of the faculty, telling them that the affected individuals would be notified within twenty days. They had gathered for a day of institutional and personal goal setting, unaware that Ricks was facing its first layoffs in more than a generation. Yet their reaction, as Hal recorded, was magnanimous:

I had prepared carefully last night, but the discussion of the announcement went better than I could have hoped for. It couldn't be pleasant, but it was reasonable and even optimistic at points. During the day I had interviews and met with faculty informally. I got reports that the faculty were working hard, writing objectives, not talking about the announcement. (January 2, 1974)

In the succeeding days, however, tender emotions showed through. As Hal privately interviewed department chairs, each of whom was asked to come with a list of candidates for layoff, one of them lowered his head and wept. The man's grief, which Hal shared, led him to recall the only answer he had received as he prayed about coming to Ricks: "It's my school." "Since I believe that," he wrote in the journal, "I can proceed with confidence that this hard process will be a blessing to us all, even those who must leave."[2]

Hal also received expressions of support from Neal Maxwell, who called from Salt Lake with the assurance that "any moves dealing with people and our manpower problems would be checked first with the prophet and the Board." Neal also urged putting human and educational considerations ahead of financial ones. Spiritual support also came in the form of tender mercies that revealed themselves in the otherwise painful analysis.

> When he identifies something that's important, because it's prompted by the Spirit, he has the capacity and the courage and the will to do it.
> —ELDER RICHARD G. SCOTT[3]

All afternoon, I met with department and division heads. My faith seemed rewarded. I've believed that the Lord loves our people and the college, and both can be served. In one of the last meetings, we saw a chance to use the surplus in one department to help avoid a cut in another. I'd felt impressed to leave that surplus, during an earlier meeting, but had been worried that I didn't know why and I might have been wrong. Today, as we saw a complementary need in another department, I felt relief, and gratitude. (January 11, 1974)

As Hal's mid-January deadline for proposing staff reductions neared, the pace and intensity of the work increased. A few of his Ricks colleagues challenged him to be a braver champion for the school. One, a decorated World War II veteran, forcefully likened the layoffs to leaving wounded comrades on the battlefield. The metaphor stung young Hal, who had never seen such action during his relatively pleasant time in the military. He pondered his older colleague's challenge as he traveled to present his proposal to Ken Beesley and Neal Maxwell.

I worried all the way to Salt Lake City, realizing my approach was to lay the problem out evenly, trusting that a fair, full view from Ken's view would give Ken the best chance to discern what the Lord wants. After reading the memo, Ken suggested a more gentle route and more thoughtful for our faculty than I would dare have argued as a partisan champion. Neal Maxwell, without first talking with Ken, made the same suggestion. They asked that I bring the recommendation to the executive committee on Thursday. I spent the rest of the day with Harden and my family in Salt Lake, elated to have my faith confirmed that the Lord leads his church and He leads in kindness. (January 15, 1974)

Two days later, Hal returned to Salt Lake to make his final proposal to the Board. Again, he had a sweet experience that strengthened his faith in the Brethren.

After flying to Salt Lake City, I met briefly with Neal Maxwell, had lunch with Joe Christensen,[4] and then was in the meeting at two. I presented Ricks College's enrollment and manpower problems. There was vigorous discussion, both of the possibilities of stimulating enrollment and of drastic reduction of staffing. At the conclusion, they formally approved a plan to eliminate a small number of positions, prepare for possible further decline of enrollment, work harder to increase the quality of academic experience for young people, and spur enrollment without changing the basic recruiting guidelines. I arrived home late and tired, after a fine supper with Harden and his family. I was grateful then, as I still am, that kind and confident men, inspired of God, lead us. (January 17, 1974)

The next Monday, Hal acted on the directions given by the Board. Notwithstanding the prophetic mandate, it was a difficult, humbling experience.

How do I describe this day? The time came to talk with the faculty members whose positions must be eliminated for next year. I can only be grateful the Brethren didn't ask that I go as far as they first suggested. It was late afternoon by the time I finished all the preliminary meetings and could talk to the people affected. If I've ever felt maladroit, this was the time. My best conversation was strained, and it failed to leave the feeling of concern the Brethren would have had me show. The worst was better not described. Such moments take more prayer, more fasting, and more skill than I brought today. (January 21, 1974)

PERSONAL STRAINS

Well before the roller-coaster ride of the 1973–1974 school year, Hal had been struggling under the crushing weight of his workload. Along with out-of-the-ordinary responsibilities such as leading the Select Committee and the Role of Ricks task force, his first year had brought other unexpected duties. The Brethren asked that he serve on the board of the Church's regional hospital in Idaho Falls, which faced serious financial and managerial challenges. From local priesthood leaders came a raft of invitations to speak to their congregations, especially to the youth. Hal filled requests from youth conference organizers as far away as British Columbia and Louisiana.

In addition to his frequent trips to Salt Lake City—sometimes two and even three times per week—the college's financial difficulties required him to hit the road as a fund-raiser. Some of the work could be done locally, in nearby towns such as tiny Newdale, whose prosperous and frugal potato farmers gave it the distinction of having the most millionaires per capita of any U.S. city. But Hal also made multiple trips to New York to call on all of the major higher education donors, including the Carnegie, Rockefeller, and Ford foundations. He also traveled to California and Europe to fulfill preexisting teaching commitments to Stanford.

In those days before the creation of airline hub-and-spoke systems, air travel took much longer, particularly between small cities. For example, on May 31, 1972, Hal's thirty-ninth birthday, he flew

from Idaho Falls to a youth conference near Penticton, British Columbia. En route, the plane stopped seven times—in Salt Lake City, Twin Falls, Boise, Lewiston, Spokane, Seattle, and Vancouver. The total flight and tarmac time was ten hours, just two hours less than he would have spent driving. The price of such frequent stops wasn't only in the scheduled elapsed time. There was also the possibility of a weather problem or other unforeseen delays at each intermediate airport. Frequently, Hal would call Kathy to say that he wouldn't be home as planned. His body craved rest, though he seldom had time for it.

Henry laughed this Saturday morning when I woke at 8:30. He said, "You get up at six all week and then sleep until now. Why didn't you get up earlier?" The honest answer would be: "Because my poor body only rouses at six from the tension of the coming day." And today was a no-tension day. (October 9, 1971)

Fortunately, Hal felt inspiration in accepting and filling his responsibilities, including those directly related to the presidency of Ricks, which he could have declined. Heaven's hand was upon him, sometimes even more than he knew. That was true, for instance, of his long trip to a youth conference in central Louisiana. The travel itself consumed two full days, with airline stops in Salt Lake City, Denver, New Orleans, and Lafayette. The return trip involved waking at 4:15 a.m. and flying with a private pilot, a local bishop, back to New Orleans. But Hal's remarks were appreciated by more than five hundred young people. And, as recorded in the journal, he "visited on the plane and during the day with Bob Hales, the regional representative and a friend from Boston."[5] Hal hadn't seen Bob Hales since the latter's graduation from Harvard's MBA program, in 1962. The day they spent in Louisiana renewed a friendship that would grow much deeper in the decades to come.

The rigor of his schedule and the extraordinary challenges facing Ricks left Hal exhausted. Things got even tougher in the late spring of 1972, when the Eyrings' fourth son, John, was born. Only days after John's birth, Kathy was diagnosed as needing emergency gall-bladder surgery. In one respect, the diagnosis was welcome: it explained the difficulty of the pregnancy, which kept Kathy down during much of the unusually harsh winter, their first in Rexburg. But it also meant a difficult postpartum summer. Hal and Kathy determined to have the surgery performed at the Stanford Hospital, and to have her and the boys spend the summer on the Hill, where Sid and La Prele could nurse both Kathy and the baby, and where the older boys could better entertain themselves.

Throughout those early years in Rexburg, Hal's workday, including time spent with the boys and in his calling as a member of the Rexburg Stake high council, rarely ran shorter than sixteen hours. In addition to attending college dinners, artistic performances, and intercollegiate athletic contests, he said yes to invitations that might easily have been declined, such as the weekend outings of the student leadership council and ritual announcements of engagements (sorority-style "candle passing" was popular among female college students). On any given Sunday, both

> **At eleven tonight I spoke briefly at the family prayers of the girls in the 6th dorm.**
> —JOURNAL, OCTOBER 19, 1971

Hal and Kathy were likely to have speaking or teaching responsibilities, usually outside of their home ward, the Rexburg Sixth. High council meetings, held on weeknights, typically kept Hal out past ten o'clock and sometimes ran until midnight.

Hal indirectly expressed his feeling of being out of control in his journal entry for Friday, December 8, 1972. The day had begun in his office at seven, when he learned that he was supposed to be in a hospital board meeting at that hour in Idaho Falls. After returning to Rexburg, he spent the workday in difficult interviews and budget meetings. Arriving at home with what he thought was time enough to dine with Kathy and the boys, he received a call reminding him of a commitment to speak to a student group who were at the moment singing hymns while they waited for him on campus. After meeting with that group, he went, still on an empty stomach, to see a three-act play being put on by the college's theater students. He intended to stay just for the first act but learned too late that there were no intermissions. Near midnight, he ended his journal entry with this incomplete sentence: "I think I'm going to sleep now, but given [six month-old] John's restlessness and my record of never being right today when I saw an end, I'll end this not with a period but a comma,"

GROWING SELF-AWARENESS

The strain on Hal manifested itself in frequent headaches and colds, as well as constant back pain that sometimes completely immobilized him. But it also had a therapeutic spiritual effect. His empathy for his Ricks colleagues and his regret at failing to serve them better turned him to personal introspection. The journal records a pattern of almost daily self-analysis, with an emphasis not only on his performance in the day's activities, as had been true at Stanford, but also on the environmental conditions and personal motives that had contributed to subpar performance.

I sense willfulness whenever I seem to be decisive. I only hope I can learn to be submissive and decisive as we try to do the Lord's will for the Church Educational System and Ricks College. (November 3, 1971)

***

Many appointments today, the backlog of weeks. Most people asked for money or favors. In most cases I denied the request, too often without the proper expressions of compassion. That carried into high council tonight. I've got a ways to go to learn kindness under fatigue. (April 5, 1972)

***

Despite a good day of working at my office and playing golf with Kathy in the evening, I managed to be too gruff and tense to give Kathy a good day. I've miles to go to learn how to be kind when I'm feeling pressures. And no other kindness makes much difference, since life is mostly pressure. (May 18, 1973)

As Hal studied his personal weaknesses, he was blessed with life-changing insights, which he recorded in the journal along with the self-criticism. Some, such as the realization that he wasn't delegating enough, should have been obvious to a professor of business management. But it took humility and faith to let go of important tasks, and he discovered that almost everything seemed important to an anxious chief executive.

In time, and through the whisperings of the Spirit, he recognized that pride was a great stumbling block both to getting things done and to feeling personal peace. That truth came home to him, literally, as he returned to Rexburg one night from meetings in Salt Lake City. While waiting for his airplane there, he read from the Doctrine and Covenants, trying to dispel the feeling of strain he had taken from the meetings. As he pulled into the garage at home, a message hit him: "You've had a cloud inside you all day because you've wanted the praise of people, rather than eternal life for yourself and the people around you."[6]

Hal also discovered less obvious truths, including one that seemed counterintuitive but would become a great source of both power and peace. It was that meekness didn't preclude accomplishing difficult objectives.

 Much of the day is best described in a comment I made at dinner in answer to Kathy's question: "How did the day go?" I said, "I was able to stay at peace inside, but I was so meek I didn't seem to get much done." I worried that it's nearly impossible for me to be poor in spirit and hard-driving. But, in a 6:30 MIA[7] meeting my worry evaporated. Because I was aware of my great inadequacies, I was guided in putting aside my prepared talk and responding to the students' questions. Clearly, the work of the Lord is a different kind of work: meekness is power, because it gives you access to the Lord's power. (April 18, 1972)

DIVINE SYNERGIES

Hal found additional power in divinely facilitated synergies between apparent intrusions in his office workday and the work itself. When seen through the lens of faith, what initially seemed to be a time sink often revealed itself as a time-saver and a uniquely valuable source of inspiration. Hal recorded such an experience in early 1973, as he approached the end of his second year at Ricks:

At ten-thirty tonight I was back to preparation of a training lesson for bishops and high councilors in the study when two girls called on the phone, insisting they had to come to the house. When they arrived, I found them in tears and remorse. They had been arrested for shoplifting in our bookstore today. After talking an hour, I felt prompted to teach them repentance from the 19th Section of the Doctrine and Covenants. They seemed so worried about parents, and courts, and friends. I urged them to get God's forgiveness. (February 13, 1973)

***

When I woke this morning, the events of last night rushed in on me, confirming what I was to teach. The girls in need had taught me a basic rule of all interviewing. When I taught the bishops and high council class from 6:30 to 8:00 I felt not only inspiration of the moment but that last night had been carefully provided preparation by the Master. (February 14, 1973)

Hal discovered another important source of synergy in an unexpected place: a basketball court. For the first time since his intramural basketball days at the University of Utah, he had started playing ball occasionally at Ricks. In the beginning, it was catch-as-catch-can, noon-hour "hoops" with Ricks colleagues during that first summer, when Kathy and the boys were still in California. The games were informal and friendly, a great combination of much-needed physical exercise and retrieval of hard-earned talents from his youth. But things got a little too serious in 1973, when he accepted an invitation from his fellow ecclesiastical leaders in the Rexburg Stake.

> A basketball game with Church leaders this morning taught me something about spirituality and competitiveness and its enemies. We played for two hours, and competitive feelings plus general lack of finesse led to more hitting and bumping than basketball is designed to produce. And my feelings heated up, as did those of several of the brethren. No fists were thrown and no oaths sworn, but my spiritual inclinations were clearly missing much of the rest of the day. Anger, even from a game, is bad stuff. (February 1, 1973)

Providentially, there was a good alternative form of exercise immediately at hand. The college had just launched a physical fitness program called "Around the World in Eighty Days." The goal was to enlist enough members of the campus community to run—in eighty frigid, wintry days—25,000 miles, a distance roughly equal to the earth's circumference. Hal decided to join this group and, significantly, to involve ten-year-old Henry and nine-year-old Stuart as well. Together, they determined to each run eighty miles, at the rate of one mile per day.

> **Running without boys is like eating without food for me.**
> —JOURNAL, MARCH 11, 1974

To his delight, Hal found that the boys could easily run not just one but two miles with him in the college field house before breakfast on school days. That put them on pace to achieve their goal, even with the inevitable "I'm-too-tired" response that one or both boys sometimes gave when he woke them at six. All three of them, especially Hal, loved the experience, and it set a pattern that persisted after the Around-the-World program ended. As well as running, the Hart Building offered a broad array of athletic venues. Particularly during Rexburg's harsh winters, the college's athletic facilities became a second home for all members of the Eyring family.

While John napped along with Kathy, the older boys and I had a sports afternoon. First, I bought them all gym shoes. Then, we went to the college where we ran, played football, high jumped, lifted weights, played basketball, and jumped on the trampoline. Henry and Stuart chinned themselves on a bar, time after time. [Five-year-old] Matthew pulled 90 pounds from the floor and pressed 100 or 120 pounds with his feet. He ran from device to device, adding weights, and saying, "Exercise is good for you." . . .

TENNIS SHOES AND SWIMMING GOGGLES

The only quiet moment was the long shower we took, arrayed around the circular column holding the four shower heads. We lazed in the steaming water. (Saturday, February 9, and Saturday, February 16, 1974)

Hal found that workouts with the boys provided more than physical exercise. On the mornings when none of them joined him, he missed the spiritual lift. When the boys were there, their conversations inspired him. That was true one night when son number four, John, was old enough to join the group. As they walked from the basketball court to the locker room, John asked, "Dad, what did you become when you grew up?"

"A teacher," Hal replied.

"I'll probably be a teacher too," John said. "But I know I'll be a dad."[8]

The college became a regular base of operations for Hal and the boys, not only for athletics but for other developmental diversions. Saturday projects continued at home as before, but new campus-based traditions sprang up as well. On school days when the boys didn't feel like an early-morning athletic workout, they joined Hal at his office to color drawings he made of a scripture story that they would then read back at home over breakfast. In the afternoons, they often walked the three blocks from Lincoln Elementary school to Hal's office and then escorted him home for dinner.

On long Sunday afternoons, when TV was banned and squabbles among bored boys tended to break out, Hal would take them to the office to work on genealogy with their personal books of remembrance. In addition to adding photocopied pedigree charts and family group sheets to books that soon grew too heavy to carry, the boys enjoyed buying "treats" from the administration building's vending machines. To preserve the spirit of the Sabbath, Hal helped them build Sunday stockpiles by buying extra supplies from the machines during the week. He was also sensitive to Kathy's needs, often leaving her at home to catch up on sleep while he and the boys were at the office.

KATHY'S CONTINUED GUIDANCE

In Hal's efforts to purify himself, Kathy was his greatest earthly ally. As she had been since their first date, on the tennis court at Harvard, Kathy remained Hal's closest confidante and essential complement at Ricks. Though the four boys, born in a short span of nine years, took all the attention and energy she could offer, she saved enough to serve as Hal's best friend and key adviser. They took up skiing and golf in Rexburg, involving the boys in both (mostly just driving the golf cart, in the latter case). And they continued to play tennis occasionally. In fact, Hal and Kathy perennially advanced to the final rounds of the college's doubles tournament. In 1975, they won, defeating the city champions, two male members of the Ricks faculty.

But Kathy's greatest gifts to Hal were spiritual. She excelled in helping him connect his grand, eternal objectives with day-to-day opportunities to serve and express love. She offered that kind of practical advice in early June 1973, when Hal returned from his long weekend at the youth conference in British Columbia, the one that took him away from home on his birthday. He recorded their belated birthday celebration with a friend, the Eyrings' family doctor, after his first day back at the college.

This long day at the office was warmed by Kathy. She missed me while I was gone, needed me with the boys, and blessed me with feelings of being loved and important to her. That made our evening especially nice, as we had dinner with Dr. Peterson and his family. His birthday and mine are within a few days.[9] Kathy rode happily around on the Petersons' motorcycles, and then we all went through their family project: a retirement home called the Golden Living Center. As we went to sleep, I told Kathy I wanted to be with her for eternity. In her special spiritual and practical way, she said, "Well, then let's take some of the people from the Golden Living Center for drives on Sunday. They'd like that." (June 5, 1973)

> Kathy has helped me see that emotions need always to start—and end—with love of God and unselfish love of others.
>
> —JOURNAL, OCTOBER 3, 1975

Kathy kept at the theme of realizing long-term spiritual goals through daily acts of loving service. On a Thursday of the following month, Hal noted this interchange between the two of them:

Kathy and I had a wonderful chat, centering on how we both were excited with the challenge of living for eternal life. She helped me see, as I have not for months, that I need the gift of love for the people I am trying to serve. (July 12, 1973)

The next day, Hal recorded his successful application of the principle Kathy was trying to teach him. After two unexpectedly difficult years at Ricks College, he was beginning to sense the effects of his efforts to be a better man.

This long day was blessed by my talk with Kathy last night. I saw a long series of people, some with grievances, and all the conversations were guided by a desire to serve them that I've not felt equaled in me in a long time. (July 13, 1973)

KATHY, THIRTY-YEAR-OLD "FIRST LADY" OF RICKS COLLEGE

nephew, Mark, sometime last week, forced her out of
our double's match this morning; within an hour she'd
sent a replacement, so I played six sets. Result: I
soaked my elbow in a tub of hot water propped on the
table in the breakfast room at grandpa's, while I watched
the b   es with the boys. Annette served the whole

13

FOLLOW THE BRETHREN

In three words,
Follow the Brethren,
Rests the most important counsel
That I could give to you.
—ELDER BOYD K. PACKER[1]

H al's capacity to labor in the kingdom was growing as a result of the trials that he and Ricks College faced in the early 1970s. His family members, especially Kathy, were among the leading facilitators of that personal growth. In addition, he was mentored by great priesthood leaders. Naturally, those included the General Authorities, one or more of whom visited Rexburg almost every month for a devotional, stake conference, or other special assignment. In the warmth and informality of the campus setting, he saw a side that deepened his admiration and understanding of them. That was true, for example, during a meeting of representatives of the Church Board of Education, including four of the Brethren:

> My contact with the four General Authorities today confirmed an impression I've had before: they combine unaffected humanity with spirituality. As the meeting ended, Elder Boyd K. Packer went from jocular participation in a conversation about why we should have a horse program at Ricks College into

giving a blessing to the college in his closing prayer that left me sure heaven heard and will answer. (April 11, 1975)

Each month, Hal also encountered the senior Brethren collectively, in meetings of the full Church Board of Education. His first meeting, the one in which President Lee asked him to make a statement, taught him a memorable lesson about the importance they place on unity in decision making. He was surprised by a style of discussion unlike anything he'd encountered in the academic and corporate worlds.

> I had never seen such frankness without rancor before, but neither had I seen people listen to each other as carefully. In a few minutes, what had seemed to me widely divergent views began to move—I thought so rapidly as to be miraculous—toward a consensus. Just as I began to think I had seen an example of joint revelation beyond what I thought possible among strong leaders, I was surprised by a statement from the chair, President Lee. He said something like this: "I sense that there is someone here still not settled on this matter. I suggest that we hold it for further thought. We can discuss it again in a later meeting."[3]

> President Lee had seen or felt, I don't know which, that there was not yet complete unity. And so an important matter was held off.
> —TALK, AUGUST 26, 1996[2]

When the meeting ended, Hal remained seated as the senior Brethren left the room. One of them, passing by President Lee, murmured "Thank you."

A BLESSING FROM BISHOP DYER

One of the Brethren to whom Hal looked first as he wrestled with his responsibilities was the bishop of his boyhood, Alvin R. Dyer. Bishop Dyer had traveled a unique path since leaving Hal's ward in 1954 to preside over the Central States Mission. In 1958, after finishing the mission, he was called as an Assistant to the Quorum of the Twelve. In that capacity, he served again as a mission president, this time from 1960 to 1962 in the Church's European Mission. In October 1967, he was called as an Apostle, though not as a member of the Quorum of the Twelve. The following spring, he was set apart as a counselor to David O. McKay in the First Presidency. With the setting apart he was given a special blessing to "be a watchman over the consecrated lands in Missouri,"[4] with which he had been intimately acquainted as he presided over the Central States Mission. In this new assignment, he acquired property in and around Jackson County and planned the construction of a Church visitors' center in Independence.

With the death of President McKay in 1970, Bishop Dyer was released from the First Presidency and again became an Assistant to the Quorum of the Twelve. He humbly accepted what might have been considered a demotion and energetically undertook his new assignment, raising funds to support missionaries who otherwise would be unable to serve full-time. He was engaged in that work when Hal went to see him at Church headquarters on Thursday, March 30, 1972.

> **Alvin Dyer was a pure soul.**
> —2011 INTERVIEW

By then, Hal was neck-deep in the challenges of leading the Select Committee and of simultaneously defining the role of Ricks and cutting its budget. He went to Bishop Dyer's office in the Church Administration building at 1:30 in the afternoon, following a morning flight from Rexburg and subsequent meetings with Neal Maxwell and Ken Beesley; it was Neal who suggested that he go see his old bishop. That night, back in Rexburg, Hal recorded his memory of a priesthood blessing that Bishop Dyer gave him. He was surprised by the extent to which it spoke of the future, as he had expected only guidance in his current responsibilities.

 As best I can recall, he mentioned, "the channeling of your thoughts as you work on educational problems by the Holy Spirit; the Spirit will testify to you when you have chosen correctly; this will come because of your humility; you will have a long life; and after this present calling you will have many kinds of service to the Church and the Kingdom." I felt the Spirit confirm to me what he said. (March 30, 1972)

Bishop Dyer's blessing, especially its reference to humility, proved immediately beneficial. Increased humility helped Hal in leading the Select Committee and the Role of Ricks task force, and particularly in capturing the members' shared views in the final reports. It also helped him respond to a surprising proposal made by Neal Maxwell on the first Monday in June 1972, when he presented his recommendation for the role of Ricks College to Neal and his associate commissioners.

Neal said, "Just last Friday we got an idea that started in a meeting, and it's mushroomed over the weekend. How would you react to Ricks College becoming a campus of BYU, as would Church College of Hawaii? We think it would solve some faculty morale problems at CCH. While we're doing it, we might bring in Ricks and make a clean sweep."

I said that I would do as the Brethren wished, but that it would take great convincing in the faculty, the alumni, the town of Rexburg, and all of Idaho. The Commissioner plans to explore the possibility in the Board meeting on Wednesday. (June 5, 1972)

Hal was justified in warning that Neal's proposal would "take great convincing" of Ricks's boosters. During the Great Depression, when the Church had proposed closing the college or giving it to the state of Idaho, its employees, alumni, and local citizens kept the institution afloat through a combination of pay cuts and donations. In the 1950s, they accepted with little complaint the demotion from four-year status back to two. But, several years later, they campaigned relentlessly to prevent a proposed move of the college from Rexburg to Idaho Falls. In the end, President McKay himself came and put the matter to rest.

Hal knew that history; among old-timers, the emotional scars still lingered. He could also imagine the reaction of all of Ricks's employees to another change in the college's status, particularly coming on the heels of budget cuts and reorganizations. The timing of this proposal, on the day Hal presented the Role of Ricks recommendation, made it all the more surprising and worrisome. Yet he responded with the humility promised by Bishop Dyer.

The following day, after sleeping fitfully, Hal conducted business back in Rexburg without mentioning Neal Maxwell's proposal to his Ricks colleagues. He had good reason to believe that the proposal would be implemented (in fact, in the case of the Church College of Hawaii, it was). The BYU name would enhance the standing of the college campuses in Rexburg and Laie, and there might be cost savings and other operational benefits to administrative coordination of the three schools.

Yet much might be lost. Having transitioned from Harvard and Stanford to Ricks, Hal appreciated the college's focus on ordinary undergraduate students. BYU represented the Church well in academic research and high-profile college athletics, but opening those doors at Ricks could prove expensive, both financially and in terms of student focus. Much more than the likely negative reaction to the loss of the Ricks name, Hal worried that the institution might lose its unique mission. But he trusted that the Lord knew that too, recalling the  words, "It's my school." He also had confidence in the members of the Board of Trustees. That night he wrote: "I see problems with the plan to make Ricks a part of BYU but feel spiritual peace, suggesting that I need not be concerned with shaping the decision of the Brethren."[5]

The next day, Wednesday, Hal was back in Salt Lake City, having been gone only forty-eight hours. This time he presented to the Board the Select Committee's report on the future of higher education in the

Church. There was no discussion by the Board of the proposal to make Ricks a campus of BYU.

> I did not use the day discussing the merger of Ricks College and BYU. Neal Maxwell had decided not to present the idea to the Board and to consider the issues further. I had been impressed spiritually yesterday that I might be at peace about the matter, even though I saw grave hazards. (June 7, 1972)

BROTHER MOORE'S WARNING

Bishop Dyer's promised blessing of humility also helped Hal respond faithfully to unexpected counsel received from another priesthood leader, his home teacher, Craig Moore. Brother Moore wasn't an obvious choice to serve the Eyring family in this role. In fact, he had won the position by default, during a meeting held before Hal and his family moved to Rexburg. As a member of the leadership of the Rexburg Sixth Ward high priests group, Brother Moore had participated in a debate about which group member should home teach the Eyrings. On the one hand, the leadership worried about assigning a Ricks College employee, who might be uncomfortable teaching his boss. On the other hand, they worried about assigning an unlettered man, who might feel intimidated by a Stanford professor's intellect. That effectively eliminated everyone in the group.

Craig Moore fell squarely in the unlettered category. Like many Rexburg boys, he had grown up planning to go to Ricks. In fact, he did attend for a few semesters, beginning in 1933. But as the Great

Depression deepened, his family couldn't afford to keep him in school. Young Craig dropped out to work the family dry farm, which comprised mostly leased, marginally productive land high in the hills east of Rexburg.

Just months after marrying a local farm girl, Lila Atkinson, Craig was paralyzed on his right side during an operation to remove a lung abscess. He learned to walk again without crutches, thanks to a knee brace and a technique of throwing the right leg forward from the hip. With the help of Lila and two adopted children, Kathy and Merrill, Brother Moore eked out a living when the family farm became his.

A soft-spoken but blunt man with no love of long deliberations, Brother Moore abruptly ended the debate about a home teacher for the Eyrings. "I'm not afraid; I'll do it," he said. Brother Moore proved true to his word, and then some. He showed his faithfulness from the beginning, helping to arrange Henry's baptism during the family's first month in Rexburg. He made his visits early in the month and kept them brief but purposeful. He was also at the ready to shuttle Hal to and from the Idaho Falls airport on short notice, whether for college business or family vacations on the Hill.

But Brother Moore's faithful ministration went beyond the expected monthly lessons and acts of service. In the winter of 1973, when Hal was struggling through the wrenching organizational changes at the college and the rigors of his personal schedule, Brother Moore placed a call to the Eyring home. Hal recorded the unusual conversation:

I received a phone call from Brother Moore, our home teacher. Among other things, he asked whether I had kept my commitment to him that I would visit some Ricks College workers, simply to learn to know them, show concern, and build their feelings of identification with the College. I laughingly said that I had it on my schedule for next Friday. His voice turned hard and cold. He said, "Now, don't you get us both in trouble.

I've been told twice now, by the Holy Ghost, to see that you did that. The first time was a month ago."

It was a moving experience for me for two reasons. First, Brother Moore is so mild and so self-effacing that I have no doubt the message came from the Holy Ghost. Second, I was chastened to realize that the same message had been coming to me, gently, for months from my own feelings, but the Lord had to send the message through my home teacher before He could get me to act. (February 25, 1973)

To his credit, a reference to Hal's earlier feelings also appears in the journal, six weeks earlier. On his first day back in the office after a long, pleasant Christmas vacation with Kathy and the boys at her parents' home, he expressed feelings of wanting to get out onto the campus.

It was good to get into the office routine again, but disconcerting, too. I've felt that the routine needs changing: less time in the office and less time working through mounds of communications other people originate. There are people I need to sit with—students, faculty, townspeople—and they are people who will not come to me. (January 8, 1973)

Hal had responded to this feeling by inaugurating open brown bag lunches, opportunities for anyone to come to talk about any subject of interest. However, few people—employees or students—took him up on the offer. Meanwhile, the tension on the campus continued to rise.

GETTING OUT OF THE OFFICE

Brother Moore's rebuke focused Hal's attention. The next day, he began to make changes in his leadership practices.

Not surprisingly, this day was spent totally with people, listening to them, and trying both to sense their feelings and draw those feelings to the purposes of Ricks College. I also began to gather pictures and materials on the individuals on our staff and faculty. I will need to learn their names and something about them, to make my visits with them personal. (February 26, 1973)

Hal's schedule didn't allow him to make any visits the next day. However, his conscience was pricked and his resolve deepened during a devotional address in which the speaker related advice given by Harold B. Lee to a newly called patriarch. The patriarch, a personal friend of President Lee, asked what he should do about the great fear he felt as he gave blessings. In the journal, Hal recorded President Lee's answer: "First I'd fast, and then I would go off by myself and pray that, as long as I lived, I would never lose that fear." Hal continued with these observations:

I've let my faith in God and the people at Ricks College give me feelings of peace and safety that have merged into slothfulness. Some words from the scriptures describe how I must be: "Anxiously engaged," and "fearing God." The peace of the gospel has to be blended with urgency and the goal of perfection. (February 27, 1973)

The following day, Hal at last ventured out onto the campus. He followed Brother Moore's instructions, taking particular care to meet the campus postmaster, Max Sorenson, a man specifically identified by Brother Moore. But Hal spent most of the afternoon simply wandering, seeking heavenly guidance.

This was the day I tried to do what both I and my home teacher felt I was prompted to do. It was his saying that the Holy Ghost had instructed him twice to get me going that got me going.

After a morning of meetings and interviews in my office, I moved out into the campus to meet with people on the campus. At noon I had lunch with two faculty members and one student who came to the open meeting. Then, I spent an hour with Brother Garrett Case and his people in the bookstore. Another

Brother
Craig Moore
March 31, 1974

hour with a man who runs our post office was the one I had committed to spend in my home teaching interview with Brother Moore. For the rest of the afternoon I spent much of the time crawling under, on, and over the boilers in the heating plant and the rest visiting with Brother Elmo Dial, the supervisor.

It's not clear to me yet what I was to accomplish. I prayed that I might know and stayed long in each location, waiting for some direction for how I should direct the conversation. While I felt peace and reassurance in the visits and still intend to continue them, I cannot yet see the end nor exactly how to do it. But I do feel both the interest in what people do and a concern for their feelings were part of what is intended to help the people I visit. (February 28, 1973)

Hal found time again the next afternoon for another visit, this one to Sister Thora Clausen, the head resident in one of the college's two boys' dorms. She gave Hal a tour of the buildings. He greeted the boys and had a discussion of dorm-management strategy with four resident assistants (colloquially known by the moniker "RA"). Then, he returned to report to Brother Moore.

When I got back to my office, I called my home teacher, Craig Moore. Among other things, I talked with him about his home teaching challenge that I should get out and spend time with working people at Ricks College. He told me this: Just before making his January visit to our home, he felt an impression, around two in the morning, that he should tell me to get out of my office and spend time with all levels of the people working in the Ricks College organization. He resisted the idea, feeling he had no right to give advice about my work. But the feeling persisted for days. When I was not in town for the January visit, he tried the idea out, briefly, with Kathy and went home even surer that he had no business giving me the challenge. He hoped I would not be there for the February visit, but I was, and he again felt the impression.

I reported that I was visiting and continuing to visit people away from my office at Ricks. Brother Moore said, "Good, maybe now He'll leave me alone." When I said I still did not see the purpose, he said, "We don't know why, but you're laying a great foundation." (February 29, 1973)

Hal continued to follow his home teacher's counsel. It cut against his task-oriented grain: wandering the campus inevitably meant ending the workday with important items on his to-do list left undone. In time, though, he began to see the unexpected fruits of his labors, as recorded in journal entries made on consecutive days two months later.

It was partly planned and partly accidental, but today was a being-with-people day. I planned to spend the morning walking around the campus, never going back to my office. I began in the Manwaring Center[6] and ended there, too. I visited with custodians, bakers, and students and even got on the roof. At noon I went to a room where I held my regular open lunch with anyone who comes. And then three hours in the afternoon were spent with two fellows who were suspended yesterday for violating grooming standards. Most of the day I felt both that I was doing what I should and real help in doing it. (April 25, 1973)

***

The blessings that follow yesterday's faith flowed again today. I spent much of yesterday with people around the campus. That was hard to do, because I felt urgency to stay at my desk. Yet I was clearly prompted, several times, to get out. And my work at the desk had been at a standstill. Today, with the richness of yesterday's experiences still with me, I was at peace enough to turn out a five-page paper for Neal Maxwell, which he asked for at noon and I had in the mail by five in the afternoon. That's a personal record for prompt writing for me, and a fruit of yesterday's faith. (April 26, 1973)

> A hard office day was broken by a visit from Brother Moore, our home teacher. He delivered the same message he has once before: The Holy Ghost had told him to warn me that I should spend more time with individuals on the faculty and staff. His visit hit with extra force because I felt the same urging.
>
> —JOURNAL, MAY 5, 1975

In the long run, Brother Moore succeeded in changing Hal's behavior. Decades after Hal's departure from Ricks, he was remembered for kibitzing with custodians and eating hamburgers with the staff of the campus grill, sitting with them on stools behind the counter. But Brother Moore had to stay at it, as Hal admitted more than two years after the original warning.

GETTING OUT OF DEBT

Heeding the counsel of his home teacher helped Hal hear and respond quickly to another important call to action that came in the fall of 1973. He stayed in Rexburg for the Church's semiannual general conference, but he watched or listened to each of the seven sessions, including the two on Friday. Even from a distance, the spirit of the conference moved him.

While I worked at my desk I listened to the morning and afternoon sessions of conference. I had to stop numbers of times because the tears clouded my vision and I couldn't write. Over and over I felt a burning testimony that they were God's spokesmen. And I felt overwhelming gratitude that I was hearing and that the Spirit was bearing testimony that they spoke the truth. (October 5, 1973)

Hal was particularly impressed by something said in the Saturday afternoon session of the conference. In a talk called "Prepare Ye," Elder Ezra Taft Benson quoted from a landmark address given in 1937 by J. Reuben Clark Jr. of the First Presidency. President Clark, speaking six months after the creation of the Church's welfare program, urged the Saints to prepare for even darker times than they were experiencing in the Great Depression. He particularly counseled them to eliminate their debts. Elder Benson quoted these lines from President Clark's message of warning:

> Let us avoid debt as we would avoid a plague; where we are now in debt, let us get out of debt; if not today, then tomorrow.
>
> Let us straitly and strictly live within our incomes, and save a little.
>
> Let every head of household see to it that he has on hand enough food and clothing, and, where possible, fuel also, for at least a year ahead. You of small means put your money in food-stuffs and wearing apparel, not in stocks and bonds; you of large means will think you know how to care for yourselves, but I may venture to suggest that you do not speculate. Let every head of every household aim to own his own home, free from mortgage. Let every man who has a garden spot, garden it; every man who owns a farm, farm it.[7]

After quoting President Clark, Elder Benson added his personal promise: "For the righteous the gospel provides a warning before a calamity, a program for the crises, a refuge for each disaster." He also added an admonition: "The Lord desires his Saints to be free and independent in the critical days ahead. But no man is truly free who is in financial bondage."[8]

Considering the full range of temporal preparations advocated by President Clark and Elder Benson, Hal might have given his family passing marks, overall. Other than a relatively small mortgage on the house, the Eyrings were already in compliance with the primary recommendations of President Clark and Elder Benson. They had been building up a year's supply of food since moving to Rexburg. Their friend Bob Todd, a professor of mechanical engineering, had helped Hal and the boys build a custom-engineered set of wooden racks for storing and dispensing canned food. The racks stood in a room at the back of the garage specifically designed for food storage. Just that afternoon, the family had driven west of Rexburg to the tiny but customer-friendly Burton Store to pick up their latest order of case goods. And, with the lawn and shrubs finally in, they were already planning the garden they would plant in the backyard the following spring.

Hal also could have questioned the financial wisdom of eliminating the mortgage, the family's only debt. Though 1973 was indeed a year of economic turmoil, with the stock market plummeting, inflation skyrocketing, and an oil embargo looming, the mortgage was actually the best possible "investment" he could own under those circumstances. Both interest rates and inflation had roughly doubled since the Eyrings had completed the house and borrowed to finish paying for it. This meant that the cost of the mortgage was shrinking in real monetary terms. A purely rational investment adviser would have told him to make only the minimum required payment against the mortgage and put any free cash into commodities such as gold or oil, where he stood to make a bundle.

Hal knew these things without seeking investment advice. But he felt impelled to follow the Brethren's counsel to get out of debt. His thoughts turned to the only financial asset, other than the house itself, that he could sell to retire a substantial portion of the mortgage. One of the companies he had helped found during his Stanford days, Finnigan Instruments, had stock that was traded by a small investment firm in San Francisco. With the stock market down by nearly half since the beginning of the year, he knew that the value of his Finnigan holdings would be down as well, even if he could find a buyer. But he determined to try.

It wasn't until the following Friday that Hal found time to call the stockbroker in San Francisco. Assuming that his Finnigan shares would be hard to sell at any price, he didn't ask the broker what their value might be. He simply declared his goal of paying off the mortgage and named the amount required to do so. The broker expressed surprise. "You know," he said, "I haven't had anyone interested in Finnigan stock for a long time, but someone called just last week. I'll get back to you." By the end of the day, a contract of sale had been negotiated. Two months later, Hal could report his compliance with Elder Benson's counsel to get out of debt.

This afternoon, I paid off our mortgage on the house with the check from the sale of half our Finnigan stock. We are completely free from debt. That's a miracle that began with the talk of Brother Ezra Taft Benson at conference. When I placed that first phone call to California, inquiring whether I could sell shares that had no market weeks before, it seemed to me an act of obedience rather than a likely source of funds. But the market for the shares had appeared. And it stayed there, through national crises and falling securities markets, long enough to pay the mortgage. (December 14, 1973)

> **Take the step and God opens the way.**
> —JOURNAL, DECEMBER 14, 1973

A VISIT FROM THE PROPHET

A few weeks after Hal's decision to get out of debt regardless of the financial cost, he and Kathy hosted President Harold B. Lee and his wife, Freda, for a day in Rexburg. The drive from the Idaho Falls airport in the Eyrings' station wagon, and the meetings that followed, gave Hal the opportunity to forge a deeper bond with this man he admired so much. He also learned an important lesson about the price of failing to honor prophetic direction, even when one feels justified in disagreeing. Later that night, he recorded his memories of their conversation on the road.

On the drive to Rexburg we talked of numbers of things, much of it about Ricks College. President Lee talked of his admiration of the way President John Clarke had not taken sides during the dispute over moving the college to Idaho Falls. He explained the situation substantially differently than I had heard before. He saw the sadness as having sprung from a violated

HAL HOSTS PRESIDENT AND SISTER HAROLD B. LEE

confidence. Before any decision had been made or any discussions held with the Board of Education, a member of the First Presidency had a private meeting with the stake presidencies of this area. The purpose was to explore feelings, and it was in strictest confidence. The next morning the Rexburg or Idaho Falls papers had the story. Feelings rose, land was purchased by the First Presidency in Idaho Falls, and all of the infighting followed. President Lee seemed to feel it unnecessary. He described with some satisfaction the story of President McKay driving to Rexburg to confirm that the college would remain. The satisfaction seemed less with the Rexburg site and more that the prophet had spoken. The indication was that the people involved would have been better advised to have faith that the prophet would speak and that the tempest was fruitless. (October 26, 1973)

In Rexburg, the Lees and Eyrings lunched with a group of college,

Church, and community leaders invited to honor President Lee. Hal marveled at the Prophet's kindness, candor, and humility.

After we ate, President Lee began to speak. It was about 1:30. He knew we had a two o'clock devotional to get to, but he talked for thirty minutes, saying, "I'm sure they won't go on without me." He spoke with power, emotion, and informality that I cannot recreate on this page. He spoke of his own calling, saying, "If you think Satan doesn't try to tempt the prophet, you're wrong. I'm his prime target on earth." He also said that he isn't elected every two or four years, but every morning. And only one vote would be needed to defeat him: the Savior's. He also said, at another point, that "We've never seen the hand of revelation rest any more clearly upon us than in the selection of your president, President Eyring." After talking of some of the circumstances of my call, he talked about the importance of not thinking about whether you have achieved "high" station in the Church or about moving to "low" position. He said that it's always moving to a higher position when the Lord directs. He mentioned that he may have had greatest impact in all his Church service as an M-Man[9] leader of difficult boys, years ago. (October 26, 1973)

After this conversation over lunch, President Lee spoke powerfully to the largest crowd, nearly five thousand, that had ever squeezed into the school's basketball arena; five hundred more watched in other campus venues via closed-circuit TV. Speaking in the midst of a crippling oil crisis and the Watergate investigation that ultimately would lead U.S. President Richard Nixon to resign, President Lee prophesied that the United States would never fall and urged optimism. That evening, Hal tried to capture the feeling of the meeting and the drive back to the Idaho Falls airport:

It's impossible for me to remember all of his message, but the spirit was remarkable. Near the end he said, "I feel an unusual spirit here." He closed with a prayer that left few eyes dry, calling down blessings on us all. We left for the airport with the audience singing, "We Thank Thee O God for a Prophet." On the drive President Lee answered my question about achieving perfection in this life. He said that the 88th section of the Doctrine and Covenants teaches we can get part but not all of celestial living here. It was a glorious day. (October 26, 1973)

A NEW STAKE PRESIDENT

Along with Brother Moore and President Lee, one of the most influential Church leaders in Hal's life was a local stake president called as the Eyrings marked the end of their fourth year in Rexburg. Initially, Hal didn't recognize the significance of the role that this man would play in his life. In fact, before the call was announced, he didn't even recognize the man as a potential stake president.

In the summer of 1975, Elder Boyd K. Packer of the Quorum of the Twelve came to Rexburg to create a new stake, the Rexburg East Stake. As a member of the high council of the Rexburg Stake, from which the new stake would be created, Hal knew that Elder Packer would ask him to suggest candidates to serve as its president. He had the feeling that he should take the task seriously.

Hal had been serious about his high council responsibilities from the beginning. The inspiration to do so came forcefully in 1972, his first year of service. He received it in answer to a fervent prayer about other pressing matters, including the approaching end of Kathy's difficult pregnancy with their fourth child, John, and the crucial Select Committee report.

After fasting since noon yesterday, I knelt to pray in my office this morning. I asked to know three things: what I might do to help Kathy, who I should offer the head administrative and head academic positions at Ricks College to (I mentioned four names), and what I should write for the Select Committee presentation. At 8:05, I received the answer: "Kathy and the baby will be well if you devote yourselves more to the kingdom." It came to my mind and heart with spiritual assurance. I went to my desk to think further about what I should do to devote myself more. I felt impressed that I should work more systematically at my high council assignment and that I should honor the Church administrators who came before me. (May 16, 1972)

In the ensuing three years, Hal had endeavored to be a good high councilor. His service was particularly appreciated by the members of his Sunday School class for Young Adults in the stake, many of whom were Ricks College students living at home. Teaching the class, just one of many high council assignments he fulfilled, proved to be among the most fulfilling.

> We came to the high school seminary building and sat on folding chairs. We came because we couldn't help but feel his love for the Savior. I wanted to know the Savior as he did.
>
> —GREG PALMER, YOUNG ADULT SUNDAY SCHOOL CLASS MEMBER[10]

Hal also invested more than he might otherwise have done in his monthly sacrament meeting addresses, audits of ward finances, and weekly high council meetings. As a result of his faithfulness to the message received in answer to a prayer for his family, Kathy and the boys were blessed both during his absences from the home and upon his return, and he was blessed with personal revelation.

It was in this spirit that Hal sought revelation in his assignment to recommend a new stake president. In fact, he received a clear answer. Yet the real benefit would accrue not to Elder Packer, but to Hal.

On the opening day of the stake conference, he went early to the Idaho Falls Temple, before Saturday projects with the boys. He'd fasted for twenty-four hours, and he prayed throughout the temple session. That night he wrote in the journal that, near the end of the session, "I saw a visual image of the face and shoulders of Bishop Peterson of the 4th Ward. That started me thinking, 'The bishops of the stake have great strength.' I thought of many other bishops, but without a visual image."[11]

Hal returned to Rexburg and, before planting a vegetable garden with the boys that afternoon, went for his scheduled interview with Elder Packer. Their meeting was brief but momentous.

> In the interview with Elder Packer, which lasted five minutes, I said only, "I have an assurance the Holy Ghost will confirm the choice when you announce it. My only spiritual impression is of the strength of the bishops." He pressed for three names in the new stake boundaries, so I named three, including Bishop Peterson. But I did not single him out: I had dismissed the first impression of the three-quarters view of his face. (May 31, 1975)

The next day, Hal recognized his mistake. He learned—indirectly—from his Ricks College colleague Charles "Tiny" Grant, a hulking but mild-mannered football coach, that he had missed heaven's clear answer to his fasting and prayers for guidance.

> Just before the main session of conference, Brother Charles Grant said, "The new president, Bishop Peterson, would like you to continue to serve on the new high council." Brother Grant and Leo Smith were sustained as

> counselors. I felt chastened, both by seeing the great power of the mantle of a stake president fall on Bishop Peterson, and by the fact I had received revelation yesterday as I saw the face of Bishop Peterson, but had translated that into a human judgment and had forgotten even seeing the vision. (June 1, 1975)

A BLESSING OF HUMILITY AND LOVE

The human judgment to which Hal fell prey had a logic, but it was faulty. The wards composing the new stake were exceptional in their strength of leadership. The bishops, for example, included several highly educated men who ran respected professional practices in town. Bishop Peterson was a successful entrepreneur, the proprietor of a Rexburg clothing shop. But he was relatively quiet and assumed a low-profile style of leadership.

Hal quickly received a personal manifestation of President Peterson's leadership strength and ability to speak at heaven's direction. It came immediately after the general session of the stake conference, when President Peterson set apart the twelve members of the new stake's high council. Hal recalled both the substance of President Peterson's personal blessing and its impact on him in the next day's journal entry:

> Because I still felt the promptings of the Spirit from my experiences this weekend, a hurried and unbroken series of meetings and appointments left me happy and grateful during the day.
>
> An unusual change in me today was a great increase in my love for the people I met as I roamed the campus. One faculty member said, "This is the best talk I've had with anyone in five years." President Peterson said in setting me apart yesterday, "Have humility and love the people." I have felt rebuked in that and assumed it would take great struggle and repentance. I seemed to have been helped instead. (June 2, 1975)

Hal recognized President Peterson's relatively mild Scotch blessing as consistent with Brother Moore's more forthrightly stated reprimands. Both men had effectively called him to repentance for his high degree of task orientation and a lesser but still substantial degree of pride; those traits combined to hamper effective ministration to the people for whom he had responsibility. Journal entries from the succeeding days show the same pattern of pained introspection, along with Hal's humble, rewarding response to the chastening that Brother Moore had first provided three years earlier:

Paperwork got only 15 minutes of my day; for the rest of the nine hours I met with people, half where they work and half in my office. Although the visits with people were productive, I had the pain in my stomach that sometimes comes from tension when I studied my card of "things to do" at five and saw that only the goals with other people were finished, not the writing and planning objectives. My heart knows those are the right priorities, but apparently my stomach hasn't heard that yet. (June 3, 1975)

***

I spent six minutes on the phone today and did more good than in the rest of the day. About ten this morning, two notes came across my desk: one urged me to help a crippled boy and the other told me a staff member was in the hospital. Usually, I'd wish I had time but feel too rushed and too inept to help. Today, I felt impressed to drop everything and call them. I wonder how many kindnesses I've put off in my life, blowing up in my mind the time and skill required when six minutes would have done it. (June 6, 1975)

Hal freely admitted both the joy that flowed from his increased service orientation and the source of inspiration that led him to it. "I follow offices in the Priesthood over me," he wrote, in a challenge to himself, "without regard for who holds them."[12] He particularly recognized the blessing of following his bishop, a soft-spoken engineer named Clayter Forsgren, as well his new stake president, President Peterson. As much as or even more than the General Authorities with whom he so frequently interacted, they set him on a path to increased spirituality.

My lesson this morning in the Young Adults class was on Gethsemane. As I sat in the class before teaching, I felt an impression to teach that Christ's sacrifice should lead us to be willing to sacrifice for Him and for salvation of our brothers and sisters. That conviction motivated me through home teaching and genealogy with the boys and, even more, during a temple recommend interview with Bishop Forsgren and President Peterson. I felt impressed to make a serious attempt to confess every unresolved sin, to show my appreciation for the Atonement by taking all the steps necessary for it to work in my life. Bishop Forsgren said, "Now, I urge you to seek direct confirmation of forgiveness from the Lord." And President Peterson said, "This will be one of the most important days in your life." (June 15, 1975)

***

I had to close my door as Elder Thomas Monson spoke at conference. I was afraid my sobbing would carry to the outer office. And yet his voice never broke. I reflected on that and dozens of other experiences in the last weeks, all teaching me the Lord would have me more the master of my emotions. Kathy has helped me see that emotions need always to start—and end—with love of God and unselfish love of others. President Peterson said it well when he set me apart as high councilman: "Be humble and love the people." (October 3, 1975)

nephew, Mark, sometime last week, forced her out of
our double's match this morning; within an hour she'd
sent a replacement, so I played six sets. Result: I
soaked my elbow in a tub of hot water propped on the
table

LET THEM STAY

As many as have come up hither,
That can stay in the region round about,
Let them stay.
—DOCTRINE AND COVENANTS 105:20

When Hal told Neal Maxwell that he would accept the offer to go to
Ricks College, Neal had replied, "It will only be for a few years."
In fact, Hal had been at Ricks for just one year before he began receiv-
ing inquiries from other prospective employers. One came from his
alma mater, the University of Utah, which needed to replace President
James C. Fletcher, who was leaving to head NASA.

Neal knew Utah and its presidential search process well, having served there as a vice president and been a candidate for the top
job himself when Jim Fletcher was selected. (Hal's father, Dr. Henry
Eyring, had written a letter of recommendation to the search committee on Neal's behalf.) Hal did nothing to discourage those who advanced his name, until Neal warned him that he was being considered
seriously and that there was a risk of his displacing other LDS candidates. Hearing that, Hal immediately withdrew.

HAL AND COMMISSIONER OF EDUCATION JEFFREY R.
HOLLAND BREAK GROUND FOR A NEW BUILDING

AN INVITATION FROM BYU

It was harder to know how to respond to an invitation from his colleague Dallin Oaks, then president of BYU, to think about heading BYU's college of business. Hal felt deep respect for President Oaks and for BYU, and the job would draw directly on his professional training. He would also be staying within the Church Educational System. And, in this case, Neal Maxwell wasn't weighing in.

> It was four before I began dictating letters and six before Iris finished typing them. One went to the chairman of a committee seeking a new president for the University of Utah. I declined his invitation to be a candidate. My duty lies here, but so does my heart. Saying, "No thanks," was no sacrifice.
>
> —JOURNAL, NOVEMBER 22, 1972

Hal made a visit to BYU in the fall of 1973. He mildly offended the members of the business faculty when they asked why he wanted the college's deanship. Hal replied that he would accept any assignment from the Brethren. Some apparently misread that statement as indicating lack of personal interest.

Notwithstanding Hal's poor showing in the faculty interview, President Oaks still wanted him at BYU. He asked to meet with Hal at Church headquarters between the Christmas and New Year's holidays. Feeling the need for President Harold B. Lee's direction, Hal requested an interview early in the morning of Thursday, December 27, the day he was to see President Oaks. Hal's journal records what did and didn't happen on that day, and why.

 President Harold B. Lee died tonight. I learned as I sat in Harden's home in Salt Lake. Harden called, from his in-laws' home, to tell me. It was ten in the evening. President Lee had died an hour earlier.

In my surprise, for President Lee had not been sick, my thoughts turned selfishly to myself. I was in Salt Lake to see him tomorrow, to get his counsel about whether I should serve at BYU as their Dean of Business, if I am asked. Dallin Oaks and Bob Thomas were to see me immediately afterward, presumably to talk about my response. I first felt loss that I would not get his advice.

But my thoughts turned next to gratitude. Kathy and I knew him, felt his love, and will always be better because of him and his wife. And my thoughts and prayers went to his wife, who must now feel as desolate as he did when his first wife died. She'll be a source of strength to everyone, yet I'd like to reach out to her if I could.

> There is a danger in deciding who your favorite prophet is, just as there is in having a favorite living General Authority or a favorite bishop of your ward or a favorite visiting teacher. The danger is that you may not listen to the most important messenger to you, who is always the one God sends to you now.
>
> —TALK, JANUARY 19, 1992[1]

My thoughts and love and prayers turned to Uncle Spencer, too. He must take up the great load as the President and Prophet, with a body that has borne more illness and operations than even President Lee's had. The Lord will gird him for it, but I'll do all I can, in works and faith, to lighten his load.

I pray for help for us all, that we may not falter in the transition. With faith in Christ and selflessness, we won't fail. (December 26, 1973)

The next morning, Hal went to Church headquarters as planned. But rather than going to President Lee's office in the four-story Church Administration Building where he had interviewed for the Ricks presidency, he met with Neal Maxwell in the new office tower. He was almost late, as the journal records:

> I barely got to the Commissioner's office by nine. Getting up was hard, because I'd talked with Harden and [his wife] LoiAnne until two.
>
> Neal Maxwell asked to meet with me first. With no preliminary conversation or emotional show about the death of the

prophet, he said, "I want to tell you what I think the prophet wanted to say to help you in deciding what to do about the BYU deanship."

I can recall only three main points. First, President Lee wanted me to have a free choice, knowing there was no priesthood call to BYU. Second, he had insisted that he make that clear in an interview with me, rather than let Neal do it. And, finally, he said, at one point in the conversations which must have covered several months, "Hal's doing so well at Ricks College, and he's just getting started." Or perhaps it was, " . . . and he's been there such a short time."

I asked Neal for his opinion. He said, "I lean toward your staying at Ricks." When I finally told him that I felt confident my contribution was to be at Ricks College, he said, "Well, now I can tell you something else that the prophet said. When I talked with him Friday, he said, "I lean towards his staying at Ricks." Apparently Neal wanted me to feel some confidence in my own insight and inspiration before giving me that last, important bit of information about the prophet. (December 27, 1973)

That afternoon Hal met with Dallin Oaks and his academic vice president, Bob Thomas. After two hours of discussion, he "promised to take their information into account, study and pray, and let them know in a week."[2] The following Sunday, he fasted and prayed about the matter, and then, the next afternoon, called President Oaks to say that he felt he should stay in Rexburg. It was the day that President Spencer W. Kimball was set apart as President Lee's successor. Uncle Spencer called ten days later to confirm Hal's decision to stay in Rexburg.

 As we sat together in the family room around nine, President Kimball called. As I remember his words, they were: "I heard you had been offered a position at BYU and have rejected it. I feel fine about that. It was nice you were asked. I believe the brighter future for you lies for you at Ricks, for the present. . . . Give my regards to your wife and children. Are

they well? . . . I saw your folks a day or two ago. Goodnight."
(January 10, 1974; ellipses in original)

CULTIVATING AN EYE FOR BEAUTY

For Hal, 1974 began on a low note, as he spent the month of January pursuing the charge from the Commissioner's office to bring Ricks's staffing levels into line with reduced student enrollments. But the Board's generosity in requiring fewer layoffs than planned signaled good things to come. Enrollment would unexpectedly rise the following fall, relieving the budgetary pressure on the college and its employees. And Hal's ongoing response to Brother Moore's challenge to get out on the campus yielded good results. People warmed to the outwardly business-minded and task-oriented young president as he chatted with them in their offices.

Things also became a bit easier for Hal and Kathy as parents. John, the baby, was now old enough to join in the older boys' rituals of work and play with their father, both at home and on the campus. One of their new rituals, creating illustrations for family scripture reading, led Hal to develop a latent talent for drawing and painting. The effect was immediately apparent in the journal, in which a rough but well-proportioned sketch of Ken Beesley marked the beginning of illustrations of daily events. Hal made room for the sketches by leaving spaces between entries or adjusting the carriage return on his manual typewriter, allowing for insertion of a drawing into the entry itself, in the style of a well-designed newspaper. The paragraph above that first sketch revealed his typically methodical approach to this new hobby:

Ken Beesley at the President's Council March 6, 1974. At the Lion House, Salt Lake City

While I waited at the Church tower for the CES Presidents' Council to begin, I visited the Church's graphic arts

department on the 23rd floor. Brother Luch, the director, spent two hours being my gracious host, educating me. (March 6, 1974)

Returning to Rexburg, Hal sought out Richard Bird, a gifted painter in the college's art department. Brother Bird mentored him throughout the Eyrings' time at Ricks and even later, when they had moved on to Utah. Hal particularly enjoyed drawing and painting as he traveled.

> When you get a watercolor working right, the feeling of illumination is like a deeply spiritual thing.
> —2012 INTERVIEW

He took postcard-sized art paper and, while waiting in an airport or taking a private moment in the home of a generous host, would capture a scene of an intriguing place or person. On a long trip, Kathy and the children might receive one of these original postcards in the mail. Upon his return home, Hal would send a similar custom-made thank-you note to his host. He found drawing and painting not only diverting but spiritually uplifting and even revelatory.

A JOB IN THE CORPORATE WORLD

In April 1974, Hal felt sufficiently on top of his responsibilities to add another one: a position on the board of directors of McCulloch Corporation, a California-based subsidiary of Black & Decker that made chain saws. The board met just four days each year, giving Hal the opportunity to keep his business skills sharp with a relatively modest investment of time. Also, he and Kathy were invited to an annual retreat for the Black & Decker board, which met in resort destinations of the type that Kathy had frequented with her parents as a young girl but that were well out of the Eyring family price range.

The McCulloch and Black & Decker executives liked Hal's work as a board member, and he developed strong personal relationships with them. In April 1976, as he was beginning his third year on the board, they offered him a full-time job as vice president and general manager of McCulloch's operations in the United States.

By then, Hal had been at Ricks for five years. He and Kathy and the boys loved Rexburg in a way they couldn't have imagined when they left the Hill. But he had implemented the changes he felt were necessary to keep the college close to its roots and to align it with its unique role in the Church Educational System. He didn't have a clear vision of new contributions he might make at Ricks. He also sensed that a change was inevitable at some time, and the McCulloch offer made him wonder whether the time had come to move on—not necessarily to the corporate world, but to whatever assignment heaven had planned.

Hal let his superiors in the Commissioner's office know of the McCulloch job offer. He still reported directly to Ken Beesley, but Neal Maxwell, who had been called as a member of the First Quorum of the Seventy, no longer served as Commissioner. That job had been filled just weeks before by thirty-five-year-old Jeff Holland, a former dean of Religious Education at BYU. Hal told Ken and Jeff of the offer, and they in turn notified President Kimball. In the journal, Hal recorded their response and his reaction to it:

> To my real surprise, President Kimball sent back word, through Ken Beesley, that the Church would not stand in the way of such an opportunity. Jeff Holland, the new Commissioner of Education, came on the line with Ken to tell me; he began by saying, in the first conversation we've had since he was named Commissioner, "Hal, I'm really not that hard to work for." We both laughed. And we agreed that the prophet wasn't urging me to leave, just making sure I had to get my own answer. (April 26, 1976)

Hal's surprise at President Kimball's response derived from multiple sources. One was the prophet's thoughtful phone call of two years before, expressing satisfaction with Hal's decision not to pursue the deanship at BYU. Another was a series of unusual personal contacts in just the preceding few weeks. Hal's relationship with his uncle had

I sat on the front row of the tabernacle in the 2:00 conference session. We rose to our feet at three and sang "We Thank Thee, O God, for a Prophet." I sang with happiness, but when I saw that President Kimball, above me, leaned so he could see me past the heads of the General Authorities and mouthed the words, "Hello, Hal," I seemed to stand on my very toes and sing my love back to him.

—JOURNAL, APRIL 3, 1976

never been warmer or more supportive, and it was natural to assume that President Kimball would want him to stay on the Church "team."

Hal got no greater support from his family for staying at Ricks, as he noted in the journal that night:

[Twelve-year old] Henry and I talked about it. He said, "Well, Dad, you may have to leave Rexburg someday, and this may be an attractive way the Lord's given you. If it is, you better not miss it." Kathy and I agreed, in our long talk after family night. (April 26, 1976)

At the time of Hal and Kathy's marriage, Uncle Spencer had prepared him to leave Stanford. The statement about being ready to "walk away easily when the call comes" had helped him respond relatively quickly and confidently to Neal Maxwell's offer of the Ricks presidency. But now he faced precisely the opposite scenario—walking away from a call to a Church school to return to employment in "the world." And neither Uncle Spencer nor anyone else was discouraging him from doing so.

President Kimball phoned the next day, as Hal wrestled to receive inspiration. If anything, what he said only deepened Hal's sense of doubt.

Kathy and I fasted today, trying to get an answer to the question "Are we going to stay in Ricks College or accept the offer in Los Angeles?" I interspersed meditation and prayer with long interviews with people in trouble. President Kimball called. Some of what he said was, "My counselors and I agree the Church should not stand in your way . . . We appreciate your marvelous service for five years . . . We are not trying to encourage you to leave." Here were some of our exchanges:

"President Kimball, I've found myself praying to find if I may stay at Ricks. I've felt a warning that I can only stay if I hit it hard. And I expect nothing in return, since it's no sacrifice."

"No, it's no sacrifice. (Chuckle) Well, that sounds like Hal Eyring. That's sweet. Hal, President Romney did say that we have men who go out to these important positions and then come back to give great service."

"I guess it would be too easy if you told me."

"Yes, Hal, that would be too easy. Keep praying, and involve Kathy with you." (April 27, 1976)

STUDYING IT OUT

Hal determined to test himself against the one impression he had felt, that he shouldn't stay at Ricks unless he had a plan for "hitting it hard." By that he meant coming up with new ideas for moving Ricks forward, rather than just following through on programs he and his colleagues had already implemented. In the beginning, facing an empty page with the words "Goals for Ricks College" written across the top felt vexingly reminiscent of days in the bathhouse on the Hill, when ideas for research papers wouldn't flow. The fact that Kathy already had her answer, that Hal and the family should stay at Ricks, didn't help.

From family scripture reading in the morning until Kathy picked me up at the office when she finished Primary, I worked on my goals for my service at Ricks College. And I tried to get direction for where I am to serve. Henry asked as we ate lunch and again at dinner, "Dad, how come you don't know, when Mom already has the answer?" I have at least received an answer to that question: I'm to write out what I will do, specifically, to move the college along next year. Then, I am to apply in prayer for the opportunity. That seemed strange to Henry, but not to me, because I know at least a little how important this stewardship is to touch lives in the kingdom. The other alternative, in Los Angeles, was explained to me over the phone in even more attractive particulars than I had imagined, but I still feel I am to seek the chance first to serve here for at least another year. My father, in another phone conversation, thought I should stay put. (April 28, 1976)

Hal made fitful but significant progress on his statement of goals for the college and himself during the first three workdays of the week of May 2. By Thursday, he had a proposal worth praying about. But the answer to his prayer surprised him, as he wrote that night:

All day I prayed about this question, "Heavenly Father, may I stay at Ricks if I will carry out this program?" Then, I tried to describe the results of the last week's analysis of what should be done. By the time I finished at my office, near eight in the evening, I felt one impression, "Go talk with President Peterson." I did, at eleven-thirty, after a long high council meeting. He listened and then said this, "God couldn't give you the answer you seek without taking away your free agency. You are being tested in the balance. Without the requirement to choose, you wouldn't make a real sacrifice." He gave me a blessing, at his suggestion, which simply said, "God loves you. And he wants you to use your agency." (May 6, 1976)

For one night, the matter seemed clear to Hal. He didn't have a clear spiritual feeling, but the balance of evidence, particularly Kathy's impression and his father's counsel, suggested that he should stay. President Peterson's blessing cleared the way for him to make that choice, even without an answer to his prayers.

The next morning, though, Kathy made things complex again:

At nine-thirty this morning, as I was about to call McCulloch and say, "No, thanks," Kathy called me. She urged me, backed by a talk by Elder McConkie, to get a clear witness of the

Spirit before I declined or accepted the McCulloch offer. That got me back on my knees, where I was when my phone call to McCulloch went through. But, since I still had no clear witness, I simply told them of facts which urged me to stay at Ricks, without giving the definite "No" I had intended since last night's interview with President Peterson. So, my stomach burned with the worry of my lack of an answer through an afternoon of working, a talk to the seminary dinner, and racquetball with Kathy until 11 p.m. (May 7, 1976)

Finally, that weekend, the spiritual confirmation came. Hal had spent Saturday gardening with the boys in the morning, attending sessions of stake conference in the afternoon and evening, and playing tennis with Kathy in the annual college tournament until late that night. He got his answer as they prayed together before bed.

Kathy and I played doubles in the field house from nine-thirty until eleven; she was banging away with power and accuracy, so we won.

We talked until late in our room. As we knelt together for our prayers, I felt impressed to pray about the decision to move or not to move. And, as I prayed, I felt the confirmation that we should stay at Ricks College and in Rexburg. (May 8, 1976)

Even when Hal's answer came, it humbled him. It was one of those important messages that came as a voice in his mind. The voice was the same one that had said, "Go!" when he prayed about marrying Kathy and, "It's my school," in answer to his inquiry about leaving Stanford for Ricks. This time, the voice said, "I'll let you stay a little longer."

In private, Kathy was typically low-key about Hal's decision. But she expressed approval publicly several months later, as she introduced Hal at the first devotional of the new school year. She

> Hal Eyring went to Rexburg not because he was uniquely needed in Rexburg, but because he uniquely needed Rexburg to prepare him for the future.
>
> —ELDER DALLIN H. OAKS[3]

noted that one of the things that had attracted her to Hal when they first met was his willingness to put Church service ahead of worldly honors.

And since we have been married, this quality has grown. He has consistently chosen to serve the Lord, even where some outside the Church may have wondered at this service. He's consistently loved the Lord and wanted to do whatever he was asked to do, either in an official capacity or whatever else the prophets or those who are in authority over him have suggested should be done. And I am grateful beyond my words to express for the tremendous influence that he's had in my life for good.[4]

THE FLOOD

A month after Hal decided to stay at Ricks, on the first Saturday in June 1976, Idaho's just-completed Teton Dam broke. Ironically, a faulty earthen structure built to prevent the frequent flooding of the Teton River created a deluge like none before. Eighty billion gallons of water roared toward Rexburg at forty miles per hour, sweeping away everything in the way.

THE FLOOD'S DEVASTATION

That morning Hal and Kathy were in the Idaho Falls Temple for the marriage of their Stanford friend Michele Howell. They had left Matthew and John with a babysitter. Henry and Stuart were working with Brother Moore on his farm in the hills above Rexburg. Roadblocks put up by state troopers kept Hal and Kathy from getting back home, though they were able to confirm by phone that the boys were all safe.

That night, on a motel room TV, they saw scenes of what newscasters described as a wall of water fifteen feet

HAL AS A PRINCETON TOWNSHIP ELEMENTARY SCHOOL STUDENT

INFANT HAL

A HALLOWEEN "MOUNTIE"

HAL AND OLDER BROTHER, TED,
WITH GRANDMA CAROLINE ROMNEY EYRING

THE EYRINGS IN THEIR PRINCETON BACKYARD

PRINCETON FAMILY PORTRAIT

HAL AND TED

SIXTEEN-YEAR-OLD HAL

KATHY AT HIGH SCHOOL GRADUATION

NEWLYWEDS BEFORE THEIR WEDDING RECEPTION

HAL'S PAINTING OF THE LOGAN TEMPLE

HAL'S RENDERING OF A CARVING SUGGESTED BY ELDER BOYD K. PACKER

AFTER TENNIS ON THE HILL, WITH PORTRAIT OF STUART

THE GUEST HOUSE AS SEEN FROM THE FORMAL GARDENS

HAL, HARDEN, TED, AND HENRY EYRING, WITH SPOUSES KATHLEEN JOHNSON,
LOIANNE BAILEY, MARILYN MURPHY, AND MILDRED BENNION

BREAKFAST IN REXBURG, WITH MATTHEW, JOHN, HENRY, AND STUART SEATED LEFT TO RIGHT

KATHY CATCHES HAL THROWING A SNOWBALL ON A TRIP THROUGH THE ALPS

A FAMILY PLAQUE CREATED BY HAL

HENRY SKATES WITH HIS PARENTS IN REXBURG

HAL AT HIS 1971 RICKS COLLEGE INAUGURATION

HAL AT THE 2005 INAUGURATION OF KIM B. CLARK (CENTER), WITH PAST RICKS COLLEGE/BYU–IDAHO PRESIDENTS
JOE J. CHRISTENSEN, DAVID A. BEDNAR, STEVEN D. BENNION, AND ROBERT L. WILKES

WITH GORDON B. HINCKLEY AND PRESIDENT DAVID BEDNAR AND HIS WIFE, SUSAN;
HAL'S COUSIN ED KIMBALL CAN BE SEEN AT THE FAR RIGHT

HAL WITH MATTHEW (IN ARMY-SURPLUS BACKPACK) AND HIS OLDER BROTHERS,
CUTTING A CHRISTMAS TREE IN THE SANTA CRUZ MOUNTAINS

KATHY AND THE BOYS IN REXBURG WITH UNCLE SPENCER, AUNT CAMILLA,
AND D. ARTHUR HAYCOCK (IN DOORWAY), PERSONAL SECRETARY TO PRESIDENT KIMBALL

FAMILY PORTRAIT AROUND THE ORNAMENTAL WELL ON THE HILL

MATTHEW, COUSIN GARY JOHNSON, AND JOHN IN GRANDMA JOHNSON'S FOUNTAIN

ELIZABETH AND INFANT MARY ON A TRIP TO EUROPE

HAL AND ELIZABETH SWIMMING AT LAKE POWELL

HAL, KATHY, AND THE GIRLS WITH GRANDMA AND GRANDPA JOHNSON

ELIZABETH STUDYING AT THE KITCHEN COUNTER
IN BOUNTIFUL

KATHY FLANKED BY ELIZABETH (ON HER RIGHT) AND MARY

GRANDMA AND GRANDPA JOHNSON'S HOUSE, SEEN FROM THE SWIMMING POOL

THE DRIVEWAY NEAR THE TOP OF THE HILL

PORTRAIT OF THE EYRING FAMILY AT HAL AND KATHY'S FIFTIETH WEDDING ANNIVERSARY IN 2012

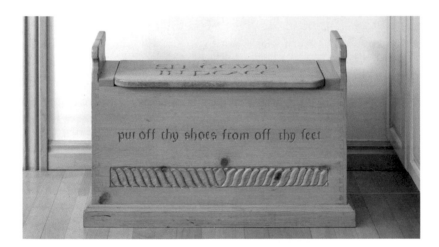

CARVED SHOE BENCH IN THE BOUNTIFUL HOME

GREETING CHURCH MEMBERS

DINING IN WEST AFRICA

WITH ELDER ROBERT C. OAKS
AND A LION CUB IN SOUTH AFRICA

HAL'S WATERCOLOR OF THE GARDEN TOMB

WITH PRESIDENT BOYD K. PACKER IN ASIA, AS A NEW MEMBER OF THE QUORUM OF THE TWELVE

A DUCK DECOY, CARVED FROM A BLOCK OF WOOD GIVEN TO HAL BY ELDER PACKER

HAL AND KATHY AT THE POLYNESIAN CULTURAL CENTER

FIRST COUNSELOR BISHOP EYRING
AT A CHURCH HISTORY SITE

HAL'S WATERCOLOR OF HAWAIIAN SURF

HAL AND KATHY VACATIONING

HAL AND KATHY IN EUROPE

TESTING HAL'S GRAVY AT A FAMILY PARTY

KATHY AT THE PULPIT

CELEBRATING THEIR FORTY-THIRD WEDDING ANNIVERSARY IN 2005

HAL WITH YOUNG TEMPLE DEDICATION ATTENDEES

HAL AND KATHY WITH PRESIDENT PACKER

SEALING A TEMPLE CORNERSTONE

PUTTING WITH GRANDSON JACOB EYRING

CONDUCTING A CHRISTMAS PAGEANT WITH GRANDDAUGHTERS
KIMBERLY, STEPHANIE, ALYSSA, AND ASHLEY EYRING

TEACHING ALL OF THE GRANDCHILDREN AT THE FIFTIETH WEDDING ANNIVERSARY

WALKING HOME FROM CHURCH WITH
GRANDDAUGHTER EVELYN PETERS

ENJOYING A CAROUSEL WITH GRANDSON JAMES EYRING

GRAND MARSHALL OF THE DAYS OF '47 PARADE

ARTIST BEVERLY WILKEY'S RENDERING OF HAL AND KATHY
AT THE TIME OF HIS CALL TO THE TWELVE

A SYMBOLIC TREASURE BOX REQUIRING TWO KEYS

KISSING AT A FAMILY GATHERING

THE NEW FIRST PRESIDENCY IN 2007

SPEAKING AT A FIRST PRESIDENCY CHRISTMAS DEVOTIONAL

THE FIRST PRESIDENCY

NEWLYWEDS FOREVER

high carrying houses and trees on its crest. Yet Hal felt a providential peace. "I slept soundly," he wrote in the journal, "knowing that the college had already been designated the disaster center and that I'd need strength for the days and nights to come."[5]

Thanks to early warning by local radio stations and the dam's breaking during the daytime, rather than at night, the immediate loss of life was limited to six drowning victims. But nearly four thousand homes were destroyed or damaged by water that ran six feet deep down Rexburg's Main Street. The neighboring community to the north, Sugar City, was entirely wiped out.

The college, on slightly higher ground than downtown Rexburg, was mostly unscathed except for a house that the flood deposited on the football field. The campus became the center of disaster relief operations, and its student dormitories were opened to 2,400 evacuees. In the ensuing months, the College would serve 386,000 free meals. Hal and his colleagues oversaw the effort to house and feed the appreciative flood victims.[6]

> Sometime near midnight, I stood near two couples in a soup line, whose lank hair and scraggly beards filled my small heart with irritation that drifters were taking our free food and lodging intended for flood victims. As the dirtiest man stood next to me, he looked up shyly and said through his dark-stained teeth, "President, we're sure grateful what the college is doing for us. We lost all we had in Sugar City. Thank you, sir."
> —JOURNAL, JUNE 6, 1976

Hal also played an informal leadership role that extended beyond the bounds of the campus. He was among the church and civic leaders who convened the day after the flood, Sunday, in the Manwaring Center. His journal outlines the disaster-relief strategy they created, in which the Church, whose members comprised 95 percent of the citizens in the most heavily affected areas, played a crucial role:

> Only Latter-day Saints could build a smooth running team from co-equal heads in Church, civil defense, and the college. By the end of the day we'd found our parts: county government

at the civil defense center will direct the efforts of search and road clearing; Church leaders will direct the people and the welfare support for them; and the college will provide the home and shelter for the victims and the nerve center for the disaster-relief efforts. (June 6, 1976)

The journal makes no mention of it, but others present at the meeting recall a statement Hal made during a discussion of Rexburg's future. One of them was Robert E. Wells, who four months later would be called as a General Authority. At the time, Elder Wells headed the Church's purchasing department and had been dispatched to Rexburg to coordinate the acquisition of relief supplies.

Early in the meeting, those who spoke expressed gratitude that the disaster hadn't been worse, particularly in terms of lives lost. But they shared a grim view of Rexburg's future. All of the town's Main Street and most businesses had been destroyed by the flood. It seemed unlikely that the college would open for the fall semester or that federal relief would come quickly, if at all. There was talk of simply abandoning the flooded areas and rebuilding the town, slowly, on higher ground.

> He turned the meeting around and established the leadership of the college.
>
> —ELDER ROBERT E. WELLS[7]

Standing, Hal gently but firmly squelched that talk and refocused the discussion on the disaster-relief efforts. He declared that the college would open for the fall on schedule and that the town should be rebuilt where it was. It was time, he said, to get moving.

That first meeting set the pattern for daily correlation among Church, government, and college representatives. Church members recognized it as drawing from principles and practices of weekly ward council meetings.[8] The local stake presidents assured government officials that their bishops would provide the same care to members and nonmembers within each ward boundary. As a result, the Church's systems for communication and coordination became an extension of all relief agencies. Government officials worked through bishops to contact affected families and begin the process of finding alternative housing and replacing losses. In the end, these officials would acknowledge the Church for doubling the speed of relief, cleanup, and rebuilding efforts.

Even the less severely flooded homes took hundreds of man-hours to clean. It wasn't enough to simply shovel, scrape, and wash away the flood's putrid mud; in most cases, carpeting and sheetrock had to be stripped and concrete floors and wooden studs dried. Here again, the Church and its members stepped for-

THE MUCK LEFT BEHIND

ward. Under the direction of President Harold Hillam of the Idaho Falls South Stake, armies of volunteers were enlisted and organized. Each day, buses brought several thousand volunteers from throughout Idaho and Northern Utah. President Peterson, whose Rexburg East Stake was largely unaffected, identified and prioritized the needs against which to deploy the volunteers. As there were no accommodations for them in Rexburg, many volunteers boarded buses in their home areas well before dawn and returned in the wee hours of the next day. By summer's end, they had donated one million hours of service.

LIFTING AND LEARNING

On the Monday after the flood, Hal began to visit the affected college employees. As he went from house to house, the starkly contrasted scenes of physical devastation and spiritual triumph lifted him.

President Peterson told the story today of one volunteer who thanked him for the chance to do a second hard cleanup task with these words, "Oh, thanks. I was afraid I wouldn't get my money's worth." He'd paid six dollars to come.

—JOURNAL, JULY 18, 1976

Muck flowed into my boots in twenty-five living rooms to-day. In those homes were the survivors; on many lots only the foundations remain. The largest proportion of homes completely swept away is in Sugar City. Allan Clark[9] and I stopped our four-wheel-drive truck first at Wilson Walker's home.[10] We took pictures and made a written description, which we signed, of his home's destruction. Gary Ball,[11] from Rexburg, was there in his large tractor, ripping away the ruined front porch. Wilson's voice cracked, as he described the force and depth of the water. His wife smiled and bid us good-bye with, "We'll have the flow-ers blooming soon." (June 7, 1976)

In the months that followed, Hal visited the home of each Ricks College employee who lost property in the flood. It was a season of strenuous service but great learning, far beyond anything he had planned for himself just that spring as he had tried to justify staying at Ricks.

Time and again, he marveled at the strength of the people. Temporal disaster seemed to bring out spiritual strength, particularly in those who had been strong already. One college employee, knowing that his home had been washed away by the flood, spent days help-ing others before finally going to confirm that all he owned was lost. Local priesthood leaders, especially the bishops, needed encouragement to look to their own fami-lies' needs and to get sufficient rest. Where nerves ought to have frayed and tempers flared, the general reaction to the disaster was increased goodwill and magnanimity.

Hal learned lessons about what it takes to be prepared for great personal trials. Seeking to understand the difference be-tween the heroic response of some victims and the betrayal of others, who left even

> One Latter-day Saint couple spoke to me in the Manwaring Center, expressing appreci-ation, "This is the third flood we've been through and we're so grateful that Ricks College has made this one the best. We couldn't have done it without your hospitality."
>
> —JOURNAL, JUNE 9, 1976

loved ones to their own devices, he commissioned a small but scientifically significant study. "There was just one thing we could find," he later told a class of graduating high school seniors.

> Those who were heroes had been the people who always remembered and kept promises in the little things, the daily things ... a promise to stay after a church dinner to clean up, or to come to work on a Saturday project to help a neighbor.
>
> Those who deserted their families when it was hard had often deserted their obligations when it wasn't so tough. They had a pattern of failing to keep their word to do little things when the sacrifice to them would have been slight and doing what they had said they would do would have been easy. When the price was high, they could not pay it.[12]

Hal marveled at the general lack of blaming the government for its faulty dam or wondering why God would allow such a disaster. Self-reliant, faithful people became all the more so. Many Church members refused food stamps offered by the government; others took them but later deducted the amount from their financial reimbursements for damage. Less than two weeks after the flood, both the government's program for dispersing food stamps and a similar relief program operated by the Red Cross were shut down for lack of takers.

> We attended a fine sacrament meeting where Bishop Forsgren bore testimony and gave advice that we should work to clean up and theorize later. He said, "Sure I've got a theory as to why I lost my business building: I built it near the river and the dam burst."
> —JOURNAL, JUNE 13, 1976

As Hal talked with government officials who had made a career of disaster preparedness and relief, he learned that the miracle of the Teton Dam flood was not just in the speed of the cleanup. The dam had broken at the best possible time of the day and week—a Saturday morning in June, when almost everyone was awake but no children were in school—thus minimizing the loss of life. And, to an unprecedented degree, people who had lived through flooding before, and who doubted that this one would be much different, nonetheless responded immediately to the warnings to move to higher ground. Even the time of year bore the mark of a loving God's concern for an obedient people: the weather was just warm enough for the cleanup effort, most of which would be complete before snow fell again in the fall.

GUIDANCE FROM THE BRETHREN

The senior-most leaders of the Church visited Rexburg as the second week of cleanup began. On Sunday, June 13, President Kimball and Elder Boyd K. Packer of the Quorum of the Twelve spoke twice to gatherings of thousands of flood victims in the Hart basketball arena. Hal was surprised by their ability to convey love while expressing only a modicum of sympathy. Their focus was on moving forward with faith, as he recorded in the journal:

Elder Boyd K. Packer, speaking in the Hart Building, told the flood victims, "Some may ask, 'What have we done wrong to deserve this?' The answer is, 'Nothing.' If you attach tragedy to sin only, how do you explain the sufferings of Christ?" And he said, "Life is a test."

President Spencer W. Kimball told the people in both meetings, "My great thanks to Heavenly Father has been that we did not lose more lives." Both he and Elder Packer said several times that parents should have family meetings and private interviews to assure that little children express fears and have questions answered. They both urged establishing usual family patterns, with prayer and family councils, and they suggested pacing for the long run; also, they recommended father's blessings for wives and children. President Kimball said, "We must get students back to the college, both for the community and so the young people may get spiritual education combined with academic learning. Yet," he said, "we must be sensitive to the needs of the survivors."

In our one moment of private conversation, President Kimball said to me: "When money begins to be given to the victims, you may see fault-finding and jealousy. It's important now to unify the people." (June 13, 1976)

President Ezra Taft Benson, the senior member of the Twelve, arrived just forty-eight hours after the visit by President Kimball and Elder Packer. By then Hal and his colleagues were exhausted. But they appreciated Elder Benson's praise and optimism, which meant all the more coming from a seasoned administrator who had directed the Church's post–World War II relief efforts in Europe.

Tension must be running me down: I laid down on my office floor around noon, closed my eyes, got up after what I thought was five fitful moments, and found an hour had passed. I arrived at the Manwaring Center just in time to shake President Ezra Taft Benson's hand and then hear him say to a meeting of stake presidents from the flood area: "I've never seen people anywhere respond to tragedy with quite the spirit I've seen here . . . I think good is going to come from this. We'll look back on this experience in years to come with gratitude."

He also said, "The Lord has a way of bringing blessing out of tragedy if we do our part. . . . Outsiders will get a testimony that this is pure religion in action, and they will inquire. . . . I promise you blessings, in the name of the Lord, from this experience, cherished blessings for you and yours." In answer to questions about whether to accept loans or other government aid, he declined to rule on specific programs, other than rejecting a dole, and said that the general principle was "The Lord desires his Church to be independent of every other institution under heaven. Let's follow that as closely as we can." (June 15, 1976)

The disaster gave Hal the opportunity to explain the Church's welfare and leadership systems to many non-Church members. Idaho Governor Cecil Andrus, who joined President Kimball and Elder Packer in speaking to the flood victims, asked Hal to write to him about the way LDS people would apply Church welfare principles in accepting aid. Journalists and federal government officials also sought to understand how a spiritual organization could achieve such impressive temporal results.

 Rain poured down outside, while I sat in my office with people from California and from Seattle who marvel at what they have seen here. The man and wife from California, writers for Readers Digest, found that a visit with stake president Robert Smith, in St. Anthony, turned the focus of their story from the flood to the Church's response. My second visitors were deputy directors for the Federal Disaster Assistance Agency. One of them said, "I've never seen such organized, rapid recovery. I credit that to your Church." (June 16, 1976)

I walked down a stairway today in the Manwaring and saw one box at eye level in a stack that reached far above my head. The stencil on it read, "Deseret Brand Peanut Butter—Houston East Stake." I thought of the good that food has done and the kindness of God to touch the hearts of people in Houston two years ago to bless us now.

—JOURNAL, JUNE 11, 1976

Hal himself marveled at the power of the Church's priesthood and welfare organizations. Like many Church members, he had filled assignments at stake farms and canneries throughout his life. Though the work imparted warm feelings, it was hard to visualize the use of the goods that he and his fellow volunteers helped to produce. The flood provided an unforgettable glimpse of the welfare system's full purpose.

CARRYING ON

Ricks College began its fall semester as scheduled. The dorms were empty, thanks to the rapid deployment of mobile homes by the U.S. government's Department of Housing and Urban Development. They were also immaculate, thanks to the tidiness of the grateful families who had occupied them. Students contributed to the ongoing cleanup and rebuilding efforts, but otherwise campus life proceeded as usual, with a full schedule of classes and athletic events.

Hal resumed his academic responsibilities, including his Brother Moore–prescribed visits to faculty members and other employees. He also continued to think seriously about the role of the college.

While Henry and Stuart greeted the day with a 6 a.m. swimming team practice, I wrote answers to questions like this: "Why should Ricks College try to keep its doors open to students of a wide academic ability, at least as shown by past performance?" When the boys came to get me at 7:30, I'd thought more deeply about Ricks College and its place in the Church than I ever had before.

Following my new schedule, I went out to the industrial sciences building to visit people where they work. As if I'd been led, I turned down a corridor I'd not noticed before and found two concerned faculty members, talking, and obviously worried. I stayed for an hour. (March 31, 1977)

Notwithstanding his outreach efforts, the results of a facultywide survey conducted in the spring of 1977 indicated that Hal's administration of the college was still a source of concern for some. Because of Brother Moore's challenge to get out among the college's employees, the news was neither entirely unexpected nor as bad as it might have been. But, after six years of giving his all, Hal couldn't help feeling stung and disappointed. Yet the journal records only feelings of gratitude and determination to increase the unity of the campus community.

Family prayers, class, lunch with the boys, and all my office work until afternoon were filled with anticipation and a touch of anxiety. At two I led a presentation and discussion to the faculty which reported to them the results of a survey of faculty attitude. I felt the Spirit. The faculty meeting, which could have increased bitterness by inviting criticism, somehow moved to a feeling of all of us working together. I could feel the help of heaven for the college. The survey clearly confirmed the counsel of our home teacher, Brother Moore, when he said he'd felt impressions in the night that I needed to get out of my office and into the work places of our people at the college. (April 14, 1977)

These challenges at Ricks didn't lessen Hal's appreciation for the opportunity to "stay a little longer," though he could have left for greener professional pastures. Since declining the McCulloch offer he'd received an equally enticing one. Bruce Henderson, renowned founder of the Boston Consulting Group (BCG), had asked Hal to open and lead a West Coast office for his rapidly growing firm. Like Hal, Henderson had attended the Harvard Business School and worked at Arthur D. Little. Though they hadn't overlapped at either of those places, Hal had discovered Henderson's brilliant management theories while at Stanford. The two had begun a correspondence, and Hal granted Henderson's request to send his chief lieutenant, Bill Bain, to recruit at Stanford. Bain hired several of Hal's standout students, including one who later helped him found his own consulting firm, Bain & Company.

When I left the house the second time this morning, just before eight, Kathy said through half-closed eyes, "This is the roughest homecoming I've had." The two feet of snow didn't help, nor did the fact that our car is held prisoner by a broken garage door spring.

—JOURNAL, JANUARY 4, 1977

The BCG offer had much to recommend it. Hal and Bruce Henderson thought alike. Both saw the potential value of theories of business management but also the need to make the theories practical. They'd been mutually impressed by one another's work, Hal introducing Henderson's influential "experience curve" in his Stanford classroom and Henderson inviting Hal to present at BCG-sponsored executive retreats in the United States and Europe.

Hal also saw in Bruce Henderson a potential mentor of the kind he had found in General Doriot and C. Roland Christensen at HBS. More than the opportunity to become a coleader of a prestigious consulting firm, he was attracted by the prospect of working with someone he deeply admired and could learn from. There was also a geographical draw: Hal would have his choice of West Coast locations, including the San Francisco Bay Area. That thought loomed temporarily large as the Eyrings returned from their annual Christmas trip to the Hill.

But Hal let the BCG offer pass, with much less deliberation than the one from McCullough. He was still feeling grateful for the blessing of staying a little longer at Ricks, and he was mindful of the source of that blessing. He also sensed there was something else coming, a professional opportunity that would make him and Kathy feel good "from the inside out."[13]

A NEW ASSIGNMENT

In July 1977, Jeff Holland invited Hal and Kathy to come, on a day's notice, to meet with him in Salt Lake City. Hal's journal entry records the essence of the conversation they had there.

> At dawn, I took Henry and Stuart swimming. By afternoon, Kathy and I were in Salt Lake having lunch with Commissioner Holland in the Hotel Utah basement coffee shop. He asked me to be Deputy Commissioner of Education for the Church. I turned to Kathy and said, "What do you think?"
>
> She smiled and said, "What is there to say?"
>
> Jeff Holland had already told us he had a letter from President Kimball authorizing him to call us to the position. (July 12, 1977)

This time, the conviction that Hal should accept the job offer came quickly, the next day, though not in the form of a voice:

> I prayed to know if we should go. My answer, instead of an assurance of success or approval, was the picture of little students, of all colors, all over the world. Along with the picture, I had a surge of love for them. (July 13, 1977)

Hal's last day on the job at Ricks was Friday, July 29. Forty-eight hours later he was on his way to Utah to start work in the Commissioner's office. Kathy clipped for him the editorial that ran in the Idaho Falls newspaper that day (see following page).

That fall, Hal's colleagues at Ricks invited the Eyrings and their extended family members back to Rexburg for a special Homecoming Week assembly and dinner in honor of his service. Four thousand students, alumni, faculty, and friends attended the assembly, which was followed by dinner for one thousand. The lavish tributes embarrassed not only Hal but also his father-in-law. As the long evening finally ended and they made their way to the exit, Sid said to Hal, with a wink, "Let's get out of here before they find out the truth."

May 31, 1984
Thursday

I wrote in the Atherton
guest house of the
Johnsons, looking down
on the trees and drive
of our first home.
Elizabeth and Mary
Kathleen watched me
blow out cand[l]
birthday cake,
dinner by Tru
Holy Ghost h
teach a Sunda
workshop in Me

June 1, 1984
Friday

Elizabeth and
the pool and
worked on a ta
Gary came b
Los Angeles a
to hear me s
time to yout
Altos.

June 2, 1984
Saturday

I towed Eliza
inflated, gree
Mary Kath
complimen
purple dress,
match to the
hair that mar
Stuart's and
sister. Grand
and I watched Stephanie
dance in a musical.

June 3, 1984
Sunday

Thanks, Dr. Eyring

Dr. Henry B. Eyring is going international, and Ricks College and all of East Idaho will miss him. As deputy education commissioner for the LDS Church, the former Ricks College president will be tilling an education garden that stretches round the world.

The combination of a keen, pervasive mind and composed graciousness has been the leadership catalyst for an unusual sprint in growth and stature at Ricks College during his presidency. The college not only grew 20 per cent to some 6,000 students, it felt the tug of Eyring excellence as well.

Many East Idahoans — especially those in the Rexburg vicinity — will remember him for another reason: for his quick conversion of Ricks College to a dramatically rescuing flood refugee center after the Teton Dam collapse had visited its terror and despair upon the valley.

Bon Voyage, Dr. Eyring, and thanks for coming.

Kathy, Elizabeth, and Mary Kathleen were dressed and packed early for our drive from Atherton to the San Jose airport. On the flight home, a stewardess made a bullseye with a glass full of orange juice on my lap. It was so cold and complete a soaking that I laughed for the rest of the trip. I used bags to shield the results as I got us to the car.

neyhaw, Mark, sometime last week, forced her out of
our double's match this morning; within an hour she'd
sent a replacement, so I played six sets. Result: I
soaked my elbow in a tub of hot water propped on the
table breakfast room at grandpa's, while I watched

15

PREPARE THE WAY

Wherefore, go to, and call servants,
That we may labor diligently with our might
In the vineyard,
That we may prepare the way,
That I may bring forth again the natural fruit,
Which natural fruit is good
And the most precious above all other fruit.

—JACOB 5:61

The Church's seminary and institute system, for which Hal assumed responsibility after concluding his service at Ricks in 1977, was poised for dramatic expansion. Under President Spencer W. Kimball's leadership the Church was growing internationally as never before, especially in Latin America. As Hal wrote one night after trying to describe his new role to fellow members of the McCulloch board of directors, "There is no way to explain 'Deputy Commissioner of Education' without talking about the gospel going to every nation, kindred, tongue, and people."[1]

Hal sensed the magnitude of the Church's international growth during a trip he took after just two weeks in his new job. Between the 14th and the 19th of August, 1977, he visited Mexico City, primarily to inspect the Church's secondary schools there. His hosts and travel guides were the Church Educational System representatives in Mexico. The senior CES man, Ben Martinez, was one of Hal's former counselors in the bishopric of the Stanford Ward. The journal records Hal's warm feelings at seeing Ben and learning of the Church's success in Mexico.

More than the air was warm as I walked into the Mexico City airport; despite my anxiety in arriving at a new city, I felt a love and optimism flood into me that remained through the bumper-to-bumper car drive into the Maria Isabel hotel. As Ben told me of the 50,000 converts per year, on a base of 250,000 members, I felt a spiritual confirmation that this country has the special blessing of the Lord. (August 15, 1977)

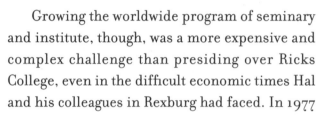

Growing the worldwide program of seminary and institute, though, was a more expensive and complex challenge than presiding over Ricks College, even in the difficult economic times Hal and his colleagues in Rexburg had faced. In 1977 more than 300,000 students were enrolled in either seminary or institute. They lived in fifty-four countries and needed curriculum in seventeen languages.[2] Serving more of the youth of the Church would require not only hiring more people and establishing operations in new countries but also simplifying the seminary and institute curriculum so as to make the tasks of translating and training less costly and more effective for learners.

In addition to seminary and institute, Hal's new responsibilities included the supervision of seventy-three Church secondary schools serving 16,000 elementary, middle, and high school students. The schools were spread across Mexico, Chile, Peru, and Bolivia, as well as all of the major islands of Polynesia.[3] Initially, each school was founded in response to a deficiency in the local public education system. The Church tradition of self-sufficiency in education dates back to pioneer times, when absence of public schools in the American West required each Mormon settlement to create its own academy, typically sponsored by the stake. In fact, Ricks College began as an academy for schoolchildren, gradually creating high school and junior college curriculum and finally dropping the pre-college grades as the state of Idaho's public school system grew. Brigham Young University and the University of Utah have similar pioneer academy origins.

Hal's feelings of closeness to his new responsibilities went beyond Ricks's origin as an elementary school and his one-year stint as an early-morning seminary teacher. His mother, Mildred, had been a member of the Church's first seminary class, at Salt Lake City's Granite High School, in 1912. In addition to appreciating what seminary had done for his mother, Hal felt personally grateful for the program. The seminary building adjacent to East High School had been a spiritual refuge for him. The early-morning tutelage of Sister Stoddard and Brother Toronto had reinforced him against the worldliness and doubts that assailed him at school. With the passing years, his gratitude had only grown.

> Your call has eternal consequences for others and for you. In the world to come, thousands may call your name blessed, even more than the people you serve here. They will be the ancestors and the descendants of those who chose eternal life because of something you said or did, or even what you were.
>
> —TALK, OCTOBER 6, 2002[4]

TAKING COUNSEL

Hal was grateful to be teamed with two administrative colleagues, Joe J. Christensen and Stanley A. Peterson, each of whom brought remarkable energy and insight to their shared task. Joe Christensen had served as an institute director at three universities, including the University of Utah, site of the Church's largest institute. In 1970 he and his wife, Barbara, were called to preside over a mission in Mexico. They served for only a few months before

JOE J. CHRISTENSEN

being brought home by Neal Maxwell, the then-new Commissioner of Church Education. Neal had admired Joe's work while they were both at the University of Utah and had tapped him to lead out in expanding the seminary and institute programs worldwide. Joe had been engaged in that work for seven years when Jeff Holland asked him to report to Hal.

Stan Peterson arrived when Hal did, in the summer of 1977. Until that time he had been dean of BYU's continuing education division, one of the world's largest providers of home-study courses for college and high school students. Commissioner Holland, who had been a fellow dean at BYU, thought to apply Stan's continuing education expertise to CES's Education Week, Know Your Religion, and Especially for Youth (EFY) programs, as well as literacy offerings for students in Latin America. A former California school principal, Stan also brought valuable experience relative to the Church's international schools.

Commissioner Holland charged Hal, Joe, and Stan to bring seminary and institute, Church schools, and continuing education together as never before. He worried about the potential confusion and redundant costs of having separate representatives of each of the three branches in the field, where they were prone to overwhelm inexperienced priesthood leaders.

> It was all over the map. I used to say that we'd sometimes have people three-deep bumping into each other at the airport.
>
> —ELDER JEFFREY R. HOLLAND[5]

To this end, Commissioner Holland cautioned Hal, Joe, and Stan against dividing up responsibilities according to these traditional categories. They determined to follow this counsel, but it required coordinating to a degree that none of them had experienced before. One result was to stretch and develop Hal as a leader.

Fortunately, Hal found it easy to respect Joe and Stan. The capacity of each man was immediately evident, and it would be manifest in subsequent assignments. Joe would go on to preside at both the Provo Missionary Training Center and Ricks College before serving ten years as a member of the First Quorum of the Seventy. Stan would, beginning in 1980, spend twenty years overseeing all three of the areas for which they then had joint responsibility.

Still, in their early months of working together, the power of the trio seemed to be a mixed blessing. On the one hand, inspired ideas flowed freely:

> Joe Christensen and I never stopped striking new ideas off each other, like sparks, in happy conversations that ranged over how to bolster young Latter-day Saints against attacking philosophy professors to new ways to meet the needs of adults who want more gospel education. We ended our talk in the car, at eleven, after a meeting with seminary and institute teachers at BYU. (August 9, 1977)
>
> ***
>
> As Joe and Stan and I sat down at nine-thirty, I asked, "Joe, what's the darkest cloud you see on the horizon?" That brought forth a flood of concern, a far-ranging discussion that lasted for four hours. At the end, we knelt together and felt a clear confirmation that we had found the new organizational

STANLEY A. PETERSON

> pattern we're to follow as we share the work of directing all the religious education, schools, and special programs of the Church Educational System. (September 15, 1977)

But while ideas flowed freely, achieving consensus on important decisions often proved difficult. The challenge of effective communication and decision making was heightened by global travel schedules. On any given workday, at least one member of the trio was likely to be out of the office and hard for the others to reach. The insights and impressions each man brought back from the field proved illuminating but not always easy to reconcile.

The leadership environment differed markedly from the one Hal had experienced at Ricks. There, he had presided over a hand-picked team of administrators with clearly defined functional responsibilities. Each of those men knew the limits of his authority, with respect both to one another and to Hal. By contrast, things were much less clearly defined and inherently more overlapping in the triumvirate that Commissioner Holland had created. It was a situation common to Church headquarters and thus beneficially preparatory for Hal; in future service, he would be glad for having had the experience of working in close intellectual quarters with strong-willed peers. But, at the time, it proved to be stretching and often uncomfortable.

> Our Heavenly Father wants our hearts to be knit together. That union in love is not simply an ideal. It is a necessity.
>
> —TALK, APRIL 5, 1998[6]

Part of the challenge stemmed from the great difference in personal backgrounds and temperaments. Joe and Stan had spent their careers in the activities that they and Hal now oversaw. They had seen supposedly revolutionary ideas for religious education come and go, in the process developing a healthy skepticism and an appreciation for continuity. Hal, by contrast, saw innovative possibilities everywhere. "The flood of impressions, exciting results from computer models and convictions from the words of prophets continued," he wrote one night. "In my life, I've never had the challenges of my work run so clearly, so insistently, so constantly in my mind and heart."[7]

Many of Hal's ideas proved invaluable, but only with Stan and Joe's help. They often found themselves in the unpopular roles of reality checking and prioritizing. As Stan observed of Hal, "He had an absolute steel-trap mind that was very creative and always moving. He could think up more ideas than you could implement."[8]

In his struggle to master a new, more collaborative style of leadership, Hal received guidance from several sources. Prominent among them were Kathy and his father, as he noted in the journal:

Kathy urged me to work more with the men I lead, and Dad counseled me at lunch at the University to be less frivolous; the good advice helped me in administrative meetings, interviews, and hours of working on the planning model for schools. (October 17, 1978)

Hal's most abundant source of leadership insight was his observation of the Brethren. Having studied organizational behavior as a professor and watched the Brethren grapple with tough issues when he was president of Ricks, he wasn't surprised to see them struggle with the same challenges of unifying groups that he faced. But in watching them he learned important lessons about the power of inspiration in achieving unity, even in the most complex situations. That was the case particularly in meetings of a subgroup of the Church's Board of Education, the "Executive Committee,"[9] which Hal attended monthly.

> The day was primarily a preparation for the Executive Committee meeting at three. Elders Hinckley, Monson, and Packer were there, along with Bishop Brown. I spoke little but learned a great deal. And I saw clear inspiration where all four members felt a common, strong position on several complicated issues.
>
> — JOURNAL, AUGUST 25, 1977

Hal also learned from meetings that didn't go so well, especially the ones he led. He saw that divergent opinions were a two-edged sword. You needed different views to make well-reasoned, inspired decisions. But without proper care, debate could cut the members of a group off from the source of inspiration and from one another.

I tried to manage and reduce conflict today in my meetings; and I saw it appear in a committee meeting I attended conducted by a General Authority. Very few people can tolerate differences of opinion without making and feeling personal attacks. Anger seems to come flying out of almost any difference, and yet if we don't work on differences we don't learn much from each other. (November 10, 1977)

As the months passed, the Eyring-Christensen-Peterson team began to gel. A big part of the reason was Hal's willingness to be less directive than he had been as president of Ricks College. More than ever, the journal became a tool for self-analysis and discovery. He noted "learning something about how to balance a 'take-charge' urge I have in me with the need to give others responsibility."[10] That contributed to breakthroughs in the assignments that the trio had received from Commissioner Holland.

Unless optimism clouds my view, meetings today seem to have brought us close to resolving three of the main organizational questions I was brought in to resolve: how our field organization will represent all of Church Education in student advising; adult religious education; and the planning and construction of buildings outside BYU and Ricks. We seem close to solving them all, and my feeling is that the Spirit softened hearts to help us negotiate; it was never hard to see what would be best, but almost impossible to see how to get people to agree. We're started. (December 2, 1977)

GROWTH AND SIMPLIFICATION

The new Deputy Commissioner and his two associates faced challenges not only of growth but also of simplification. Commissioner Holland charged them to reduce and simplify the Church's religious education curriculum. Seminary lesson manuals, for example, had grown so copious that presenting all of the material in each lesson could preclude reading the scriptures upon which the lesson was based. In addition to this spiritual liability of bloated manuals, there was also the practical problem of translating them into dozens of languages. Simplification was needed, both to allow for affordable translation and to increase the teaching focus on the scriptures and essential gospel doctrines.

There was a similar need for prioritization and simplification in the Church's system of primary and secondary schools. Though the schools were beloved by the students and parents who benefited from them, they were growing increasingly expensive; they would only become more so with the advent of computers in the classroom. And with the slow but steady emergence of public alternatives in many countries in which the Church operated schools, Commissioner Holland and his colleagues had to justify offering educational services. It was rapidly becoming true that they were not truly a last resort but merely a preferred alternative to the schooling that Church members could obtain at no additional cost.

The question of whether the Church should provide higher quality alternatives to existing public schools was a difficult one not only internationally but in the United States. Members whose children attended public schools with declining moral and physical safety standards naturally hoped that the Church could create educational safe havens. Their argument for help became especially poignant during the era of court-ordered busing in the United States. In 1971 a Supreme Court ruling allowed federal courts to order that students be bused to schools far from their homes for the sake of racial desegregation. The Church received particular pressure from members in Los Angeles beginning in 1977, the year that the California Supreme Court required that city's school board to create what became a drastic plan for desegregation through forced busing.

The Church Educational System had faced a similar crossroads not long before. When Neal Maxwell had become Commissioner in 1970, he had immediately recognized the impossibility of serving the Church's 200,000 college-aged members solely through BYU, Ricks, Church College of Hawaii, and LDS Business College, which had a combined capacity of fewer than 35,000 students. Knowing that the Church couldn't afford to expand or create college campuses to meet the needs of all members, Commissioner Maxwell had promoted the rapid growth of institutes during Hal's time at Ricks.

By 1977, Commissioner Holland and the Board had come to a similar realization: the Church couldn't be a provider-of-last-resort for primary and secondary schooling and in fact didn't need to do so in many of the countries in which it operated schools. As institute was doing for college-aged students at non-Church schools, seminary could provide the spiritual education for students attending public elementary and secondary schools. This approach would allow CES to serve all young Church members, thanks largely to the success of the home-study seminary program, which had been proven under the direction of Joe Christensen. Hal performed quantitative analyses of the options:

In the long hours today, some alone and some with the Commissioner and the zone administrators, I began to build mathematical models of the alternatives the Church faces in building schools or closing them, selecting religious education programs for different age groups, and doing it all in the face of a desire of the Brethren to simplify. Just thinking through the way I would build mathematical models has made me do more careful analysis than I had done before. (October 10, 1978)

Though the overall strategy felt right, it still left Hal, Joe, and Stan to make hard decisions about school closures. Even where the decisions were analytically justified and spiritually confirmed, they were painful to implement, as Hal recorded after a special meeting of the Board.

I joined in the meeting of Board members, General Authorities responsible for South America, and Chilean priesthood leaders; we told them that the Church schools would be closed because public education has become adequate. They were loyal, despite a personal loss. (March 30, 1978)

The pain of school closures was softened somewhat by prophetic calls for new learning opportunities for Church members throughout the world. In June 1978, President Spencer W. Kimball announced that priesthood and temple blessings would be extended to all male members of the Church. That fall, in priesthood leadership meetings held in connection with general conference, President Kimball called for the blessings not only of the gospel but also of formal education to be taken to the world, including Africa. Later that weekend, in the Tabernacle on Temple Square, Elder Boyd K. Packer, a member of the Board of Education, lifted Hal's sights regarding the opportunities, particularly in Mexico.

Elder Packer ended our eight o'clock meeting with the priesthood leaders of Mexico by saying: "I have had a feeling since I came in this room that there are opportunities we've never dreamed of that will come. The limitations we have known on the schools in Mexico will go, although some will go painfully. I am not sure how quickly this will happen." Then as the meeting ended, he said: "The Lord will bless us. He is brooding over his Church in Mexico. Great things are ahead." He went to some trouble to see that I was seated on the second row in the Tabernacle before he took his seat on the stand. (October 1, 1978)

Hal, Joe, Stan, and those who worked with them eagerly responded to the prophetic call for increased educational opportunities for Church members. Their simplification of the religious education curriculum led to a 90 percent reduction in the materials used for teaching seminary, which were used by both professional instructors and volunteers called to teach early-morning seminary. By reducing translation and printing costs, this streamlining made it possible to broaden seminary and institute opportunities around the world.

The more he immersed himself in this work, the more Hal's love for seminary and institute and the Church schools grew. Though he regretted leaving Kathy and the boys for lengthy trips to distant parts of the world, he thrilled to see the positive effects of education on the members of the Church. He also admired the sacrifices of the Church employees who made possible the activities of the schools, institutes, and seminary programs. They and their families lived on modest incomes and moved frequently, with inspiring willingness and gratitude.

Above all, Hal felt love for the students that he and his colleagues were serving. The picture of little children of all nationalities and the feeling of love that had come to him when he prayed about leaving Ricks proved visionary. Particularly as he traveled overseas, he experienced frequent confirmation that he was still on the Lord's errand.

We had dinner with Seoul Mission President F. Ray Hawkins at the Mission Home, and then went back to the hotel for a family home evening with wives and children of our men. In our small hotel room, the children crowded into a line in one corner and sang, in Korean, "Give, Said the Little Stream," "I Am a Child of God," and "I Hope They Call Me on a Mission." The wives and children went into my room, while we visited with the men. Then the children came back bearing pears and apples and oranges, all carefully cut and prepared on plates for us to eat. We shook all of the hands of the parents and the children as they walked down the hallway at the end of the evening. The last ones turned to bow towards us. I bowed back. (October 31, 1978)

TEACHING AND LEARNING FROM YOUNG MEN

During his global service as Deputy Commissioner of Education, Hal also developed an increased capacity to love the youth in his own neighborhood. Upon arriving in Utah in the fall of 1977, the Eyrings became members of the Bountiful 46th Ward. The ward, high in the hills above the pioneer town's Main Street, was growing rapidly. Ripe for division, it had more priesthood leadership than it needed. Hal's first call was to serve as one of four Sunday School greeters.

When the ward was divided five months later, Hal received a call to serve as Scout Committee Chairman of the new 48th Ward, presided over by Bishop Norman Dobson. Suppressing doubts about his own Scouting status (he was a Second Class Scout) and his claustrophobic fear of sleeping in tents, he accepted the call eagerly.

Bishop Dobson mentioned in my temple interview combined with tithing settlement that they were thinking of calling me to help with the Scout committee. I was surprised, and pleased, to hear my name read in sacrament meeting as Scout Committee Chairman. The Scoutmaster told me on the way out I'll get to start my winter camping on the way to Cache Valley in February. (January 8, 1978)

Less than a year later, Hal accepted a related call to serve as an adviser to the deacons quorum. His main duty was teaching Sunday lessons, though he also assisted with weekly Scouting activities. The teaching proved unexpectedly productive and pleasant. He found that inspiration flowed as much in the presence of a handful of

HAL'S SON MATTHEW, ONE OF HIS SCOUTS

twelve- and thirteen-year-olds as it did in Ricks College devotionals with thousands of college students, or in discussions with the General Authorities.

I felt impressed to teach from the 19th verse of the 130th section of the Doctrine and Covenants to my deacons quorum. In the sacrament meeting, which was put on by seminary students from Bountiful High School, one of the most impressive talks quoted that same verse. The deacons looked around at me in the meeting, obviously surprised. I was too, although I know now that it was the Holy Ghost which had taught me to prepare the boys to be taught again, later. (February 25, 1979)

Hal tried to show the same respect for the deacons quorum president that he did the Brethren. As he would remember in a 2006 general conference talk, he "made a habit of seeking the counsel of the one with the charge from God by asking him, 'What do you think I should teach? What should I try to accomplish?'" He explained, "I learned to follow his counsel because I knew God had given him responsibility for the teaching of his quorum members."[11] The deacons reciprocated Hal's respect, engaging actively in the discussions he led. One young man who struggled with chronic illness sent a tape recorder with a fellow quorum member on days when he couldn't attend.[12]

Camping, though not his favorite activity, benefited Hal as well as the boys. Around the campfire and on long hikes he found informal teaching opportunities that were otherwise hard to create, even with the best classroom curriculum. In addition to growing closer to the boys, he gained personal insights. He came to see himself as not so very different from these twelve- and thirteen-year-olds. He realized, for instance, that the temptations common to youth, such as seeking the approval of peers, were hard to outgrow.

Twenty scouts, on three tiers of bunks, shouted and laughed in the semi-dark until three in the morning. At first I called "Knock it off," now and then, to no avail. Afterwards I began to listen. I noticed how much the calling back and forth was cued by each boy trying to get approval; if one nonsense line got a laugh, you could count on it coming again. I'd been so like them earlier in the day, when I glowed at the praise of Commissioner

Holland; he tapped the side of his head and said, "You're smart," when I had anticipated a problem. I'll be tempted to seek that again. (February 10, 1979)

In the 48th Ward Hal also gladly accepted the assignment to serve as a home teaching companion to his oldest son, Henry, who had just turned fourteen. As in Rexburg, Hal fulfilled the assignment as though it were his most important calling, second only to his duties as husband and father. One evening in early 1978, as they were returning from a home teaching visit, Henry gave Hal reason to believe that perhaps he was making progress as a priesthood leader.

After a series of difficult meetings, and before going home to sign a sale agreement on our Rexburg house, I lettered a visual aid for Kathy from Mosiah 3:19: "Becometh as a little child."[13] I'm not sure that scripture is working on me, but something must be; as we left our home teaching visit together tonight, Henry said, "You've changed more in the last six months than in your six years in Rexburg." He attributed it to travel and fatigue. I think he sees the change in the positive direction. I think. (March 21, 1978)

nephew, Mark, sometime last week, forced her out of
our double's match this morning; within an hour she'd
sent a replacement, so I played six sets. Result: I
soaked my elbow in a tub of hot water propped on the
table in the breakfast room at grandpa's, while I watched
the boys with the boys. Annette served the whole

16

HEARKEN UNTO THE LORD'S SERVANT

For I will send my servant
Unto you who are blind;
Yea, a messenger to open the eyes of the blind,
And unstop the ears of the deaf;
And they shall be made perfect notwithstanding their blindness,
If they will hearken unto the messenger, the Lord's servant.

—JOSEPH SMITH TRANSLATION, ISAIAH 42:19–20

His employment at Church headquarters increased the frequency and intimacy of Hal's interactions with the Brethren. Working with one or more of them almost daily, he gained greater appreciation for their goodness and deeper understanding of their way of thinking.

He was especially grateful to see his uncle President Spencer W. Kimball more frequently. But his first formal meeting with the prophet, the September 1977 gathering of the Board of Education, reminded him of his uncle's fragile health, as he noted in the journal:

During the first hour of the meeting, President Kimball spoke once; at the moment Jeff Holland introduced me and my associates, Joe and Stan, President Kimball said, "For the Board, I want to say how much we appreciate all you have done and will do." A few minutes later, as the discussion of an important issue continued, Joe leaned to me and whispered, "The President isn't well." His eyes seemed glazed. Moments later, he leaned to President Tanner and whispered, "I must leave." When he could not rise, a group of us carried him in his armchair to his office. As we did, he kept saying, "Oh, this is terrible to inconvenience you." We laid him on his office sofa, where security men began to give him oxygen. President Kimball said to us all, "Go back to the meeting." We did, where the discussion continued without reduced quality, despite the sound of ambulance sirens. . . . His whole concern, when death seemed near, was for our convenience and that the work of the kingdom go forward. (September 7, 1977)

THE MODEST VOICE OF A PROPHET

It wasn't the first time that Hal had seen President Kimball put concern for others ahead of his own needs at a moment of great personal distress. That had happened several years earlier, in Rexburg. As was typical of that more relaxed time, the prophet had flown to Idaho Falls with no security escort, and Hal and Kathy had met him at the airport in their station wagon. They could see immediately that President Kimball was in pain. The chronic heart problem that plagued him had flared up. They suggested that he at least rest and even consider canceling his speaking engagement, but he demurred, asking only for an opportunity to take his heart medication.

At the pulpit of Ricks's Hart auditorium, the mantle of prophecy lifted President Kimball as he preached the doctrines of the Atonement and repentance, drawing from his book *The Miracle of Forgiveness.* But Hal could see sweat on the prophet's brow and the clenching of his hands on the podium, as though he were holding himself from falling. It seemed that he was literally risking his life to call the students to repentance.

President Kimball spoke for more than an hour. As he finished, he expressed regret to the congregation that he would not be able to stay and shake hands. After the closing prayer, Hal took his uncle's arm and shepherded him carefully from the stage. When the prophet asked quietly, "Do you think they heard me?" Hal replied, with admiration not only for the sermon but for the strength required to give it, "You were wonderful, President Kimball."

The prophet literally turned on Hal. He grabbed Hal's coat lapels and said, through teeth clenched in pain, "Don't tell me that. That's not what I mean. I want to know if you think they could *hear* me." President Kimball's concern, Hal realized, was not for the quality of his performance or even for his own life. He worried only whether his listeners had been sufficiently moved to repent.

> President Kimball is never flamboyant. He does not underline his talks. He just gives them.
>
> —TALK, APRIL 6, 1981[1]

Though President Kimball's health slowly declined during Hal's four years as Deputy Commissioner, there were ample opportunities for him to view the prophet's modest but powerful mode of ministry. That happened in monthly Board meetings as well as more private settings, such as when President Kimball ministered to Hal's father, Henry, who had cancer. Always, the prophet melded confidence with humility, firmness with gentleness. The lesson stayed with Hal, influencing his own speaking style.

SEEING THE LORD'S HAND IN THE WORK

Watching the senior Brethren make difficult decisions increased Hal's admiration for both their personal capabilities and their ability to receive revelation. He was blessed to see beyond logical explanations for their wisdom; he recognized heaven's helping hand in the work. For example, in a meeting in which his father's cousin President Marion G. Romney seemed very confident of his knowledge of Mexico's constitution, Hal might have ascribed that to President Romney's having spent the first fifteen years of his life in the Mormon settlement of Colonia Juarez, in northern Mexico. Later in the

COLONIA JUAREZ TITHING OFFICE

same day, just a month after coming to work at Church headquarters, he could have similarly explained away a story about an unexpected ray of sun in Poland. The journal records his choice to see instead the Lord's power being poured out on His anointed servants.

I saw one prophetic miracle today and heard about another. President Romney, in an interview in the paneled President's Conference Room at 47 East South Temple, asked Brother Ben Martinez, "Do you know that the constitutional risks in this proposed reorganization in Mexico are real?" As he asked the question, I realized that neither legal counsel nor his vast experience were telling him; he knew with a certainty from another source.

In my earlier meeting with Commissioner Holland, he recounted to his staff a conversation he'd had today with President and Sister Kimball: they had described the experience of dedicating the land of Poland in a park last week, of the sun breaking through to beam on the prophet, and of the hospitality of the government. That's a special miracle in a Communist land, although it may someday seem ordinary. (September 6, 1977)

Hal was lifted by similar stories he heard in his travels around the world. He learned of the great need for inspiration at the geographic frontiers of the Church, where membership growth was rapid and conditions differed markedly from those in the relative strongholds of the western United States. He saw the Brethren lifted at all times, but particularly as they led the Saints on these frontiers, where human wisdom often proved inadequate or flat-out wrong. It was then that their gift of prophecy shone most clearly.

Frank Bradshaw, CES Zone Administrator for Asia, shared a story with me as we left Japan today, which was a perfect capstone to our trip. When President Kimball held a conference in Korea, he announced a temple in Japan and promised the people in Korea that they would be able to travel to that temple when it was constructed. Even the faithful priesthood leaders said, "Oh, President Kimball made a mistake there. He doesn't understand our government." Ho Nam Rhee, our man in Korea and also a stake president at that time, said, "You have faith; the prophet said it would happen." We learned on our trip to Korea, that, after years of restricting even the priesthood leaders from going out of the country for conference in Salt Lake City, the country has just announced that it will allow passports and exit visas for all citizens. The starting date is 1980, the year the temple will be opened in Japan. (November 7, 1978)

The Brethren themselves set the example for seeing the Lord's hand in events that might have been rationalized as mere coincidence. A month after attributing inspiration to President Romney and seeing divine forces behind the Church's warm welcome in Communist Poland, Hal recorded an observation made by Elder James E. Faust:

In a meeting where I sought guidance on what countries we should study for introducing Church education, Elder Faust told this story to show how much attention the Lord and President Kimball give the opening of new countries to missionary work. Several months ago, President Kimball told Elder Faust to have a substitute for a couple who had been called to be the first missionaries to a European country. He repeated the warning in five different conversations within a week's time. Two weeks later, the husband died. Elder Faust, who said President Kimball seems to get such detailed instructions often, had to find another couple. Elder Faust, by the way, declined to name a single country for us to study. (October 4, 1977)

From Elder Faust's answer to the inquiry about countries to study, which Hal could have incorrectly interpreted as a non-answer, he drew a lesson not only about seeing the Lord's hand in the work but also about the burden on the Lord's servants to give their best effort, and especially to heed counsel. In a self-effacing way, Elder Faust had taught Hal that he wasn't going to do his job for him. In addition, by sharing the painful story of his own failure to act on President Kimball's repeated instruction, he gave an implied warning. Hal determined to increase his responsiveness to the Brethren's counsel, even when it seemed to be mere advice rather than a clear command.

 I felt the power of prophetic foresight today. In the Executive Committee meeting Elders Hinckley, Packer, and Monson all seemed deeply occupied by the erosion of the dollar against foreign currencies. Elder Packer said, "We must simplify the programs of the Church. The day will come that we must. So it's better to do it now, when we can be thoughtful, rather than slash when we're forced to." I had not seen the problem of a worldwide, growing Church financed by dollars losing their buying power. In this, and other things, they gave quiet advice, never demanding we comply, but repeating the advice over and over. With that spur, I made a series of moves to increase the power and reduce the costs of our programs. (September 5, 1978)

> If you and I will study the scriptures and pray and tune our hearts and ears, we will hear the voice of God in the voice of the people that He has sent to teach and guide us and direct us.
>
> —TALK, APRIL 7, 1985[2]

ELDER PACKER'S MENTORING

With Hal's appointment as Deputy Commissioner, he came into close and frequent contact with Elder Boyd K. Packer. Elder Packer was, both educationally and professionally, a product of the Church Educational System, having earned a doctorate from BYU and served as the senior administrator over the seminary and institute programs. As a member of the Executive Committee of the Church's Board of Education, Elder Packer met with Commissioner Holland and Hal twice each month.

This frequent contact with Elder Packer wasn't new for Hal. He had attended these Executive Committee meetings as president of Ricks College. Moreover, Elder Packer had visited Rexburg many times while the Eyrings were there, notably when the Rexburg East Stake had been created and he had asked Hal's opinion of candidates to preside over the new stake. But being located at Church headquarters meant that Hal could see Elder Packer not only in occasional board meetings but also privately, with a focus on particular projects and questions.

Hal sought such a private meeting just a month after arriving in the Commissioner's office. That day's journal entry summarizes the detailed instruction he, Joe, and Stan received after rehearsing a presentation they were preparing to make to all of the Church's regional representatives[3] and General Authorities. The meeting was set to occur three weeks later, in connection with general conference.

In the late afternoon, Joe, Stan, and I made a presentation to Elder Packer. He listened to what we expected to present to the regional representatives, taking notes in the half light. When we asked for his comments, he said, "Do you really want feedback?" We said, "Yes," knowing how frank he can be. He walked to the front, began by telling a mission-field story as illustration, and then told us for forty minutes how to redo our message. His directions were to present seminary as the most powerful tool the priesthood leaders have to promote missions and celestial marriage. When Joe said that might offend other auxiliaries and even the General Authorities who would be listening, Elder Packer said, "Don't worry about politics or people. You just please the Lord. He has little trouble with His servants' being too strong. Most of His difficulty is in getting them going." Much of Elder Packer's concern was that we say how much more powerful daily teaching is than weekly. And he said, "Half the problems in the Church occur because the members don't know the gospel."

As we stood digesting his suggestions, he came back in and said, with a smile, "I just had a thought on the elevator. Make the presentation yourselves. You have the stewardship. Prepare so much that you work through at least one night. Have it criticized in at least a two-hour rehearsal. Then rewrite it completely. That may produce the excellent teaching you must exemplify for seminary." (September 7, 1977)

The journal records the seriousness with which Hal and Joe responded to each of Elder Packer's instructions, from being personally involved in the presentation to rehearsing and rewriting it. Hal worked through more than one night while traveling to and from the South Pacific, where he toured schools and saw firsthand evidence of the value of daily seminary instruction in the lives of students in Fiji, Samoa, and Tonga. He and Joe also determined to involve a group of seminary students from the Salt Lake Valley so that the regional representatives and General Authorities could have a similar experience.

My jet lag came back again at four this morning; that's when I got up for a dress rehearsal with the seminary students for our regional representatives' seminar on Friday. The sleepy students put their heads down on their desks while Joe Christensen and I went through our parts under the concerned eye of Elder Holland. (September 27, 1977)

The benefits of precisely following Elder Packer's instructions were realized on Friday, September 30, the day before the start of general conference. President Kimball opened the training meeting for regional representatives and General Authorities with a powerful address on missionary work, emphasizing the responsibilities of each member of the Church. That night Hal reflected on the presentation that he, his colleagues in the Commissioner's office, and the well-prepared seminary students made after President Kimball's address.

Our students shone during our presentation, as they answered questions from the scriptures, some asked by regional representatives in the audience. After the seminar, Jeff Holland saw Elder Boyd K. Packer in a crowd. Elder Packer, who criticized our earlier version of the presentation, smiled at Jeff, licked his right finger, and put an imaginary mark on the imaginary scoreboard in front of him. His approval made my heart warm. (September 30, 1977)

As a result of Hal's faith-fulness to counsel given in situations such as this one, Elder Packer recognized in him a worthy pupil, and the two formed a close working relationship, one facilitated by, but not limited to, their regular interactions in CES meetings. Elder Packer went out of his way to teach Hal,

BOYD K. PACKER AND HAROLD B. LEE WITH HAL AT HIS 1971 RICKS COLLEGE INAUGURATION

and Hal paid special attention. He found Elder Packer's mentoring to be like that of his mother, Mildred: the counsel you got was pointed and sometimes painful, but well worth the price paid.

During the morning, I spent an hour with Elder Packer and Commissioner Holland. I asked a question at the end of Elder Packer's presentation which brought a smile from him and a quiet comment, "That's a pretty good question from a guy no smarter than you." His answer taught me that "treating every member of the Church equally" means meeting his needs in a way appropriate to his or her needs and country, not imposing the same chapel designs, the same organization structures, or the same programs on everyone everywhere. Giving a member in Peru what is preferred on the Wasatch Front can be giving him less than giving him a simpler building and program suited to him. And it can cost a lot more. (January 11, 1978)

***

In the Executive Committee of the Board, we discussed a quick decision made by an officer of the Board, without asking for advice. Elder Packer leaned over to Elder Monson and whispered, "There is safety in counsel." (March 16, 1978)

A PROJECT FOR MEXICO

In August 1978, President Marion G. Romney, Second Counselor in the First Presidency, invited Hal to his office. He asked Hal, who had been at Church headquarters for one year, to serve under Elder Packer on a task committee for the First Presidency. He praised Elder Packer this way: "He's right for the task. He's an educated man. And he's got horse sense. That's more important."[4]

The task of the special committee headed by Elder Packer was to plan for the educational needs of Church members in Mexico, whose numbers were growing by tens of thousands each year. Hal's fellow committee members included William R. Bradford, a member of the Seventy with responsibility for Mexico, and F. Burton Howard, the Church's legal counsel in Mexico City.

> We will come from every nation and many ethnic backgrounds into the kingdom of God. And that prophesied gathering will accelerate.
>
> —TALK, OCTOBER 5, 2008[5]

Hal joined Elder Packer and these brethren for a tour of Mexico in late September of that year. As during a similar trip the year before, Hal was inspired by the growth of the Church and the goodness of its members in Mexico. Elder Packer taught him the significance of bringing thorough data and unbiased analysis to bear on questions that would ultimately require inspiration to answer.

By example in a committee meeting, Elder Boyd K. Packer taught me how to listen and teach with soft questions. And in a phone conversation afterwards, he taught me that neither politics nor personalities should limit the search for the Lord's preferred solution when the salvation of men is concerned. (September 1, 1978)

***

Elder Packer introduced our discussion today by saying, "When we have full information, we will be agreed." And he proceeded to ask hard questions and make assignments to be sure we got full information. He asked us to be frank, and so I ran some risks by asking some hard questions myself. I spoke freely. (September 18, 1978, Mexico City)

Hal used mathematical modeling techniques, learned as a graduate student at the Harvard Business School, to project the needs for Church education in Mexico and the costs of providing it. Though he had done similar analysis for the Select Committee seven years before at Ricks College, this time he ran the models on a computer, determined to use the latest analytical technology. Battling to master the computer while simultaneously gathering and analyzing data made the work that much harder, but he felt the importance of investing for the future.

Having completed an initial computer analysis in October, Hal spent November and December writing a report for the committee to present to the First Presidency. His hopes of finishing before the Christmas holiday proved vain, though he felt gratitude for Elder Packer's continued support and confidence.

> I said to Elder Packer: "Does inspiration come more easily for administrative problems or for helping individuals in their struggles?"
>
> He replied: "He seems to let us struggle and work on all the problems we face."
>
> —JOURNAL, SEPTEMBER 27, 1978

As we ended our five hours of discussions about Church schools in Mexico, Elder Packer asked me to write another draft of our final report by tomorrow. He and Elders Bradford and Howard had ranged so broadly in our discussion that I'll be challenged to catch enough that we can agree tomorrow, the last day before Elder Bradford returns to Mexico City. Elder Packer knew we needed unity and that I needed help; he called on himself to close with prayer, asked for unity, and then said, "Bless Brother Eyring as he writes for us. He is a man susceptible to revelation. We've seen that in his life." I hurried to my office. (December 19, 1978)

The work continued in the new year. Hal put in long hours on the report, even as he and his colleagues traveled to collect the data needed to support the analysis and recommendations. But extraordinary effort yielded dividends that went beyond the report itself. Those included a deepening friendship with Elder Packer, increased appreciation for prophetic direction, and growing enthusiasm for the work of Church education.

 I began at six this evening to write the report about Mexico. At just before two I went to bed. (Thursday, January 11, 1979)

***

I wrote the fifth draft of the report to the First Presidency about Mexico by eight. My secretary Connie Sherwood was typing as I pulled on my coat for the dash to Elder Packer's office. He liked the work enough to call members of the committee, one in Mexico, to hear it. I went home to sleep at one, with the sixth draft on Elder Packer's desk. By the sixth draft, spiritual help came. (Friday, January 12, 1979)

***

Elder Boyd K. Packer called quietly to me, through the motel door, at five thirty this morning. He talked about Mexico with Commissioner Holland and me after we'd shaved. As we left Elder Packer's room, he invited us to pray with him. Near the end, he said, "We'll take rebuke and instruction if we're wrong. We love the truth." (Friday, January 19, 1979)

***

Kathy and I sat in the beamed-ceilinged kitchen at Elder Packer's. She visited with Sister Packer while he and I worked on the committee report to the First Presidency on Mexico. As we left, Elder Packer coaxed three large geese with grain. They had flown in to visit his geese, pheasants, and peacocks, all housed in an aviary. All but one: as he showed me his shop in a barn, one peacock flew out by me, its wings whirring like a giant pheasant would sound. The Packers were kind. (Monday, January 22, 1979)

**

The Executive Committee asked their hardest questions of us during budget review. I take that as sincere interest. "Whom the Lord loveth, he chasteneth." (Wednesday, January 24, 1979)

**

Elder Packer created a Mexico Educational Council today. He handled potentially sensitive feelings faultlessly. On the flight back to Salt Lake City, he left his seat to come back to me. As he taught, he described the quiet force God puts in the world for good: humble visiting teachers in a country and parents conducting family home evenings. And then, after twenty minutes of such stories, he said, "Sometimes, when I'm on my knees, I feel almost crushed to the floor with gratitude that I have a Father like that." (Wednesday, February 28, 1979)

HITTING STRIDE IN THE COMMISSIONER'S OFFICE

In May 1979, Hal was approached again about the deanship of BYU's college of business. He and Jeff Holland both felt that too much lay ahead of them in religious education to break up the team. The journal records the confirmation of that decision, received through prayer:

The answer came clearly to my mind, not as a voice, but unmistakable. It was, "You'll have to work hard to know as much about leading the schools, seminaries, and institutes of the Church as you do about business." I take that as assurance I must work to qualify for my present job. (May 30, 1979)

Hal's work apparently qualified him not only for his present job—supervision of seminary, institute, and Church schools—but for other special assignments. In addition to Elder Packer's Mexico committee, he was asked to join Jeff Holland in defining the role of the Church

Educational System in the Church at large. He also received assignments to think and write about religious education curriculum, with special emphasis on young people. One of these assignments came to him as a member of the Church's Sunday School general board, to which he was called in 1980. Though the additional assignments made his already busy schedule the more so, they sparked his interest and confirmed the feeling that he was in the right place.

The black and blue paint was still wet on my large charts when I walked to the Executive Committee meeting at two. I only had thirty minutes to describe our analysis and plans for all the international programs. After I was done, Elder Packer said, "I've never seen anyone get so much from charts in so little time." Elder Hinckley, the committee chairman, said, "What you've presented today, and at the last meeting, is the type of analysis we've needed for a long, long time." They asked me to rethink the main assumptions of all our overseas programs. I was too tired, after the meeting, to begin again, but I'm starting to feel the excitement of the new challenge. (December 14, 1979)

Hal also saw evidence that he had been divinely prepared for his work as Deputy Commissioner of Education. Even during the years in rural Rexburg, his assignments and travels had led him to think broadly about the world and its future. And the interweaving of his current assignments seemed to be more than coincidental, as he wrote while attending a meeting of the Black & Decker board at the Biltmore Hotel in Santa Barbara, California.

During the Black & Decker strategy meetings today, the talks were focused on the United States economy and on the social and economic futures of nations around the world: Japan, Brazil, Mexico, Thailand, and the countries of Europe. I found myself making notes about what it meant for the Church. And that led to this thought: The Lord may have known I would leave Ricks College to take a worldwide assignment. The appointment to the McCulloch board was clearly miraculous. And the miracle seems to have more purpose now. (October 18, 1979)

A similar confirmation of the divine design in his work came six months later, during a trip to visit seminary and institute leaders in Asia:

I awoke in the hotel room in Tokyo feeling that I had received this message: It is no accident that I am responsible for the seminary and institute curriculum of the Church, for the youth curriculum in the Sunday School, and assigned to special materials for youth from the First Presidency. The Lord has given me those three assignments simultaneously so I can make a special contribution to my family and to the Church. (May 6, 1980)

A TEST OF FAITH

Hal was set apart as a member of the Sunday School general board by Elder Hugh W. Pinnock, his dear missionary friend, shortly after returning from that trip to the Far East in May 1980. As Elder Pinnock set Hal apart, he blessed Hal to be effective through "great changes" that would come in his life, and to be relieved of his anxieties and make "magnificent contributions." Kathy sat nearby, holding six-month-old Elizabeth, a long-awaited first daughter.

While traveling in Texas the following week, Hal received word from his office that Elder Pinnock wanted him to call. When they connected, Hugh said, "I felt something when I set you apart to the board. We need to talk." They arranged to meet two days later. The journal records the gist of their conversation then.

Elder Pinnock said, with great seriousness, "I felt that you would have a major, difficult change in your life as I set you apart." I told him that I had felt a spiritual confirmation of that part of the blessing. I asked if I should feel a foreboding. He said, "Oh, no, that change will be difficult, but positive, very positive. Until I gave you that blessing, I felt sure you would be the next Commissioner of Education. Now, I'm not sure. Perhaps it is something else, some other call." (May 21, 1980)

Elder Pinnock's reference to "the next Commissioner of Education" had its roots in the announcement, made several weeks before, that Jeff Holland would replace Dallin Oaks as the president of BYU. It was natural to assume that Hal would succeed Commissioner Holland. He was the most senior of the operating executives reporting to the Commissioner who wasn't presiding over a Church university or college. And, thanks to his experience at Ricks and the preceding three years supervising the seminary and institute programs and Church schools, he had firsthand knowledge of all the major arms of CES—higher education, primary and secondary schools, and religious education.

But Elder Pinnock's statement, "I'm not sure," proved prescient. The Board didn't immediately appoint a new commissioner, and Hal was left to wonder. June passed with no word. In July, Hal began to pray more fervently that his will in the matter would align with heaven's. On a Friday in mid-July, he received an answer to his prayers.

Near the end of the day, I finished reading the Book of Mark. I then locked the door and prayed. I felt three impressions about the uncertainties in my life: that I would be tested by the way the Board of Education will pass by me as they choose a new Commissioner of Education, as would occur if they chose Bruce Hafen, the president of Ricks College; that I should be pleasant, supportive, and dedicated to my assignment; and, that I will be moving to a new assignment in the East, probably in business or government and within the year. I appreciated the lifting of my vision and the help it will give me to be generous. (July 18, 1980)

The Board's decision in August to appoint Hal as "acting" Commissioner seemed to bear out his impression about being passed by. The way he learned about the temporary assignment fit the apprehension of being tested. The summer ended with no word about his role in the Commissioner's office, even as he conducted meetings on Jeff Holland's behalf. At the beginning of August he left with the family for a summer vacation on the Hill. Upon returning, he spent his first morning back in the office reading and responding to accumulated correspondence. One letter in the stack informed him of his new, temporary responsibility. Oral confirmation didn't come for another week, when Elder Gordon B. Hinckley, executive chairman of the Board, mentioned it in an August 21 meeting.

> I have come to understand that to try our faith is not simply to test it but to strengthen it, that the witness which comes after the testing strengthens that faith, and that God's preparation includes in the plan for deliverance the timing that will best strengthen our faith.
>
> —TALK, AUGUST 20, 1996[6]

Two days before, Elder Packer had called Hal to his office to respond to Hal's request for counsel on a seminary matter. After reassuring Hal regarding a decision that he, Joe, and Stan had made, Elder Packer shared ideas about a talk he was preparing for delivery at BYU. The following day, he invited Hal back. Hal sensed he was there for reasons that went beyond the talk.

Elder Packer asked me to his office again today. He'd done two complete redrafts of his talk for BYU next week. In addition, he had pages of other ideas written and redrafted but not yet woven into the talk. His masterful sermons are the result of labor. And his phone rang every two minutes. He took some of my suggestions down in notes. But I was impressed that I was there to be taught. The talk is about success not being measured by position or wealth. (August 20, 1980)

Elder Packer continued to involve Hal in the painstaking talk preparations. When he and Kathy heard the talk delivered the following week to four thousand BYU employees and their spouses at the Marriott Center, it was a fourth reading for Hal, though significantly different each time and in the end polished beyond his expectation. He was deeply moved:

I cried as the Spirit bore testimony to me. So did Elder Packer, near the end, something I've not seen before. (August 27, 1980)

In the ensuing days, Hal carried on with the usual juggling of professional, family, and ecclesiastical assignments. In addition to doing Saturday projects, attending Sunday Church meetings, and celebrating the Labor Day holiday with Kathy and the children, he worked on a general Sunday School writing assignment, something Elder Packer was helping him with.

On Wednesday, September 3, Hal attended the monthly meeting of the full Board of Education, including all three members of the First Presidency. One item of business caught him by surprise, as Hal recorded later that night:

President Kimball put his arms around me and whispered in his husky voice, "I'm very proud of you." The meeting had just ended in which the Board had elected me Commissioner of Education. Elder Monson had made the motion, saying, "I move it, with great enthusiasm." Then, Elder Packer said, with a smile, "Well, if you're for it, I'll second." (September 3, 1980)

The unexpected new assignment would change the course of Hal's professional life. He would not be leaving Church employment as he had supposed. But perhaps more important in the long run was a spiritual insight Hal gleaned. As his feelings of surprise and relief at being named Commissioner yielded to introspection, he saw that the long, hard experiences of the summer had been designed for his benefit. The designers of those experiences included the Lord's servants, particularly Elder Packer, as Hal recognized that night in the journal:

> I had not expected it. Although I had seen hints, my experience after prayer on July 18 convinced me that I would not be chosen. That humbling experience had moved my feelings from some irritation to complete acceptance that I would support happily whomever the Board named. That hammering of my ego to proper size was helped by my being invited to hear Elder Packer's talk three times and then in its final delivery. After the second interview, I realized with a shock that Elder Packer knew who would be the Commissioner and yet he kept asking me to hear a talk teaching that money and position have no bearing on real success. My only explanation for my July 18 experience is that, like a much smaller version of Abraham and with only my ego to sacrifice, I was being tested. (September 3, 1980)

nephhw, Mark, sometime last week, forced her out of
our double's match this morning; within an hour she'd
sent a replacement, so I played six sets. Result: I
soaked my elbow in a tub of hot water propped on the
table in the breakfast room at grandpa's, while I watched
the b   ng with the boys. Annette served the whole

17

INCREASE LEARNING

A wise man will hear,
And will increase learning;
And a man of understanding shall attain unto wise counsels.
—PROVERBS 1:5

It didn't take Hal long to appreciate Jeff Holland's work as Church
Commissioner of Education and to understand why he had wanted
a strong deputy, someone who could think strategically and move
the Church Educational System toward long-term objectives. The
Commissioner, Hal quickly learned as he assumed that role, spent
much of his time reacting to individuals whose urgent needs couldn't
wait. Fortunately, the Spirit guided in that kind of interpersonal fire-
fighting as well as in strategic analysis and decision making, as he
noted after one of his first days on the job:

> At one point, I had one General Authority on one line and
> another on hold. A man was waiting outside my office with a
> personal disaster, and yet I felt peace and satisfaction in the
> midst of tumult. I knew it mattered, and I knew the Spirit was
> helping. (October 1, 1980)

Hal was blessed to have strong, experienced associates with whom he shared a common vision of the future of the Church Educational System. But the new duties of the Commissioner filled his professional and personal plate to overflowing. In addition to his work with the deacons quorum in the Bountiful 48th Ward, he continued to serve on the general Sunday School board, for which he was drafting a new handbook and leading weekend training meetings, often outside of Utah. And with the addition of Elizabeth to the Eyrings' family of four increasingly independent boys, the complexities of home life had never been greater. Hal typically took the bus to work so that high schoolers Henry and Stuart could have his car to get to early-morning swimming workouts and late-afternoon tennis matches. For them, that meant picking Dad up at the office when he worked past the last bus departure.

> At the end of the workday I left my office for Sunday School board. I went home twenty minutes after midnight, with a completed third draft of the Sunday School Handbook. And with a cold coming on.
>
> —JOURNAL, OCTOBER 14, 1980

HARD DECISIONS

As he had at Ricks College in 1971, Hal assumed his new leadership role in CES during a time of global economic and political difficulty. In 1980, the year of Ronald Reagan's election as President, the United States and much of the world was plagued by high inflation and unemployment, an Iranian hostage crisis, and an increasingly expensive Cold War with the Soviet Union. Hal saw the effect on businesses from his position on the board of McCulloch, whose sales of chain saws declined by 40 percent as financially strapped customers postponed purchases in the hope of better times ahead.

The Church faced economic constraints at a time when the need for education had never been greater. The population of young Church members was growing rapidly, thanks largely to a boom in convert baptisms, particularly in Latin America and Asia. In the United States, pressure to build Church schools came as a result of a general trend toward secularism and recent judicial decisions to force racial desegregation via busing. Hal observed the pressure on LDS students firsthand during an October 1980 trip to Los Angeles, where one of the most aggressive busing schemes had been mandated.

I spent a long day learning about the problems in the Los Angeles public schools. I saw a chapel that priesthood leaders want to lease to a private school. I also visited a private school. It's crammed into the house and bungalows which were the home of the movie comic Stan Laurel, of Laurel and Hardy. And then I ate supper with a driver of the buses students must ride to integrated schools. I finished the night in four home evenings of families whose children are being forced to ride buses. (October 27, 1980)

Hal's heart ached for the schoolchildren who spent hours each day on buses and whose parents could not afford expensive private school tuition or relocate to areas beyond the busing mandate. But he felt that creating Church schools wasn't the answer. In addition to the financial impracticality, there were spiritual reasons for Church members to remain integrated in their communities. The Brethren had instructed the Saints throughout the world to build Zion where they were. Elder Bruce R. McConkie had made the point powerfully three years before, in an address to Church members in Lima, Peru:

We are living in a new day. The Church of Jesus Christ of Latter-day Saints is fast becoming a worldwide church. Congregations of Saints are now, or soon will be, strong enough to support and sustain their members no matter where they reside. Temples are being built wherever the need justifies. . . .

This then is the counsel of the Brethren: Build up Zion, but build it up in the area where God has given you birth and nationality. Build it up where he has given you citizenship, family, and friends. Zion is here in South America and the Saints who comprise this part of Zion are and should be a leavening influence for good in all these nations.

And know this: God will bless that nation which so orders its affairs as to further his work.[1]

Hal sensed that the fiscally prudent thing, denying the members' request for private Church schools, was also the right thing spiritually. His continued study during the second day of the Los Angeles trip confirmed that impression and gave him courage in addressing priesthood leaders in the evening. The presiding authority in that meeting was Elder Vaughn J. Featherstone of the Seventy.

My day included going with students as they were bused twenty-five miles, attending superb classes in an integrated public school, hearing a school superintendent describe the chaos of starting school under court orders, and walking over the school of a private operator who must find millions to buy land to handle the growth of his Pacific Palisades private school.

In the evening I spoke to priesthood leaders. They came to the Santa Monica Stake center from the San Fernando Valley, Orange County, and all over Los Angeles. I prayed before that I would be able to do three things: teach them the truth; build their faith in their leaders in the priesthood; and help them accept that the Church would not give them Church schools. Elder Featherstone asked them to sustain and accept that decision of the Board. I shed a tear and so did he to see them all raise their hands. (October 28, 1980)

Though Hal didn't mention it in the journal, Elder Featherstone made a promise to those disappointed priesthood leaders. "If you will support this decision," he said, "the busing problem will be resolved." At the time, this statement seemed bold, almost reckless. Public school desegregation had been mandated by the California State Supreme Court, and a popular proposition to limit the court order had been declared unconstitutional. Yet, less than six months later, Elder Featherstone's promise was fulfilled when the State Supreme Court revisited the issue, let the popular proposition stand, and effectively ended forced busing.

Though the economy would gradually rebound, the need to focus financial resources on the construction of chapels, temples, seminaries, and institutes required the closing of forty Church schools. Nearly all were in Mexico and the countries of South America, where the Church was growing rapidly. Providentially, the public schools in those countries had improved since the founding of the Church schools. Like their counterparts in Southern California, the members in Mexico and South America faithfully sustained the Brethren's hard decision.

> There will come times when the Lord's prophet will ask us to do more with less. Knowing that will come, we must and will find ways to improve and to innovate that require little or no money. We will depend more upon inspiration and perspiration to make improvements than upon buildings and equipment.
>
> —TALK, SEPTEMBER 18, 2001[2]

IDEAS OLD AND NEW

As in his other Church Educational System assignments, Hal could see evidence of a divine hand in his work as Commissioner. Experiences and insights from his time in Rexburg and the Deputy Commissioner's office prepared him for this new role. In particular, the years he had spent imagining and modeling the future of Church education proved invaluable. Yet heaven kindly kept him from making too much of his knowledge, as he observed in the journal after an important meeting in early December:

> I said to Kathy this morning, "I slept more on the night the Teton Dam broke." My presentation to the Church Coordinating Council was over by nine fifteen. I spent the day working and wondering why I'd had things taken from my memory that I'd planned to use in the question and answer period. My answer may have come late in the day. Elder Maxwell, who had been in the meeting, said, "Your presentation raised issues we may not

have been ready to put our arms around. You were certainly frank. It was near profound." All that suggests he thought I'd said enough, or more. Perhaps that's why I couldn't remember other things I'd wanted to add. (December 3, 1981)

The following spring brought a change in the journal. The preceding ten-plus years of entries had been only left-margin justified, and most had at least one typographical error, typically an overstrike of a single letter and occasionally an entire x-ed out word. Each letter had its own visual character—some broad and dark, others wispy—a telltale sign of keys struck with varying force on Hal's portable manual typewriter. But the entry for Friday, April 10, 1981, was markedly different: right- and left-justified, typo-free, and machinelike.

Hal had been tinkering with computers since his Stanford years. Back then, he joined other faculty members in queues for the university's massive mainframe computers, which could perform research analyses far faster than even slide-rule aces like Hal's father, Henry. As Deputy Commissioner, Hal had gained access to the Church's smaller but even more powerful minicomputers, manufactured by Digital Equipment Corporation, the company he would have monitored had he gone to work for Harvard's General Doriot rather than taking an academic career path. It was on these minicomputers, still hulking machines by today's standards, that he built his first models of CES growth.

More recently, the Church had given him a portable personal computer, a "luggable," that allowed Hal to tweak his growth models at home. He had also purchased his own desktop machine, a Radio Shack TRS-80, on which he used a program called VisiCalc to keep the family budget, along with a daisy wheel printer. Both Stuart and Matthew joined Hal in learning to use these new machines. Hal and Stuart took a course together in BASIC programming; when Stuart became fairly proficient, Hal lured him away from his part-time job as a Hotel Utah busboy to build more-advanced growth models (on Hal's dime, rather than the Church's).

Hal's personal interest in computers and technology not only facilitated his CES work, it also drew the attention of the Brethren. He was assigned to participate in a Utah Board of Education study of a statewide computer network for faculty members, students, and parents. He also found his mind drawn to the potential use of satellite technology in the Church.

Yesterday, I began to get an idea of what the Church's satellite system might contribute. For two hours, I wrote a draft about the ideas. It was still so rough that I printed just one copy from the computer and took it to my meeting of the Church Audiovisual Committee. I felt an urging to read it in the meeting, despite an almost equally powerful feeling of fear. When Elder Ballard invited me to read it, he said, "Teach us." That scared me more, but as I read the Spirit touched me enough that my voice broke at one point. Afterward, Elder Didier said, "Thank you for the inspiration." And Elder Ballard convinced me to leave the rough draft with Elder Paramore for distribution to the Committee.[3] My understanding of it is still misty, but I know the Lord has prepared an opportunity related to the growth of the Church, the small numbers of living prophets, the need for

> President Hinckley called. He was able to give me instructions quickly because of letters I'd written to him yesterday, describing alternatives and making a recommendation. The letters were improved by calculations from Stuart's computer program. Stuart came in again today to work on a new one.
>
> —JOURNAL, APRIL 6, 1982

CHURCH BUILDING WITH SATELLITE DISH

members to know the gospel, and the satellite system. (February 23, 1984)

Hal's awareness of technology trends and the potential benefits to the Church allowed him to imagine exciting possibilities. It also qualified him for inspiration and assistance from heaven-sent helpers.

On the flight to New York, a member of the Church with his own telecommunications company insisted on sitting next to me. He spent the five hours designing a two-way interactive teaching system with me, using television, computers, and radio. That unusual good fortune buoyed me up on the all night flight to London. (January 9, 1984)

***

Selective perception works. Since I'm working hard on the use of high technology in education, everyone I see and everything I read suggests ideas about innovation. It may be more than selective perception; heaven may be steering what I need my way. Or it may be both. Visitor after visitor to my office brought more help. (May 24, 1984)

SERVING THE BRETHREN

In his new role, Hal had to balance his personal exploration of emerging technologies and ideas for innovation with the administrative responsibility of representing the Brethren in all matters of Church education. Working with them was a pleasure, notwithstanding the difficulty of the challenges they faced together.

Despite the Brethren's kindness, Hal felt impelled to serve them with everything he had. Doing that, on top of other professional and family responsibilities, sometimes required burning the candle at both ends.

I was so tired from late-night computer work that I slept on my office floor for twenty minutes. Maybe some of the fatigue was from frustration. Arrangements I'd made for the First

Presidency came undone because I'd failed to be sure everyone who might decide to change things knew what the First Presidency had decided. Most pain in organizations comes from someone not getting the word. (April 14, 1981)

***

I was called into a meeting of the First Presidency today. Because I had expected the President's secretary to discuss the item with them, I had not read it carefully. That led to an error, which I caught as I spoke. But I thought I sensed their disapproval that I had not done my homework. The feelings of chagrin and determination to do better have stayed with me. (July 14, 1981)

By giving his all with pure motives, Hal qualified for extra help. He recognized it as it came. His journal records many divine interventions, such as this one:

I had a piece of paper in my hand as I left for an appointment with Elder Ballard. On it were instructions for what I was to tell him. As I sat in his office, I felt impressed that I shouldn't say anything about the matter but that CES administrator Dave Christensen should handle it by talking to another man. I learned later that Dave was talking to that man at the very moment I had the impression, had learned the data on the sheet were wrong and would offend Elder Ballard, and was thinking, "Oh, how can I stop Commissioner Eyring from saying anything to Elder Ballard?" (May 1, 1981)

Hal met more frequently than ever before with the senior

> In a series of meetings, I met with six members of the Quorum of the Twelve and talked on the phone with a member of the First Presidency and the President of the Quorum. That, and phone calls with other General Authorities about difficult questions, left me feeling I'd had a glimpse of heaven in the way they treated me, each other, and the problems we addressed. Some of the problems gave me a glimpse of another place.
>
> —JOURNAL, FEBRUARY 15, 1985

Brethren. Observing their wrestles with important and often diffi-cult decisions increased his already high regard for their penetrating insights and pure hearts. He saw firsthand their compassion for the members of the Church and their confidence that the Lord would move the work forward according to His timetable, no matter how great the apparent obstacles.

Elder Hinckley leaned across his desk and said to the Executive Committee: "I see no way we can help these people financially, and yet I remember the story President Lee told." And then he recounted a time when President Lee declined to help some members of the Church who had unwisely invested, worried about it all night, and then said to his counselors the next morning: "Yesterday, Harold B. Lee spoke. Now, today, the Lord will speak." And they sent help. That led us to find a way to help some people in difficulty. I felt a confirmation that it was right in the meeting and again when I called the man with the good news. (March 20, 1981)

***

President Kimball conducted the Board of Education and Board of Trustees meeting this morning. When Elder Hinckley concluded his report of a trip to Russia he said, "The Lord will have to make some major changes before our work can go for-ward." Very mildly, President Kimball said, "He'll do that, but in His own time, don't you think?" (June 3, 1981)

Hal continued to enjoy what he felt was a particularly close relation-ship with Elder Boyd K. Packer. They traveled together occasionally, and they interacted frequently at Church headquarters. As before, their association blended the professional and the personal. The common theme, whether they were teaching seminary and institute instructors in Brazil or carving wood in Utah, was an emphasis on sacred matters and the joy of shared spiritual experience:

Elder Packer said to our CES administrator for Brazil, who was about to start a training meeting: "You may never have

Brother Eyring and me here again. You can teach each other anytime. We'll take the time this morning and leave what we have." And so for four hours we taught. And as he spoke, an idea would come to me and he would say, "Brother Eyring now has something to say." And while I spoke, I knew what he would say next. (October 28, 1981)

***

Elder Boyd K. Packer invited me to his office when I said that I need guidance on my duck decoy carving. As I sat down, he pulled a finished decoy from under his desk and said, "Here, you can keep this as a guide until you finish yours." And then he sketched the next cuts on my carving, cradling it against his chest. He smiled and wiped sawdust from the vest of his blue suit as we talked about the Church Educational System. (May 31, 1982)

***

Matthew handed me the phone at six this morning and said, "If you take this, you'll be talking to Elder Packer." We talked about a problem he'd been on for hours and planned to stay with for the weekend. This must be one of the few weekends he'll be home this year. Yet he's working, full blast. (April 30, 1983)

***

My writing gave way at 2:30 to a pleasant interview with Elder Boyd K. Packer. He met me at my car, where he examined the carving the boys and I have started. He suggested we consider painting the flowers, the birds, the house, and the temple in the style of some Swiss and Austrian carvings. And then we talked in his office. In the midst of the long conversation, he paused and spoke in a tone that I know means he spoke for more than himself. He promised me a spiritual gift of ideas forming in my mind beyond anything in my previous experiences. And he promised that I would not be confounded by intellectuals. (November 8, 1984)

TAKING COUNSEL AND RECEIVING INSPIRATION

In his work with the senior Brethren, Hal occasionally earned their unreserved praise, a sign that he was learning to think as they did. He recorded one such triumph in early 1982:

> I went from reading Mosiah with the family to writing a letter for the Board meeting today. When I read it to the Board, Elder Monson said, "You should have been a diplomat. You told him what you wanted but made him feel good." After the meeting, President Hinckley suggested I make the salutation more formal, saying, "This letter will be referred to again." (March 3, 1982)

Yet even when he hit the mark, heaven kept Hal humble, providing evidence that he was only one of many receiving divine help.

> At the end of a long day, I took the pages I'd written to a member of the Quorum of the Twelve. He was joined by another member of the Quorum. It was clear that they had arrived at the conclusions of what I had written sometime last week. That gave me great reassurance that I was, as one of them said, "bang on," but it reminded me again that prophets can have staff work done by the Holy Ghost just a little faster than by me. (March 20, 1985)

Hal was also humbled by occasional impressions to disagree with his colleagues in the work, including the Brethren. He recorded such an instance after a meeting of the Executive Committee of the Board of Education, which included several members of the Quorum of the Twelve:

> The Executive Committee Meeting, held in the high-ceilinged First Presidency conference room, dealt with issues of such substance and complexity that I had to speak, always with some difference from the others who spoke. That made for a long afternoon. (April 26, 1983)

Hal made a careful study of the right way to express a contrary opinion. Sometimes, he found, discretion—including silence—was the better part of valor. Often, though, he felt impelled to speak, even at the risk of giving offense and incurring disfavor. In those cases, he learned, the key to success was speaking with pure motives. Only then could he and his colleagues attain the unanimity necessary to receive inspiration.

Elder Thomas Monson said quietly, "Well done," at the end of our presentation to the Executive Committee of the budget for the Southern hemisphere. I didn't wade in with my opinion in a discussion among the Brethren. I remained silent because I judged my view would raise heat but not persuade. (September 22, 1981)

***

My productive writing was interspersed with one high and one low. The high was a pleasant 30 minutes with President Hinckley. The low was to learn secondhand that I had displeased a senior General Authority. It took some careful reflection to be sure I was sad about it for the right reasons. (March 15, 1982)

***

My meeting with the First Presidency tested my ability to give counsel without stepping over the line to "steadying the ark." After hours of reflection, I am at peace. (March 24, 1982)

***

I felt the influence of the Holy Ghost in our Board meeting. The Board made decisions which can dramatically improve the quality of seminary and institute teaching around the world for years ahead. I've learned to know the signs: spirited and clear discussion, and then perfect unanimity. (May 2, 1984)

In seeking to increase his value as an adviser to the Brethren, Hal took lessons from Kathy and the children. That was true even of little Elizabeth, whose outward sweetness overlaid a surprising inner determination. He discovered the strength of that determination at a poignant time. In the spring of 1982, when Elizabeth was two and a half, Kathy miscarried the pregnancy of a hoped-for sibling and playmate for Elizabeth. At a difficult, unexpected moment, Elizabeth taught Hal a lesson in giving counsel.

I dressed Elizabeth, telling her we were going to the hospital to get her mother. When she resisted me at two different points, I pushed. Kathy had told me tales of her independence, but I knew my charm and charisma would prevail. They didn't. At last, when she decided to do what I had been ordering, she carefully picked up a toy, helped me play with it, and then did what I asked. She seemed to be showing me, "I'll do it with you, not because you give orders." Spirits arrive in this world with personalities. (April 2, 1982)

Hal also learned from miracles of assistance that he recognized as divine gifts. He found that, as he respected the agency of others and exercised faith, even the most difficult dilemmas seemed to resolve themselves. He attributed those miracles of resolution to their divine source. He also observed how heaven honored the efforts of those who were doing their best, notwithstanding the inadequacy of the effort to the particular task.

I saw evidence again today that God steers his kingdom even while we have free agency. I've been working for days on finding a way to correct one of our people. Today, I learned that a member of the Quorum of the Twelve had, without any contact with me, persuaded the man to ask for help. I have no doubt that I am responsible for what I do, but I also know that Heavenly Father has many ways to get his work done: he is not at the mercy of my performance. (April 22, 1982)

***

Amidst crisis after crisis, a lesson kept being taught me: "God is very kind, very patient." I saw it in a decision of the First

Presidency and Quorum of the Twelve reported in a memo. And that colored the way I reacted to some failures of people which ordinarily would be easy to condemn. But today I seemed acutely aware of how slow Heavenly Father is to reprimand more than we can bear. (July 5, 1983)

> People in authority may call you to a position of leadership. You may be given great powers to discipline and to reward those you are to lead. But your power to lead them will at last be granted by their choice to follow you, without compulsion.
>
> —TALK, APRIL 23, 1998[4]

Increasingly, Hal recognized that he was the beneficiary of the same divine forbearance and generous assistance. One powerful confirmation came in the fall of 1983, at a time when the Church Educational System was facing serious challenges in an overseas location. A message received as the day dawned confirmed that the Commissioner of Education was being honored by heaven, yet still had things to learn about accessing the full power available.

Yesterday, I woke with two fully formed messages in my mind. They helped me today. One was this: "The difficulties you've had in your work were not necessary. Had you been petitioning me for guidance, I could have warned you." And the other was the contents of a letter I am to compose to our CES men in one part of the world. It will solve all the problems which seemed to be overwhelming us. The ideas were not in a dream, but they were in my mind as if delivered in my sleep. I have had this experience before, I recognize its source, and I am grateful for it. (October 17, 1983)

nephew, Mark, sometime last week, forced her out of
our double's match this morning; within an hour she'd
sent a replacement, so I played six sets. Result: I
soaked   elbow in a tub of hot water propped on the
table   breakfast room at grandpa's, while I watched

18

LABOR DILIGENTLY

For we labor diligently to write,
To persuade our children,
And also our brethren,
To believe in Christ,
And to be reconciled to God;
For we know that it is by grace that we are saved,
After all we can do.
—2 NEPHI 25:23

Hal's term as Commissioner, from 1980 to 1985, was a time of test-ing both at work and in his personal life. Among the notable chal-lenges was the passing of his father, Henry. In the summer of 1981, the Eyring family learned that their patriarch had little time to live.

Henry had battled cancer off and on since the late 1960s. The can-cer initially took hold in the prostate, at a time when Henry was nurs-ing Mildred through the final months of her life, teaching a full load of courses during the day and sleeping at the hospital on most nights. He delayed seeking treatment for himself until after Mildred's passing. The cancer spread gradually but persistently through the 1970s, not-withstanding aggressive treatment with innovative therapies, including radiation treatment at Stanford University while Hal and Kathy were still there.

SOMETHING ABOUT CHARACTER

By the time the Rexburg Eyrings moved to Bountiful in 1977, it was clear that Henry would ultimately lose the battle. Yet he fought on, greatly aided by his second wife, Winifred, whom he married two years after losing Mildred. In his final six months he authorized his doctors at the University of Utah to administer one experimental form of treatment after another. He would neither admit the inevitability of defeat nor alter his schedule of teaching, travel, and research. Among the standing duties he refused to relinquish was a monthly lunch with his sons, Ted, Hal, and Harden.

My father showed me something about character today. He was having trouble with the arrangement the doctors have used to carry away his urine. He was to see the doctors at two for repairs. But he came to lunch at the University of Utah Panorama Room, where faculty and public could see the moisture on his pants. He's working hard to convince the University he is able to continue full-time teaching at eighty. He must have been both embarrassed and concerned for his career, but he came to lunch because he'd promised his sons. (July 9, 1981)

Henry's courage and good humor from July to December of 1981, when he finally succumbed, left an indelible mark on the family members, friends, and medical professionals who served him during that time. Hal's journal records the kind of stories that proved memorable and moving for so many.

During the day, Winifred called to report the doctor's prognosis, delivered today, that my dad won't live until Christmas. When we talked about my giving him a blessing, I said I had no car to get to their home. She said, "Oh, tonight would be better anyway. You see, he's teaching his class at the university now." I smiled. (July 17, 1981)

***

As I walked into the University of Utah hospital, I met one of Dad's Chinese co-workers. Winifred told me, when I got to the room, that Dad and his associate had just finished a research proposal. Dad lacks a sense of the tragic: he was writing research proposals when he almost died of a heart attack last night from the strain of chemo-dialysis. I talked with Winifred, Ted, Elder Neal Maxwell, and Dad—when he was conscious—about another operation. I felt impressed, as did Winifred, that we should go ahead. After six hours, they came to wheel him to the operating room. He smiled at me. I think my being there helped. Then he began to sing, "Yo-ho-ho, fifteen men on a dead man's chest." The attendants all laughed. But they shrugged in puzzlement when he said, very distinctly, and his arms folded on his chest, "Jim Hawkins." I'll have to get out my copy of Treasure Island, but I think Dad was remembering the boy in that story. Dad couldn't have seen the book since he was twelve. And then he said, "Wheel out the dead man," with a smile. An hour later he was out of surgery, with the operation successful.

Dad's former stake president and the secretary to the First Presidency, Francis Gibbons, came by to see him before the surgery. He brought a book inscribed to "one of the greatest men I've known." He also said that Dad's grandfather had been one of only two men not General Authorities invited to a revived School of the Prophets in St. George in about 1880. That pleased Dad. And then President Gibbons said, holding Dad's hand, "I love you." Elder Maxwell had said that to me earlier. I've learned that those facing the unknown appreciate your presence, your praise, and the words, "I love you." (July 31, 1981)

***

At noon I spent an hour helping my dad go home for a visit. I thought he was too tired to know I was there. He took at least twenty minutes to walk into the house, with me under one arm and Winifred under the other. He spoke only once, as I left. He said, "I couldn't have made it without you." I did for an hour what he's done for me over my whole lifetime. (August 27, 1981)

***

Kathy and I visited Dad at his home. For the first time in weeks he was quick and pleasant in conversation. He gave me advice about my talk to the faculty of BYU tomorrow. And he said to Kathy, "Hal wouldn't be half the man he is without you." Kathy said that proved how sharp he was. (August 31, 1981)

In the final months of Henry's life, the pain intensified. But so did his spiritual learning experiences, many of which he shared with Winifred and his sons as they watched over him through long, tortured nights. Henry often sought solace in prayer, sometimes even dragging himself out of bed to kneel on the floor. Ever a teacher, he shared with Hal the lessons learned.

I drove to my father's house at eleven to stay for the night. We talked after he woke from several hours of pained sleep. Dad, who speaks like a child now, had been terribly troubled. He said, in a clear, almost youthful voice, "I've got the answer. God doesn't want to break me down. He wants people with courage. I'm so grateful for the plan." (September 17, 1981)

After months of all-night vigils by Winifred and her stepsons, the end finally came at Christmastime. Aggressive chemotherapy had de-

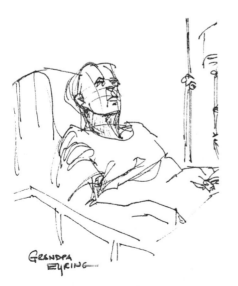

GRANDPA EYRING

stroyed Henry's kidneys, and an innovative attempt at internal dialysis, with filtering of the blood occurring inside the abdominal cavity, was failing. Winifred, Ted, Hal, and Harden conferred with Elder Maxwell, who had blessed Henry several months before with "time to complete some things." Elder Maxwell suggested that Henry's work in this life was now complete. Yet Hal's father managed to teach him more lessons before leaving.

All of our family went with me to see Dad, who was suffering, in the hospital. I stayed for over five hours, as we wrestled with the decisions about whether to try more dialysis and blood transfusions. Elder Neal A. Maxwell had given him a blessing at noon, before we arrived. By phone, he helped us decide. His counsel to me was, "There is so much more he can do over there." (December 24, 1981)

***

I sat with Dad and Winifred late into the night. In his delirium, he swore a little at the pain, including an expression I remembered from childhood, "Oh, hell, HAL-y." Later, as if talking to himself, he said distinctly, "Study hard, then next day do the best you can." And very late in the night he cried, "May this hour pass." (December 25, 1981)

> I hope you'll also remember, as I always will, the scientist Henry Eyring on his knees, when the questions that really mattered yielded to the method for finding truth he'd learned as a little boy at his mother's knee in Old Mexico. This was long before he took the train to Tucson, and Berkeley, and Madison, and then on to Berlin and Princeton to use the scientific method to create theories that changed the scientific world. What he learned on his knees brought him peace and changed my life.
>
> —TALK, NOVEMBER 18, 1986[1]

The following afternoon Henry died. Hal didn't speak at his father's funeral, which was attended by nine members of the Quorum of the Twelve Apostles and the three members of the First Presidency. After the funeral, which Hal described in the journal as "the finest I've ever attended," he dedicated the grave. "My voice broke only once," he wrote:

That was when I felt the Holy Ghost remind me, as I prayed, that my father had called out to his "Papa" in his greatest pain. I prayed that the memory of Dad's kindness and strength would strengthen us someday. (December 30, 1981)

Evidence of Hal's fondness for his father appeared for months afterward in the journal, in the form of more than a dozen press clippings and letters from Henry's scientific and ecclesiastical colleagues. There was also this entry, made on a Sunday night two months after his father's passing. It suggests a beginning to the end of grieving:

I spent the afternoon preparing two talks, gave them in our family meeting, and then again later. The first was given to Lowell Bennion's[2] ward in East Millcreek. The second was to President Hinckley's study group, all missionaries from England in 1934 through 1936. I talked about my father and laughed more than I cried. (February 28, 1982)

"JUST START WRITING"

Desk landscape
March 29, 1974
Henry & Matthew's pencil holders

Hal would continue to benefit from his father's insights and counsel throughout his life, particularly in times of uncertainty and struggle. He increasingly encountered such struggles as he wrote for public audiences. Paradoxically, Hal enjoyed writing when it was for himself, as in the journal, or for one of the Brethren. In those instances, he often felt inspiration flow, and with it, words beyond his own:

Bishop Brown[3] barely had five minutes to read the draft I'd handed him. I'd been working since five a.m. but only writing for ten minutes. To my amazement, he approved and said, "You don't know how much I depend on you." (December 10, 1982)

***

I rushed back to my office to labor on the document for Elder Maxwell.[4] Five minutes before he called, I felt a complete change in what we should do. And when I sat down with him, he proceeded to name the nine main ideas which had come to me, none missing, and none added. (June 15, 1984)

Hal felt similar inspiration in leading discussions on the Brethren's behalf, particularly in classroom-style settings, which drew on his teaching experiences at Stanford and Ricks. But when the audience became a group rather than an individual, he felt greater pressure, just he had in Palo Alto and Rexburg. And the sense of pressure intensified when the audience was the Brethren themselves. In their presence, he found that presenting ideas was better viewed as an opportunity to learn than to teach.

My nervousness peaked between one and two, as I sat in the Quorum of the Twelve's room listening to them teach the nine members of three Area Presidencies testing a new decentralization of the Church. When my turn came to lead a case discussion, I felt an assurance come that all would be well, and it was. Each member of the Area Presidencies participated, making always wise and sometimes witty suggestions. Only Elder McConkie remained of the Twelve to observe. He said afterwards, "I have only one complaint. You didn't let me sleep." And then, also with a warm chuckle, he said, "I felt I was learning at the feet of Gamaliel."[5] (October 10, 1984)

***

I began my presentation to the Quorum of the Twelve today using a scripture as my theme. My tongue was clumsy. That lasted throughout the hour. What they said and asked was inspired. And they supported our religious education both by praising it and pledging to help it. But, unlike some other times in my life where I've been blessed in performance, my ability seemed constrained today. Hours later, I began to see the blessing: by speaking less well, I listened more, learned more, knew that I was in the presence of prophets, and had one of the great experiences of my life. I'd forgotten that it's hard to get your ego fed and learn at the same time. (April 13, 1983)

As the Brethren assigned Hal to speak in increasingly large and formal settings, such as BYU devotionals, held in the 23,000-seat

Marriott Center, the pressure at times became almost unbearable. At Stanford and Ricks, he had appreciated the need for preparing thoughtfully so as to qualify for inspiration. But those forums were much smaller, and even a talk to a larger audience, such as a group of Ricks College students gathered for a devotional, wasn't broadcast or published. A BYU devotional, by contrast, would reach a much broader audience, particularly when the speaker was the Church's Commissioner of Education.

Thus, Hal began to write out talks that before he might have delivered from only an outline, supplemented by impressions of the moment. Now he started his preparation sooner, and he worked harder and worried more. The labor of talk writing became reminiscent of hard days and nights spent in the bathhouse on the Hill, trying to produce research papers and books for the sake of earning tenure at Stanford.

> At ten, my secretary carried the completed manuscript of a chapter to the Deseret Book Company.[6] The relief I felt triggered resolutions: I'll get drafts started early for every talk and every writing assignment. Before you have a draft, there is a terror that nothing will come. After you have a draft, it is like holding wood or clay in your hands and knowing you can hack and shape. My dad used to watch me fuss and read "just one more book." He would say, "Just start writing."
>
> —JOURNAL, JULY 2, 1984

In writing for devotionals and other Church-related audiences, Hal had the advantage of addressing spiritual subjects and drawing upon eternal principles, rather than spinning business theories. Yet the very seriousness of the subject matter and the faithfulness of the audience created a weight of its own, which pressed on him more than ever. Inspiration came, but at a higher price, and sometimes not until the last moment. That can be seen in a series of journal entries from early 1983 during the days leading up to a BYU devotional address.

 Each conversation during the day seemed to teach me something about the talk I'm trying to prepare for Tuesday's devotional at BYU. I'm not sure if Heaven gives the inspiration when you need it or that the terror of having to say something publicly makes you listen better, or both. But the help arrives. (February 3, 1983)

***

When I got home at two in the morning, Stuart didn't mention his successes at a high school debate tournament in Phoenix. He just got to work bridge building[7] while I wrote at the computer. He came in to show me his bridge at four, saying he was going to bed. I looked up what seemed minutes later and saw light coming through the window. (February 7, 1983)

***

For the first time in my life that I can recall, the Holy Ghost left me to the end struggling with a talk. Kathy and I sat in the president's reception room at the Marriott Center while I chopped my draft of the fifth or sixth version. Numb from fear and fatigue, I stepped to the podium and began to talk. Ideas and feelings took me away from the text, and so I did what no BYU Devotional speaker but LeGrand Richards has done in years: I spoke on live television from the heart. But I did feel something happen at the end. Kathy said afterwards, "I've never heard you bear testimony with that power before." I don't

MARRIOTT CENTER AUDIENCE

understand yet. Perhaps I was allowed to struggle so long to appreciate what Henry is passing through as a new missionary in Japan; or perhaps I have not appreciated the easy help in the past; or perhaps it was to let those who heard see the difference between a stumbling Hal Eyring and the Spirit manifest at the end. Whatever, my body aches, and I am very, very subdued. (February 8, 1983)

A NEW DAUGHTER AND NEW CHURCH CALLINGS

Hal's work, with its frequent travel and special assignments from the Brethren, had always required the support of the whole Eyring family. By 1983 that included four maturing boys and three-year-old Elizabeth, who was as strong a personality as any of her brothers, as Hal recorded after a twelve-hour day at Church headquarters:

> I'd done my homework for the Sunday School Board meeting at five. That improved my mood and increased my contribution. Kathy seemed content to let me go back to the office for another computer run, even when I called at after eight. She's genuinely happy when I do something useful for the kingdom. Elizabeth was a little less happy when I called. She said, "Come on home." And she helped me hang up my clothes, as she often does, when I got there. (March 8, 1983)

In April 1984, Hal and Kathy welcomed their sixth and last child, Mary Kathleen. Kathy was nearly forty-three, and the pregnancy was a

KATHY WITH ELIZABETH AND BABY MARY

difficult one. In February she slipped and fell hard on the Eyrings' steep driveway; the fall triggered contractions, and Kathy was hospitalized briefly. She and Hal gave thanks when Mary, another redhead, joined the family in perfect health. Their joy was shared by many others who had watched over Kathy and the Eyring family during the pregnancy.

Several months after Mary's birth, Hal received an invitation to meet with Elder James M. Paramore, a member of the First Quorum of the Seventy and a former counselor in the Church's general Sunday School presidency. As a member of that general board, Hal had worked with and developed deep admiration for Elder Paramore. Hal's journal records the interview that he and Kathy had in Elder Paramore's office:

At 3:15, I met Kathy and Mary Kathleen at my office elevator, rode downstairs with them, and walked across to the Church Administration Building. Elder James M. Paramore invited us into his office. He asked if his secretary could hold Mary Kathleen for a minute. Then we knelt in his office and he prayed. He excused Kathy, interviewed me, and then invited her back into the room while he called me to be a regional representative. I am to take three regions in Northern Utah with 13 stakes. Kathy walked Mary Kathleen around the office while Elder Paramore set me apart. Among many promises, I remember that I would receive counsel on ideas about the gospel from my children. And I was promised health if I was faithful. As he spoke, I had the thought that he was speaking the exact words the Lord would use. (September 20, 1984)

> Elder Asay's wife, Colleen, called this morning. Kathy was her counselor in the stake Relief Society presidency until a few months ago. Sister Asay said, "I had a dream last night. Kathy is in the hospital. What's wrong?" When I talked with Kathy, she was touched to hear of Sister Asay's concern. I was touched by heaven's concern. And I wondered how much I could be learning from my dreams if I lived closer to the way Sister Asay does.
>
> —JOURNAL, MARCH 26, 1984

The new calling brought an end to Hal's seven years of formal service to Scout aged young men. It also meant leaving Kathy and the children on Sundays to visit with his thirteen stake presidents, located in Brigham City and Utah's Cache Valley. But Hal took joy in traveling to what he considered "protected places" where unusually faithful Saints qualified for unusual blessings. He found that meeting with a stake president in that leader's home produced a feeling of standing on sacred ground.

Hal took a minimalistic approach to directing the stake presidents.

In his usual studious way, he made many visits and asked questions to understand the conditions in each stake. But he gave little advice to the presidents, each of whom he recognized as holding the keys of leadership for his stake. That approach derived from gentle but pointed guidance he had received from his friend and mentor Elder Neal Maxwell, whom he had sought out shortly after the call to serve as regional representative. Hal expressed concern about the number of stakes for which he had received responsibility. "How can I have significant impact in thirteen stakes?" he asked. With a wry smile, Elder Maxwell replied, "You can't. That's *why* they gave you thirteen stakes."

Hal had been in his new calling for less than six months when he began to feel spiritual stirrings. Some came in response to challenging problems at work. Others resulted in decisions to reorder the Eyring family's financial affairs.

The phone brought me more problems, all interesting, and all beyond my human powers to solve. For some reason, heaven is giving me a push toward getting revelation far more than I've felt in years. (March 12, 1985)

***

In my office this morning, I locked the door and knelt down to get some guidance. I'd learned yesterday that System Industries, a company I founded, was in financial straits. I still own 15,000 shares. I asked in prayer whether I should sell part of our holdings. A clear impression came into my mind immediately, "Don't trust in the arm of flesh." By early afternoon I had all the shares in the hands of my broker for sale. And he will sell the rest of my holdings in Finnigan Instrument Company, which I also started. I believed not that I had been told what to do financially but where I should invest my attention. For years I have daily made calculations estimating the security those investments might provide, usually when I felt insecure. By switching to less speculative investments and ones where my ego is not involved, I can spend time and get assurance in better ways. Kathy sustained my decisions. (March 13, 1985)

Three weeks later, Hal was preparing to enjoy general conference, set to open on Saturday, April 6. For Hal and his fellow regional representatives, training meetings began the day before. His reveille that day came particularly early because of a matter of business between the Church Educational System and the Presiding Bishopric's office that had to be resolved before the weekend. A seven o'clock meeting set the stage for an unexpected new assignment.

At three this morning I was awakened by an uneasy feeling. I felt an impression that I should not contend against a senior person in the Presiding Bishop's shop in a meeting scheduled for seven. Because I arrived before seven at the office of Elder Maxwell and because others had not yet gathered, I was able to handle the problem quietly. Later I sat in the Assembly Hall with all the mission presidents in the world and all the regional representatives. As we came back from a break, one of the security men said to me, "President Hinckley would like to see you in his office." I walked along the wall of the temple grounds, on South Temple, in the bright sunlight. I reviewed the problems he might want to discuss with me, but none seemed worth his time on the day before conference. And then I thought, "If it is a call, it has to do with the Presiding Bishopric."

President Hinckley greeted me, sat behind his desk, and said, "Do you have any questions about your faith and worthiness?" And then he said, "Tomorrow morning your name will be presented as first counselor to Bishop Robert Hales in the Presiding Bishopric." A tear came to my eye. I realized that God had been gentle with me again and I said, "There is no man who would be easier for me to follow than Elder Hales." Then, as if he had all the time in the world, President Hinckley talked pleasantly about how he'd enjoyed being fifty-one. (April 5, 1985)

In one respect, Hal's call as a General Authority would simplify his life, making his professional work and Church calling one. But his service in the Presiding Bishopric would be a time of challenge and personal growth beyond anything he'd yet experienced.

19

THE BISHOP AND
HIS COUNSELORS

And inasmuch as ye impart of your substance unto the poor,
Ye will do unto me;
And they shall be laid before the bishop of my church
And his counselors, . . .
Such as he shall appoint . . .
And set apart for that purpose.

—DOCTRINE AND COVENANTS 42:31

W hen Hal told President Hinckley that there was no man easier for him to follow than Elder Hales, he meant it. As both of them would say that weekend in general conference talks, they had known one another nearly all of their lives. In 1932, the year before Hal's birth in Princeton, New Jersey, Robert D. Hales was born in New York City. The Saints of New Jersey and New York occasionally gathered to hear from Church authorities visiting from Utah. If such a meeting were held on a day other than Sunday, it might be followed by a softball game, in which "Bobby" Hales demonstrated the athletic prowess that inspired realistic visions of playing for his favorite team, the New York Yankees.

At the University of Utah, Hal and Bishop Hales both partici-pated in intercollegiate athletics, the one high jumping and the other pitching for the baseball team. Both also joined the Air Force Reserve Officer Training Corps. A year older than Hal, Bishop Hales graduated first, in 1954. He then went to flight school and became a jet fighter pilot. Though Hal finished at Utah in 1955, his tour of duty in the air force was shorter, and so he was the first to enroll at the Harvard Business School, in 1957. Bishop Hales arrived the next year with his wife, Mary.

In addition to seeing one another on the HBS campus, Hal and Bishop Hales interacted as priesthood leaders. While Hal served as a counselor to Wilbur Cox in the New England District presidency, Bishop Hales presided over the district's Weston Branch. The district was made a stake in the spring of 1960, as Hal was graduating with his doctorate and preparing to go west to Stanford. Bishop Hales was called to serve as a counselor to President Cox, the new stake president.

> Bishop Eyring and I have known each other since boyhood. He is a man of God. Sitting in this audience today is Wilbur Cox. Both Bishop Eyring and I have served as counselors to him in a stake presidency. He molded us in a way in which we have been blessed.
>
> —BISHOP ROBERT D. HALES[1]

Hal and Bishop Hales had also spent the preceding four years serving together on the general Sunday School board, Hal as a board member and Bishop Hales as a counselor in the Sunday School general presidency. Hal had observed and felt impressed by Bishop Hales's work as a General Authority.

I was still at my desk at six, writing but also listening through the wall to the meeting Elder Hales was conducting with his regional representative from Germany and German-speaking Switzerland. I could feel the mantle of his office on Elder Hales, who I knew twenty-five years ago as a baseball player at the University of Utah and a student a year behind me at Harvard. (April 1, 1983)

***

Elder Robert Hales came to my office at nine, when I called him. I'd finished a draft proposal for a major change in the Sunday Schools of the Church. President Pinnock had asked

Elder Hales, his counselor, to prepare it. And Elder Hales had asked me for a draft. He and I worked, first at a table and then at my office computer. Others of the general board joined us. I ran what must have been the tenth draft at noon, just before I rushed to a tennis match with my brother Harden. (October 14, 1983)

As his second counselor, Bishop Hales chose Glenn L. Pace, who headed the Church's Welfare Department and had a strong background in accounting and finance. Neither Bishop Hales nor Hal had worked closely with Bishop Pace before his call to the Bishopric. But they quickly came to appreciate not only his business sense but also his moral character.

> Bishop Pace was never calculated; he had rock-ribbed integrity. He wouldn't pretend on anything.
>
> — 2012 INTERVIEW

SUSTAINING THE BISHOP

President Gordon B. Hinckley, then Second Counselor to President Spencer W. Kimball in the First Presidency, invited a sustaining vote for the new Presiding Bishopric in the first Saturday session of general conference. After the second session, he set Hal and his fellow bishopric members apart. President Hinckley noted that he had chosen to do so on April 6, the anniversary of the Church's founding.

The members of the new bishopric went to work immediately. On the Monday morning after general conference, they gathered with the other General Authorities and their spouses for a special sacrament meeting on the top floor of the Salt Lake Temple. With them were most of the 188 mission presidents of the Church, who had been called to Salt Lake City for training in the use of a new set of missionary discussions. Kathy joined Hal, who sat next to Bishop Hales. Later that night Hal recorded a special experience shared with his old friend and new priesthood leader. Together they found special meaning in 2 Nephi 9, in which Nephi's younger brother Jacob teaches the doctrines of the Atonement, Resurrection, and Judgment.

As I sat on the east stand, waiting for the sacrament meeting to begin, the thought came to me that in such settings, with the presidents of 30,000 missionaries, it would not be remarkable if the Brethren should speak in tongues. I asked Bishop Hales for his Book of Mormon and whispered to him, "I feel impressed to look at 2 Nephi 9. Don't ask me why." He read over my shoulder.

After the sacrament, Elder Asay began to speak with the greatest power and majesty of language I had ever heard from him. When it had continued to happen, speaker after speaker, I realized that I was witnessing a miracle.

In two meetings during the afternoon, our first with the Presiding Bishopric staff, Bishop Hales said, "My counselor gave me this scripture today." And then he used 2 Nephi 9 in ways I had never understood before. (April 8, 1985)

In addition to sharing spiritual insights, Hal learned from Bishop Hales's executive skills and style, garnered in four of the world's most innovative corporations. In the fifteen years between his graduation with an MBA from the Harvard Business School and his call as a General Authority in 1975, Bishop Hales had risen through the ranks at Gillette to become president of its Papermate division, moved to Max Factor as a vice president, and presided over first Howard Hughes's television network and then personal-care products maker Chesebrough-Pond's. He had what Hal called "street smarts," the ability to predict and respond effectively to situations likely to catch even

BISHOP ROBERT D. HALES

well-educated and highly intelligent executives by surprise. In fact, these street smarts were the product not only of intuition and past experience but also of discipline in getting firsthand understanding before taking action. Bishop Hales was a practitioner of one of President Thomas S. Monson's maxims: "Get the facts, or the facts will get you."[2]

Along with world-class business skills, Bishop Hales had also gained unusual experience as a Church leader. His military and business assignments had taken him to areas in which the Church was small and needed strong priesthood leadership. In addition to serving as bishop of the Boston Stake's Weston Ward, Bishop Hales presided as a bishop in Chicago, Illinois, and Frankfurt, Germany; he also served as a branch president in Albany, Georgia, and Seville, Spain. Later, he was the regional representative for Minnesota and Louisiana (where he met Hal at a youth conference in the early 1970s). Then, in ten years as a General Authority, he presided over the London Mission and had responsibility for the Europe Area, an assignment in which he worked closely with Elder Thomas S. Monson supporting Latter-day Saints in the Soviet Bloc countries of Czechoslovakia, East Germany, Hungary, and Poland.

On top of unusually strong business and ecclesiastical experience, Bishop Hales brought great energy and enthusiasm to the Presiding Bishopric. Hal's record of their first week together, including the Monday that the General Authorities typically take off from work to rest from their weekend stake conference assignments, reveals his admiration for the Bishop.

My first set of Presiding Bishopric meetings were a humbling revelation. Bishop Hales taught me more about the value of directness in one of our meetings today than all the leadership books I've ever read. The mantle of his calling is a thrill to see. (April 9, 1985)

***

Bishop Hales found time to meet with us between meetings to give us our assignments within the Bishopric. I was touched both by his kindness and the confirmation I felt that the tasks I was given were ones I'd been prepared for by circumstances unknown to Bishop Hales. (April 11, 1985)

***

Kathy and I fixed pancakes, eggs, and bacon for breakfast. I drove John and Matt to school, and then took Elizabeth to the library. We drove home for her to change. Then I drove around Bountiful to pick up her classmates and dropped them at Linda's Little Learners.

By ten I was on the phone. And by eleven I was at the office. Bishop Hales had urged we spend Mondays at home, but I didn't have the hang of it. After hours of interviews and phone calls in my office on the eighteenth floor, the Bishopric went to the temple. (April 15, 1985)

LONG HOURS

The members of the new Presiding Bishopric shared a passion for their work. They often worked not only on Mondays but also during July, a month reserved to allow the General Authorities to rest from their travels and weekend labors. Late nights were even more common for this Bishopric.

Hal felt the burden as a father of young children. By this time, Henry and Stuart had left for college. But teenagers Matthew and John were still at home. And Elizabeth and Mary, respectively ages six and one when their father joined the Bishopric, presented Hal and Kathy with the female version of the child-rearing opportunities and challenges they had faced when he was bishop of the Stanford Ward.

Bishop Hales had no children at home, but his family history of heart troubles and personal history of hard work meant that he too paid a price for the long hours at the office and the globe-trotting travels. Still, along with Bishop Pace, they were committed to giving their all.

My twelve-hour office day began with chairing a committee for the University of Utah and ended in a conversation with Bishop Hales, who quit at seven because his doctor called him at five to complain. He was in the hospital until Friday. (September 17, 1985)

***

After I dropped Matt off at Temple Square to work on the grounds crew, I prepared for my eight o'clock meeting on the Church Membership Information System and then a Bishopric meeting, our first for several weeks. I'm supposed to be on vacation, but the Bishop seemed to appreciate the chance for us to all be in a room again. (July 15, 1986)

***

Bishop Hales left for San Francisco. He will conduct a stake conference over the weekend, but he'll start with a round of golf at the Olympic Club in San Francisco on Friday afternoon. That's the first break in his 70-hour weeks I've seen in a long time. Bishop Pace left for Canada by noon. That left me with an afternoon to ponder my talk for conference. (March 18, 1988)

Hal's new call weighed heavily not only on him but also on Kathy. A journal entry she made one month into the new assignment reveals her sense of awe and concern, but also her gratitude for blessings received in Hal's absence.

This month has been quite eventful. At the last April conference, Hal was called and sustained to be the First Counselor in the Presiding Bishopric. It came as quite a surprise to us both. I must admit, however, that for several weeks before his call I had been reading Elder Maxwell's books as well as Elder Packer's and had felt, more strongly than usual, my failings and shortcomings. These feelings were intensified when Hal was called to be a General Authority on Friday, April 5, by President Hinckley. Hal called afterwards on the phone, and I could hardly recognize his voice as he told me. I was in a haze for the rest of the day.

So many people, especially the other Brethren and their wives, were so kind, expressing their best wishes and congratulations about Hal's calling, and I kept feeling so unworthy and nervous about so many things, not the least of which was Hal's travel schedule. He has been so good to help out around the house, and I wasn't sure I could handle everything on weekends without him.

Last weekend was Hal's first conference assignment, to Winslow, Arizona. He left Friday night, and while we all missed him, we were really blessed while he was gone.[3]

COMPLEMENTARY PERSONALITIES

Hal's relationship with Bishop Hales was close and constant, but not tension free. In fact, in important ways, it was tense by design. For all of their similarities of background, Bishop Hales had chosen in Hal a first counselor of markedly different training and temperament.

The athletically gifted son of a New York artist, young Bob Hales had grown up dreaming of pitching for the Yankees. Until injuries ended that dream at the University of Utah, it had seemed within his reach; he starred at Utah and spent several summers playing semi-professionally. When the door closed on a major league baseball career, Bob joined the air force ROTC unit on campus. After graduating, he served four years as a jet fighter pilot. While Hal used complex equations to painstakingly calculate the likelihood of a nuclear bomb going off when it shouldn't, Bob had to make his life-or-death calculations literally on the fly.

Hal's mathematical background and dinner-table discussions with PhD-trained parents prepared him for great success in the classroom at the Harvard Business School. Bob, a year behind, also did well in his formal studies. But he truly excelled in the job market, where he was recognized by prospective employers as one of the great marketing minds of his generation. He could paint innovative ideas for new products and marketing schemes as though working with his father's brushes and canvas. Rather than relying solely on the static, dated numbers provided by accountants, he developed a feel for a company's operations and customers by going to the field himself. At his own request, his initial assignments at Gillette included working factory floors and stocking drugstore shelves with razor blades. It was there, on the front lines of business, that he gained the practical insights about the company and its customers that allowed him to rise to the top so quickly.

Hal, meanwhile, had decided that it was the study and teaching of business, rather than business itself, that motivated him. While Bob Hales put his holistic intuition and take-charge style to work in one major corporation after another, Hal lived the deliberate, analytically conservative life of a scholar. He put those tendencies to good use at Ricks College, where falling enrollments required

> **So, you're going to be a *professor*?**
> —BOB HALES TO HAL EYRING, UPON HEARING OF HIS DECISION TO ENROLL AS A DOCTORAL STUDENT, 1959

frugality measures, and in the Commissioner's office, with its need for long-term planning and organizational controls. Bob and Hal had much in common, including deep respect for one another. Still, for two graduates of the same prestigious MBA program, their paths and personalities could hardly have been more different.

> **So, you're going to be a *salesman*?**
> —HAL EYRING TO BOB HALES, UPON HEARING OF HIS DECISION TO GO TO WORK FOR GILLETTE, 1960

Bishop Hales understood these perspective and personality differences when he prayerfully chose Hal as his first counselor. In addition to being sure of the inspiration behind the call, he foresaw the benefit of complementing his creative, can-do style of leadership and decision making with a more measured, cautious one. During his ten years as a General Authority, the Brethren had called on him several times to scale back or refocus the Church's business operations, among them large welfare farms and the Utah & Idaho Sugar Company. He knew something of Hal's similar experiences with Ricks College and the Church's hospital in Idaho Falls, which in 1975 had become part of the new Intermountain Healthcare Corporation. Hal's cautious perspective might help the Bishopric avoid unjustified expansion, a natural tendency in almost all large organizations.

In the temple meeting of the General Authorities, Bishop Hales was asked to bear his testimony. He talked of the love he had for his father. Then, he said that he'd been in the room where we were, praying to know whom he should call for his counselors. Then, with emotion in his voice, he said: "I want you to know that I know the Lord loves my counselors."

—JOURNAL, MAY 1, 1986

Bishop Hales had also observed the Brethren's concern for sound judgment in the Church's affairs, especially those that consumed tithing funds or affected its public reputation, as did so many of the operations reporting to the Presiding Bishopric. He knew the Brethren expected well-communicated proposals that anticipated and mitigated every conceivable risk. To this end, Hal was an ideal teammate. Beginning with the 1971 report on the future of higher education in the Church, Hal had spent the preceding decade and a half studying, debating, and writing up major proposals for the Brethren's consideration, often taking the analysis beyond what most executive decision makers would consider the point of diminishing returns. That had been the case in the writing Hal had done on behalf of the Sunday School general presidency.

In the Bishopric, Bishop Hales benefited from Hal's complementary traits. Hal tended to challenge any bold new idea, at least upon initial introduction. They would spend more time arguing its merits and demerits than Bishop Hales would have with a less analytical, skeptical, and courageous counselor. The consequence was often tense debate and, sometimes, frustrating delay. But the end result would be

May 31, 1984
Thursday

I wrote in the Atherton
guest house of the
Johnsons, looking down
on the trees and drive
of our first home.
Elizabeth and Mary
Kathleen watched me
blow out candles on my
birthday cake, after a
dinner by Trudie. The
Holy Ghost helped me
teach a Sunday School
workshop in Menlo Park.

June 1, 1984
Friday

Elizabeth and I played in
the pool and then
worked on a talk. Uncle
Gary came back from
Los Angeles again today
to h
time
Altos

June
Satur

I tov
infla
Mar
com
purp
matc
hair
Stua
siste
and
danc

June 3, 1984
Sunday

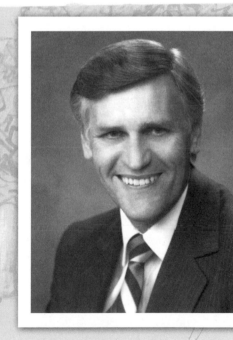

THE PRESIDING BISHOPRIC

Kathy, Elizabeth, and Mary Kathleen were dressed and
packed early for our drive from Atherton to the San Jose
airport. On the flight home, a stewardess made a bullseye
with a glass full of orange juice on my lap. It was so cold
and complete a soaking that I laughed for the rest of the
trip. I used bags to shield the results as I got us to the car.

a finely crafted proposal for action that the Brethren could easily comprehend and fully trust.

In the Bishopric's debates, Hal pushed as hard as anyone. Yet he knew when to defer, as Bishop Pace would recall: "He would argue very, very convincingly. He wouldn't give when it came to principle. But he could always sense when the Bishop had heard our opinions, and he would not overstep."[4] With time, Hal grew to appreciate not only Bishop Hales's respect for the Brethren to whom they reported but his ability to discern their preferences. Hal confided to the Bishop, "I've learned something through the Spirit and watching you. Often I think you're telling us what President Hinckley has told you. And then I realize that you've never seen him on the subject. But you've learned to think like him."[6]

> At the end of the day, I don't ever remember a time when they weren't supportive and didn't come together.
>
> —BISHOP H. DAVID BURTON, SECRETARY TO THE PRESIDING BISHOPRIC AND LATER PRESIDING BISHOP[5]

Hal's journal records how members of the Bishopric followed the Savior's injunction to resolve their differences quickly, while they were "in the way."[7] Sharing a desire to serve Him, they found themselves tapping into a common source of inspiration and insight. Soon the casual friendship that Hal had enjoyed with Bishop Hales over forty-plus years deepened into a bond of brotherhood.

Through our long series of discussions about a new custodial program for the Church, the tension rose. Just before six thirty, I was alone in my office and knelt to pray. The strong impression came to me to go to Bishop Hales's office. When I did, I found him there, at his desk. And I talked with him long enough to ease the strain that had developed between us as we had wrestled over decisions, starting from opposite viewpoints. (December 19, 1985)

***

During the day, I walked to a scheduled meeting with the Twelve, paused on the doorstep, and felt constrained not to go in. I slipped into a nearby, empty office and waited until I saw Bishop Hales through the glass of the door. I found that he had felt, for some reason he couldn't explain, not to go in either. We learned that staff had invited us incorrectly and that it would've been difficult for us and the Twelve had we walked in to that particular meeting with their having no way of knowing why we were there. (August 27, 1986)

***

As I prayed in the First Presidency meeting, I saw in my mind the Presiding Bishop, who was at the University of Utah in a trying situation at that very minute. My heart went out to him. That brought emotion to my voice and a plea for the Bishop that probably puzzled both President Benson and President Monson. Bishop Pace understood. The picture I saw was of Bishop Hales as a little boy, as his father might have seen him, and what I felt was a desire to protect him. The bravest of us may look more childlike and vulnerable to heaven than we suppose. (June 10, 1988)

***

Through the two hours Bishop Hales and I talked, I felt every few minutes a clear impression that he was the Lord's Presiding Bishop. Even as I looked at his face, I saw more than a man or my friend. (November 27, 1990)

> He's the consummate counselor. It doesn't get any better.
> —ELDER ROBERT D. HALES[8]

PROVIDENTIAL PREPARATION

Like Hal's assignments at Ricks College and in the Commissioner's office, the move into the Bishopric put him in roles he'd never filled. Those included oversight of the Church's financial investments, construction of chapels and temples, and information technology (IT) operations. Yet he was well prepared, particularly for one who hadn't come up through the departments reporting to the Presiding Bishop or worked full-time in the business world, as Bishop Hales had done. For example, though Hal had never overseen a financial investment portfolio remotely as large as the Church's, he had studied investment theory as a business school student and professor. And, during his six years at Ricks, he had presided over the facilities planning and construction attendant to a doubling of the campus infrastructure. When he received an assignment to work with President Hinckley in temple construction, on top of his responsibilities for new chapels and stake centers, he saw heaven's hand in preparing him.

President Hinckley said he would look to me in the selection of sites and the construction of temples. At that moment, and in the hours afterward, I realized that I have been prepared for this assignment in recent days and in opportunities going back to a high school class in architecture. (August 17, 1987)

Hal likewise appreciated the depth of his preparation to oversee the Church's burgeoning information technology activities. It went beyond his recent work with personal computers or his late-1950s encounter with Ken Olsen's then-revolutionary DEC minicomputers. During his summer at RAND, in 1963, he had met scientists from the Advanced Research Projects Agency (later DARPA), who were conceiving what would become the Internet.[9] At Stanford, he had helped Ed Zschau create System Industries. That company made peripheral devices, such as printers, for DEC computers, which were the mainstay of the Church IT department.

Hal was blessed beyond his awareness of the technologies themselves. He sensed their application to activities of great importance to the Church, such as education and family history. As a Harvard graduate student in the late 1950s, when only visionaries such as Ken Olsen appreciated the vast potential of computers, he found himself at a social event with an IBM marketing executive who had been drinking. Learning that Hal was from Utah, the tipsy man declared, "I've just returned from Salt Lake City!" He then described visiting the Genealogical Society of Utah, forerunner of the Church's Family History Library, where he saw patrons working with microfiche and carrying card files. "I've found out why computers were invented," he exulted. "It's to do things only those people will ever want to do."[10]

> I always had the feeling that computing was going to be a very important multiplier of our powers to do the things that would matter very much in the kingdom.
>
> —2012 INTERVIEW

Notwithstanding providential preparation, Hal's initial years in the Presiding Bishopric proved to be a time of learning and stretching. As in other new assignments, much of the learning was spiritual. Through personal reflection on his performance and the whisperings of the Spirit, he was taught the value of an open mind and a soft heart.

President Benson asked Elder Bangerter[11] to pray, mentioning that Elder McConkie and his family needed the blessing of comfort.[12] That began to melt my heart, and then Elder Bangerter began to pray over me, the newest member of the council. Since yesterday I've been praying to know which applicant to choose as my secretary. No answer had come. But in that moment I felt an answer. I called Kathy from the airport, on my way to Rexburg, to tell her I'd learned something about revelation. At least for me, the problem is to get my heart softened. (April 17, 1985)

***

Last evening I felt impressed to give a man an assignment, despite his past performance. This morning I learned that he and his wife had been in the temple last night, and had prayed and had fasted in the hope that God would touch my heart. As soon as I made the assignment, the solution to a series of problems appeared. It was clear that God was guiding the whole process. (March 19, 1986)

***

Kathy returned from speaking to a conference of women in a nearby stake just as Stuart took me to the airport. President Moss, of the Ammon Stake, met me in Idaho Falls. When I got to my room at ten, I tried the advice I'd suggested in my last talk: I read the Book of Mormon, thought about my gratitude for the Atonement, and then asked in prayer if there was anyone I could help. Henry came clearly to mind and then this instruction: you could bless him if he saw more often in you an example of how the gospel will bring peace in this life. (April 25, 1987)

***

I ate lunch with former secretary to the First Presidency Elder Joseph Anderson, who, at nearly one hundred, remembers with clarity conversations he had with President Heber J. Grant. And the conversations all display President Grant in kindness and good humor. I wonder if any secretary of mine would recall me with such generosity. (December 15, 1987)

***

I spent the morning in a General Authority training meeting from eight until noon. I learned to see opportunities in place of problems. And I learned how the Savior taught by asking questions to which He knew the answers. (September 27, 1988)

INSPIRATION IN THE WORK

As Hal wrestled with the breadth and magnitude of his Bishopric assignments, he often received help beyond his own capacity. That was true, for instance, on a trip to Nicaragua. One of Hal's assignments was to inspect an uncompleted chapel in a small town called El Rosario. More than a decade before, the Church had begun work, laying a foundation and building a baptismal font. But a violent revolution and ensuing civil war had prevented completion of the chapel. With the end of hostilities, Bishop Hales sent Hal to see whether the Church could build, on the old foundation, a structure serviceable for the Saints and fitting to the local architecture.

On a Sunday afternoon, Hal and his local hosts drove the thirty miles from Managua to El Rosario and found the building lot, dusty and overgrown with weeds. Hal felt that the site and foundation might work. The next step was to find the right architectural style. His journal entry notes the inspiration that attended the search for a good model:

We drove up and down streets, looking at each building, trying to feel if it looked like the type of building the Lord would want in Rosaria. We saw block, wood, plaster, and even brick construction. But none seemed right. Finally, as we were about to leave, I said, "Let's just try this street." So, we turned left on a street which fronted the town square. We passed five buildings. And then, wedged between taller buildings was a house no larger than a child's playhouse. There was no sign of life. The rough boards above brown block ended at the tin roof. But I said, "Stop. That's it." As we looked, a young man in white shirt and tie came out of the house, walked to the car, and invited us to come inside. In a tiny room not more than 10 feet by 10 feet sat 21 members of the Church on a few chairs. The sacrament, under a white cloth, was on the only table. We listened and watched as the man conducting bore his testimony. Eyes shone with faith. As we left, the man who met us said, "The man conducting built this house. It is his. He is a carpenter. If the Church ever wishes us to build on the lot, we are ready." Among hundreds of buildings, one stood out. It was the only place in the village where the Saints of God were met in sacrament meeting. (March 11, 1990)

Though Hal frequently enjoyed inspiration in his Bishopric assignments, he had humbling experiences as well, reminding him who was really in charge. One of those came in connection with the announcement of a temple to be built in Bountiful, Utah. President Ezra Taft Benson made the announcement in early 1991, more than five years after Hal received responsibility for temple construction. To say that it caught him off guard would be a gross understatement, as he told a group of BYU–Idaho students in Rexburg some twenty years later.

Bountiful was never on the list of recommended or even possible temple sites during the time I was doing the work for the prophet of God. In the late 1980s, in fact, a brilliant man working for the Presiding Bishopric and for me prepared a list, using careful statistical analysis, of one hundred places deserving temples. I delivered it to the President. Based on the criteria we used to make that list, Bountiful, which is where my family and I then lived, would not have appeared in the second or third hundred possibilities.

Not many weeks after I sent the list of one hundred sites to the President, our son John, the one born in Rexburg's old Madison Memorial Hospital, came home from the Bountiful seminary. He announced with some enthusiasm, "A dad in seminary today told me that the Church has purchased a site for a temple on Bountiful Boulevard." I said to him with great emphasis, and some annoyance, "John, I am in charge of evaluating and buying sites for temples. If you look as if you even think that unfounded story might be true, people will believe it."

Within a day or two, my wife said that she had heard in Relief Society that the Church had purchased a future temple site in Bountiful. I told her, "Kathy, I am in charge. That is an unfounded rumor, and you mustn't even appear to believe it."

The next day in the media, the Church announced the

purchase of a temple site in Bountiful. I called Clair Bankhead, who worked with me buying temple properties and sites. I asked, "Clair, why didn't you tell me?" He said, "President Benson told me to buy it and not to tell anyone. So I did what the prophet asked."

When John came home that day after hearing the news, he said with a smile, "Now I know what it means for you to be in charge."[13]

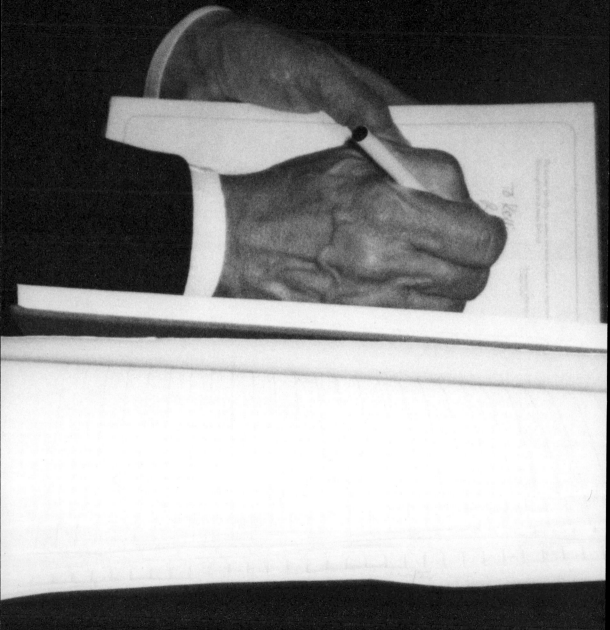

nephew, Mark, sometime last week, forced her out of
our double's match this morning; within an hour she'd
sent a replacement, so I played six sets. Result: I
soaked elbow in a tub of hot water propped on the
table breakfast room at grandpa's, while I watched

20

LET HIM HEAR

He that hath ears to hear,
Let him hear.
—MATTHEW 11:15

Hal's work in the Bishopric meant frequent meetings with the senior Brethren, particularly the members of the First Presidency, Presidents Benson, Hinckley, and Monson, as well as the new President of the Quorum of the Twelve, Howard W. Hunter. Hal had known them long enough to see their human frailties. But he had also seen in them the qualities of the Savior. And he had heard them speak as prophets. He knew that at these times they, like the Savior, rarely thundered their pronouncements or cited divine authority. Thus, from the beginning of his service in the Bishopric, he was on the alert for such moments of quiet instruction.

An important one came in the fall of 1987, during a meeting of the Investment Committee of the Church, which included the First Presidency and President Hunter. Hal and the Bishopric's team of investment professionals had just concluded a presentation of their current investment positions and strategy for the future. It was a great time to be in the financial markets. After decades of disappointing returns, the stock market had broken through to all-time highs. The year 1986 seemed to vindicate U.S. President Ronald Reagan's economic strategy of tax cuts and heavy defense spending, as the Dow Jones Industrial Average, the broadest measure of stock market growth, rose by roughly 12 percent. Then, beginning in January 1987, the market soared another 40 percent.

Like the majority of professional investment managers, Hal and his team saw little reason to doubt the sustainability of this beneficial trend. Inflation was relatively low, and government spending wasn't the only source of economic vitality: businesses were also doing well. From a long-term historical perspective, the growth seemed overdue, barely enough to compensate for the preceding twenty years of economic stagnation.

Hal had been paying the price to have an expert's opinion about the market and its future. The Church had become a large enough investor that representatives of the major investment banks regularly visited Salt Lake City. Most of these visitors, such as his Harvard Business School roommate Powell Cabot, hailed from New York. But Japanese bankers also came from Tokyo.

> From eight until almost five I attended the first Garn Institute meeting in Washington, D.C. The subject was international finance. Senator Jake Garn of Utah kicked off the program, and after that we heard the Assistant Secretary of the Treasury, assorted heads of New York and Tokyo investment banking houses, and James Baker, Secretary of the Treasury.
>
> —JOURNAL, JANUARY 12, 1987

Hal and his team likewise traveled widely in search of the best available market information.

Given his hard-earned expertise, Hal might have been tempted to ignore a conversation that the Brethren conducted among themselves after his team's presentation, which had advocated a steady course designed to make the most of the market's growth. As though Hal and his group weren't present, President Hunter turned to his brethren and said, "I've got a feeling that stock prices are little high." Presidents

Benson and Hinckley concurred, citing similar feelings. Yet the conversation seemed to be a private one. The Brethren concluded the meeting without giving any specific instructions.

Hal immediately reassembled his team back in his office and asked, "Did you hear that? The Brethren are concerned. Should we be?" Hal's team responded affirmatively to his rhetorical question. They began to discuss a strategy for selling stocks to capture the gains of the past eighteen months and limit the Church's downside investment risk. But the team recognized a problem: the Church's holdings were so substantial that selling large blocks of stock quickly could "move the market," overwhelming the normal demand from buyers. They agreed to begin selling steadily in small amounts that wouldn't have a price-depressing effect. The move out of the market didn't make sense in purely rational terms, but Hal and his colleagues decided to pick prophecy over rationality.

Several months later, on Monday, October 19, the stock market crashed. It fell by nearly 25 percent in a single day, more than any daily decline in history, including the panic of 1929 that presaged the Great Depression. The media quickly dubbed the event "Black Monday." It would be another two years before the market slowly rallied to pre-crash levels. During that time, the Church slowly reinvested, not only preserving its earlier gains but redoubling them.

Several months after the crash, the chief investment strategist for one of Japan's largest investment banks came to Salt Lake City. Through an interpreter, he said, "Of all of our major clients, you Mormons are the only ones who saw the crash

> He's the ultimate Samuel: "Speak Lord; for thy servant heareth."
> —ELDER ROBERT D. HALES[1]

coming. How did you know?" Hal could only reply, "We are led by wise men."

"THE REMARKABLE EXPERIENCE OF BEING TAUGHT BY PROPHETS"

President Benson and his counselors soon recognized what Elders Maxwell and Packer had known for the better part of fifteen years—that Hal Eyring was a good man to give an ad hoc assignment to, especially if it required writing. Though many of these assignments came on top of his regular Bishopric duties, Hal appreciated the opportunity to serve. He saw this work with the Brethren as both a blessing and a fulfillment of Kathy's vision of the kind of professional contribution he might make if his heart was right. His above-and-beyond-the-call attitude reinforced the Brethren's perception of Hal as someone who gave much and expected little in return.

Elder Hunter conducted the Temple and Genealogy Executive Council. When I made what seemed to me a modest suggestion, Elder Hunter said, after a pause: "What Bishop Eyring said makes good sense to me." From that came an assignment to write a major report, on a topic far afield from the assignment of the Presiding Bishopric. Years ago in Atherton, Kathy asked if I shouldn't leave Stanford and do studies for the Brethren. She had remarkable foresight. (May 8, 1985)

***

Last night, President Monson gave me an assignment. I delivered it to him this morning just before eight. He smiled and said, "I like the way you do things." President Benson called during the morning. As I sat beside President Hinckley in a meeting at the end of the day, I felt gratitude for the remarkable experience of being taught by prophets. (January 21, 1986)

Notwithstanding the joy of being taught by the Brethren and receiving their approbation, the work was taxing and, at times, trying. Hal sometimes sacrificed sleep to fill special assignments, only to have his work critiqued or contradicted. Always, the Brethren were supportive of him personally. That helped him accept the correction and even celebrate it.

Just before I left my office for the First Presidency meeting I prayed and felt impressed to read the 124th section of the Doctrine and Covenants. And somehow that told me to be more modest about the analysis I had done as the basis for a recommendation. When I made my presentation and then asked for guidance, they used my analysis to make the opposite decision, because they saw two issues I had missed. I was grateful for prophets, for the Doctrine and Covenants, and for that prayer. (May 22, 1987)

> We know He has placed servants to offer us both His covenants and His correction. We see the giving and the taking of correction as priceless and sacred.
>
> —TALK, OCTOBER 21, 1997[2]

Even as he learned to take correction from the Brethren, Hal came to appreciate what Kathy called "the One Sure Source" of approval. He realized that the Brethren themselves looked to heaven in judging his recommendations. Thus, serving them and the Church well required that he do the same. Hal was grateful for Kathy's support in practicing this principle even when it didn't immediately produce the praise of which he hoped to be worthy.

When I talked with Kathy after my presentation to an Executive Council, I told Kathy that I'd felt the approval from heaven but not particularly from the Brethren. She said, "Well, you've got what's best." (June 12, 1985)

> I don't think the thought ever enters his mind, "What needs to be done to be compatible with what others are thinking?" He just divines what the Lord's telling him through the Holy Ghost, and he does it.
>
> —ELDER RICHARD G. SCOTT[3]

PRESIDENT EZRA TAFT BENSON

While learning through personal reflection and inspiration, Hal continued to learn from the Brethren. Particularly in his frequent interactions with the First Presidency—at least weekly in a formal meeting with the Bishopric, and often more frequently in ad hoc meetings and personal discussions—he saw the power of priesthood keys manifested strongly, even in seemingly small matters.

That was true of the prophet of that time, President Ezra Taft Benson, whom Hal had known for almost thirty years. President Benson had shown great kindness to Hal during the lonely years at Harvard before Kathy arrived. Probably out of admiration for Henry and Mildred, whom he knew through their work on the general boards of the Sunday School and Relief Society, respectively, then-Elder Benson of the Quorum of the Twelve invited young Hal, the doctoral student, to visit his family in Washington, D.C. From 1953 to the end of Dwight D. Eisenhower's two terms as U.S. president in 1961, Ezra Taft Benson served both in the Twelve and as President Eisenhower's secretary of agriculture. During that time he invited Hal to take the train from Boston to Washington for visits that included tours of the White House and Camp David, the presidential retreat in Maryland.

Only a little more than a decade later, they were working together in the service of Church higher education, Hal as the young president of Ricks College and Elder Benson as a member of the CES Board of Trustees. Hal admired Elder Benson's zeal for education and his championing of required college courses on the Book of Mormon and the principles of American history, economics, and government.

Seven months after Hal's call to the Presiding Bishopric, President Benson succeeded Spencer W. Kimball as the President of the Church, with Gordon B. Hinckley and Thomas S. Monson as his counselors. Hal was immediately impressed by the combination of power and humility demonstrated by the new prophet.

May 31, 1984
Thursday

I wrote in the Atherton
guest house of the
Johnsons, looking down
on the
of our
Elizab
Kathleen
blow out
birthday
dinner b
Holy Gh
teach a
workshop

June 1,
Friday

Elizabeth
the poo
worked
Gary ca
Los Ang
to hear
time to
Altos.

June 2,
Saturday

I towed
inflated,
Mary
compli
purple
match t
hair tha
Stuart's
sister.
and I w
dance in

June 3, 1984
Sunday

PRESIDENT EZRA TAFT BENSON

Kathy, Elizabeth, and Mary Kathleen were dressed and
packed early for our drive from Atherton to the San Jose
airport. On the flight home, a stewardess made a bullseye
with a glass full of orange juice on my lap. It was so cold
and complete a soaking that I laughed for the rest of the
trip. I used bags to shield the results as I got us to the car.
Henry, Matthew, and John were waiting happily at home.

In the monthly meeting for General Authorities, the final testimonies were given by the First Presidency. Elder Dean Larsen[4] said of President Benson's testimony as we left: "We heard a prophet speaking as a prophet." I had felt it too. (March 6, 1986)

***

President Benson began our meeting with the First Presidency by asking, "Do you think the meeting went well yesterday?" He spoke with quiet modesty. I could hardly believe that he could speak with such prophetic power yesterday and yet be so humble today about it. (March 7, 1986)

Hal and Kathy saw President Benson's prophetic power again during the dedication of the Denver Colorado Temple, which they were privileged to attend with him.

Kathy sat directly in front of the speakers in the celestial room of the Denver Temple. I sat in the last chair on the stand, where I saw the speakers from the side. President Benson spoke in the first session from a prepared text. Then he put aside the other talk he had prepared for the second and third sessions. And those talks were completely different from each other. The first was a sweet memory of a spiritual experience in his family. He said afterwards that someone in the 1600-person audience, somewhere in the temple, needed it. In the next session, he repeated over and over again that he had a testimony of the Lord's pattern for succession in the Presidency. And then, he suddenly thundered, "This Church is true. And if you don't believe it, why don't you get out of it?" Then, he went on quietly. Kathy and I later shared the same impression: he had been told by inspiration to rebuke someone in that audience. It was a powerful manifestation of prophetic power. (October 24, 1986)

Hal learned that President Benson could be a tough taskmaster. The prophet's love for the Lord and for the members of the Church seemed to drive him to do the very best he could for them. He naturally expected the same of his colleagues, and his direct executive style could sting. Yet Hal still found himself drawn to this great priesthood leader. His prophetic mantle was undeniable. And he seemed to reciprocate Hal's love.

President Benson greeted me with a smile and the question, "Well, have you repented?" He had asked me to fix something yesterday and he hadn't forgotten. I took care of it in the rush of activities before noon. (April 29, 1988)

***

President Benson bore his testimony last today. He stood with a smile upon his face and said this: "It's been a wonderful meeting. I think it has gone on long enough. I have but one thing I'd like to say. The Lord loves you." And then he leaned forward and said with measured emphasis: "And I know whereof I speak." Then he closed in the name of the Savior. (March 3, 1988)

> I bear you my testimony that Ezra Taft Benson is a prophet of God. I bear you my testimony that he loves us. If I should not meet with him again, the last incident I will remember is his hand on mine, reaching out to thank me for holding a door. He noticed me. He felt for me. He understood me. I think that is a gift of God, not available only to a prophet but to all of God's children who exercise their faith to receive the gift of the Holy Ghost.
>
> —TALK, AUGUST 27, 1991[5]

***

President Benson greeted me as he came around the table before the Appropriations Committee:[6] "Young man, you always come to meet me, don't you?" I hadn't realized that the warmth of his greeting before each meeting must be drawing me toward him as he approaches. (March 15, 1988)

ELDER PACKER'S CONTINUED MENTORING

Though Hal was now reporting directly to Bishop Hales—and, through him, to the First Presidency—Elder Boyd K. Packer continued to be a mentor to Hal in a sweet mix of Church matters and personal interests, particularly wood carving. In both cases, the training Hal received was hands-on and in the moment, in the style of a master teacher. This personal guidance enhanced Hal's ability to contribute in his new assignment.

 I'd blocked out the morning for testing a new Church membership program on an IBM PC, but when Elder Packer called I jumped at the chance to visit with him in his office. He showed me a bird carving he is just completing; it is so real you want to touch it to see if it's stuffed and so perfectly designed that it's a work of art from any angle. He loaned me a carved Canvas Back duck as a model for one of my projects. And he gave me counsel on how to guide effective computer development in the Church. (July 9, 1986)

***

At eight I met with the Council on the Disposition of Tithes, which was defined by the Lord in the Doctrine and Covenants to be the First Presidency, the Quorum of the Twelve, and the Bishopric. From ten until two I met with the ten General Authorities who direct the work of the Temple and Genealogy departments. Elder Packer spoke, as did Elders Faust and Oaks, all with great spiritual power. In the discussion, we seemed to be laboring, and then I knew what was to be in the statement of purpose we were trying to write. Just as it came into my mind, Elder Packer called on me. He smiled, as if in recognition, as I made the suggestion. That warmed my heart; perhaps I heard what he heard. (December 12, 1986)

> I awoke from a dream in which Elder Packer asked me the question I am to answer in my talk in the Denver Temple.
> —JOURNAL, OCTOBER 17, 1986

***

Elder Packer took a minute between meetings to look at one of my carvings for Christmas and sketch out a suggestion for finishing it. (Wednesday, December 9, 1987)

***

Elder Packer called a little after six this morning. He asked if I could meet him in his office just after seven. When I walked in, he opened a brown grocery sack and pulled out a carving. Last night, despite pressures on him I can only imagine, he'd taken a piece of wood, carved a part of the design on a gift I'm using for Kathy's family, and then stained it with colors so that I could use it as a guide. And then he gave me the sack, which had tubes of the colors I would need. (Thursday, December 10, 1987)

LABORING DILIGENTLY TO WRITE

Another constant in Hal's life was the struggle of writing talks. He spoke extemporaneously often, with relatively limited preparation or undue concern. But sermons likely to be published weighed more heavily than ever. As a General Authority, he felt the responsibility of speaking to all Church members, representing the prophet and the Lord. Perhaps to compensate for his increased sense of obligation and concern, inspiration sometimes seemed to flow more freely. For example, on April 6, 1986, the one-year anniversary of his first general conference address, he received a fully formed address in his mind, though he had no assignment to speak.

 When I woke at six, I had a full sermon on the promises of God in my mind, scriptures included. I knew it wasn't that I was to speak. As the sessions went on, I realized that what I had been given was addressed by others, a nice confirmation. (April 6, 1986)

A similar gift of insight came that fall, as the next general conference approached. While preparing to perform the temple marriage of a nephew, Hal was led to Mosiah 26, which, as he noted in the journal, "doesn't seem to be about marriage."

But I was clearly told to talk to the couple from that passage, urging them to build faith in the Savior in their children, to avoid even the hint of dissension even in what they felt was a reasonable difference between them, and to pray often. And I told them that the Book of Mormon and that chapter would teach them other things if they will never stop pondering them. (September 3, 1986)

> For behold, this my church; whosoever is baptized shall be baptized unto repentance. And whomsoever ye shall receive shall believe in my name; and him will I freely forgive.
>
> For it is I that taketh upon me the sins of the world; for it is I that hath created them; and it is I that granteth unto him that believeth unto the end a place at my right hand. . . .
>
> Yea, and as often as my people repent will I forgive them their trespasses against me.
>
> —MOSIAH 26:22–23; 30

In the succeeding days, thoughts of Mosiah 26, with its promise of divine mercy for repentant sinners, even those as once-wayward as Alma the Younger and the sons of Mosiah, stayed with Hal.

I had felt since yesterday that I would be asked to bear testimony in the temple meeting of General Authorities today. I was, and it became clear that I had been given Mosiah 26 for today as much as for the marriage yesterday. The First Presidency also read my name to be a speaker in the last session of general conference. Back in our Bishopric offices, Bishop Hales and Bishop Pace gave me a blessing. As Bishop Pace spoke, a theme for the talk came into my mind. (September 4, 1986)

Even with the benefit of an inspired theme, the hope of repentance for those who seem hopelessly lost, Hal struggled through September. The journal chronicles the creation of multiple full drafts, with Kathy providing heavy editing of each:

I woke with the clear impression to discard the latest draft of my conference talk and write without even notes. In two hours at the office I wrote a new, nineteen-hundred-word draft. By six I had revised it four or five times, between interviews. At home, Kathy made editorial suggestions while I ate supper with Matt and John. (September 24, 1986)

The real test came, though, one week before general conference, when the talk had to be given to those who would translate it. For a few hours, Hal was caused to wonder whether he was teaching false doctrine. Even after receiving confirming witnesses and making the translation deadline, he would have to make truly last-minute changes.

I had twenty minutes before the First Presidency meeting to revise the talk which was due at five to the translators. Before noon, one of the Brethren came in to say that the draft of my talk touched him and yet he wondered if I might be challenged about the basic premise, which I took from a conference talk of President J. Reuben Clark. It is that the spark of faith never completely dies, in anyone. His question troubled me even more when I read a chapter in a book written by another General Authority that emphasizes a "point of no return." I walked over to lunch. First, I met Elder Ashton,[7] who told me that the premise of my talk was true. And then I sat at lunch with Elder Packer who opened the Book of Mormon and said, "I will teach you from the scriptures that it is true." And then he shared a statement he'd written today on a scrap of paper which he felt inspired to use in his talk. It fit perfectly what I have been impressed to say. I got moist eyes thinking about how closely the Savior directs conference. I turned in my talk before five with a happy heart. (September 26, 1986)

***

I slept restlessly, still puzzled that the Spirit had told me to drop both humor and stories from my conference talk. During the morning session, I learned that Elder Tuttle, who has cancer, was to speak unexpectedly.[8] He spoke without notes before me, bearing what may be his last testimony. And Elder F. Burton Howard[9] followed me, telling stories directly parallel to the ones that I'd felt impressed to drop from my talk. I learned that God sets the melody for conference and asks us each to play the notes He needs. (October 5, 1986)

Hal's next general conference talk, delivered in April 1988, was no easier to write. Those who heard that talk, "Because of Your Steadiness," might remember its poignant central metaphor of a young boy dreaming of soccer success. The boy kicks a ball time and again toward an imagined goal, giving his all to make the dream come true. Only Hal and Kathy knew that he had been driven to a similar limit to qualify to receive the metaphor and the talk built upon it.

My appointments filled the day until five. Then, I called Kathy to tell her I was going to the room in the temple where the Bishopric have lockers. It contains three chairs and a table. I called Security to warn them I was there so as not to scare one of our men on his rounds, who would see a light through the glass door. Early in the evening I felt I was told the disjointed drafts I've been writing were parts of the talks that others will give in the priesthood session where I speak. I prayed and wrote for four hours and still

From the islands of the Pacific to the highlands of South America, I've seen boys working to turn dreams into reality. In fact, I've seen it so often that it merges into one image, one picture. It's of a small boy, maybe nine or ten, in shorts, barefoot, and with a torn shirt. He's on a patch of dirt, alone, and he's looking down at a white-and-black-checkered ball. He takes a step toward it, his leg swings through, and the ball shoots off, about seven feet above the ground, where it might zip past a goalie into the net—except there's no goalie and no net; there's just the boy and the ball. And then he runs to the ball, puts it in place with his foot, and kicks it. And he does it over and over again.

You don't know where he lives, but you know that he'll take the ball home with him and that more than likely he keeps it near the place he sleeps. He sees it when he gets up and when he goes to bed. He may even dream about that ball shooting toward the goal.

—TALK, APRIL 2, 1988[10]

nothing came. Finally, after I'd been fasting more than 25 hours, I knelt again and pleaded, saying I'd give up any ideas of mine and would do it heaven's way. I began to flip, it seemed randomly, from page to page in the Book of Mormon and the Doctrine and Covenants. When I'd filled a page, I could see that the references were related and combined to make a message to an audience. On the way home I realized that what I was to talk about was new to me. Perhaps I could not have been given that if I hadn't been brought to some feeling of dependence. (March 22, 1988)

Hal's feelings of dependence as he labored diligently to write would only grow. The "experience curve" that makes most repetitive tasks easier to accomplish with practice seemed, in his case, to be inverted. With each new assignment to speak came an increased sense of the Lord's high expectations and standard of effort.

KATHY'S SERMONS

In these writing struggles, Kathy continued to serve as Hal's best source of encouragement and editorial counsel. Like him, she had a gift for writing. That was recognized by the wives of the other General Authorities, who met each month at the Church Office Building. They selected Kathy as their secretary. In addition to helping with the selection of speakers for the monthly lunch meetings, she kept formal minutes. Her work was valuable to the group and also a source of inspiration to Hal in his writing labors.

Kathy was a gifted writer in her own right, though she preferred to avoid the public-speaking limelight. Her most powerful sermons were the ones she gave at home, mostly by actions rather than words. Perhaps even more than the full attention she gave her children,

Kathy's greatest gift was a plain, undeniable testimony of the powers of good and evil at work in the world. She invested only a modicum of effort in prescribing or regulating the children's behavior. A poor report card from school, for example, provoked little if any reproof, though a good one might earn a loving smile. Likewise, she worried no more about the children's choice of clothes than she did her own. But she continually taught the fundamental principles of the plan of salvation, particularly the differences between right and wrong and the invisible forces enticing her children to one or the other.

The teaching became especially intense when Kathy sensed that one of the children was heading toward spiritual danger. As on the tennis court, when this kind of competition threatened, she grew fiercely serious. Her voice, which never rose except in childlike laughter, dropped lower still and grew firmer, as did the set of her jaw. With a solemn, piercing gaze she would warn in the starkest terms of the dangers she foresaw. Though rarely long, the sermon offered no invitation to rebuttal. None would have been accepted: even a moment's worth of such a warning seemed like eternity and left the hearer glad for its end.

Kathy shared a generic, extended version of such a sermon with the congregation that heard Matthew speak as he left for a mission to Santiago, Chile, in the summer of 1988. Matthew, she knew, had already received and internalized the message; thus, she made only a passing reference to him and his missionary service. Her greater

> Kathy called, just as I was leaving for another training meeting of the General Authorities. She had given me earlier her draft of the minutes she takes for the luncheon of the wives of General Authorities. She asked me to read them to her. And then, she proceeded to ask for criticism to get it straight. After a few minutes, she had what she wanted. As I thought about it later, I realized that the reason Kathy is so frequently mentioned by the other wives as a great writer of minutes is that she is teachable: she seeks counsel, instead of praise. And she is that way in everything.
>
> —JOURNAL, MARCH 27, 1990

concern was for several of Matthew's friends, who were struggling in their decisions to serve a mission or even to be worthy of one.

Without speaking to them directly, Kathy ministered to these young men as though they were her sons. They received the same kind of message that the Eyring children—and Hal—valued so much. Kathy was both complimentary and encouraging, but she was also stark in her portrayal of grave moral dangers and high spiritual stakes.

> I believe that a mother can be given insights and promptings as to what each of her children can do to prepare for future opportunities and challenges. As a child quietly listens to these insights and tries to follow the righteous counsel he receives, it can be wonderful preparation for his future.
>
> —TALK, MAY 8, 1994[11]

This morning I would like to talk to you youth about a choice you made many years ago in the premortal world while you were living with your Heavenly Father. As you were being taught the principles of the gospel, you made a decision that has affected your entire life here on earth. You made the choice to follow your Heavenly Father, to be obedient to His commandments.

Because of your faithfulness, our Father in Heaven gave you great opportunities and blessings. He gave you the opportunity to come to this earth at a special time in a special place. He gave you the opportunity to come into a family where you could hear the truth taught, where you could live in a country which allowed you to go to church and hear the gospel preached, and where you could have the freedom to choose how you would live and what you would believe.

It is difficult for you to imagine how strong and courageous you were in keeping our Father in Heaven's commandments. I use the word *courageous* because there were those around you who chose to follow Satan. As you know, there was a war between the followers of Satan and the followers of Heavenly Father. The main objective of those who followed Satan was to try to get you to come over to their side. It is hard to comprehend the strength with which you fought to stay true to your Father in Heaven.

Having painted a picture of a tense spiritual battlefield, Kathy used plain language and concrete metaphors to pull away the mask of the adversary's sophistries and subtleties.

Those same spirits who you fought against in heaven are here on earth today. They are still waging war against you. This attack is so deceptive that some of you do not even know you are at war. The weapons used are not machine guns or missiles—at least, these are not the primary tools. The weapons are generally more subtle. If I were to ask you what these weapons are, many of you would answer that they are certain kinds of movies and TV shows and magazines and songs, and you would be right. He also encourages us to skip our prayers or Church meetings or to criticize each other, especially our leaders, and to do anything that leads us away from Christ to Satan's side—first, by enticing us to think evil, and then by tempting us to do evil. He tempts not only young people but adults as well.

And so, once again, during this time on earth we must make the decision to follow our Father in Heaven. All of us have made daily choices that help to lead us toward Heavenly Father, but there are some who have made a total commitment to always try to keep His commandments. This is the commitment for which we pray in the sacramental prayer each week—that we may always keep His commandments. Those who have made this choice are not perfect, for everyone makes mistakes, but they have made the decision that they will try as hard as they can to obey Heavenly Father and have walked away from situations that they knew were surely in Satan's territory. Others are still watching, waiting to make that choice.

To those of you who may be waiting, we are told that this decision that we must make again is the most important one we will ever make in this life. Just as our choice in heaven determined the circumstances under which we would come to this earth, so it will now determine where we go in the next life . . . for an eternity. In the heavens there are realms of unbelievable beauty and of joy greater than we can imagine. There are also realms of spiritual squalor and poverty which would make us miserable . . . forever.

There is an interesting thing that happens as we wait to make the choice of where we would like to spend the eternities. The longer we wait, the greater the chance that Satan and his forces have to pull us spiritually into their territory. It is somewhat like a tug-of-war with Satan and his legions. While we would never think of taking hold of the rope and then simply watching and waiting as Satan tugged us toward him, yet that is essentially what we are doing when we allow ourselves to think for any length of time on thoughts that we know are impure. For just as surely as Satan can pull on that rope, he can pull our thoughts, dragging us into a spiritual mire until we rationalize that listening to a pornographic song is simply entertaining, that watching a dirty movie is simply humorous, that criticizing a ward or stake leader is simply trying to improve the Church, until step by step Satan has us unexpectedly and sometimes unknowingly in his grasp.

Kathy ended her brief address by putting Matthew and his friends in the company of spiritual heroes, and by bearing her personal testimony of the doctrines and observances of salvation.

We get something of the strength of our opponent on the other end of the rope by reading an account of the Prophet Joseph Smith, who struggled literally with his foe as he prayed in the Sacred Grove.[12] Such is the power of Satan.

But a simple prayer, a contrite plea such a young boy offered can call down the powers of our Father in Heaven so that Satan is bound. Even if you find yourself closer to Satan's side than you would desire, you may in sincere repentance ask our Father in Heaven for the Savior and His infinite atonement to help pull you back into safe territory. King Lamoni's father offered such a prayer as the missionary Aaron was preaching to him.[13] This Lamanite king made the choice that we all must make if we are to return to our Father in Heaven, the choice to give away all of our sins to know God.

Our prophet, Ezra Taft Benson, has told us of a simple yet powerful way to help give us this desire. It is to read the Book of Mormon, not all at one sitting, but a chapter or a few verses each night so that daily we may be reminded of our promise to serve the Lord so that all of our choices may be according to His will. Obedience to the teachings in the Book of Mormon will bring the power of our Heavenly Father to help us daily make the right decisions.

Matthew will be asking the people in Chile to make the choice to follow our Father in Heaven. This is a choice that he has made. You have all been faithful and courageous. You have won the first battle. You can win the next battle.

I bear you my testimony that God does live and that the Book of Mormon is true. I can remember many years ago sitting in a small dormitory room on a Sunday afternoon reading the first few chapters of the Book of Mormon, seeking to know if it was true. I will never forget the peaceful assurance which came to me that it was the word of God, and that assurance has made all the difference in my life. I pray that tonight you may have that experience and that it may make all the difference in your life.[14]

THE END OF THE BISHOPRIC ERA

Hal's service in the Presiding Bishopric, which ultimately lasted seven and a half years, was a time of growth and blessings for both him and Kathy. The older boys and their wives finished school and moved away from Utah. But they returned often to visit, bringing grandchildren. Matthew and John served faithfully as full-time missionaries. The stories they shared in letters became material for lessons Elizabeth and Mary taught to their parents in family home evenings. Everyone was in good health, both physically and spiritually.

Though Hal wrestled in talk writing, he hit his stride as what Bishop Hales called the "consummate counselor." His Bishopric responsibilities allowed him to apply at large scale the theories of business and science that he had studied and taught in his twenties and thirties. Combined with his fifteen years of service in the Church Educational System, his Bishopric experiences prepared him for almost any new assignment the Brethren might give.

But when change came in the fall of 1992, it wasn't to something new. Rather, Hal was sent "back to school."

BRIGHAM YOUNG
UNIVERSITY

neph**ew**, Mark, sometime last week, forced her out of
our double's match this morning; within an hour she'd
sent a replacement, so I played six sets. Result: I
soaked **my** elbow in a tub of hot water propped on the
table **in the** breakfast room at grandpa's, while I watched
the b****** ***es with the boys.** Annette served the whole

21

A HOUSE OF FAITH,
A HOUSE OF LEARNING

Organize yourselves;
Prepare every needful thing;
And establish a house,
Even a house of prayer,
A house of fasting,

A house of faith,
A house of learning,
A house of glory,
A house of order,
A house of God.

—DOCTRINE AND COVENANTS 88:119

In the general conference convened on October 3, 1992, Hal was released from the Presiding Bishopric and called as a member of the First Quorum of the Seventy. With the move to a new ecclesiastical position came the return to a former assignment, Commissioner of Church Education. As he had from 1980 to 1985, Hal would again direct the Church's schools, seminaries, institutes, and colleges and universities.

It was a pivotal time for the Church Educational System, especially at the collegiate level. With the Church's membership growing rapidly, interest in attending its three largest post-secondary institutions—BYU, Ricks College, and BYU–Hawaii—had never been greater. Yet because of the high cost of operating these institutions, which relied on tithing funds to cover well over half of their expenses, the Board of Education had felt the need to cap enrollments. The inevitable result was the denial each year of thousands of spiritually worthy and educationally qualified applicants.

ENTRANCE TO BYU CAMPUS

At the same time, BYU in particular was coming into its own as a major research university, with faculty success being judged not solely on teaching effectiveness but also on the publication of original ideas. This form of scholarship weighed heavily in hiring and tenure decisions, naturally affecting the intellectual profile of the faculty and the balance of their academic activities. BYU was becoming not only harder to get into but also more intellectually sophisticated and research focused.

In general, BYU's increased sophistication was a great asset to both the university and the Church. The melding of high-quality scholarship with religious faith and gospel doctrine was a double benefit to students, whose BYU experience strengthened their commitment to the Church while preparing them for success in future professions and as parents. The campus regularly received visits from respected scholars, business leaders, and government representatives from around the world, creating opportunities to share gospel insights and establish important friendships.

But the increase in scholarship also created new complexities for both BYU and its sponsoring institution. For example, faculty members seeking forums in which to present and publish their research occasionally found themselves among scholars whose views challenged gospel doctrines and even the Church itself. The participation of BYU employees in such forums risked lending credibility to these challenges and creating doubts among Church members at large. In response to these concerns, the Church issued a "Statement on Symposia," encouraging LDS scholars to "be sensitive to those matters that are more appropriate for private conferring and correction than for public debate."[1]

BYU also faced well-intentioned prodding from the mostly non-LDS academicians who came periodically to review the institution's accreditation status. In 1986, these accreditation representatives encouraged BYU to clarify its position on "academic freedom," the long-held tradition of protecting university scholars from institutional limitations on their research inquiries or statements deriving from their research findings. University administrators responded in the fall of 1992 with an academic freedom statement similar in most respects to those of nonreligious institutions. Yet, consistent with the university's unique mission to engender faith in the restored gospel, the statement differed in an important respect: it proscribed expressions contradicting fundamental Church doctrines, attacking Church leaders, or constituting illegal activities or other violations of the school's honor code.

MESSAGES OF ENCOURAGEMENT AND EXHORTATION

The new statement on academic freedom satisfied not only the vast majority of BYU faculty members but also the external accreditation team that returned to evaluate the university several years later. However, some faculty members openly challenged the statement. The rare public rift between the Church and even a minority of its employees drew local and national media attention. It also drew the attention of the Brethren.

In the October general conference in which Hal was called to the Seventy, Elder Boyd K. Packer addressed the theme of Church education in a talk called "To Be Learned is Good If . . ."

Addressing the employees of Church universities and colleges, Elder Packer complimented the majority for their combination of intellect and faith. But he also challenged faculty members to remember that their greatest contributions would be made not through personal scholarship, but through nurturing students.

Our faculties and staff are a miracle—men and women who have the highest academic degrees, many of them having been acclaimed for outstanding achievement. They are at once men and women of humility and faith.

We are grateful for teachers who will challenge students to high scholarship but would not even think of undermining testimony or acting in any way subversive to the progress of the Church and kingdom of God.

Because of such quality teachers, our schools can be unsurpassed in meeting the standards set by those who accredit schools, yet unique in mission, and contribute much to the Church even though a growing number of eligible students cannot enroll.

Because salaries of faculty and staff are paid from the tithes of the Church, there is a standard for them as well. A Church university is not established to provide employment for a faculty, and the personal scholarly research is not a dominant reason for funding a university.

Elder Packer also added a particular warning for a group of students and faculty members he characterized as "a very few."

Our purpose is to produce students who have that rare and precious combination of a superb secular education, complemented by faith in the Lord, a knowledge of the doctrines He has revealed, and a testimony that they are true.

For those very few whose focus is secular and who feel restrained as students or as teachers in such an environment, there are at present in the United States and Canada alone over 3,500 colleges and universities where they may find the kind of freedom they value. And we are determined to honor the trust of the tithe payers of the Church.[2]

Less than two weeks after general conference, President Gordon B. Hinckley, then First Counselor in the First Presidency, spoke on behalf of President Ezra Taft Benson at a BYU devotional in the Marriott Center. His remarks, titled "Trust and Accountability," paralleled those of Elder Packer. He began with a compliment directed to the majority of the faculty and students.

First, I want to thank you for the strength of your desire to teach and learn with inspiration and knowledge, and for your commitment to live the standards of the gospel of Jesus Christ, for your integrity and your innate goodness. I am confident that never in the history of this institution has there been a faculty better qualified professionally nor one more loyal and dedicated to the standards of its sponsoring institution. Likewise, I am satisfied that there has never been a student body better equipped to learn at the feet of this excellent faculty, nor one more prayerful and decent in attitude and action.

There may be exceptions. There doubtless are. But they are few in number compared with the larger body.

President Hinckley noted the BYU community's success in its "continuing experiment on a great premise that a large and complex university can be first class academically while nurturing an environment of faith in God and the practice of Christian principles." He also praised the faculty for being men and women of faith as well as learning, and for their service in the Church. Yet he reiterated the possibility of exceptions, and upon such individuals he pronounced a gentle Scotch blessing.

I repeat, there may be exceptions. But I think those are few. And if such there be, I am confident that in their hearts they feel ill at ease and uncomfortable, for there can never be peace nor comfort in any element of disloyalty. Wherever there is such an attitude there is a nagging within the heart that says, "I am not being honest in accepting the consecrated tithing funds of the humble and faithful of this Church. I am not being honest with myself or others as a member of this faculty while teaching or engaging in anything that weakens the faith and undermines the integrity of those who come to this institution at great sacrifice and with great expectations."[3]

A CHARGE TO THE NEW COMMISSIONER

Hal heard both of these messages in person, and he recognized them as including a charge to him as Commissioner. He knew that BYU stood at a critical crossroads. It was coming of age as one of the

world's leading universities, with a dual mission of faith and academic excellence. The rate of increase of academic excellence was profound, by design: under Presidents Dallin Oaks, Jeffrey Holland, and Rex Lee, the university had substantially raised its academic standards for both faculty and students. But the vast majority of faculty members had received their graduate education at universities where faith wasn't considered a natural or even a welcome part of academic inquiry. In establishing an expectation of world-class scholarship melded with gospel principles, BYU was pushing its faculty to go where no institution had gone before, and where even the most faithful and accomplished scholars had not been formally trained to go.

Hal wasn't fearful when a few openly questioned the Church's right to protect its doctrines or require conformance to standards of conduct on its campuses. He believed what President Hinckley had implied, that such individuals would feel uncomfortable and either reconsider their views or leave BYU. Rather, he was determined to create the right vision of the university's future as a unique place of scholarship and faith. That would be critical not only in guiding current faculty members in their work, but also in selecting new ones. In the ensuing ten years, half of the faculty, many hired during the collegiate boom of the 1960s, were likely to retire. Faculty hiring decisions and the guidance provided to the new hires would determine the university's course for the coming generation.

Hal's training prepared him well for the work to be done at BYU. But it wasn't his academic background that would prove most useful. The more important training had occurred in his parents' home, where he had seen living examples of the intertwining of reason and faith. Henry and Mildred had been hardheaded thinkers; merely sitting at the dinner table with them was as intellectually challenging as participating in research seminars at Harvard. Yet while rational analysis enhanced his parents' faith, in the end the analysis bowed to that faith.

Throughout his life, Hal had emulated his parents' example of faith. He sought to merge reason and faith, confident that the two were compatible and ultimately reinforcing. But he knew that, at least by mortal minds, they ultimately could not be treated as equal, as he noted in a journal entry:

> In a Board of Trustees meeting, a BYU professor described his discovery of a mummy, buried in Egypt in the early Christian era with clear evidence that the person had received the temple ordinance as we know it today. In an independent presentation, a member of the Twelve in a later meeting read from a manuscript, translated into English in 1914 and therefore unavailable to Joseph Smith, which gives clear evidence that the temple ceremony as we know it was known to the Lord's apostles in Palestine. I was interested, but my testimony rests on personal revelation; if physical evidence sways us one way, then contrary evidence must, too. (May 6, 1987)

Providentially, Hal had already given a speech at BYU that offered guidance in blending scholarship and faith. In August 1991, while still a member of the Presiding Bishopric, he had spoken at the invitation of President Rex Lee at the annual university conference for BYU employees. The theme of that year's conference was drawn from 2 Corinthians 3:17: "Where the Spirit of the Lord is, there is liberty."

Hal introduced his remarks, titled "Teaching Is a Moral Act," by noting that everyone in the audience was both a teacher and a student. Citing personal experiences, Hal recalled the paradoxical dual temptations of the learning process—fear and hubris.

> I suppose all of us as students and as teachers see that interesting swing, which we all seem to make at times. Sometimes we

feel so overwhelmed that we are sure we can't learn; at other times we know so much that almost no one can teach us. I don't think we are looking for some middle ground; that is not what we are looking for. Rather, there is another place, almost a magic place, not halfway between being terrified and being vain, but another place where both vanity and fear are muted, not simply balanced.

Hal described seeing his father occupy that "magic place" once at a meeting of the American Chemical Society in New York City:

My father was presenting a paper at this meeting. In the middle of his presentation, someone stood up and interrupted him. This man stood up in front of everyone and said, "Professor Eyring, I have heard you on the other side of this question." I am not reproducing the sting that it had to it. It had a cut to it. I could feel the electricity. I thought: "Oh, I am seeing my father attacked in public, and I know he has a temper. Oh dear, oh dear. What might happen here?" At least, I knew if I had spoken to him that way, I would have had quite an experience. But Dad laughed in the most pleasant way. He chuckled and said: "Oh, you are right. I have been on the other side of this question. Not only that, but I have been on several sides of this question. In fact, I will get on every side of this question I can find until I can understand it." And on he went in his presentation, as happily as could be. Now that was much more than a clever rejoinder. That was a glimpse for a moment of that

> It seems clear to me that the Lord used the Prophet Joseph to restore His gospel. This is the important thing for me.
>
> As a devout Latter-day Saint the important fact for me is that the Lord is directing the affairs in His Universe, not exactly how He does it. Whether or not some organic evolution was used or is operating seems to me to be beside the point. He is infinitely wise. I just work here. If He told me in detail how He works I'm sure I wouldn't understand much of it.
>
> —DR. HENRY EYRING, IN LETTERS RESPONDING TO CONCERNED CHURCH MEMBERS[4]

happy place which I think is best described this way: He took delight in struggling with what he *didn't* know because he had no feeling of limits on what he *might* know. That made him not only a powerful learner, but someone who was not in much danger of quitting because he was afraid or fearful. He was also not in much danger of feeling that he knew so much he couldn't be taught.

> Let no man deceive himself. If any man among you seemeth to be wise in this world, let him become a fool, that he may be wise.
>
> —1 CORINTHIANS 3:18

Having tied teaching and learning to humility, Hal linked it also to faith. He did so by citing probably his most influential professor, C. Roland Christensen of the Harvard Business School. Professor Christensen had chaired Hal's doctoral dissertation committee, making him the most significant academic figure in Hal's life during his five years at Harvard. But their relationship went much deeper than that. In addition to guiding Hal in his research and teaching activities, Professor Christensen had taken a strong interest in Hal's personal life. He had assumed the role of trusted mentor, so much so that, as Hal pondered marrying Kathy, he took her to meet Professor Christensen and was pleased to receive enthusiastic approval. Though they hadn't seen one another for years, Professor Christensen had, just the month before the 1991 BYU conference, sent Hal a copy of a book called *Education for Judgment.* In it, Professor Christensen declared teaching to be a "moral act," with faith as its "indispensable dimension."

Hal noted that the greatest benefit of the BYU faculty's research could come in helping them to have faith in their students and to enter into the students' world of discovery, with its feelings of vulnerability and the need for humility.

The teachers who will make the difference are the ones who somehow can enter into that world with the student and feel what they feel, know what they fear, care about their fear, and help them move through the fear to learning. Research, of the right kind, can take a teacher into a world like the one a student must enter.

If your research makes you feel very, very bright, or very, very good, or very, very famous, or very, very valuable, that could get in your way as a teacher. If, on the other hand, your research makes you feel very, very vulnerable, very, very anxious to know more, and if you read other people's papers as often as you read your own, if you thrill when someone else gets an idea that makes yours look a little less important or even wrong, if all this seems like a wonderful game to you, then think how you can bless your students.

Hal also addressed the subject of academic freedom. He did so with a personal story, drawn from his final years at Stanford, when the university was torn by student protests and faculty demands for greater power. He had accepted an assignment from the dean of the Stanford Graduate School of Business, Arjay Miller, to represent the school on a universitywide faculty committee. To his dismay, he discovered that the committee intended to wrest power from newly appointed president Kenneth Pitzer. In fact, the effort succeeded: President Pitzer's term in office would last only nineteen tumultuous months. Hal told the audience at BYU of his surprise at the faculty committee's desire to undermine President Pitzer's authority.

I was invited to join a coup in an academic situation. Other people, who were working in the same situation I was, decided that they had had enough of what they saw as a dictator. They wanted me to help get him ousted. I remember getting the phone call and being absolutely stunned because oppression had never occurred to me. I told the caller that I was not interested in the coup. I literally did not feel oppressed. And I tried to figure out why.

I will tell you what I learned about myself and about you. Somebody, somewhere along the line, must have trusted me and said: "Look, Hal, I will exert my authority upon you this way. I believe in you. I believe that God can correct you, so I will point out the consequences of your behavior and then not push you very hard." As a result, I have always felt free, even when some people tried to push me.

Hal concluded by explaining why freedom from authority, or even protection from intrusive authority, had never been of much concern to him:

> I believe not so much in the perfection of my bosses or my critics as I believe that I am still a child with lots to learn. Most folks can teach me something. No one can really take away the freedom that matters to me, and most criticism from human beings awakens an echo of a rebuke I've already felt from the Holy Ghost.[5]

GETTING TO KNOW THE BYU FACULTY

When Hal was called for the second time as Commissioner of Education, one year after giving his "Teaching Is a Moral Act" address, he made BYU a leading personal priority, involving himself directly in its affairs at the invitation of President Rex Lee. While fulfilling weekend conference assignments as a General Authority, he dedicated many of his Mondays to interviewing faculty leaders in Provo, an hour's drive from his home in Bountiful. Ultimately investing almost a year in the effort, he interviewed more than one hundred faculty leaders of colleges, departments, and groups. In addition to teaching him much, the interviews communicated his appreciation and admiration.

> It impressed me that he would spend that much time, that he was interested in me and my work. What I mostly remember is this powerful spirit of being part of the kingdom.
>
> —ALAN L. WILKINS, BYU ORGANIZATIONAL BEHAVIOR DEPARTMENT CHAIR AND LATER ACADEMIC VICE PRESIDENT[6]

Hal also met with faculty members collectively. Among those invited were university-appointed leaders and members of the Faculty

Advisory Council, who were nominated for service by their faculty peers via popular election. In these meetings he took all questions, giving frank answers not only as the Commissioner of Education but also as a former professor. His straightforward, respectful dialogue with the faculty won their respect.[7]

Yet all the while, pressure mounted. The small minority of faculty and students who chafed at perceived limits on their freedom became more vocal. They took their concerns to the media, both in Utah and nationally. In March 1993 the *New York Times* ran a lengthy article under the heading, "Faith and Free Speech Wrestle for Dominance in Brigham Young Case."

This critical media attention, combined with disruptive demonstrations on the campus itself, led some to question Hal's failure to take quick, decisive action to restore order. The critics among the faculty and students were easy to identify, and the costs of their activities were borne by not only the supportive majority of the BYU community but also the Church itself. It would have been easy to justify clamping down on the dissent.

Instead, Hal worked with BYU administrators to strengthen the vast majority of faculty and students, who were devoted to the vision of President Hinckley and the many others who had spoken prophetically of BYU's unique potential. As part of that effort, he helped a university "self-study" team publish a collection of talks they called *Educating Zion*. This volume began with founding President Karl G. Maeser's address "History of the Academy," delivered in 1891. Also included were talks by David O. McKay, Spencer W. Kimball, and Boyd K. Packer.

At the annual university conference in August 1996, Hal built on these inspired statements with a talk he called "A Charted Course." This title derived from a landmark address from *Educating Zion*, one given in 1938 by President J. Reuben Clark Jr., First Counselor in the First Presidency. The title of President Clark's talk was "The Charted Course of the Church in Education."

Hal began his "Charted Course" address by noting that he had just reread the foundational documents collected in *Educating Zion*. "What struck me," he said, "was their consistency across long periods of time and with each other. I was struck with the recurrence of the idea that putting religious faith first will enhance our achievements as a university." Then Hal noted something important but only implicit in the talks in *Educating Zion:*

> What was not said in those documents, perhaps because it was understood by the audiences, was that the religious faith of which they spoke was faith in a revealed religion, one with living prophets and with faith that God reveals his will to his servants. That makes the idea a bold proposition, given the histories of other universities and the prevailing views in much of the academic world.

Hal explained why the leadership of prophets, which might be considered a liability for a university charged with secular excellence, is in fact a treasure:

> Not only does the Board of Trustees give consistent direction, based on a deep understanding of universities as they have been and of this one as it is, but it gives direction out of unity far beyond a product of counting votes and far above a process of coalition bargaining.
>
> Those patterns of leadership from the Board, so valuable to this university, will never be lost, because of their source. The consistency of view, the grasp of things as they really are, and the unity are not dependent on any individual or even on a cluster of individuals. The view stays consistent and facts are made clear and the unity comes because the inspiration of God is the source. He really calls His servants. He knows the past, the present, and the future. He knows what is best for His children.

And He inspires His servants. Members of the Board of Trustees will leave and others will come. But there will be consistency and steady purpose. The patterns of such value to the university will continue because they are independent of the people involved. Religious faith, faith in a revealed religion, does not require some sacrifice in the effectiveness of a university; it allows enhancement. Only for someone who believed that the mark of a great university is the lack of wise and consistent leadership would such a board be anything but a treasure.[8]

Hal's patient efforts, along with those of many others, particularly BYU presidents Rex Lee and Merrill Bateman, soon yielded the hoped-for results. The optimistic emphasis on BYU's divine mission and prophetic guidance galvanized the faculty and students. As President Hinckley had predicted, a few faculty members chose to leave. But the supposed "wrestle" between faith and free speech that made headlines in 1993 gave way to an unprecedented era of faithful, first-rate scholarship. Part of the success derived from extra effort invested in the hiring of new faculty members, a process Hal focused on. Increased emphasis on the role and importance of faith produced an outstanding group of young professors, many of whom had attended BYU as undergraduates and achieved academic success in doctoral programs at the leading research universities.

> He was looking for people who were both proficient in their academic discipline and loyal and faithful in the gospel. He wanted people who would be good role models for the students.
>
> —JAMES D. GORDON, BYU ASSOCIATE ACADEMIC VICE PRESIDENT FOR FACULTY[9]

The new hires further increased BYU's distinctiveness as a religious research university. A 2002 study of four of the largest such institutions—BYU, Baylor, Boston College, and Notre Dame—found that the faculty in Provo were unique. "Brigham Young faculty are distinctively committed to their school's religious tradition," a trio of non-LDS scholars concluded.[10]

Gratified and inspired by this trend, in 2001 Hal gave a talk called "A Consecrated Place" at the annual university conference. In it he drew upon remarks made at BYU a quarter-century before by President Spencer W. Kimball. President Kimball cited the dream of a man named Charles Malik. Dr. Malik, a Lebanese philosopher and diplomat, had earned a PhD at Harvard and presided over the United Nations General Assembly. A deeply religious man, Malik had ventured that "one day a great university will arise somewhere—I hope in America—to which Christ will return in His full glory and power, a university which will, in the promotion of scientific, intellectual, and artistic excellence, surpass by far even the best secular universities of the present, but which will at the same time enable Christ to bless it and act and feel perfectly at home in it."

Having quoted these words, Hal observed,

> Malik spoke with certainty of a time when the Savior will return in glory to this earth. He described a place—a university—where the resurrected Lord would join with the students and the faculty and all who labor there. The Master will feel perfectly at home there.
>
> That would seem beyond our reach if after reading this quote President Kimball had not then said: "Surely BYU can help to respond to that call!"

Hal described what it would take to qualify for the Savior's presence, and he complimented the members of the BYU community for their efforts to do so:

> We know something of what a place must be like for the glorified Savior to feel perfectly at home. Of one thing we can be sure: those who labor there and all associated with it will have long before consecrated it to Him and to His kingdom.
>
> His plan of redemption has always required men and women to consecrate all they have and all they are to the service of God. They covenant to do that. And then He tests them to see how sincere they are and how much they are willing to sacrifice. That test

may be different for each of us, tailored for us alone, but it will be enough for the Master to prove our hearts.

Those who welcome Him at that university will have met and passed the tests. He will be at home, perfectly at home, because they will not only have said the words, "This is the Lord's university," but they will have served and lived to make it so. They will have made it a consecrated place, offered it to Him, and in the process they will have been sanctified. What they will do to prove their consecration will have allowed the Atonement to change who they are.[11]

> The journey toward being a consecrated place is a long one. We have not arrived, but we are moving on the path. Those everyday tasks to which you now will give your all—because you give your all—are changing this school, and they are allowing the Lord to make a change in you. There will be tests ahead—not because God doubts us but because He loves us. I have every confidence that we will pass the tests and that surely BYU will respond to the call to be a consecrated place.
>
> —TALK, AUGUST 27, 2001[12]

A CALL TO THE TWELVE

At the time Hal bore this testimony of BYU's great potential and progress, he did so as a member of the Quorum of the Twelve Apostles. The call to the Twelve had come unexpectedly on the last day of March 1995, a Friday. That afternoon he received a message inviting him to meet with President Gordon B. Hinckley in his office. Hal knew that there was a vacancy in the Quorum. President Howard W. Hunter had passed away exactly four weeks before, and James E. Faust had joined Presidents Hinckley and Monson in the new First Presidency. The members of the Church expected that the resulting vacancy in the Quorum of the Twelve would be filled on April 1, the first day of general conference.

However, President Hinckley's initial question seemed to rule out the possibility that Hal would be affected by these developments. "So, Hal," President Hinckley began as they sat down in his office, "how do

May 31, 1984
Thursday

I wrote in the Atherton
guest house of the
Johnsons, looking down
on the
of our
Elizab
Kathleen
blow out
birthday
dinner b
Holy Gh
teach a
workshop

June 1,
Friday

Elizabeth
the poo
worked
Gary ca
Los Ang
to hear
time to
Altos.

June 2,
Saturday

I towed
inflated,
Mary
compli
purple
match t
hair tha
Stuart's
sister.
and I w
dance in

June 3, 1984
Sunday

PRESIDENT GORDON B. HINCKLEY

Kathy, Elizabeth, and Mary Kathleen were dressed and
packed early for our drive from Atherton to the San Jose
airport. On the flight home, a stewardess made a bullseye
with a glass full of orange juice on my lap. It was so cold
and complete a soaking that I laughed for the rest of the
trip. I used bags to shield the results as I got us to the car.
Henry, Matthew, and John were waiting happily at home.

you feel about your service as Commissioner of Education?" Putting aside any thoughts of the vacancy in the Twelve, Hal joined President Hinckley in a thirty-minute conversation about the challenges and opportunities facing the Church Educational System. There was a mix of both. For example, though BYU was fulfilling its academic and spiritual mission as never before, its president, Rex Lee, seemed to be slowly losing a long battle with cancer. A new president might be needed soon.

Systemwide, there was also the challenge of demographic growth. Students were applying to the Church's universities and colleges—and being turned away—in record numbers. The problem was particularly acute at BYU and Ricks College, large institutions that between the two of them had, until the 1970s, accepted nearly all high school graduates willing to live Church standards of behavior. Now, due to the growth of the Church and enrollment caps necessitated by the high cost of providing higher education, well-qualified applicants were being denied by the thousands. Ricks College, generally assumed to be much less selective than BYU, was in fact turning away nearly half its applicants. Faithful, tithe-paying parents who as youngsters had never worried about getting into a Church college now found their highly qualified children being shut out.

President Hinckley, a longtime member of the Board of Education, understood this challenge well. It troubled him deeply. But the conversation apparently convinced him that Hal was doing the Commissioner's job as well as anyone could. In fact, President Hinckley concluded that Hal could continue to play that role and take on an additional assignment. Making his first reference to the vacancy to be filled the next day, he said, "Well, I think we'll have you continue as Commissioner as you join the Twelve."

President Hinckley instructed Hal briefly from section 112 of the Doctrine and Covenants, in which the Lord challenges the Twelve to take the gospel to the "ends of the earth."[13] He specifically tasked Hal with learning what it means to feed the Savior's sheep. Yet the charge to the newest member of the Twelve was brief and to the point, in the style Hal had come to expect from President Hinckley. Returning to his own office, he immediately went to work on a general conference talk, which he delivered the next day after being sustained as a member of the Quorum of the Twelve Apostles. The talk, called "Always Remember Him," contained just one allusion to his new responsibility.

> Over the last hours I have come to understand other blessings from "always remembering him."
> —TALK, APRIL 1, 1995[14]

A NEW UNIVERSITY

Hal's simultaneous service as Commissioner and as a member of the Twelve wasn't unprecedented. David O. McKay, John A. Widtsoe, and Joseph F. Merrill had all headed Church education as Apostles. However, in 1995 Hal's executive responsibilities for CES, with a direct reporting line to the First Presidency, stood in contrast to the assignments of the other members of the Twelve, who worked entirely under the direction of their Quorum president. Recognizing this, and wanting to demonstrate his fealty to the Quorum, Hal worked up the courage to ask President Hinckley privately how long he would continue to serve as Commissioner. President Hinckley replied, "Probably another year or so."

When a year had passed, Hal waited expectantly for a release. After several months with no word, he again sought out President Hinckley with the question, "How much longer?" The Prophet's terse, stern reply caught him off guard: "We'll let you know, Hal." Hearing what he interpreted as irritation in President Hinckley's voice, Hal decided that he had asked that question for the last time.

Serving as the lone member of the Quorum with such an external responsibility not only placed an unusually heavy workload on Hal, it sometimes left him feeling like an odd man out. Yet his respect for the First Presidency's direction resulted in blessings of strength and insight in all of his Church work. It also put him in a position to contribute to an unexpected change at Ricks College.

In the spring of 2000, following a meeting of the Board of Education, President Hinckley asked Hal to come to his office. Inviting him to close the door and sit down, President Hinckley said, "Hal, couldn't we serve more students at a lower cost by making Ricks a university? What problems do you see?" Hal was more than surprised by the question. During his time as the president of Ricks College, he had been asked repeatedly by faculty, students, alumni, and other boosters whether and when a return to university status might occur. The president's job, both then and in the decades since, was to say diplomatically but firmly something to the effect of, "Don't even think about it."

Temporarily stunned, Hal fumbled for a moment and then began enumerating the additional costs of granting bachelor's degrees at Ricks. Even if the new year-round program worked, he observed, adding junior- and senior-level courses would require more faculty. They would need offices, and that would mean adding buildings; so would providing classrooms for the additional students. "No, President," Hal concluded, "it will cost you more, not less."

"No it won't," President Hinckley shot back. "It will cost me less *per BYU graduate*." He then went on to outline a bold innovation, one not unlike the creation of small temples. He had in mind a new kind of university. Though it would bear the BYU name, its mission and operating model would be different. In becoming a four-year institution, Ricks College would cease its participation in intercollegiate athletics. It would also eschew the graduate degree programs, publication-oriented scholarly research, and faculty rank common to large universities such as BYU.

Instead, the new university, BYU–Idaho, would remain focused on undergraduate education. In fact, it would be designed to serve *more* undergraduate students by operating year-round and using computer and Internet technology to offer additional learning opportunities without building new classrooms. By creating a less-expensive four-year school with the BYU name, the Church could make a BYU education available to many more of its members at an affordable cost.

The task of creating this university fell to a team of Ricks College administrators and faculty members under the direction of BYU–Idaho President David A. Bednar. Hal had first met President Bednar, then a regional representative living in Arkansas, in 1995 when the two were assigned to conduct a stake conference. Hal felt impressed that his junior companion, a professor of business at the University of Arkansas, might be a candidate to head Ricks College. When the presidency of Ricks opened in 1997, Hal recommended David Bednar to President Hinckley.

On Tuesday, June 20, 2000, President Hinckley and Hal stood together at a lectern in Salt Lake City and announced the creation of BYU–Idaho. The written statement explaining the unique nature of the institution included just twenty-one sentences. Though Hal went immediately to work with President Bednar and his team, he let a year pass before going to Rexburg to offer a fuller public explanation of the Board's purposes and expectations.

"A STEADY, UPWARD COURSE"

Hal gave his landmark address, "A Steady, Upward Course," on September 18, 2001, just three weeks after delivering "A Consecrated Place" to the employees of BYU in Provo. But in those three weeks the world had been turned upside down. On September 11, terrorists had toppled New York's Twin Towers and killed thousands. In the wake of the attacks and resulting uncertainty, Hal would have been justified in cancelling his scheduled devotional address at BYU–Idaho. Yet he saw the timing not as prohibitive but as providential. In addition to delivering the remarks he had been preparing for weeks, which he had vetted with President Hinckley, Hal began by exploring the role of change in Heavenly Father's plan.

Each of us finds ourselves asking: "What other parts of my world that I thought were stable have now become uncertain?" No wonder that you and I have heard and read so often in the last few days "everything has changed." But at least two things will help us take courage and find direction.

First, change is part of life. For instance, growing up and growing older are adventures in change filled with uncertainties and surprises. And second, God, through prophets, prepared us to expect changes to accelerate in the world.

Having established the inevitability of change, Hal pointed out its potential benefits:

> Although we face an increase in challenges, there is another change sweeping the earth. It is a flood of opportunity. The steady flow of invention is an example. A generation ago there were no small computers. But now university campuses connect them with fiber-optic cable, and that cable may be replaced soon by wireless technologies. There are now tens of thousands of people taking BYU courses through Web technology. There was no Web a few years ago. The cell phones which figured so touchingly in the tragedies of last week did not exist a generation ago. The list of powerful and helpful new technological miracles goes on and on, and the rate of innovation is accelerating. We will live for better or for worse with rapid change and the uncertainty it brings. You and I want to make that change work for the better for us and not for the worse.
>
> You're going to change tremendously, and the world around you is going to change. The purpose of the gospel of Jesus Christ is to change you so that you're not trying to resist change. You're trying to have change take you where the Lord wants you to go.

Given all that had happened at the new BYU–Idaho in the preceding year, including the elimination of intercollegiate athletics and the

Each of us wants to live in a world of change where our personal reaction to it is not only productive but where it enhances the best of what we are.

—TALK, SEPTEMBER 18, 2001[16]

replacement of the Ricks College name, it was easy to cite the members of the university community as sterling examples of responding productively to change.

> The people who serve here have found a way to make changes—great and rapid changes—that will enhance, not replace, the best of what the school has always been. Because of that, I can with confidence make you a promise. When you return in some distant future, you will find great innovation has become commonplace, and yet, amidst all the changes, the school will have retained and enriched the basic characteristics that blessed your life.

Hal also complimented the administrators and faculty of BYU–Idaho for literally putting the Savior first in the mission statement they had submitted to the accreditation body empowered to grant, or deny, university status.

*Northwest corner of Kirkham, where a new theatre in-the-round may be attached.
March 29, 1974*

> The first goal, stated boldly and plainly in the prospectus, is to "build testimonies of the restored gospel of Jesus Christ and to encourage living its principles." That choice to put the Savior and His purposes first is the primary basis of my confidence in the future.
>
> Every innovation, every change, will be measured against this test of the heart: How would this proposed change build testimony and true conversion to the restored gospel of Jesus Christ in the heart of a student? True conversion comes by gaining sufficient faith to live the principles of the restored gospel of Jesus Christ. Some potential and proposed innovations will help that to happen. There will be other innovations proposed that

would be less helpful or might even hinder. The cumulative effect of change here will be to build testimony and accelerate true conversion.

Hal explained how putting the Savior first at BYU–Idaho would make the institution a place of outstanding teaching and learning, notwithstanding the lack of traditional faculty scholarship and graduate programs. And he promised the fulfillment of a declaration made by President Bednar that the university would "play a pioneering role in understanding learning [and] teaching processes."

> That will happen because the Savior is and will be the great exemplar. He was a teacher. His work and glory was to lift others. He taught His disciples not to set themselves as being better than others, but to be the servants of all. Only a faculty who believe those things could see a blessing in serving without academic rank.[15] Only a faculty with hearts set on the Savior could believe that they could keep growing as teachers in their changing and challenging fields without graduate programs.
>
> That pioneering role as a leader in understanding learning and teaching will come to pass. I, as a servant of Jesus Christ, testify to you that I know that will happen. Even with these apparently humble and even paradoxical standards of what we will be and who we will be, that miracle will occur and this institution, in the world, will become a place that people know of because of the insights that will come as we come to understand the teaching and learning process here. I so testify.[17]

FRUGALITY, INNOVATION, AND LEADERSHIP

In addition to making the Savior preeminent, Hal identified a second key to fulfilling the potential of the new university: frugality. When he announced the creation of BYU–Idaho, President Hinckley had made several references to the financial efficiencies that the institution's unique operating model would facilitate. Filling the classrooms year-round and using online learning technology would give

BYU–Idaho a natural cost advantage. But Hal's experience as Ricks College's president had taught him that frugality was important both at the institutional level and also for individuals. Frugality, he explained, was a quality of mind and heart, and it was crucial not only to making a BYU–Idaho education affordable but to realizing the spiritual potential of the university.

The school will enhance another of its characteristics which will carry it safely through turbulent times, and it will come from showing students by example how to live with great faith. That characteristic is frugality. Listen to the words of President Bednar speaking to the faculty and staff during this time of change:

"There is a responsibility to be prudent in the management of the resources, and there are places where we need to improve. If there is an example of *use it up, wear it out, make it do, or do without*, we are that place. If we ever lost that, we would be in trouble. So we need to be careful what we ask for."

Now those of you who are young don't understand all that was in that statement. I was the president of Ricks College. I couldn't understand. I couldn't understand why the Brethren were always coming to me, the men who lead the Church, when I was the president, saying: "What more can we do for you? What more can we do for you?" I didn't understand that. I now do. They knew this place, and they knew we wouldn't ask. They knew we'd make do.

Hal ascribed the tradition of frugality at Ricks College to its founders, members of the Bannock Stake who in 1888 established a frontier academy to educate their children.

They built this school in their poverty. The first principal, Jacob Spori, housed his family in an unheated grain storage shed in his first winter because that's all they had. The people here have treated all they had as the Lord's and

Spori Building

always counted it as enough. And they have used it as if it was the offering of the poorest widow to her Lord and to His kingdom. Nor have they felt badly treated when the Lord asked them to take less and yet give more. Because of that faithful obedience and sacrifice, I certify the Lord has poured out His Spirit here.

I want you to know that the reason those people from the Board of Education used to say, "Hal, isn't there something more we could do for you up there at Ricks College?" is that they were almost afraid we wouldn't ask; that we might run just a little too lean, just a little too hard, trying to do the best we could with what we had; just afraid we might overdo it because that's who we were.

I testify to you this beautiful campus that you see now is the reward from a loving God and His Board of Education that said: "We know those people. We know what they're like. They're out of a pioneer heritage, and they don't think that the things they have mean much. It's what they are. And they think they can do a very great deal without very much."

Hal described what he termed the practical benefits of the Ricks College tradition of frugality, referring to "turbulent times" like those of the moment:

There will be a practical benefit, in turbulent times, from that frugality borne of faith. There will come times when the Lord's prophet will ask us to do more with less. Knowing that will come, we must and will find ways to improve and to innovate that require little or no money. We will depend more upon inspiration and perspiration to make improvements than upon buildings and equipment. Then hard economic times will have little effect on the continuous innovation that will not cease at this school, even in the most difficult times.

Now I testify to you that that blessing is both a practical one and a spiritual one. It's practical because then the Lord will provide when we do need something, and He'll provide generously because He trusts us. But it has another benefit as well. I testify to you that that spirit of sacrifice, that spirit of trying to give just a little bit more and ask a little less brings down the powers of heaven. You will be learners. Your teachers will teach better than their natural capacities would ever allow them to do because the powers of heaven will come down. They will come down because of your faith.

Finally, Hal added a special blessing, which he described as prophecy, regarding the students of the new university:

> They will become lifelong teachers in their families, in the Church, and in their work, and they will bless others wherever they go by what they have learned about innovating with scarce resources and treating all they have as if it were the Lord's.
>
> You can imagine the joy of an employer or a Church leader when such a graduate arrives. The graduates will be at personal peace by having kept the commandments. They will be natural leaders who know how to teach and how to learn. They will have the power to innovate and improve without requiring more of what money can buy. Those graduates of BYU–Idaho will become—and this is a prophecy that I am prepared to make and make solemnly—those graduates of BYU–Idaho will become legendary for their capacity to build the people around them and to add value wherever they serve.
>
> I hope I live long enough to someday meet some employer who employed one of you and says, "Where did that come from? I've never had such a person. Why, people just flock around that person. And they want to follow. They don't have to be led; they're seeking to go where that person wants to go. And they come up with new ideas. I don't know where that comes from. They seem to find a better way, and the budget doesn't go up. I can't understand it." And I'll smile and say, "Well, come with me to Rexburg. And I may not be able to show it to you, and I may not be able to prove it to you, but you'll feel it." There will be a spirit here, I so testify, because of the love of God for all of His faithful children. And those blessings will be poured out here in rich abundance.[18]

A RELEASE . . . AND NEW CHALLENGES

In early 2005, President Hinckley finally released Hal as Commissioner of Education. By then he had served for nearly ten years as a member of the Quorum of the Twelve. The Church Educational System was strong and stable, with its two largest institutions, BYU and BYU–Idaho, on particularly innovative paths. BYU's academic reputation continued to grow, even as its faculty members involved more undergraduate students in mentored research. Research output increased, as did the number of BYU graduates going on for advanced degrees. The faculty had begun to prove, as Hal had said they might, that their research could be conducted so as to benefit their students, and that faith could enhance their scholarship.

BYU–Idaho also grew. Creating a third full semester and offering online courses allowed the university to admit nearly everyone in an expanding applicant pool, without a proportional increase in classrooms or full-time faculty members. The size of the student body increased while annual financial support from the Church remained roughly the same. The new university also grew in reputation. Thanks in part to an institutionally sponsored internship program, some students began to be recognized for their leadership potential, as Hal had promised, even before graduation. Accounting department chair Keith Patterson recounted the following at a BYU–Idaho devotional:

> As BYU–Idaho became a university, I must admit that I was quite skeptical about competing with other universities, with much more prestige and recognized names, for employment and internship opportunities, especially in the accounting area. Many of our accounting students struggled to find good internships in the early semesters of our transition. Some even had to accept nonpaid opportunities just to land an internship.
>
> In January of 2005, I became the Accounting Department Chair. In March of that year, I went on my first internship expedition to New York City. As part of the trip, I made arrangements

to visit our three interning students and their Big Four accounting firm.

During the office visit I was able to talk with one of their managers. She said to me, "Where is this BYU–Idaho? I had never heard of it before your students came on board. And where did these kids come from? They are wonderful. They work hard. They are willing to accept any assignment given. They are always helping one another. They are constantly cheerful and have a smile on their faces. And they don't come to work on Monday mornings hung over."

My thoughts quickly turned to President Eyring's prophecy, and while fighting back the tears, all I could quietly say to her was, "Come with me to Rexburg!"[19]

In hindsight, Hal would recognize the value of doing double duty as Commissioner of Education and member of the Twelve. In addition to being viewed as a prophet, seer, and revelator as he guided the employees and students of the Church Educational System, he received the gift of prophecy. The gift came, he realized, largely because it was needed by those he was assigned to lead. Traveling as Commissioner among university faculty members and seminary and institute instructors around the world, he was lifted for their sakes. He was reminded of that whenever he returned home, where learning to be an Apostle took real work.

neyhaw, Mark, sometime last week, forced her out of
our double's match this morning; within an hour she'd
sent a replacement, so I played six sets. Result: I
soaked my elbow in a tub of hot water propped on the
table the breakfast room at grandpa's, while I watched

22

FEED MY SHEEP

Now, I say unto you,
And what I say unto you,
I say unto all the Twelve:
Arise and gird up your loins,
Take up your cross,
Follow me,
And feed my sheep.
—DOCTRINE AND COVENANTS 112:14

Hal had no premonition of his call to the Quorum of the Twelve Apostles. At the time, in the spring of 1995, he was serving in relative obscurity for a Seventy, not as a member of the Presidency of the Seventy or an Area President but as second counselor in the California Area Presidency. Others, though, received signals of what was coming. One was Elder Neil L. Andersen, a fellow Seventy. Elder Andersen, who had served in that capacity for just two years, attended the meeting of the General Authorities on the Thursday before general conference opened. By tradition, they gathered in the First Presidency council room on the fourth floor of the Salt Lake Temple.

The Seventy, who had no assigned spots, were seated in folding chairs behind the armchairs of the First Presidency and the Quorum of the Twelve. That day, Elder Andersen found himself sitting behind an empty armchair. It was the seat of the junior member of the Twelve, vacated as James E. Faust had been called into the First Presidency and the Apostles junior to him had each moved one seat to the right to fill the opening. Gazing at that empty twelfth chair, Elder Andersen had the impression, "The person sitting on your right will be called to fill the vacancy in the Quorum of the Twelve." He was surprised by the thought, which came out of the blue and caught him off guard, as he hadn't noticed who was next to him. He turned to his right and saw Hal Eyring. Touching his colleague's arm, he said, "Elder Eyring, it's an honor to sit next to you."[1]

TWELFTH MAN

Two days later, Hal was sustained by the members of the Church as the newest Apostle. President Gordon B. Hinckley ordained and set him apart as a member of the Quorum of the Twelve Apostles on the following Thursday at the regular meeting of the First Presidency and the Twelve, which happened to fall on April 6, the anniversary of the founding of the Church and the date on which Hal was first sustained as a General Authority. In his words of blessing, President Hinckley noted that Hal's training had been beneficial in his ministry and given him "standing among some groups of people." But he declared Hal's new calling to be above any worldly honor or authority. He also assured Hal that his forebears were proud and that they had added their confirming voice in the call.[2]

While Hal continued to perform his responsibilities as Commissioner of Education, he undertook the training of a new member of the Quorum of the Twelve. That included traveling with senior members of the Quorum on their assignments. The lengthiest of those trips was one with the new Acting President of the Quorum, Boyd K. Packer, who took Hal with him on a tour of Japan.

The two of them had made many similar journeys, and President Packer had always used their time together as an opportunity to school Hal. But now the focus of the training was on the Apostleship. President Packer particularly pushed Hal to speak with greater sensitivity to the Spirit's direction and to the way listeners would hear his words. In each of dozens of meetings with Church members and full-time missionaries, President Packer challenged Hal to probe the feelings of his heart and simultaneously to imagine himself standing at the back of the room, judging the likely effect he was having on the congregation.

After each meeting, President Packer assessed Hal's performance. He reminded Hal that he now spoke not only for the Church but to all of its individual members, many of whom knew no English and had little formal education. In this new position, any worldly eloquence or the slightest desire to impress would block communication with both the Spirit and the hearers. President Packer also reminded Hal that an Apostle must be capable of speaking not only in the gentle, storytelling style he tended to favor but also in the direct, leave-no-doubt manner of Old Testament prophets such as Elijah and Jeremiah.

Upon their return, President Packer encouraged Hal to speak up in Quorum meetings, often calling on him to render his opinion on an issue before even the most senior members had spoken. Hal appreciated the spirit of those invitations from his longtime mentor. But he accepted them with greater awareness and caution than he might have done as a young Stanford professor or as a new counselor to Bishop Robert D. Hales. He was sensitive to both the size of the Quorum and also its respect for seniority and experience. The four senior-most members, President Packer and Elders David B. Haight, L. Tom Perry, and Neal A. Maxwell, had a combined tenure of more than eighty years. In fact, Hal felt special respect for all members of the Quorum, regardless of their experience in that body. The two just above Hal in seniority, Elders Hales and Holland, had supervised him in previous positions, and he felt deep appreciation for their talents. He was truly the Quorum's junior man.

In responding to President Packer's invitations to speak, Hal was concerned about more than his junior status. He knew that his unique background in both Church education and the Bishopric would allow him to offer expert opinions on many matters that came before the Twelve. But he had learned that inspired decisions could come only from a group united by the Spirit. One man's expertise—and the confidence that came with it—could be more divisive than helpful.

Yet he also knew that it wasn't enough to simply agree for the sake of agreement. The issues faced by the Church's leading councils, like those at the local level and within families, are often multifaceted and full of seeming contradictions. Hal appreciated that finding inspired answers would require not just feeling mutual goodwill but making the most of the different perspectives each council member brought to a matter.

Hal was blessed to have experienced such complex conversations since boyhood. His parents had seen most things in life at least slightly differently—and some things very differently. At the dinner table each night, Mildred and Henry would discuss the events of the day, from family- and Church-related matters to science and politics. Given their divergent personalities and viewpoints, the discussions often resembled debates, with Hal and his brothers encouraged to join in.

We can't have feelings of resentment or irritation. Harmony is air to the Spirit. But what we're after is not just a uniform idea. We have to learn how to get in a room on a terribly difficult problem, all thinking very different things to start with. And then, in time, suddenly or maybe slowly, we have the mind of the Lord.

—2011 INTERVIEW

Hal recalled a discussion from election night 1944, when Franklin D. Roosevelt stood for an unprecedented fourth term as President of the United States. Henry, pleased by President Roosevelt's success in reviving the national economy and leading the war effort, felt that a fourth term in office was well deserved. Mildred disagreed, objecting to the President's inefficient government programs and political high-handedness. When Henry announced that he had already voted for Roosevelt, Mildred, who had no driver's license, quietly left the house. She walked to a polling booth and cast a vote for Republican challenger Thomas Dewey, thus negating the effect of Henry's ballot. Years later, Elder Russell M. Nelson accurately observed of Hal's upbringing, "His father would have cultivated that kind of freedom of speech in their home. And his mother would have insisted on it."[3]

A STUDENT AGAIN

Yet along with a lifetime's training in argumentation, Hal entered the Twelve conscious of Patriarch Gaskell Romney's promise of his being a peacemaker, a promise he had cherished and tried to realize since boyhood. As much as possible, he wanted to meld these roles, sharing his unique ideas in ways that would help unify, rather than divide.

One way to do that was to emulate the students he had found most helpful when leading case discussions at the business schools at Harvard and Stanford. In those discussions, students were motivated by more than personal ego to comment in each class session: a large fraction of the end-of-semester grade hinged on daily classroom participation. Seeking to maximize their participation scores, many students adopted a practice of commenting often, with the goal of demonstrating their intellectual prowess. These students might keep an arm raised for the better part of an hour, ready to make a comment prepared before class with the goal of impressing the professor.

But Hal kept his eye on students of another kind, the ones who shared his desire to move the whole group toward clearer understanding of the problems under discussion. These students cared more about learning than about scoring points or "solving" the case. They paid attention to the direction of the discussion, sensing opportunities to add when things seemed to be moving forward productively or to take a new direction when the discussion was bogging down. They were vital allies to a discussion leader, and Hal took care to identify them early in the semester. He literally looked to these students at critical junctures in each class session, trying to read their faces for signs that they might know where he hoped the discussion would go. He valued the contribution one of them might make more than the brilliant but self-conscious comments of the dozens with hands in the air.

As a member of the Quorum of the Twelve, Hal discovered how challenging it was to be such a student. The complex issues that come before this group are vital to the Church and its members. Even more so than in the Church Educational System or the Office of the Presiding Bishopric, the issues brought to the Twelve often involve a complicated mix of temporal and spiritual concerns.

Resolving these issues, Hal found, required not only sharp analytical skills but also inspired judgment. For example, there were delicate balances to be struck between the general need for uniformity in the Church and specific instances warranting exceptions. Likewise, the Quorum frequently grappled with questions of fairness, where the principle of general accountability seemed at odds with individual mercy. And, in many decisions, there was the critical matter of timing—moving in an inspired direction at the right pace, neither too quickly nor too slowly.

Hal discovered a natural urge to simplify these complexities for the sake of making decisions and taking prompt action. He also found that personal experience, including one's current assignments, could be a two-edged sword, a source of both valuable insight and dangerous bias. For example, in addition to his ongoing responsibilities for CES, as a member of the Quorum, Hal received assignments to sit on committees overseeing family history and public affairs. He found that his special knowledge of these causes could fuel desires to protect or to advance them. He came to appreciate his colleagues' warnings not to allow his "stand" on an issue to be influenced by where he "sat."

Fortunately, with twelve unusually bright and experienced minds in the room, a one-sided or self-interested view never got far before meeting strong counterarguments. Yet such opposition, though beneficial, could trigger personal feelings of hurt and even lasting resentment. Hal was surprised by the power of what he called "pride of authorship," the temptation to defend his own statements simply because he had made them. Though there was no formal grade at stake, hc sometimes found himself feeling like a student with a personal agenda, rather than a selfless seeker of truth.

TUTORING AT HOME

In his efforts to succeed in this new "classroom," Hal received special help at home, where the gender balance had flipped. Until the arrival of Elizabeth, in 1979, Kathy had been outnumbered by Eyring men five to one. But now, thanks to the birth of Mary and the gradual departure of the four boys, Hal lived in a feminine world.

He adapted admirably, particularly for a man raised with only brothers. In educating and entertaining four sons, he had learned to carefully plan rigorous physical activities; the key to keeping them engaged was unrelenting motion. The girls, by contrast, appreciated intellectual creativity. They delighted in conversation, preferring spontaneity to structure. Still a task-oriented male at heart, Hal split

HAL PAINTS WITH GRANDDAUGHTER REBECCA

the difference with conversational games such as twenty questions and what he called "made-up stories." The girls helped him make the transition to this new, more introspective and spontaneous world.

Mary asked, "Will you tell us a made-up story?" I said that I couldn't because I had to have time to think of a story. Elizabeth said, "Here, I'll give you two words and you make up the story around them." She thought for a minute and then said, "The words are 'corral' and 'agate.'" The moment she said them I saw a dusty ranch in Arizona, on a high desert plateau, and a little girl coming out of the log house to look up at the distant, purple mountain. And I just knew that girl would find an agate somewhere on that mountain. Then, sure enough, I had a story. And it seemed real to me, not made up. (March 2, 1990)

Hal adapted to the girls' preferences in other ways. He turned Saturday projects from construction and yard work to cooking and organizing closets. With the same methodical study he had applied to drawing and carving, he became an accomplished baker of bread and maker of gravy.

As a General Authority, Hal traveled on most weekends, and so Monday became family project day. When Elizabeth and Mary returned from school, he was ready with the ingredients for whole wheat bread. The girls helped him mix and knead dough. Then, while they waited for the dough to rise and bake, he would carve letters into a small wooden bread board, cut out in advance, for the purpose of making a gift. In each board he carved the words "J'Aime et J'Espere," French for "I Love and I Hope." He would also add the initials of a recipient, usually a neighbor facing a trial of health or sorrow. When the bread was ready, Hal and the girls took a loaf with the board to the neighbor's home.

On the weekends, the girls helped Hal prepare for his stake conference assignments. Elizabeth served as valet, folding a clean white shirt (buttoned to minimize wrinkles) and ensuring that he remembered everything from toiletries to the outlines for his talks.[4] Often, she packed a snack for the road.

Mary, five years younger than Elizabeth, focused more on spiritual preparation. Though fifty years her father's junior, she was a perceptive and outspoken spiritual guide. The journal records her influence on two consecutive weekends in 1990, when she was just six:

> Because Elizabeth and I had taken too long sharpening one of our carving tools, my nervousness rose as the time for my plane approached. Mary felt my irritation, I guess, because she stopped us all with, "Let's pray before we go." Kathy, Elizabeth, and I knelt with her. She was mouth. Her prayer included this line: "Bless Daddy that he will know what to do to help the people in St. George." In the evening of the stake conference, I realized that her prayer was being answered in two ways: I knew what to say; and I felt the love of God, both Mary's for Him and His for me. (Saturday, February 10, 1990)

***

> During the evening session of the Plano (Texas) Stake conference, which was on harmony in the home, I thought of Mary Kathleen. She had heard me speak in a businesslike tone the other day, walked quietly toward me, and said, "Don't speak with a mean voice." She had heard what I hadn't; and she reminded me what the real standard of love is. And then, when I got to my room in the stake president's home, I took out the piece of bread which Elizabeth had baked and included in the bag she packed for me. I shared it with my host and hostess. (Saturday, February 17, 1990)

VISITING THE STAKES

Hal missed Kathy and the girls as he traveled, yet he relished his assignments to meet with Church members around the world. He particularly enjoyed stake conference assignments. He found that his work with the stakes brought outpourings of insight and love.

He also found, though, that the blessing of feeling love for stake members and knowing what to tell them had to be earned. Whenever possible, he would arrive early in the city or town in which the conference would be held. Before the first meeting, he would drive the streets of that community, sometimes with the help of a cab driver, studying the buildings and observing the people.

> When we'd drive in a taxi cab, he'd sit in the front seat, next to the cab driver. And immediately he would start asking him questions, getting acquainted with him, engaging him in a most effective way.
>
> —ELDER L. TOM PERRY[5]

Hal tried to imagine the daily lives of the people and the forces with which they might struggle. The gamut of conditions was always wide, even within a single community. Each stake was likely to include members beset with poverty and despair, as well as others for whom ease and self-satisfaction might be the great spiritual dangers. But, as he studied and prayed, revelation came.

Elder Neil L. Andersen was a member of the Seventy and Hal's junior companion when they shared such an experience. In April 1998, three years after Elder Andersen's impression that Hal would be called to the Twelve, they spoke together at a multistake conference in Pleasant Grove, Utah. At the time the economy and the stock market were soaring, riding unbridled enthusiasm for the alluring possibilities of the Internet. Many Church members in that area worked for booming high-tech companies and were enjoying rapidly rising incomes. It was a time and place of great optimism.

But driving the well-kept streets of aptly named Pleasant Grove, Hal had feelings of wanting to warn the Saints of difficulty

VIEW FROM STAND

ahead. In his remarks at the conference, he cautioned them to avoid living beyond their means and to reduce their financial indebtedness. Elder Andersen would later observe that this caution made little sense at the time: "Everything in the economy was shooting upward. And some believed that the developments of the Internet meant that classic economic cycles as we knew them were over."[6]

In fact, for the next two years, Hal's counsel would seem unfounded and even foolish. The stock market continued to rise at unprecedented rates. Yet six months after Hal's warning, in the priesthood session of general conference, President Hinckley gave similar counsel to exercise caution, noting "a portent of stormy weather." Finally, in the spring of 2000, the market collapsed, as did many high-tech companies, setting off a wave of job losses. The warnings against financial overextension came early, but they proved providential to those who heeded them.

> It was about money, but not really. It was about pain and peace. I had a feeling: "I want you to have peace; I don't want you to have pain. Be careful."
> —2012 INTERVIEW

Elder David A. Bednar shared a similar experience with Hal on a stake conference assignment in Canada. In this instance, they arrived too late for any advance study or even to confer with the stake presidency before the first session of the conference. In that session, Hal found himself led from one apparently unrelated subject to the next, with no opportunity to make orderly transitions. By the time he finished, he had spoken for forty minutes on five different themes. Sitting down, he told Elder Bednar, "I have no idea where that was going; it was all over the place."[7]

After the meeting, Elders Eyring and Bednar were finally able to spend a few minutes alone with the stake presidency. The stake president said, "Elder Eyring, there were some things I had hoped to visit with you about this morning that our members needed to be aware of." He then pulled out a small piece of paper, from which he read the five topics Hal had addressed.[8]

KEEPING IT SIMPLE

During this time Hal's style of public speaking evolved. He felt a growing desire to represent the Savior and to speak so as to be easily translated to a global audience. In general, he tried to be simpler and softer in what he said. To this end, living with three spiritually sensitive females proved highly beneficial. Interacting with them helped Hal recall the soft, plain-spoken style of the great mentors in his life, beginning with his mother, Mildred. That can be seen in a 1990 journal entry, recorded when his youngest child, Mary, was six years old:

Mary Kathleen and I were upstairs, reading the Book of Mark together. My turn came on the verses where Jesus first forgives a palsied man's sins and then, when he senses the unjust censure of the scribes, he heals the man. I decided to give it life, so I read the words with dramatic emphasis, thinking Mary might find it more believable: "I say unto thee, Arise, and take up thy bed and go thy way into thine house." I waited a second. Mary said, softly, "When Jesus spoke then, he didn't use that kind of power language, did he?" Immediately, I remembered the modest voice of President Kimball when he blessed the sick. And I said, "No, Mary, I'm sure he didn't." (December 28, 1990)

In addition to speaking more softly and modestly, Hal tried to speak more simply. That went beyond using shorter words and sentences. It included sticking to the simplest, plainest doctrines. As Commissioner of Education, he had for many years taught the Church's religious educators to emphasize the most fundamental truths of the gospel. In 1993, he reminded them of Gordon B. Hinckley's unmistakable charge, delivered thirty years before at Brigham Young University.

Teach the simple, straightforward truth that came out of the vision of the boy Joseph Smith. Teach the reality of that vision and the manifestations that followed, that brought into being the restored Church of Jesus Christ—The Church of Jesus Christ of Latter-day Saints.[9]

In a 1999 general conference talk, Hal shared his growing appreciation for the power of such simple teaching, along with a warning against well-intentioned attempts to risk more innovative and potentially more intriguing approaches.

> Because we need the Holy Ghost, we must be cautious and careful not to go beyond teaching true doctrine. The Holy Ghost is the Spirit of Truth. His confirmation is invited by our avoiding speculation or personal interpretation. That can be hard to do. You love the person you are trying to influence. He or she may have ignored the doctrine they have been taught. It is tempting to try something new or sensational. But we invite the Holy Ghost as our companion when we are careful to teach only true doctrine.
>
> One of the surest ways to avoid even getting near false doctrine is to choose to be simple in our teaching. Safety is gained by that simplicity, and little is lost.[11]

He's anything but a showman.
—ELDER D. TODD CHRISTOFFERSON[10]

The change in Hal's speaking style was evolutionary, a gradual shift that had been occurring for years and was merely accelerated by his call to the Quorum of the Twelve. But it was a real achievement for a former professor trained at the most elite business schools. In his twenties and thirties, he had competed for the respect of demanding reviewers of his research papers, brilliant MBA students, and savvy, hard-driving business executives. Professional success had required always having new theories and quick answers, elegantly and powerfully expressed.

By contrast, his experiences in speaking as a special witness of the Savior taught him that revelation depended on childlike willingness to be guided, with no personal agenda and no desire to impress through either novel ideas or flowery phrasing. The rush of pride that had accompanied a new insight in the university classroom or an executive boardroom now became a warning signal. As he told a worldwide audience of the Church's seminary, institute, and university religion professors, he learned to step back from any apparently new discovery that came to him in the process of preparing a talk. Upon further study, he would inevitably find not only that a truly inspired idea was not new, but that another Church leader had said it better—"more simply and with even more evidence of God's love."[12]

> He won't say something he doesn't feel or something we don't know or something that hasn't been revealed.
>
> —ELDER QUENTIN L. COOK[13]

Along with teaching simply, Hal increased his emphasis on encouraging listeners with love and optimism. From his mother and other plain-spoken mentors, he had learned the value of setting high expectations. As a college student, he had been disappointed by Mildred's response to the best report card he ever showed her. Somehow, he had managed during one semester as a physics student to get all A's. She looked at the report and said nothing. Crestfallen, he asked, "What do you think?" She replied, "That's what we expect of you."

Through the years, Hal not only got over his disappointment, he learned to appreciate his mother's high expectations as a compliment and a testimony of his eternal potential. "Sometimes the greatest kindness we could receive," he told a group of BYU students in 1997, "would be to have someone expect more from us than we do, because they see more clearly our divine heritage."[14]

At the same time, Hal was grateful for his father's gift of building people up, in anticipation of life's knocking them down. Though he never fully believed his father's overly generous compliments, they inspired him to believe in himself.

Thus, in his talks to the members of the Church, Hal sought to convey both high expectations and genuine confidence in their ability and desire to rise to those expectations. He did both, simultaneously, by ascribing to his listeners the desire to be better. For example, he began a talk titled "Come unto Christ" with the statement, "You have moments when you want to be better than you have ever been."[15] Often he would pay the additional compliment of joining his hearers in that desire to be better.

COUNSELING WITH THE QUORUM

Hal's experiences in addressing the Saints in their stake conferences and in larger gatherings such as general conference helped him find the right way to speak in meetings of the Quorum of the Twelve. Much as he would prepare for a stake conference by arriving early and observing the physical and spiritual environment, he also learned to get the lay of the land before speaking in Quorum meetings. That meant not only reading the briefing materials prepared to facilitate discussion of scheduled topics but also studying those discussions as they unfolded in the meeting.

> You and I would like to know how to control our wants and increase our gratitude and generosity. We are going to need that change. Someday, in our families and as a people, we will live as one, seeking each other's good.
>
> —TALK, SEPTEMBER 30, 1989[16]

His background as a classroom teacher and student proved helpful. He appreciated the importance of listening carefully to each comment made by his peers. Rather than focusing on his own thoughts about a topic, he tried to attend to his colleagues. He observed both their words and the tone with which they spoke. This helped him understand the emotions behind the statements being made.

In understanding his colleagues, Hal appreciated the effects of past personal experiences. In Elder Hales's case, the intertwining of their lives gave him firsthand understanding of many of the experiences that had shaped this great leader. But Hal was also blessed to have known many other members of the Quorum before any of them were called as General Authorities. Elder Maxwell was the Commissioner of Education who changed the course of Hal's life in 1971. That was also when he began his association with Elder Oaks and Elder Holland, who were drafted into CES service by Elder Maxwell at the same time as Hal.

May 31, 1984
Thursday

I wrote in the Atherton guest house of the Johnsons, looking down on the trees and drive of our first home. Elizabeth and Mary Kathleen watched me blow out candles on my birthday cake, after a dinner ⟨...⟩ Trudie. The Holy Gh⟨...⟩ teach a⟨...⟩ workshop⟨...⟩

June 1, ⟨...⟩
Friday

Elizabet⟨...⟩ the po⟨...⟩ worked ⟨...⟩ Gary c⟨...⟩ Los Ang⟨...⟩ to hear⟨...⟩ time to⟨...⟩ Altos.

June 2, ⟨...⟩
Saturda⟨...⟩

I towed⟨...⟩ inflated⟨...⟩ Mary ⟨...⟩ compl⟨...⟩ purple ⟨...⟩ match ⟨...⟩ hair that marks her as Stuart's and Matthew's sister. Grandpa Johnson and I watched Stephanie dance in a musical.

June 3, 1984
Sunday

THE QUORUM OF THE TWELVE AT
THE TIME OF HAL'S CALL

Kathy, Elizabeth, and Mary Kathleen were dressed and packed early for our drive from Atherton to the San Jose airport. On the flight home, a stewardess made a bullseye with a glass full of orange juice on my lap. It was so cold and complete a soaking that I laughed for the rest of the trip. I used bags to shield the results as I got us to the car.

His awareness of other Quorum members went even further back. Elder Nelson was the gifted surgeon who had preserved his mother's life in the late 1960s. And he had first encountered Elder Haight as he courted Kathy, almost ten years before that. At the time, Elder Haight was president of the Palo Alto Stake, where Kathy's parents lived. On Hal's first visit from Boston to Palo Alto, his in-laws hosted a dinner. Sid and La Prele invited their good friends Dave and Ruby Haight as part of an informal team assembled to vet Hal as a son-in-law.

Of course, Hal had known all his fellow Quorum members for many years, having interacted with them in his work as a member of the Presiding Bishopric and as Commissioner of Education. Through shared Church service assignments he had learned about the experiences that had shaped their perspectives, from schooling, to mission or military service, to professional training. Though careful not to fall prey to stereotyping, he was sensitive to the way a professor, such as himself, might view things differently than a business entrepreneur, an engineer, a lawyer, or a doctor would.

Hal quickly gained a reputation among his colleagues for thinking carefully before he spoke up. They could tell that it wasn't a matter of shyness, that he was pondering both the merits of the particular issue at hand and also the best way to introduce his own thoughts. They appreciated his desire to enlighten while simultaneously enhancing unity.

At the same time, Hal became known for boldness, particularly given his junior status in the Quorum. Thanks to the remarkable longevity of the

> Sometimes he just sits quietly, but you know what's going on in that magnificent mind is pondering, weighing, and organizing.
> —ELDER RICHARD G. SCOTT[17]

> He has a tendency to be really cautious until he fully understands. . . . He's trying to see things as they are.
> —ELDER M. RUSSELL BALLARD[18]

fourteen men senior to him, he would occupy the twelfth chair for more than nine years, longer than any man since John A. Widtsoe. But he didn't let that status stop him from contributing. He was careful not to weigh in when his opinion would add little—as he would have been regardless of seniority. Yet when, after careful deliberation, he felt the need to speak, he did so boldly.

Hal felt gratitude for his Brethren's measured reaction to his boldness. He was amazed at their ability to depersonalize even a strenuous debate. That was particularly true of his longtime colleague Dallin H. Oaks, who left the University of Chicago for BYU as Hal departed Stanford for Ricks College. He had admired Elder Oaks from the beginning. But in the Quorum, that admiration reached new heights. Hal found that he could challenge Elder Oaks with a contrary argument and, if his facts were good, be not only heard but actually thanked for the correction. Like all of their Brethren, Elder Oaks sought not to win an argument, only to find the truth. In that, Hal's first impression of him was more than borne out.

 I walked over to my 7:30 meeting with the Commissioner and the presidents, arriving on the dot. The discussions ranged over 22 agenda items until three in the afternoon, with only a ten-minute break. The tribute to Neal is that not five minutes seemed wasted or fruitless. Dallin Oaks has a precious combination: he is without pretense and smart as a whip. The humility allows him to ask questions, and his mind gobbles up the answers. He will grow at a breathtaking rate. He's the living argument for the effectiveness of being teachable. (August 13, 1971)

> Sometimes he has engaged me, where we had a different opinion on a matter. I've always found that exhilarating and helpful because he is so bright.
> —ELDER DALLIN H. OAKS[19]

Even in his boldness, Hal remained responsive to correction. That was true not only in Quorum discussions but in formal assignments to work on specific problems. In that work he gave his all—and then, when directed, more.

In the first meeting of the day I reported to a committee on my weeks of work on a difficult problem. I expected that my recommendations would be accepted and the task ended. Instead, President Packer and Elder Oaks saw more that could and must be done. So, instead of a load being lifted, more was added. I felt joy to know that the Lord wanted more done and trusted me to do it. It was clear that what was asked for was given by revelation. Continuous revelation seems to mean continuous work. (November 18, 2005)

Hal was particularly responsive to correction when it came from the Spirit. Elder David A. Bednar saw that in 2001, three years before becoming a member of the Quorum of the Twelve. At that time, Elder Bednar was president of the just-created BYU–Idaho. President Bednar hosted Hal, in his role as Commissioner of Education, on a visit to Rexburg. They toured the campus, which included several recently completed buildings. President Bednar shared the new university's plans for additional buildings, as well as the creation of many new faculty positions.

President Bednar believed that all of this had been approved by the Church Board of Education, headed by President Gordon B. Hinckley. But Hal interpreted the approval as provisional, an authorization only to explore expansion, not necessarily to execute it without further review. "We never agreed to this much space, this much money, or this many people," he declared. President Bednar expressed willingness to change direction, despite months of planning and preparing for the growth. But he expressed his view that everything was within the scope of what the Board had previously approved.

Hal spent the night in the Bednars' home, in a basement guest room. When he came up for breakfast the next morning, his first words were, "President, I was rebuked by the Holy Ghost last night."[20] He didn't ask to see the minutes of the Board meetings in which the university's growth had been discussed, though his memory of those discussions hadn't changed. In the night he had been told to let the

> When things are a little stressful, he finds ways to see things from a different viewpoint and take into consideration what others think. That's helping to be a peacemaker, when you take that which others feel is important and significant, and weigh it before you judge it.
>
> —PRESIDENT DIETER F. UCHTDORF[21]

BYU–Idaho administrative team proceed at heaven's direction. For Hal that message settled the matter, without regard to minutes or memories.

Elder Dieter F. Uchtdorf, who entered the Quorum on the same day as Elder Bednar, was among those who observed Hal's responsiveness to correction. These two new Apostles, whose addition finally relieved Hal of his junior status, saw the beneficial effects of the preceding nine and a half years. They observed in their colleague a bright, opinionated man nonetheless open to reason and eager to learn the Lord's will. Hal was becoming known as a peacemaker.

In April 2005, Hal completed his tenth year as a member of the Quorum. The milestone was marked partly by his release as Commissioner of Education. President Hinckley, who had ended discussion of the matter nine years earlier with the words, "We'll let you know, Hal," finally did.

Late in the day, President Hinckley called me to his office. He asked how long I had served as Commissioner of Education. I said that I didn't know. President Hinckley smiled and said, "It's been a long time." I apologized for not knowing the number of years and explained that I didn't think about such things partly because my father had always said, "Work your heart out every day doing the best you can and the future will take care of itself." President Hinckley then asked if I was ready to be released. I answered with a smile, "I want to do whatever you want me to do." President Hinckley said that the release would be given.

Kathleen took the news with a smile when I got home. (January 11, 2005)

In addition to Hal's release as Commissioner, there would be another marker of his tenth anniversary as a member of the Twelve: a serious trial of health. And other trials would follow. He was entering a new phase of service to Church and family.

Kathy's left elbow, as injured she was playing with an
nephew, Mark, sometime last week, forced her out of
our double's match this morning; within an hour she'd
sent a replacement, so I played six sets. Result: I
soaked my elbow in a tub of hot water propped on the
table in the breakfast room at grandpa's, while I watched
the box with the boys. Annette served the whole

23

STAND BY MY SERVANT

Therefore be diligent;
Stand by my servant Joseph, faithfully,
In whatsoever difficult circumstances he may be
For the word's sake.

—DOCTRINE AND COVENANTS 6:18

Since his thirties, when Mildred and Henry were diagnosed with cancer, Hal had known that the same fate awaited him. When his younger brother, Harden, underwent treatment for prostate cancer, the disease that ultimately killed their father, Hal felt certain that his time would likewise come. It did, in the spring of 2005.

Hal's doctor was pragmatic. The prostate cancer, he said, was in its early stages and likely to advance slowly; it wouldn't begin to create real trouble for perhaps ten years. By then Hal would be in his early eighties, a reasonable life expectancy for even the healthiest of men. At that age he was as likely to die from some other cause. Thus, foregoing treatment was a valid option, one that came without the potentially life-altering side effects of treatment, particularly radical prostatectomy.

Hal and Kathy consulted with other doctors and with his Brethren. Neither he nor she felt comfortable taking no action. They ultimately decided on surgery as the course most likely to preserve Hal's life and potential to serve his family and the Church for a long time.

The surgery was successful, but it took a greater toll than expected. Hal didn't recover his strength for more than six months. Stake conference visits and mission tours with which he had hoped to celebrate recovery had to be postponed or canceled. Even after he resumed his usual schedule, it was with occasional pain and persistent fatigue. The frustratingly long recovery period, though, brought unexpected benefits. Hal had time to reflect on his service and the reasons for which heaven might be willing to extend it.

Among other things, he pondered a conversation from the year before with his friend and mentor Neal Maxwell. Elder Maxwell had been diagnosed in 1996 with an aggressive form of leukemia and given a prognosis of a year or two of life, at best. He beat that target by more than six years, not succumbing until July 2004.

A few weeks before his passing, Elder Maxwell invited Hal to his home for a final interview. Neal offered counsel for Hal's future service, delivering a message at once complimentary, gentle, and trenchant. Neal said, "Hal, you have a great mind and a gift for perceiving risks. But if you're going to reach your full potential to contribute in the kingdom, you're going to have to become as good at seeing possibilities as you are at seeing pitfalls. We need you to be a problem solver, not just a problem spotter."

> Trained as I was, at the Harvard Business School and around the dinner table at my home, I almost always shot holes in things—not trying to destroy, but to identify imperfections.
>
> —2013 INTERVIEW

Elder Maxwell's counsel, given by a supervisor and senior colleague of more than thirty years, hit home. Had Hal wanted to argue the point, he could have done so forcibly. As the Commissioner of Education, for example, he had helped to solve two of the Church's most complex higher education challenges: melding faith with scholarship and serving more students at an affordable cost. That work had required keen analytical understanding of difficult problems, but also the patience and kindness to help others understand and take action on their own.

Hal knew, though, that Elder Maxwell was talking about the even more complex challenge of problem solving as a member of the Church's leading councils. For nearly ten years Elder Maxwell had watched Hal in weekly meetings of the Quorum of the Twelve and the First Presidency. Neal had admired Hal's courage in advancing well-reasoned opinions, even in the face of strong and sometimes heated counterarguments. But Hal tended to speak more by way of caution than of support.

Hal didn't argue with Elder Maxwell in this last interview. His motives went beyond deference and the desire to part amicably from his generous mentor. He knew that Elder Maxwell was right. Throughout his term in the Quorum he had felt the burden of being one of its more notable naysayers. Elder Maxwell's challenge to become a problem solver aligned with Patriarch Caskell Romney's charge to be a peacemaker: ultimately, his ability to promote opinions among his Brethren depended on his joining them in solving problems. Thus, he welcomed Elder Maxwell's clear, actionable agenda for personal change.

I saw two such men—changed men—negotiate for a place in a cafeteria waiting line a few years ago. One, the younger man, tried to get the older man to go ahead of him, because he thought the older man's time was more valuable than his. But the older man refused. They were negotiating their disagreement as I watched, both determined that the other would go first. I remember that the older man won his point. His name was Spencer W. Kimball. The younger man must have thought that the time of the President of the Church was more valuable than his. But I suppose President Kimball thought that the younger man's stomach needed something in it sooner than his did. There was disagreement and negotiation. But think of what a disagreement that was, and think of the smiles on their faces as they found, together, a path of peace.

—TALK, FEBRUARY 6, 1994[1]

A LAST-MINUTE ASSIGNMENT

In September 2007, Hal received an assignment to practice his problem solving and peacemaking skills under unusually challenging circumstances. That year, September 11, the six-year anniversary of the terrorist attacks in New York City and Washington, D.C., was also the 150-year anniversary of the Mountain Meadows Massacre. Descendants of the victims of the massacre, along with others dedicated to preserving the memory of the tragedy, planned to gather for a historic commemoration.

The Church had decided that it would be represented at this commemoration and respond to long-standing calls for a formal statement about its involvement in the massacre. Initially, Hal was not scheduled to participate. Elder Marlin K. Jensen, a member of the Seventy and Church Historian, would represent the Church and read a prepared statement approved by the First Presidency. Elder Jensen was an excellent choice, a representative deserving of respect not only as a General Authority but also as an expert on the history of the awful events at Mountain Meadows.

However, during the weekend before the Tuesday commemoration, Elder Jensen became gravely ill, to the point of needing hospital care. On Monday, with less than twenty-four hours' notice, Hal received a phone call from the office of the First Presidency. He

> I had grown up in the mission field where there was only a tiny branch, which met in my home. Then my family moved to where there were stakes and large wards and chapels and quorums of boys who all seemed to know so much more than I did about what priesthood holders do. They had in that ward a complicated pattern for passing the sacrament. I felt almost certain that I would make a mistake when my turn to pass or prepare the sacrament came.
>
> In my fear and desperation, I remember going outside the chapel to be alone. I was worried. I prayed for help and for some assurance that I would not fail in serving God in His priesthood.
>
> —TALK, OCTOBER 6, 2007[2]

was assigned to stand in Elder Jensen's stead and read the Church's statement.

At the time, Hal was working on a general conference address to be delivered three weeks later. He was struggling with the theme, "God Helps the Faithful Priesthood Holder." He had in mind two personal memories. One was of the fear he felt in passing the sacrament for the first time in Utah after moving from New Jersey.

The other memory was of an assignment from the First Presidency to fill in for Elder Maxwell at a national conference of leaders of churches in the United States. Hal had arrived in Minneapolis, site of the three-day conference, with no knowledge of his role but with feelings of trepidation about the conference theme: reducing competition among religious denominations. His concerns mounted when he learned that he was assigned to speak multiple times on the need for a restoration of the true Church through Joseph Smith. When he reported his fears in a phone call to President Hinckley, the prophet replied simply, "Use your best judgment." That led to a sleepless night, as Hal would recall.

> I prayed through the night. Somewhere near dawn, I was sure I was to say about the Restoration not, "This is what we believe happened to Joseph Smith and why we believe it happened," but, "This is what happened to Joseph Smith, and this is why the Lord did it." In the nighttime I was given no assurance of the outcome, just a clear direction—go forward.
>
> To my amazement, after my talk the ministers lined up to speak to me. Every one of them, one after another coming to me, told essentially the same story. Each of them had met a member of the Church somewhere in their lives that they admired. Many of them said that they lived in a community where the stake president had come to the aid of not just his members but of the community in a disaster. They asked if I could take back their greeting and their thanks to people I not only didn't know but had no hope of ever meeting.[3]

At home working on this talk when the phone call from the First Presidency's office came, Hal recognized another opportunity to practice the principles he planned to preach. He immediately left for Southern Utah, where he met his distant cousin Richard Eyring Turley, Assistant Historian to the ailing Elder Jensen. They spent the night planning and praying, as Hal had done in Minneapolis. Of particular concern was the fact that the statement he would read the next day stopped just short of a formal apology, using the word *regret* to express the Church's feelings about the tragic brutality and loss of life at Mountain Meadows. Moreover, the statement would disclaim involvement by senior Church leaders in Salt Lake City, notably Brigham Young, in the planning of the massacre. And the Church would not accede to requests from the victims' relatives that the Church-owned monument site be turned over to the federal government or to a private trustee.

The broader context of the commemoration prompted additional concerns. Three weeks earlier, a cinematic interpretation of the massacre had appeared in theaters nationwide, with an Academy Award–winning leading man playing the role of a murderous bishop acting at the direction of Brigham Young. Five months before that, in April, PBS[4] had televised a four-hour documentary, *The Mormons*, in which the massacre featured prominently. The atmosphere of the commemoration could hardly have been more charged.

In the event, though, Hal felt deeply blessed. In front of the aggrieved relatives, many of whom had traveled from their homes in Arkansas, he read the statement as it had been prepared and approved. His only unique contribution was a sensitive, sober tone. His voice broke as he expressed the Church's "profound regret" and as he invoked a blessing of love and forgiveness upon all present. The audience responded with unexpected graciousness, rising in a standing ovation as he finished. Many of the victims' relatives embraced Hal tearfully.

A VACANCY IN THE FIRST PRESIDENCY

At the time, a few thoughtful observers saw Hal's assignment to speak at Mountain Meadows as a portent that he would be called to fill the vacancy in the First Presidency created in early August of that year by the death of President James E. Faust. Hal, though, was not among them. He had no such inkling, and certainly not a feeling strong enough to overcome the illogic of the idea. Though he was no longer the junior man in the Twelve, thanks to the addition of Elders Uchtdorf and Bednar, a tenth man was little more likely to be brought into the First Presidency than a twelfth. Nothing like that had occurred for more than forty years, when N. Eldon Tanner, then the eleventh member of the Twelve in seniority, was called as second counselor to David O. McKay. By long-established tradition, counselors tended to be chosen from among the more senior members of the Quorum. That tradition had held in the forty-four years since President Tanner's appointment. Presidents Hinckley, Monson, and Faust had been called into the First Presidency as, respectively, the fourth, second, and third most senior members.

Hal also gave no thought to such a possibility because he revered and even idolized President Faust. The two had begun their full-time Church service at roughly the same time, in the early 1970s. Hal had several times hosted President Faust on visits to Ricks College. From the beginning, he had admired President Faust's self-effacing but steady manner.

Hal's friendship with President Faust grew especially close during a 1982 trip to the Holy Land, Egypt, and the lands of Paul's travels. For two weeks they studied and taught the gospel together, joined by family members. In a general conference address he gave years later, Hal recalled a lesson about priesthood keys learned from President Faust on that trip.

> I'm one of your newer leaders. I fill a special position among the Brethren. There has to be one who is the least and the most inadequate, the one who has the least to offer. I fill that position quite well.
>
> —ELDER JAMES E. FAUST[5]

I spoke in an ancient theater in Ephesus. Bright sunlight flooded the ground where the Apostle Paul had stood to preach. My topic was Paul, the Apostle called of God. The audience was hundreds of Latter-day Saints. They were arranged on the rows of stone benches the Ephesians sat upon more than a millennium before. Among them were two living Apostles, Elder Mark E. Petersen and Elder James E. Faust.

As you can imagine, I had prepared carefully. I had read the Acts of the Apostles and the Epistles, those of both Paul and his fellow Apostles. I had read and pondered Paul's Epistle to the Ephesians.

I tried my best to honor Paul and his office. After the talk, a number of people said kind things. Both of the living Apostles were generous in their comments. But later, Elder Faust took me aside and, with a smile and with softness in his voice, said, "That was a good talk. But you left out the most important thing you could have said."

I asked him what that was. Weeks later he consented to tell me. His answer has been teaching me ever since.

He said that I could have told the people that if the Saints who heard Paul had possessed a testimony of the value and the power of the keys he held, perhaps the Apostles would not have had to be taken from the earth.[6]

President Faust continued to mentor Hal until his passing. Often, the teaching came by way of personal example. Hal appreciated his remarkable mix of apostolic boldness and humble ministration. Even after President Faust became Second

Stuart blessed the sacrament today in the ship's lounge. Matthew passed to those on the stand, starting with Elder Hunter and Elder Faust. Elder Faust bore testimony that he, like the brother of Jared, could say that he knew the Lord lived. When Kathy thanked him later for sharing something so sacred with us, he smiled and turned away without comment.

—JOURNAL, SUNDAY, OCTOBER 17, 1982,
  SAILING FROM FLORENCE TO CAIRO

Counselor to President Gordon B. Hinckley, in 1995, he continued to show special solicitude not only for Hal but also for Kathy and their family. As Kathy's mother, La Prele, entered her nineties and declined in health, President Faust regularly greeted Hal with the question, "How's Grandma?" When La Prele passed away at age ninety-six, President Faust called with his condolences before Hal and Kathy had begun to communicate the news, which they had just received themselves. Somehow, he already knew.

President Faust continued to teach Hal personalized, one-on-one lessons, like the one in Ephesus. Several weeks after his call to the Twelve, in the April general conference of 1995, Hal received an invitation to visit President Faust, who had been called into the First Presidency in the same conference. They met in the Second Counselor's office, a spacious, high-ceilinged corner room on the first floor of the Church Administration Building.

"Hal," President Faust began, "I've been watching you. You've seemed sober lately." He continued tenderly, "Has it happened yet? Are you doubting your worthiness to serve?"

In fact, Hal had been feeling overwhelmed with the weight of his new assignment, so much so that he had begun to doubt his worthiness. He was touched that his friend and mentor had noticed, and his hopes swelled at the prospect of confessing his doubts. But as he leaned forward eagerly, President Faust held up a hand to stop him. Pointing a finger toward the ceiling, he said, solemnly, "Don't ask me if you're worthy; ask Him."

> He knew, and I have come to feel, that only the Father, His Beloved Son, and the Holy Ghost can provide the assurance we all need to go forward boldly in our service. It is not what we have done that matters. It is how our hearts have been changed through our faithful obedience. And only God knows that."
>
> —TALK, JUNE 24, 2010[7]

LILA MOORE'S "VIBES"

The combination of his junior status and his deep respect for President Faust made it all but impossible for Hal to imagine succeeding him in the First Presidency. Others, though, were more susceptible to spiritual impressions about the matter. One was Lila Moore, the widow of Craig Moore, the Eyrings' faithful home teacher during their six years in Rexburg. Craig had died in 1994, and Lila had been living alone in their home for more than thirteen years. By the fall of 2007, she was nearing age ninety and confined to a wheelchair. She passed her days watching and listening to sermons on the television and radio, taking special delight in talks by her favorite General Authority, Henry B. Eyring. Though thirty years had passed since the Eyrings left Rexburg, her connection to Hal was still strong. He had returned to preside at Craig's funeral, and he always stopped to see her on visits to BYU–Idaho, giving her special bragging rights among members of the ward.

Lila was also visited regularly by Hal's eldest son, Henry, who had returned to work at the university. On the first Sunday of September in 2007, three weeks after President Faust's passing, Lila ended Henry's visit with a surprising declaration. "I've been having vibes about a new assignment for Elder Eyring."

The word *vibes*, Henry knew, was Lila's self-effacing shorthand for her spiritual impressions. Filling the many hours of daily isolation with contemplation and prayer for her loved ones, she often received words of comfort and guidance to offer them. Henry himself had been a beneficiary. But this particular "vibe" seemed beyond the pale of reason. In fact, it took Henry several seconds to realize what she meant. When he overcame the shock, he began struggling for a gentle way to disabuse her of the notion.

"Lila," he said, "it's natural for you to admire Elder Eyring and feel that he's qualified for any calling. But he's a very junior Apostle. You've been blessed with a feeling of approval and love for your friend. But this calling will go to an equally good man who is more senior."

Lila hardened her gaze. In a low voice, with teeth slightly clenched, she said, "*I know my vibes.*"

Lila didn't let the matter drop. In the succeeding weeks she delivered the same message several times, with enough force that Henry finally felt obliged to convey it to his father. Hal responded with a rueful chuckle and said, "Well, Lila may know something, but President Hinckley doesn't seem to."

In fact, the prophet's treatment of Hal had changed recently, but not in an encouraging way. Far from displaying the kind of personal approval that might have been inferred from the assignment to speak at Mountain Meadows, President Hinckley seemed more cool toward Hal than before.

PRINCE HAL

That uncertainty shaped Hal's response to a phone call that came to the Eyring home on the Thursday evening before general conference. He had left the office a bit before five o'clock and driven home. After parking the car, he walked down the Eyrings' steep driveway to retrieve an empty garbage can. He was wheeling the can up the driveway when Kathy stepped into the open garage with a portable phone.

"Hal," she called, "it's the phone for you."

"Can you take a message?" he replied.

"It's the office of the First Presidency," Kathy said with a note of urgency. "I think you'd better take it."

Hal grasped the phone in one hand, still holding the garbage can in the other. He heard the secretary to the First Presidency, Michael Watson, say, "President Hinckley would like to talk to you." After an uncomfortable silence on Hal's end, President Hinckley came on and declared, without introduction, "I'd like to ask you to join President Monson and me in the First Presidency."

At what otherwise might have been a moment of profound thoughts and feelings, Hal faced an analytical dilemma. President Hinckley hadn't spoken his name, either first or last. Given the improbability of his being called to the First Presidency, he had to wonder whether Brother Watson had connected President Hinckley to the wrong man. It had happened before. Each member of the Twelve has his own speed-dial key on the main phones in the office of the First Presidency. More than once, Hal had taken a call for someone else due to an inadvertent mistake in dialing. This, he thought, could be one of those times. It was a chance he couldn't take.

"President Hinckley," Hal blurted out, "are you sure you're talking to the right person? This is Hal Eyring."

"I know who this is!" President Hinckley replied. The ensuing conversation was short. Hal accepted the call, saying he would do anything President Hinckley asked and that it would be an honor to serve with him and President Monson. President Hinckley bade Hal good-bye with no more explanation or expression of emotion than he had offered in calling him into the Twelve. Hal put the garbage can away and shared the news with Kathy.

Two days later, President Hinckley invited a sustaining vote of the new First Presidency and of Quentin L. Cook as a new member of the Quorum of the Twelve Apostles. He offered no verbal comment on Hal's selection. But, after presenting all of the General Authorities and general officers of the Church, President Hinckley stopped on his way back to his seat. Raising the cane that he had used for several years, he ceremoniously touched Hal on each shoulder.

Photos of the gesture soon appeared on the Internet. Many viewers saw the humor in the "knighting," but Hal appreciated its deeper significance. President Hinckley was an amateur scholar of the works of William Shakespeare. More than once, he had challenged Hal, the physics student and business professor, to become familiar with great literature in general and Shakespeare's work in particular. Hal had made only fitful attempts, and he was embarrassed when President Hinckley occasionally asked about his progress.

Hal knew just enough Shakespeare, though, to recognize the double meaning when President Hinckley referred to him as "Prince

Hal." He knew that title was a good-natured insult. Shakespeare's Prince Hal, the future Henry V of England, was a young ne'er-do-well, a bright but irresponsible idler whose conduct besmirched his father's reputation and cast doubt on his own fitness to reign. Hal, the self-doubting junior Apostle, could never fully convince himself that there wasn't more than just good-natured ribbing in President Hinckley's jovial use of the Prince Hal label. His doubts had grown during the preceding weeks, when the President's behavior toward him had been inexplicably cool. But now, President Hinckley's symbolic knighting made the Shakespearean reference sweet: With the touch of a wooden cane on each shoulder, the Prophet assured "Prince Hal" that he had come of age.

PRESIDENT HINCKLEY "KNIGHTS" HAL

A PREMATURE PARTING

Hal felt warmly welcomed by his new colleagues in the First Presidency. He knew both President Hinckley and President Monson well, though in different contexts. His relationship with President Hinckley was task based. When they were together, it was to get something done, usually in the service of the Church Educational System or, from 1985 to 1992, the operations of the Presiding Bishopric, such as temple construction.

Hal had also worked on projects with President Monson over the years. But most of their time together had been spent in meetings, particularly the weekly Thursday meeting of the First Presidency and the Quorum of the Twelve. From 1992 to 2004, when Hal was the junior member of the Twelve, he had sat immediately to President Monson's right. For nine and a half years, they were literally knee-to-knee during discussions of such matters as plans for small temples, the construction of the Conference Center, and the creation of BYU–Idaho.

They also sat side by side during a lunch following the meeting, and the tradition of serving plates by seniority gave President Monson a weekly opportunity to tease Hal. Dishes would be served first to President Hinckley and then to President Monson, on his right. The movement after that, though, was all counterclockwise: back to President Faust, on President Hinckley's left, and then to the members of the Quorum of the Twelve by seniority, with Hal last. President Monson delighted in reminding Hal of his risky position in this system. "Oh, Hal," he might say, "those potatoes look awfully good; I hope they save some for you."

The deep personal ties among the members of the new First Presidency produced an immediate unity and camaraderie. Hal relished his daily association with Presidents Hinckley and Monson. Sadly, though, it would be short-lived. President Hinckley, then in his ninety-eighth year, was finally succumbing to the physical effects of age. On January 27, 2008, less than four months after the creation of the new First Presidency, he passed away.

On February 2, a day when Hal had planned to join President Hinckley in Rexburg for the dedication ceremonies of the new temple adjacent to the recently expanded BYU–Idaho campus, he instead joined President Monson in the Conference Center, to eulogize the prophet who had conceived all three of those facilities. Hal praised President Hinckley for his unmatched work ethic and his trademark optimism:

> He is in the spirit world today among the noble prophets who have lived on the earth. He is surely aware of our sorrow and our sense of loss at our separation from him. He knew at the end of his life the pain in his heart of losing someone he loved. If we told him of our grief, he would listen carefully, and then I think he would say something like this, with sympathy in his voice but with a sound in it that would bring a smile to our lips, "Oh, it will work out."[8]

Hal ended his tribute to President Hinckley with a passage from Shakespeare's *Henry V*, which he had been reading in honor of the prophet. The passage is a prayer offered by Henry V, the young Prince Hal now grown into a surprisingly valiant, faithful king. In King Henry's prayer before the pivotal Battle of Agincourt, Hal Eyring found a metaphor for preaching the gospel against apparently overwhelming odds, as President Hinckley had so often challenged him and the Church at large to do.

> *O God of battles! steel my soldiers' hearts;*
> *Possess them not with fear; take from them now*
> *The sense of reckoning, if th' opposed numbers*
> *Pluck their hearts from them!*[9]

FIRST COUNSELOR

Two days after President Hinckley's funeral, on Monday, February 4, 2008, the Church announced via press conference that President Monson had chosen Hal and Dieter F. Uchtdorf as his First and Second Counselors, respectively. Hal was grateful for President Monson's vote of confidence. It would have been unusual but not unprecedented to have called another member of the Twelve "over" Hal to serve as First Counselor, or to have released him altogether from the First Presidency; he was still junior to nine members of the Quorum of the Twelve, each of whom could have served well. President Monson announced his decision to the Brethren of the Twelve in a meeting in the Salt Lake Temple on Sunday, February 3. His generous show of support heightened Hal's desire to give his all in the new calling.

Two days later, though, it appeared that Hal might have little or nothing to give President Monson and the Church. Early on a Wednesday morning, he collapsed as he jumped up from his basement computer. He had been writing for several hours when he glanced at the clock and realized that he'd have to hurry to avoid being late for work. The next thing he knew, he was lying in a heap on the floor, his

I had prayed extensively about my decision, and I had studied this matter very carefully, considering seniority and then considering the talents which I felt were needed at this time and those who would make a nice compatible Presidency. I felt inspired to choose Brother Henry Bennion Eyring to be my first counselor. He had been the second counselor to President Gordon B. Hinckley for just a short time before President Hinckley died. Then I chose Dieter Friedrich Uchtdorf, a convert to the Church and a member of the Twelve since October 2004 and a native of Germany, to be my second counselor. Brother Eyring comes from a family of scientists and educators, and Brother Uchtdorf was chief pilot for Lufthansa Airlines and formerly a stake president in Germany.

—PRESIDENT THOMAS S. MONSON[10]

right ankle tucked awkwardly under his folded legs. He got to his feet and made it to the office on time, though not without difficulty and considerable pain in the ankle.

Hal worked a normal office day until midafternoon, when the pain in his ankle finally prompted him to have it checked by a doctor. He learned that it was broken. More worryingly, over the ensuing days he continued to experience moments of complete or partial blackout. Fortunately, he could feel them coming on and always managed to find a chair before losing consciousness.

Though these episodes naturally terrified Hal, President Monson handled one of them with typical aplomb. The First Presidency were hosting the Israeli Ambassador to the United States in their offices. After a pleasant conversation, the group rose to take their places for a commemorative photograph. Hal could feel a blackout coming on and quickly reseated himself. Not missing a beat, President Monson enthused, "That's a great idea, Hal: We'll take this photo around you!"

Hal underwent several batteries of medical tests without learning the cause of his persistent problem. He was gripped with fear of another fall and only slightly less worried by the prospect of a long-term limitation on his ability to serve. Ironically, the stress attendant to these feelings seemed, if anything, to worsen the problem.

A welcome breakthrough in the case came when Elder Russell M.

Nelson, a pioneering heart surgeon, suggested that Hal be wired and continuously monitored for abnormal heart function. Twenty-four hours later, Hal's doctors had a conclusive diagnosis: his heart was stopping and restarting itself, sometimes after dangerous delays of nearly ten seconds. At last there was something to be done. Though potentially lethal, the problem was easily fixed with the insertion of a pacemaker.

Still, Hal wasn't out of the woods. The pacemaker required adjustments. It took several weeks to find the right balance between too fast and too slow, the one producing exhaustion and the other more fainting spells. In the meantime, general conference loomed. Hal wanted to play his part as a member of the First Presidency; that would mean speaking twice and conducting at least one of the five sessions. As the first weekend of April approached and the right pacemaker setting proved elusive, he worried about merely walking to the Conference Center pulpit and remaining upright for the seventeen minutes required to deliver a sermon.

A PROCEDURAL MISTAKE

During the anxious weeks leading up to general conference, Hal continued to go into the office and perform his normal duties. At that particular time, one of those duties was the calling of members of a new general Young Women presidency. The experience proved pivotal for Hal. He would simultaneously commit a serious error and learn what it meant to serve President Thomas S. Monson well.

One of the sisters who came to his office was expecting her call to the Young Women presidency, based on spiritual impressions. Though well qualified, she was overawed by the new assignment. Hal felt immediate empathy. Because of his heart troubles, he was experiencing similar anxiety at that very moment. He was eager to provide comfort and to share his confidence in the inspiration behind the call and the sister's capacity to lead. Having extended the call, he set her apart with special words of blessing. The effect was immediate and powerful: the new presidency member would later report that she slept peacefully that night for the first time in weeks.

Hal, by contrast, had an entirely sleepless night. Shortly after the sister left his office, he realized that he had set apart a Churchwide auxiliary leader who hadn't yet been sustained. The setting apart was thus of no effect; worse, it was an inexcusable breach of priesthood procedure. Panic gripped and all but overcame him. Committing such an error would be a serious failure in the administration of any Church President. But of all the priesthood leaders Hal had ever worked closely with, President Monson was the most concerned about proper procedure, particularly in the exercise of priesthood authority.

President Monson had grown up in Salt Lake City's Pioneer Stake, then presided over by Harold B. Lee. No man since Joseph Smith had done more than President Lee to formalize and codify Church procedures. He had begun that work as a stake president, when he and his counselors had created the forerunner of the welfare program. Later, as a member of the Quorum of the Twelve, he had led the Priesthood Correlation Committee, the body that first coordinated all the auxiliaries, activities, and curriculum of the worldwide Church.

At age twenty-two, President Monson had become a bishop in the Pioneer Stake, serving under leaders trained to President Lee's exacting standards of procedure. Just fourteen years later, upon joining the Twelve, he directly observed and contributed to President Lee's work of Churchwide correlation. Having supervised the printing operations of the Deseret News before his call to the Twelve, President Monson brought a printer's eye for detail to the procedures being codified in new leadership handbooks.

Hal had seen that eye for detail firsthand in his few months of service in the First Presidency. President Monson came to every meeting having not just scanned but scrutinized all materials provided in advance. If a new handbook or instructional manual was to be approved, President Monson had read every word. If the calls of priesthood leaders from around the world were to be ratified, he had comments about

May 31, 1984
Thursday

I wrote in the Atherton
guest house of the
Johnsons, looking down
on the
of our
Elizab
Kathleen
blow out
birthday
dinner b
Holy Gh
teach a
workshop

June 1,
Friday

Elizabeth
the poo
worked c
Gary ca
Los Ang
to hear
time to
Altos.

June 2,
Saturday

I towed
inflated,
Mary
compli
purple c
match t
hair tha
Stuart's
sister.
and I w
dance in

June 3, 1984
Sunday

PRESIDENT THOMAS S. MONSON

Kathy, Elizabeth, and Mary Kathleen were dressed and
packed early for our drive from Atherton to the San Jose
airport. On the flight home, a stewardess made a bullseye
with a glass full of orange juice on my lap. It was so cold
and complete a soaking that I laughed for the rest of the
trip. I used bags to shield the results as I got us to the car.

more of them than Hal could believe. President Monson even reviewed the minutes of the Presidency's past meetings, often correcting the details of a particular discussion or assignment.

Hal had also seen President Monson express deep displeasure with errors such as the very one he had committed in performing a setting apart before the required sustaining. Requests for guidance in such matters routinely came to the office of the First Presidency. Often, the question was whether to reperform ordinances in the proper order or to simply let matters stand. In many cases, substantial time had passed, the error having gone undiscovered or even hidden for years. President Monson could barely contain his dissatisfaction with such cases. "If priesthood leaders just read and followed the Church Handbook of Instructions," he would sternly say, "we wouldn't have such problems."

A LASTING LESSON

These thoughts kept Hal from sleeping on the night after his mistake. He considered only briefly trying to somehow hide it. Instead, he resolved to make an immediate confession. Better, he thought, to have President Monson lose faith in his competence than to attempt to live a lie. When dawn finally came, he went to the office early and waited for President Monson to arrive, standing just outside the elevator door through which he would come.

The prophet, who arrived as usual precisely at seven thirty, amazed Hal with his response to the confessed mistake. "Oh, Hal," he chortled, "I've done worse than that myself. It won't be any problem at all. We'll just have you reperform the setting apart after the sustaining at conference."

President Monson's magnanimity overwhelmed Hal. Yet he couldn't help wondering whether he had been forgiven for his mistake but not for his incompetence. He was still subpar physically, and now President Monson had reason to doubt his judgment. He feared that the prophet might not trust him to carry his full load as a counselor.

These fearful thoughts so occupied Hal's mind through the day that he almost missed a hidden message from President Monson. In the several meetings they attended together, President Monson was his usual jovial, storytelling self. Since joining the First Presidency, Hal had learned to listen carefully to these stories. Often, they seemed to be mere personal reminiscences, bearing little or no relationship to the business at hand. But, through careful attention, Hal had discovered that frequently the stories served the purpose of parables, providing gentle but incisive instruction for those with ears to hear.

On this day, though, the exhausting events of the past twenty-four hours and doubts about his standing with President Monson consumed his thoughts. In a meeting with a group of General Authorities and senior Church employees seeking guidance from the First Presidency, he let his mind try to process what had happened and what it could mean for his future service. In this distracted state, he might have missed the significance of one of President Monson's stories, shared apparently for the benefit of others, had it not been new to him.

President Monson told the tale of receiving a middle-of-the-night phone call when he was the twenty-eight-year-old general manager of the Deseret News Press. The caller was a police department captain, who said, "We just found a palletful of your papers in the Jordan River. What do you want us to do with it?"

Young Tom Monson said, "I'll be right there." He met the police officers at the river, confirmed that the pallet was indeed his, and arranged to have it taken back to the company's press facility. A cursory study there solved the mystery of the soggy papers. That night the press had been running a special issue commemorating the sesquicentennial of the birth of Joseph Smith. On the front page of the papers dumped in the river, Tom found an obvious typesetting error. He surmised that the error hadn't been discovered until a pallet's worth of papers had been printed. The mistake was an expensive one, and someone had tried to hide it.

The next morning, Tom called in his night supervisor, a longtime colleague and friend. Without presenting the evidence, he asked, "Did anything unusual happen last night?" The supervisor replied, "No." Tom asked again and received the same assurance. Then he led the man to the pallet and got the expected confession. Tom fired the supervisor on the spot, with this explanation: "We all make mistakes; that's part of the cost of business. But I can't afford to employ a man I can't trust."

In concluding this story, President Monson expressed the sorrow he felt in having to let the dishonest supervisor go. The fellow had a family to feed, and he had performed well for many years. But he couldn't have put the pallet of newspapers into the river all by himself, which meant that other employees knew of the dishonest act. For the good of the organization, dismissal was the only answer. President Monson beamed, though, as he reported having recommended the fellow for rehiring many years later.

The lesson wasn't lost on Hal. Though nothing more was said of the matter, even on the day when he reperformed the setting apart, he never forgot President Monson's message. He hadn't been chosen as First Counselor for his intellect or skill, and he wouldn't be dismissed for any failure of capability. But his fealty to the truth was everything to President Monson. Hal resolved to be true at all costs.

He was grateful for the knowledge that President Monson, like the prophets before him, didn't expect perfect performance. President Hinckley had often said, "Do the best you can." But President Hinckley had clarified that by saying, "I want to emphasize that it be the very best. We are prone to be satisfied with mediocre performance. We are capable of doing so much better."[11] Hal's study of past prophets, which had intensified since his call to the First Presidency, taught him that doing one's best was the steady standard for performance, as expressed in a talk he delivered in May in Leeds, Utah.[12]

> Kathy and I drove out across the valleys and between the red-rock cliffs. We thought of the hardships faced by the faithful Saints who answered the call of Brigham Young to gather here and

carve a living from the desert. Among them were John Bennion, Henry Eyring, and Miles Romney.

Brigham Young made countless trips by buggy through the settlements. At every stop he examined the progress made and then praised or chastised.

Whether he praised or chastised the people depended upon his perception of the effort. Their accomplishments did not seem to matter as much as their attitude toward the struggle.

Prophets are like that and so is God. All you have to do is the very best you can. That will be enough.[13]

THE NEW FIRST PRESIDENCY

Having almost missed the message in the parable of the unfaithful night supervisor, Hal recommitted to weighing President Monson's every word, including words spoken without clear connection to the business at hand, or even in apparent jest. In so doing, he began to find more guidance than he had imagined possible. As he replayed President Monson's statements in his mind, inspiration came to his heart.

Hal also strove to rise to Elder Maxwell's problem-solver challenge. President Monson frequently remarked that he had never seen three more different personalities in a First Presidency. He apparently meant that as a compliment, and Hal made every effort to qualify for it. It was true that he and President Monson and President Uchtdorf saw many issues from different viewpoints, as one might expect of a printer, a pilot, and a professor.

Hal had first worked with President Uchtdorf during a mission presidents' seminar in Rome, when Hal was a member of the Twelve and President Uchtdorf was serving as an Area President in Europe. They shared a common educational background, President Uchtdorf having graduated from a prestigious MBA program in Switzerland, IMEDE, that Hal's Harvard Business School mentor C. Roland Christensen had helped found.

THE FIRST PRESIDENCY

They also shared German heritage. The Eyring family's ancestral home, Coburg, lies less than a hundred miles from Zwickau, the home of President Uchtdorf's boyhood. Though Hal knew little German, his great-grandfather Henry Eyring made the first translation of the Doctrine and Covenants into that language while serving as a missionary there. That Henry Eyring, like Dieter Uchtdorf, was a young convert who rose from poverty and served the Church faithfully throughout his life.

Hal was impressed by President Uchtdorf's skill as a leader and his graciousness as a host. Together they walked Rome's most famous landmarks, including the Spanish Steps, which Hal recognized from one of Kathy's favorite romantic movies, Audrey Hepburn and Gregory Peck's *Roman Holiday.* Hal stopped to paint a small watercolor, with President Uchtdorf waiting patiently. While he painted, Hal said over and over, "Oh, I wish Kathy were here." As he

In showing his love for the country, for the people, and for the architecture by painting these things, he showed me that he related to other parts of the world in a very deep, spiritual, emotional way.

—PRESIDENT DIETER F. UCHTDORF[14]

was finishing, President Uchtdorf passed Hal his cell phone. "Kathy would like to talk to you," he said, smilingly broadly. When the phone conversation was over and the watercolor finished, Hal made a gift of it to President and Sister Uchtdorf.

For three years, from October 2004 to October 2007, Hal and President Uchtdorf had sat next to one another in meetings of the Quorum of the Twelve. In that setting, among so many senior colleagues, they had mostly observed and spoken when invited to do so. Now, though, President Monson expected them to weigh in on every matter of significance, particularly when they felt concerned about the trend of a discussion. The two counselors found that praising their President's views won them no favor. "That's not the point," he would say. "Let's focus on what's at hand."[15]

Hal saw many things differently than his colleagues in the First Presidency did, as he had done in the Presiding Bishopric and before that with Joe Christensen and Stan Peterson in the Church Educational System. But he benefited greatly from his experiences in those other trios. In discussions with Presidents Monson and Uchtdorf, Hal worked to see the possibilities revealed by their differences of opinion, rather than the apparent problems.

Time and again he was blessed to see the prophetic mantle on President Monson. He recognized heaven's kindness in showing him, from his boyhood, the power of that mantle as it had rested on many men. Each had been different, and none had been perfect. But in all cases, particularly that of President Monson, Hal could respond as he did to Harold B. Lee's question about President Joseph Fielding Smith, "Do you think that such a great man as this is the prophet of God?"

"I'm sure of it."

> I thank the Lord for wonderful counselors. President Henry B. Eyring and President Dieter F. Uchtdorf are men of great ability and sound understanding. They are counselors in the true sense of the word. I value their judgment. I believe they have been prepared by the Lord for the positions they now occupy.
>
> —PRESIDENT THOMAS S. MONSON[16]

nephew, Mark, sometime last week, forced her out of
our double's match this morning; within an hour she'd
sent a replacement, so I played six sets. Result: I
soaked my elbow in a tub of hot water propped on the
table in the breakfast room at grandpa's, while I watched
the ball games with the boys. Annette served the whole

24

CLEAVE UNTO HER

Thou shalt love thy wife
With all thy heart,
And shalt cleave unto her
And none else.
—DOCTRINE AND COVENANTS 42:22

Even as he grew more comfortable with his role in the First Presidency, Hal began to find that his greatest problem-solving challenge lay yet ahead, at home. For several years, Kathy had been complaining of memory lapses. Medical testing in 2005 revealed no physical evidence of the common conditions that might produce dementia. Hal and Kathy hoped that her increased forgetfulness was just that, the kind of normal memory loss incident to aging. At the time, that seemed more than just a vain hope. Remembering appointments and phone messages had never been Kathy's forte. She was famous among the family for writing notes to them and to herself on countertops, on the wall next to the kitchen phone, and even on her hands. Her new symptoms, though more serious, could be interpreted as mere extensions of these idiosyncratic and endearing traits.

But by 2007, the evidence of unusual memory loss couldn't be denied. Particularly at stressful times such as the weeks leading up to general conference or a Church-related trip, Kathy would have to ask repeatedly about what she called "the order of march"—meaning what was going to happen when and what would be expected of her. Though Hal did his best to answer these repeated questions as if each were new, they both knew the truth.

Kathy had been looking for these frightening signs for almost twenty years. That age was when they first began to appear in her father, Sid. In his case, occasional forgetfulness and disorientation became chronic and then fully debilitating. For the last few years of his life, Sid lived at home on the Hill with round-the-clock nursing care, unable to recognize visitors or to recall any but the most deeply etched memories. Touchingly, the latter included Primary songs such as "I Am a Child of God" and "Jesus Wants Me for a Sunbeam," which his caregivers sang with him to the end.

THE RETURN OF A WRITER

The beginning of Kathy's serious memory loss coincided with the emptying of her family nest. Mary, the youngest child, married in 2005, when Kathy was sixty-four. As a student at BYU, Mary had spent weekends and summers at her parents' home and was particularly close to her mother. They shared a passion for literature, Mary's major field of study, and often traveled together when Kathy visited her mother, La Prele, in California.

In the forty-five years since the birth of her first child, Kathy had been a mother in the most focused sense. The four sons born between 1963 and 1972 were followed by daughters Elizabeth and Mary, but not without an emotionally painful delay. Kathy miscarried while skiing in 1974 and nearly died

KATHY WITH MARY AND ELIZABETH

from loss of blood before an ambulance could get her off the mountain and down to a small hospital that providentially had four liters of blood of her type. She pined for another child, half-blaming herself, until Elizabeth's birth in 1979.

Elizabeth's arrival—and Mary's, four and a half years later, after another miscarriage—had allowed Kathy to feather a more feminine nest. In addition to Saturday projects of grocery shopping, bread making, and household organizing, she helped Hal lead the girls in a new activity: newspaper publishing. In the early 1990s, with the four boys out on their own, Hal decided to take his journal writing in a different direction. Rather than speaking in the first person and focusing primarily on the events of his own life, he and Kathy would involve the children more, both as writers and as readers. Elizabeth and Mary became copublishers of *The Family Monthly News Currents.* They sought contributions from their brothers and sisters-in-law and added articles and artwork of their own to this new, weekly publication. Hal supplemented the *News Currents* with personal letters to the boys and their families.

Kathy likewise became an author of messages for her posterity. Particularly as Mary went off to school, leaving Kathy alone at home during the morning and early afternoon hours, she had time to apply her remarkable gifts of reasoning and writing. She had made a similar attempt, with notable success, when John was starting school. A novel she began writing in the late 1970s and completed shortly after Elizabeth's birth won a statewide prize for young adult literature. But Kathy put her own writing on hold to focus on the girls' development, just as she had stopped playing competitive tennis to nurture the boys.

Still, the brilliant writer remained. That can be seen in letters Kathy wrote to her missionary sons. She learned that they responded best to humor, particularly when the missionary work was difficult. In those times, the boys were likely to receive a clipping from their favorite newspaper humorist, Dave Barry, or hers, Erma Bombeck.

But better than either of these was an original story from their mother, who combined the best of both of those more famous names.

Oldest son Henry received such a lifting letter during the first week of January in 1984, several months before Mary's birth. Henry was serving in Japan, and he knew from the experience of the preceding year that the weeklong New Year's celebration would allow for few teaching opportunities. Kathy knew that too. She also appreciated that Henry would be thinking of the family during Christmas, which they had spent at Grandma and Grandpa Johnson's home on the Hill, where the holiday was celebrated like nowhere else. She opened that week's letter with an empathetic reference to the cold weather Henry would be working in, followed by a personal story with a self-deprecating twist to lift his spirits:

Dear Henry:

I'm sure you've read in your father's journal his account of our Christmas in California. It rained or was overcast much of the time, but cleared enough the last few days that when we hit the Bountiful snow and ice it was a letdown, to put it mildly.

I doubt, however, that you read in the journal about our stopover in Las Vegas. The boys were delighted when our flight from San Francisco to Salt Lake was canceled and we were rerouted through Las Vegas. Visions of slot machines danced through their heads, and they were more than disappointed when, after having landed in the City of Vice, they dashed to the machines, only to find that no minors were allowed to play. That left only two possibilities for the making of their fortune—your father and me. I was reluctant at first to be used in such a manner. (I mean, can you imagine the sight of a respectable forty-two-year-old pregnant woman squandering her food money on the machines?) I was only convinced to do so when I realized that this could be an eternal object lesson, slot machines being notorious for cheating folks.

For five or ten minutes I waited behind a wrinkled, tattooed man who was softly swearing at the machine after having inserted fifty-five nickels with no reward. You can probably guess what happened after I had deposited no more than twenty-five cents. (I must admit the sound of rushing coins was music to my ears.) I guess I'll just have to wait for another opportunity to provide an object lesson for the boys.[1]

John, whose mission in Holland presented many of the same challenges and disappointments Henry faced in Japan, got a similar boost as his second Christmas approached. Kathy sent an envelope that included her letter, the wedding announcement of one of John's high school friends (a girl named Meagan), and several clippings from a novelty gift catalog.

Dear John:

It's getting to be that time again. Christmas present-sending time. I'd love to know what you need that you can't get (besides deodorant) over there. So write immediately to let me know. To encourage you to respond to this request, I've included pictures of several items I'm considering giving you as presents (the catalog items, not Meagan—she's been unavailable since the 17th). If I don't hear from you within one week, you may find in your stocking Christmas morning a deluxe nose-hair trimmer and a pair of headlight slippers . . . and they are ABSOLUTELY NOT RETURNABLE.[2]

Kathy singing carols—

Another way in which Kathy supported her missionaries was to look for and report missionary experiences of her own. In marrying Hal she had foregone full-time missionary service, which seemed to be referenced in her patriarchal blessing. But she had been a member missionary throughout her life, bravely and lovingly sharing her testimony even in the most unlikely places, such as the tony Castilleja girls' school and cynical Berkeley, where her professors tried unsuccessfully to shake her faith.

It was natural for Kathy to seek similar experiences to report to her missionary sons. She shared with John an example of such an effort, made while traveling by plane to visit Stuart and Carol in Philadelphia, where Stuart was pursuing a graduate degree.

I had an interesting experience on the flight to see Carol and Stuart last month. The morning of the flight I awoke at 5:30—early for me—and as I said my morning prayers, I prayed that I might sit next to someone whom Heavenly Father wanted to hear the gospel. As I boarded the plane, I could hardly wait to see who that someone was. It was Johnny Carson's aunt. Not a quick convert. I visited with her the entire flight, sacrificing a movie I really wanted to see, in hopes of warming her up. I wrote a letter to you, mentioning that you were on a mission in Holland and how sad it was that no one wanted to hear your message about the Church.

I asked her if she would like to hear about the Church. She said, "No." There was a Mormon lady who came into the grocery store which she and her husband owned in Montana and drove them crazy by telling them about all the things her church wouldn't let her buy from their store. I said a silent prayer. Then I bore my testimony that the Church was true and that it would change her life if she would listen to the message. She looked at me strangely and then said, "I'll listen to the missionaries when they come to my house." I said, "Oh, you can't wait for them to come to you. I'll send them." She gave me her name and address, and as soon as I finish this letter, I'm writing the mission president in Montana to give him her name.[3]

> At sunset, we walked again, exploring the grounds of the Royal Hawaiian, which look much as they must have done when Kathleen was taken there at ten by her parents. She remembered trying to convert her Hawaiian surfing instructor. She said that he told her, at the end of her visit, that he was making progress keeping the Word of Wisdom.
>
> —JOURNAL, DECEMBER 25, 2004, IN HONOLULU, HAWAII

Kathy's gift for trenchant, witty observation carried over into the successor to *The Family Monthly News Currents*. When Mary left for college, Hal shifted to a new format for communication with the Eyring children and grandchildren, who by then were spread across the country and the world. Each night, he would enlist Kathy in creating a one-page summary of their activities, accompanied by one or two photos. He called this nightly publication the "Family Journal: The Small Plates," a reference to the smaller record on which Nephi captured the more sacred experiences of his people. Hal endeavored to include at least one inspirational event in the new "Family Journal," which he disseminated electronically. The entry always ended with a verse or two from the Book of Mormon, taken from his nightly reading with Kathy.

Not every day, though, brought an inspiring experience that he could share without concerns for confidentiality, which applied to most of his work at the office. On those days, Kathy's wry wit could make even ordinary events sparkle.

> Without a doubt, the highlight of my day was taking two pictures of Hal in his office. I'm sure that if I offered them to the *Church News* they would hire me immediately.
>
> Next to picture taking, our two trips to Target would rank high in shared excitement. Hal bought heavy white hangers again, which would only surprise those of you who have been in his closet. It can hardly hold another hanger. In fairness, however, he is afraid that Target will quit making them. His shirt drawer is filled with unopened white Huntington shirts, which he bought for the same reason, and—I am not making this up—they did go out of business. What does "type-A personality" mean? Fortunately for the Johnson side of our family, we have

type-Z, which will make our lives less thrilling, but we will live longer because of it.[4]

Kathy also applied her talent for writing in the service of her parents and siblings. As Sid and La Prele aged, she assumed a leading role in organizing family reunions, including birthday and wedding anniversary parties. She often emceed these events, working from scripts of her own creation. The typical one fused a deft mix of family history and anecdotes, spiritual themes, and music, including popular songs with lyrics modified by Kathy to fit the occasion.

Among her most complex and time-consuming writing projects were personal histories of her parents. Though the family engaged professional writers for the biographies of Sid and La Prele, Kathy both instigated and facilitated the projects, helping her parents to retrieve memories their forward-looking minds had all but forgotten. In Sid's case the work was particularly delicate and time-consuming, due to his progressing dementia.

> To Kathleen Johnson Eyring, who began the long task of compiling her father's history by interviewing the reluctant JCJ,[5] who admittedly procrastinated getting started on his colorful life story. With La Prele's provocations and Kathy's astute, probing questions, a good portion of his career was recorded on tape. Those facts and quotes were invaluable to the writer, and are used extensively throughout the book.
>
> Without her early work, many of those recollections, which not only tell of his work, but illustrate his inherent sense of business, might have been lost. Her rich contribution to this publication is acknowledged with sincere love and appreciation by her parents.
>
> —ACKNOWLEDGMENT IN *THE LIFE OF J. CYRIL JOHNSON*

CLOSING DOORS

In addition to being entertaining and informative, Kathy's later writing reflected an increasing focus on the truths she considered most fundamental. Throughout her life, she had been faced with a wide range of choices. Her parents' wealth, connections, and encouragement to see the world opened the doors to a life of spending, socializing, and travel. Likewise, her intellectual gifts and access to the finest schools allowed her to explore the life of the mind. She was truly in a position to consider not only graduate school but also a career outside of the home.

However, Kathy consistently closed these doors. In fact, the life of privilege she had walked away from became a source of disarming humor as she responded to speaking requests, which became more numerous with Hal's rising public profile. Those who didn't know Kathy except as the wife of a highly educated senior Church leader were prone to be surprised by her folksy, self-effacing manner, all the more so as they gathered from the power of her remarks that she possessed an intellect equal to her husband's.

> Three of my sons were fortunate enough to live near my parents long enough for a close bond to form between them, and our trips to California will always remain their favorite summer vacation. I must add that it didn't take them long to learn that if they arrived at Grandma's in slightly worn-out clothes Mother's first outing with them would be to a clothing store.
>
> I, too, was a constant recipient of her generosity, and never left Grandma's without either a new outfit from the store or something from her closet. It took me a while to figure out that when she beckoned me to her wardrobe, showed me a dress still bearing the price tag, and said offhandedly, "I'm not sure why I ever bought this dress," the chances were she had a daughter in the back of her mind who she knew could wear it.
>
> I'll never forget the time I walked into church late, down to the front row, where my daughter was sitting. She looked at my new dress and said, loudly enough for the people in ten pews to hear, "Did Grandma buy that for you, or is it one of hers?" She knows that those are the two most likely possibilities when I wear a new dress.[6]

Kathy tended to disarm listeners not only with self-deprecating comments but also with her focus on the simplest doctrines and observances of the gospel. The sisters of Kathy's ward, who gathered to hear her speak to the assigned topic of the Relief Society's Pursuit of Excellence Program, would have experienced that winning combination. She began her remarks with this admission:

I woke after a night of praying to know what I should do. To my surprise, the answer seemed practical and personal: help Kathleen plant flowers and help her buy groceries, so that we can have pleasant suppers on the patio. I had expected answers like: "Start on those 12 major talks you must give before Christmas," or "Find a solution to holding the youth of the Church close to the gospel." So, remembering Mosiah 7:33[7] from last night's reading, we went to work with all diligence.

It was sunset before we put in the last flowers. Neighbors came by to praise and visit. Perhaps the instruction about what to do was about people, not flowers and groceries.

—HENRY B. EYRING JOURNAL, JULY 17, 2008

Several months ago, I had just finished reading King Benjamin's great address to his people in the book of Mosiah. He had spoken so eloquently of service, and I was so enthused that I wanted to do some great service for the Savior to show my gratitude to Him. I can't remember what the specific service was, but as I recall, several of my ideas were in the different categories of the Pursuit of Excellence program. I prayed with sincerity that I might be inspired to know what I should do. I was awaiting an inspired answer.

I had been praying for several minutes when, as clear as clear, came the answer. It was not just what I had expected, but it was an unmistakable feeling:

"There are dishes in the sink to be done. You have children who will be home for lunch. Give them love as well as lunch. You have a missionary in the field. He could use a letter of encouragement, as could your husband when he comes home this evening."

And there was my answer. Not exactly as I had intended

it, nevertheless clear. Without that answer, I might have set a wonderfully altruistic goal, thinking I was doing what the Savior would have me do only to find my life further complicated by goals and obligations which I felt frustrated trying to meet. That does not mean that I will never perform that great service which I had in mind. I may when my circumstances are different, but not now.[8]

MOTHERHOOD ABOVE ALL

Kathy's prompting to think of the dishes in the sink and the children coming home for lunch was part of a lifelong pattern. It wasn't so much that she closed the other open doors, but that the door of motherhood, and of supporting Hal, loomed ever larger and more inviting in her life. Particularly as she cherished the two girls born after the grief of miscarriages, she found greater satisfaction than she had imagined as a young bride, when childbearing was only one of many enticing possibilities. She spoke of that satisfaction often, both privately and publicly, as in this talk:

KATHY AT THE FAMILY MEETING

> Some time ago, a woman left her children with a babysitter, giving the sitter bedtime instructions. She explained that she always put the children to bed by reading each one several stories and then singing to them.
>
> Later that evening, when the woman returned home, the sitter said, "You know, you don't have to go through all that bedtime trouble. All I did was turn off the light and put them in bed. You've gotten them into a habit they expect from you, but if you're just firm about it you can put them right to sleep."
>
> The woman looked at the sitter for a moment without saying anything. "She doesn't understand," she thought to herself. "I don't want to put them to sleep. I want to love them to sleep."[9]

Motherhood, with the eternal perspective it provided on the choices faced by her children, became Kathy's dominant focus, both in her daily life and in her public addresses. The focus didn't diminish as her youngest, Mary, started school. In fact, as Kathy told a group of Bountiful High School seminary students, sending her children out into the world increased her sense of the truths that matter most and her desire to share them with her sons and daughters.

> Last fall I took my five-year-old to kindergarten. She is the last of my six children, and for those of you who are the youngest in your family, or who have watched your youngest brother or sister go to school for the first time, you know that this is a traumatic experience, particularly for your mother.

> The first few weeks when my daughter was at school were very lonely ones for me. Not to be able to sit down and read to a little preschooler cuddled on my lap was very difficult for me. And you can imagine, that the first day she left for school, the most important knowledge I wanted her to get was the knowledge of how to get home. I counted a great deal on the teacher walking my little girl down the hall after school, taking her outside to the bus, showing her which of the three or four buses was the one she was to get on, and explaining to her where she was to get off. If she didn't gain that particular knowledge, it didn't matter to me if she were to learn calculus or Latin, it would have meant nothing to me. The most important knowledge for her to get was how to get home.

> As I was preparing this talk, I thought that this must be how our Father in Heaven feels as He sends us down to earth. As wonderful and exciting as all the knowledge in the world is, if we don't learn how to come back home to our Father in Heaven, who loves us and waits literally with open arms to greet us, then all the knowledge of the world we gain won't mean much.[10]

Kathy's lifetime of motherhood not only increased her love for her children, it also enhanced her sense of the love and longings of our heavenly parents. She built on the image of a Heavenly Father's open arms in an address to Saints in Pachuca, Mexico, whom she visited on assignment with Hal.

Elder Eyring and I have six children, four boys and two girls. I can remember many years ago taking my two young girls to a zoo in Salt Lake City to watch the animals. It was late in the afternoon on a very cold day. Dark rain clouds covered the sky, and a strong wind blew leaves around us and the animals. I remember watching a mother hen running back and forth across our path trying to gather her young chicks under her wing. All her little chicks but one ran to snuggle under her wings for protection against the cold wind. As she tried to lift her wing to comfort this little chick, he would run the other way, stop, and then turn to look at his mother. There was nothing she could do to get him to come under her wing. The baby chick stood watching his mother as the cold wind blew around him.

I thought to myself, "Why doesn't this little chicken run under its mother's wing, where it could be sheltered from the cold, stinging wind? What keeps him from going to his mother for comfort?"

We have all been outside on a cold day and have felt the sting of the wind on our bodies. The wind and cold are not the only things that can hurt us. When we are sick and lonely or sad, we hurt. Like a mother hen, the Savior wants to help us. He wants to comfort us. And He can comfort us. When the Savior appeared to the Nephites after His resurrection and after the terrible destruction upon their land, He said:

"O ye people of these great cities which have fallen, . . . how oft would I have gathered you as a hen gathereth her chickens under her wings, . . . and ye would not" (3 Nephi 10:4–5).

The Savior wants to comfort not only those people whose lives were spared in this land in ancient times, He wants to comfort us, each one of us now."

As the Eyring children grew and began to leave home and establish families of their own, Kathy's longing to be with them eternally grew.

She wondered and worried about whether she had done enough while they lived under her roof. She took comfort in the image, provided by the scriptures, of Heavenly Father's expressing a similar concern. And she became all the more grateful that she had followed the counsel of prophets and the promptings of the Spirit to focus her life on her children.

As she told one congregation of Latter-day Saint women:

> Within the soul of every one of God's daughters He has placed a desire to be with her family eternally. More than anything else our Father wants this desire to burn brightly within us, and more than anything else Satan wants to extinguish it.
>
> I think of the beautiful allegory of Zenos, in the book of Jacob, where the Lord tenderly nourishes, prunes, and fertilizes the tame and wild olive trees—that is, His children—so that they may be forever with Him. Over and over, when the trees become corrupt, He says to His servant helping Him: "It grieveth me that I should lose [this tree]. But what could I have done more in my vineyard? Have I slackened mine hand, that I have not nourished it? Nay, I have nourished it, and I have digged about it, and I have pruned it, and I have dunged it; and I have stretched forth mine hand almost all the day long." And Zenos records that "the Lord of the vineyard wept" (Jacob 5:46–47, 41).
>
> What mother does not have sympathy, cannot feel agony as the Lord weeps and says of His earthly family, "What could I have done more?"[13]

> The longings to be with family, either born or unborn, burn brightly in the hearts of all good mothers and would-be mothers. Deep in my soul I can feel the whisperings of a loving Heavenly Father who has said, "This is my work and my glory, to bring to pass the immortality and eternal life of man." He wants to be with His family.
>
> —KATHLEEN JOHNSON EYRING[12]

Among the spiritual treasures Kathy left her family—probably thinking it would never be seen—is a parable. It is written in her elegant hand on two sheets of unlined paper. Only a few words and phrases show signs of editing.

A woman looked out at her yard. "It is bare," she thought. "I shall plant seeds." Each day she watered and cared for the seeds, and they grew and bore beautiful blossoms.

One day a local merchant came to her. "I need someone to care for my shop," he said.

"But my garden and flowers . . . who will tend them?" she asked.

"Oh, they are sturdy enough to care for themselves during the day," he said, "and you can water them at night when you return home. You will make enough money to buy the very best food and supplies that they need."

"Staying at home day after day does become tedious," she replied. "Perhaps you are right."

So she left her garden. Each day the sun beat on her flowers, and each night she came home and hurriedly watered them, too tired to remove the unsightly weeds that had grown in between the stems. "Oh, how we wish we were cared for as before," cried the flowers.

Time passed, and holes appeared in the garden fence where boards had been broken and left to decay. Travelers passing by said, "Perhaps we can take these flowers and nurture them in our gardens. Surely they will not be missed." So they took the flowers and their roots and cared for them, and the blossoms gave great joy to all who saw them.

The woman, tiring of her work at the shop, returned to care for the garden. "My only real joy has been my flowers," she said. "And the moments I spent caring for them were the happiest of my life," she recalled as she ran down the path leading to her garden.

But when she drew near, she became aware for the first time of the broken fence and saw with a shock that her precious flowers were gone.

And she wept.

A SETTING STAR

Kathy's role as the spiritual center of the Eyring home made her growing loss of memory all the more poignant for her husband and children. Yet she had spent decades preparing them for such challenges, though this particular one had been unanticipated.

The burden of Kathy's disease fell most heavily upon Hal. Even as her memory of recent events faded, her native intelligence and sense of independence remained. So did her desire to be with Hal and to be treated as his equal. They agreed never to speak between themselves of her condition and to carry on as before. Kathy would continue to keep the home without outside help. She would also join him on many days at the office, where she was accustomed to reading and resting on a reclining chair when he was in meetings. They would continue to go out for dinner on most nights.

This arrangement would have been challenging for any husband, but Hal's position as a member of the First Presidency made it the more so. For many years, he had been doing the grocery shopping, a task Kathy disliked because of the strain it placed on her memory and the frustration she felt upon returning home and realizing that she had forgotten

We all will face difficulties for which we must prepare. Time itself will bring the difficulty of age. Age may bring the challenges of ill health. The approach of the Savior's coming will bring the challenges of the last days. All of us are preparing. I cannot promise that we will be spared difficulties, although President John Taylor said, "It will only be a little compared with the terrible destruction, the misery and suffering that will overtake the world." What I can promise you, because God has promised this, is that if you are righteous you can have peace in the midst of difficulties and the assurance of eternal life in the world to come.

—KATHLEEN JOHNSON EYRING[14]

KATHY RESTS

many items. Thanks to Hal's faithfulness in performing this task for her, Bountiful residents knew that a trip to one of the local supermarkets at the end of the workday offered as good a chance for meeting a senior General Authority as standing all day on Temple Square. Hal budgeted extra time, knowing that he'd be invited to stop and chat in each aisle.

The heavier schedule and increased profile of his new calling made the old patterns harder to maintain. More of his workday was filled with meetings, and Kathy was alone more often in the office. Eating out offered less privacy and took more time, as fellow diners came to shake hands and take photos. Though Kathy continued to keep the house, even routine tasks began to confuse her, requiring Hal to assume more of that responsibility.

Hal was blessed in bearing the new weight. Part of the blessing was a heightened sense of Kathy's goodness and its lifelong effect on him. Another part was the emotional bond they continued to share.

 Kathleen was paid great tributes today. At the end of the Quorum meeting, which ranged over many issues, we were asked to express our feelings of Thanksgiving. The closing testimony was in the exact words of Kathleen's sacrament meeting talk on Sunday. And then, in an interview with a member of the First Presidency I was given an assignment with the statement that he had faith in whatever I did, and that, "I have the same confidence in your wife, Kathy." It was clear to me that the Lord was confirming how inspired her talk had been by giving the key parts of it to one of his Apostles in today's Quorum meeting. And a member of the First Presidency can see in Kathleen what

After dinner we watched the movie "Forever Young," with Mel Gibson. The romantic ending is of young love reunited. The music at the end of the film, as it was in the beginning, was Billie Holiday singing, "The Very Thought of You." We, Kathleen in tennis shoes and I without shoes, danced on the basement carpet until the last note.

—JOURNAL, JANUARY 5, 2005

I had seen when she appeared in the crowd coming out of the Cathedral of the Pines in New Hampshire many years ago, the first time I ever saw her. (November 22, 2005)

Hal and Kathy also received herculean support from the families of two sons, Stuart and John, who moved with their large families back to the Bountiful area in 2006, just as Kathy's condition took its turn for the worse. Stuart and his wife, Carol, moved into his parents' ward, and Carol was assigned to be Kathy's visiting teaching companion. Carol and John's wife, Jennifer, coordinated efforts to provide a dinner opportunity each night of the week. They also joined Kathy's neighbors in visiting the Eyring home on days when she didn't go into Hal's office.

> We are gathered in Dad's office for the second session of conference, which he is conducting. Mother is singing along to "Did You Think to Pray?," reclining with face turned heavenward in her favorite chair. She is smiling beatifically, eyes closed, as though already in heaven.
>
> —HENRY J. EYRING[15]

Those who served Kathy enjoyed her loving spirit, which grew sweeter and more ethereal. The connection to the Divine that had always lain at the core of Kathy's heart could increasingly be seen in her face. That was especially true as she sang along to the familiar hymns of the Church. As for her father, Sid, Kathy's memories of sacred tunes and verses learned in childhood outlived all others.

DRIVING MISS KATHY

Notwithstanding Kathy's sweetness and the unstinting support of family and friends, Hal's personal burden grew. The greatest burden was the gradual loss of his wisest and truest confidante. He had always relied on her clarity of spiritual and temporal insight. Even in their early married years, when their age difference was pronounced, her unfailing wisdom had guided him. Now that guidance was slipping away.

The day got off with a lurch: Ed Zschau tried to reach me during my morning shower. When he finally got to me at noon, he told me that the Bendix offer to buy Finnigan Instrument Corp. was off. That meant Ed was liable to lose 280,000 dollars in receivables and 400,000 in projected sales for this year, and I'd lose my investment in Finnigan. Kathy didn't panic: her statement was, "Roger [Sant] will think of something. He'll be finding other deals." Sure enough, she was right. (September 24, 1970)

The burden of caregiving also increased. The agreement never to speak of Kathy's illness was put to the test in unanticipated ways, as when Kathy would don a dress inside out on a Sunday morning just before they were to leave for church services. He was torn between the promise and his knowledge that, in earlier times, she would have been mortified by the mistake.

Hal found inspiration and hope in one of their favorite movies, *Driving Miss Daisy*. He and Kathy had enjoyed uplifting movies since their earliest days of courtship and marriage. With the advent of video rentals, they began to watch happy romances at home on evenings when time permitted. Hal liked stories in which an apparently underqualified male suitor won the hand of a beautiful heroine. That was the way he saw his marriage to Kathy. He particularly liked the Disney movie *Aladdin*; he cheerfully called himself the lucky "street rat" whose marriage to a princess had made him a prince.

Kathy's memory loss pushed this metaphor to a new extreme, requiring Hal to re-win her hand daily and sometimes hourly. Even when she recognized his role as her guide and caregiver, she sometimes resented it. In the struggle to help Kathy make decisions and participate in essential activities, Hal kept foremost the goal of preserving their love. She made it easier by maintaining the calm, childlike demeanor that had characterized her life. Yet each day brought myriad moments when pushing a disagreement had the potential to create a serious, possibly permanent rift.

At these moments, Hal looked to a new movie hero, the humbly faithful chauffeur in *Driving Miss Daisy.* In that Academy Award–winning picture, the son of a wealthy widow hires a man to be her driver, after she crashes the car in an accident that might in other circumstances have been fatal to her and others. The widow, Miss Daisy, resents the driver, Hoke, as a symbol of her growing incapacity. Hoke responds to her suspicion and harsh treatment with pleasant long-suffering. Over the years they grow ever closer emotionally. But Miss Daisy's dementia-induced confinement to a nursing home separates them physically, except for occasional visits that Hoke makes at his own expense via taxi, having lost his own ability to drive.

In a closing scene of the movie, during one of Hoke's visits when she is unusually alert and coherent, Miss Daisy takes his hand and says, "Hoke, you're my best friend." Initially, Hoke protests. But then he consents, "Yes'm." As Hal worked with Kathy, especially in the stressful moments, he held that scene in mind as his goal.

ALWAYS FAITHFUL

Just as Kathy foreshadowed her own challenges when she preached, "We all will face difficulties for which we must prepare," Hal had given a talk that proved prophetic and motivational for him. In 1998, when Elizabeth graduated from Bountiful High School, he spoke at the school's nondenominational commencement service. He drew the title of his talk from a Latin phrase, "Semper Fidelis," the motto of the United States Marine Corps. In English, he explained, it translates "Always Faithful."

Hal gave that charge, to be always faithful in keeping promises, to the graduating high school students. He warned that it would not be easy in the most difficult moments, but that they could prepare along the way, in the "little things."

At some time and place, and perhaps more than once, the price you will be asked to pay to be faithful to your promises will be everything you have and are. That will come to you not because God is cruel nor far away, but because He has purposes for you.

But you don't need to be fearful, wondering how you will do in the test, if you just remember a single word: "Always." Always faithful. That word "always" sounds hard if you focus only on the supreme moments of testing. But the power to pass the great tests is built into the daily grind. If we are faithful in the little things—always, day in and day out—we will be faithful in the great things.

Hal cited marriage as one of the promises that would bring great tests, drawing upon the image of new brides and grooms. He saw such young couples daily from his office window, then on the second floor of the Church Administration Building, looking north and west toward the Salt Lake Temple.

Religions across the world and over time share a common understanding of what good people promise to do. One commitment is that we will do unto others as we would have them do to us. Whether we chose to rec-

HAL AND KATHY AFTER GENERAL CONFERENCE

ognize it or not, that is the promise we make whenever we form an association with others. We always hope it will be kept by them in return. But whether others recognize and keep their commitment or not, we have accepted the obligation to rise to that standard ourselves.

You can see easily how great tests will come from that commitment. Just think of what it will take to keep that commitment in marriage. From my office window I see brides and grooms every day having their pictures taken among beautiful flowers and shooting fountains. The groom often carries his bride in his arms, at least for a few staggering steps, while the photographer shoots wedding pictures. Every time I see that I think of couples I have known who, in time—sometimes in a very short time after the wedding day—had to carry each other in other ways when it was hard. Jobs can be lost. Children can be born with great challenges. Illness can come. And then habits of having done unto others as we would have them do unto us, when it was easier, will make us heroes and heroines, in those trying times when it takes more than we thought we had in us.

Hal left the young graduates with another foreign-language phrase, this one in Spanish: "Vaya con Dios." He had learned that phrase with Kathy as they prepared testimonies to give in their travels in Spanish-speaking countries. Though he couldn't match her near-perfect pronunciation of that phrase, a gift that impressed even native speakers, he appreciated its meaning: "Go with God."

Now, you can see that my farewell of, "Go with God," is more than a hope for a good trip. It is practical counsel. You can travel with Him as your companion if you know the rules of the road and follow them. Hard times will come on your journey. You will find yourself tested to be true to your promises, time and time again. Some tests will be easy. Some will be hard. Some will require that you sacrifice, or seem to sacrifice, all you have to keep your promises to others and to God. He will give you the power to be faithful in the great tests by giving you greater faith as you choose to be always faithful when the sacrifice is less. He has a greater purpose for you than smoothing your way. His purpose is to build your faith through allowing you the chance to test and prove it and in the process to know not only that He goes with you but that you are approved.

The Savior's disciples wondered about that testing to the point of sacrifice, when He was still with them before His death and Resurrection. He said in answer to Peter's question:

"And every one that hath forsaken houses, or brethren, or sisters or father, or mother, or wife, or children, or lands, for my name's sake, shall receive an hundredfold and shall inherit eternal life."[16]

My farewell tonight will come back to you someday if you can just remember three words of Spanish and two of Latin. My farewell to you as you go out the door is, "Go with God." Vaya con Dios. And my promise is that you can invite Him to go with you along the way. To do that you must only do a simple, everyday thing. Be faithful to your promises with others and with Him in all the small tests. Always faithful. The words in Latin: Semper fidelis. And then you will not go alone and I will not worry about you.[17]

Hal's testimony as he bade farewell to the graduates contained a promise that applies equally to us as we conclude our walk with him.

I give you my personal witness that God is perfectly faithful. He will be perfectly faithful to you. He is close and He is kind. He knows the road ahead. He knows us and our capacity. When He asks us to make promises, He provides a way to lift us up to the capacity to keep them. I leave you my blessing and my promise that you will have the power to be always faithful, that you will then go with God, and that you may know that your path is approved by Him.

Vaya con Dios, mis amigos.

ACKNOWLEDGMENTS

We express gratitude to the many contributors to this work. They include all of the individuals quoted, as well others who provided valuable insights and suggestions but are not named. We hope that all who shaped the contents of this book will see evidence of their contributions and take well-deserved satisfaction.

We particularly appreciate the labors of Rebecca and Elizabeth Eaton, who helped their father sift and organize source materials. Many of these materials were provided by the three secretaries who served President Eyring during the term of the project. Sheila Kartchner, who retired in 2012, worked with President Eyring for five years, having served Presidents Thomas S. Monson and James E. Faust as Second Counselors in the First Presidency for more than two decades. Sheila was succeeded by Jenny Pederson, who applied her great organizational skills to finding documents and historical treasures that had been presumed lost. Marcia Barrett, who has been President Eyring's secretarial taskmaster and the Eyring family's traffic controller for seventeen years, helped us carve out the time we needed to spend with him.

Special thanks go to Sheri Dew, who suggested that this book be written, and to Emily Watts, who made sure that it wasn't written too badly. Emily also orchestrated the Deseret Book team who created the wonderful visual layout and helped bring the book to life: Jana

Erickson, Sheryl Dickert Smith, Richard Erickson, Kayla Hackett, Elizabeth Alley, and Rachael Ward.

With deepest appreciation we thank Dianne Hansen Eaton and Kelly Child Eyring for their loving guidance and support.

NOTES

INTRODUCTION

1. "The Extra Dimension of Ricks College: A Conversation with President Henry B. Eyring," *Ensign*, April 1975, 25.
2. Henry B. Eyring, "The Perfect Gift," First Presidency Christmas Devotional, December 2, 2012.
3. Interview with Roger Sant, January 4, 2011.

CHAPTER 1: HONOR THY FATHER AND THY MOTHER

1. Mildred Bennion Eyring, *My Autobiography*, private publication in family's possession, 77.
2. Ibid.
3. *Mormon Scientist: The Amazing Story of the Life and Faith of Henry Eyring* (DVD, 2008), Special Features, President Eyring Interview.
4. As quoted in Gerald N. Lund, "Elder Henry B. Eyring: Molded by 'Defining Influences,'" *Ensign*, September 1995, 10.
5. *My Autobiography*, 36.
6. *My Autobiography*, 6.
7. Henry J. Eyring, *Mormon Scientist: The Life and Faith of Henry Eyring* (2007), 107.
8. *My Autobiography*, 18.
9. Ibid., 17.
10. Ibid., 67.
11. Ibid., 78–79.
12. Ibid., 78.

13. Ibid., 83.
14. *Mormon Scientist: The Amazing Story* (DVD), President Eyring Interview.
15. Henry B. Eyring, "Listen Together," BYU fireside, September 4, 1988.
16. *My Autobiography*, 10.
17. *My Autobiography*, 48.
18. Interview with Russell M. Nelson, December 11, 2012.
19. *My Autobiography*, 99–100.
20. Ibid., 79.
21. Ibid., among funeral transcripts.
22. *Mormon Scientist: The Amazing Story* (DVD), President Eyring Interview.
23. *My Autobiography*, 79.
24. Ibid., among letters.
25. Henry B. Eyring, "A Child of God," BYU devotional, October 21, 1997.
26. Ibid.
27. Ibid.
28. Henry B. Eyring, "Faith in Mother's Discipline," *The Instructor*, September 1970, 322–23.

CHAPTER 2: ASK GOD IF THESE THINGS ARE NOT TRUE

1. Steven Harvey Heath, "Henry Eyring, Mormon Scientist," master's thesis, Department of History, University of Utah, June 1980, 27–28.
2. Extracted from Henry J. Eyring, *Mormon Scientist: The Life and Faith of Henry Eyring* (2007), 296–98.
3. Ibid., 299.
4. Ibid., 303.
5. Henry B. Eyring, "Listen Together," BYU devotional, September 4, 1998.
6. Mildred Bennion Eyring, *My Autobiography*, 96.
7. Ibid., 96–97.
8. Letter included in *My Autobiography*, 5 (third section).
9. Henry B. Eyring, "An Enduring Testimony of the Mission of the Prophet Joseph Smith," *Ensign*, November 2003, 90.
10. Henry B. Eyring, "Come Unto Christ," BYU fireside, October 29, 1989.
11. Henry B. Eyring, Chesapeake Virginia Stake priesthood leadership meeting, January 25, 1997.
12. Henry B. Eyring, "Ears to Hear," *Ensign*, May 1985, 76.
13. Eyring, "Come Unto Christ," October 29, 1989.

14. Henry B. Eyring, "Waiting Upon the Lord," BYU fireside, September 30, 1990.

15. *My Autobiography*, 85.

16. Rebecca M. Taylor and Henry B. Eyring, "Friend to Friend," *Friend*, April 1997, 6.

17. *My Autobiography*, funeral remarks.

18. *My Autobiography*, 94.

19. Henry B. Eyring, "Child of Promise," BYU fireside, May 4, 1986.

20. Henry B. Eyring, "The True and Living Church," *Ensign*, May 2008, 23.

21. Henry B. Eyring, "Choose to Be Good," BYU devotional, November 12, 1991.

22. Letter from an East High School classmate, October 14, 1987.

CHAPTER 3: SEEK LEARNING

1. Interview with Richard G. Scott, April 13, 2011.

2. Mildred Bennion Eyring, *My Autobiography*, 92.

3. Henry B. Eyring, "Teaching Is a Moral Act," BYU Annual University Conference, August 27, 1991.

4. Ted Eyring, as quoted in Robert D. Hales, "President Henry B. Eyring: Called of God," *Ensign*, July 2008, 10.

5. Henry B. Eyring, "Gifts of Love," BYU devotional, December 9, 1980.

6. Gerald N. Lund, "Elder Henry B. Eyring: Molded by 'Defining Influences,'" *Ensign*, September 1995, 10.

7. Henry B. Eyring, notes for a devotional address delivered Tuesday, August 24, 1971.

8. Henry B. Eyring, untitled address, Ricks College, July 6, 1971.

9. Eyring, "Teaching Is a Moral Act," August 27, 1991.

10. Interview with Henry B. Eyring, May 24, 2011

11. *Mormon Scientist: The Amazing Story of the Life and Faith of Henry Eyring* (DVD), Special Features, President Eyring Interview.

12. "Raising Expectations," Church Educational System satellite broadcast, August 4, 2004.

13. Henry B. Eyring, "Learning in the Priesthood," *Ensign*, May 2011, 62.

14. "Welfare and Service: For All Times and All Seasons," lds.org/prophets -and-apostles/unto-all-the-world/welfare-and-service-for-all-times -and-all-places.

15. See Sheri L. Dew, *Go Forward with Faith: The Biography of Gordon B. Hinckley* (1996), 148.
16. Henry B. Eyring, "A Legacy of Testimony," *Ensign*, May 1996, 62.
17. Spencer W. Kimball, "Planning for a Full and Abundant Life," *Ensign*, May 1974, 86.

CHAPTER 4: LIFT UP YOUR HEART AND REJOICE

1. A district is the geographic equivalent of a stake, though with fewer members.
2. Henry B. Eyring, "Hearts Bound Together," *Ensign*, May 2005, 77.
3. Henry B. Eyring, "Watch Over and Strengthen," *Ensign*, May 2000, 66.
4. Henry B. Eyring, untitled address, new mission presidents seminar, June 24, 2010.
5. In those days the GMAT was called the Admission Test for Graduate Study in Business.
6. Harvard University, "Report of the President of Harvard College and report of departments," 1956–1957, 387.
7. Henry B. Eyring, "'Write Upon My Heart,'" *Ensign*, November 2000, 85.
8. Quoted in *Famous Lines: A Columbia Dictionary of Familiar Quotations*, Robert Andrews, ed. (1996).
9. Interview with George Montgomery, April 19, 2012.
10. Henry B. Eyring, "Education for Real Life," *Ensign*, October 2002, 20.
11. Henry B. Eyring to Stuart Eyring, undated letter sent in fall 1991.
12. Henry B. Eyring, BYU commencement, August 18, 1972.
13. http://www.nytimes.com/1987/06/03/obituaries/george-f-doriot-dies-at-87-molder-of-us-businessmen.html.
14. Harvard University, "Report of the President of Harvard College and report of departments," 1956–1957, 396.
15. Spencer W. Kimball, *The Teachings of Spencer W. Kimball*, ed. Edward L. Kimball (1982), 386.
16. Eyring, "Education for Real Life," 18–21.

CHAPTER 5: LOVE THY WIFE

1. Henry B. Eyring to Mildred Bennion Eyring, letter, October 6, 1955. In Mildred Bennion Eyring, *My Autobiography*, 5–6 (third section).
2. Henry B. Eyring, "The Family," BYU fireside, November 5, 1995.

3. Interview with Henry B. Eyring, May 24, 2011.

4. Clyde W. Lindsay, *Daddy Lindsay: A Man with a Vision*, private publication in family's possession (1954), 32.

5. Kathleen Johnson Eyring, personal notes in author's possession.

6. *The Life of J. Cyril Johnson*, private publication in family's possession (1982), 87.

7. Interview with Craig L. Johnson, April 8, 2011.

8. Kathleen Johnson Eyring to La Prele Johnson, letter, December 1992.

9. Kathleen Johnson Eyring, "Gratitude," talk given November 20, 2005.

10. Kathleen Johnson Eyring, Introduction to Ricks College devotional, September 7, 1976.

11. Henry B. Eyring, "'Write Upon My Heart,'" *Ensign*, November 2000, 86.

CHAPTER 6: BE FRUITFUL

1. There wasn't: the prize for Economic Sciences was created in 1968.

2. Henry B. Eyring, "To Choose and Keep a Mentor," BYU Annual University Conference, August 26, 1993.

3. Ibid.

4. Kathleen Johnson Eyring, remarks at La Prele Johnson's eightieth birthday party.

5. Interview with Roger Sant, January 4, 2011.

6. Interview with Ed Zschau, May 18, 2012.

7. Henry B. Eyring, "Education," Ricks College devotional, January 11, 1977.

8. C. Roland Christensen, David A. Garvin, and Ann Sweet, *Education for Judgment: The Artistry of Discussion Leadership* (1991), 117, 118.

9. Alfred Sloan was an innovative executive who built General Motors into the world's largest company and established the Sloan School of Management at MIT.

10. Douglas McGregor, *The Human Side of Enterprise* (2005), 65–66.

11. Warren Bennis, *On Becoming a Leader* (2009), 43.

12. Interview with Ed Zschau, May 18, 2012.

13. Henry B. Eyring, "To Know and to Love God," address to CES religious educators, February 26, 2010.

14. Henry B. Eyring, "Volunteerism in Hostile Times," University of Southern California baccalaureate address, May 9, 2002.

CHAPTER 7: FATHERS ARE TO PRESIDE

1. Mark 9:35.
2. Elder Henry D. Taylor was an Assistant to the Quorum of the Twelve Apostles at the time he ordained Hal a bishop; he later became a member of the First Quorum of the Seventy.
3. Henry B. Eyring to Henry J. Eyring, undated letter, circa 1983.
4. Oscar A. Kirkham was a General Authority and a beloved Scouting leader during Hal's boyhood.
5. Henry B. Eyring, "Help Them Aim High," *Ensign*, November 2012, 60.
6. Isaiah 40:31.
7. Henry B. Eyring, "Blessed Are the Peacemakers," BYU fireside, February 6, 1994.
8. Henry B. Eyring, "A Discussion on Scripture Study," *Ensign*, July 2005, 25.

CHAPTER 8: A BISHOP TO BE APPOINTED UNTO YOU

1. Interview with Scott Cameron, January 7, 2011.
2. Interview with Dale E. Miller, counselor in Stanford Ward bishopric, May 18, 2012.
3. Henry B. Eyring, "Conversations with a Bishop," *New Era*, June 1986, 49.
4. Journal, anonymous Stanford Ward member, October 5, 1970.
5. Henry B. Eyring, "Rise to Your Call," *Ensign*, November 2002, 76.
6. Henry B. Eyring, "Feed My Lambs," *Ensign*, November 1997, 82.
7. Skyline Boulevard is California State Road 35, which climbs the Coast Ranges and at its summit offers simultaneous views of the Pacific Ocean and San Francisco Bay.
8. Henry B. Eyring, "Come Unto Christ," BYU fireside, October 29, 1989.
9. Ibid.
10. Notes for talk delivered April 11, 1971; from the 1971 journal.
11. Eyring, "Rise to Your Call," 76.
12. From transcript of audio recording in author's possession.
13. Interview with Bob Todd, counselor in Stanford Ward bishopric, June 15, 2012.
14. From transcript of audio recording in author's possession.
15. Bishop Miller, Hal's former bishopric counselor, had been called to preside over this new single student ward.
16. Eyring, "Rise to Your Call," 77.

CHAPTER 9: COME, FOLLOW ME

1. Journal, December 19, 1970.
2. Henry B. Eyring, "Where Is the Pavilion?" *Ensign*, November 2012, 72.
3. Henry B. Eyring, "Faith and Keys," *Ensign*, November 2004, 28.
4. Journal, January 8, 1971.
5. Henry B. Eyring to Kathleen Johnson Eyring, letter from Scanticon, Aarhus, Denmark, August 24, 1970.
6. Aarhus is a city on the sea in Denmark.
7. Kathleen Johnson Eyring to Henry B. Eyring, letter from Atherton, California, August 26, 1970.
8. Interview with Roger Sant, January 4, 2011.
9. Interview with Henry B. Eyring, August 17, 2012.
10. Journal, February 2, 1971.

CHAPTER 10: A SCHOOL IN ZION

1. Interview with Henry B. Eyring, May 24, 2011.
2. Psalm 40:1–3.
3. "News of the Church," *New Era*, May 1971, 7.
4. Henry B. Eyring, "Education for Real Life," *Ensign*, October 2002, 14.
5. This building was later named for John L. Clarke.
6. Journal, June 17, 1971.
7. Henry B. Eyring, "Waiting upon the Lord," BYU devotional, September 30, 1990.
8. Notes for devotional address, dated Monday, July 5, 1971.
9. Henry B. Eyring, untitled address, Ricks College devotional, July 5, 1971.
10. Ibid.
11. Ibid.
12. See John 14:26, 16:13.
13. Eyring, untitled address, July 5, 1971.
14. Notes for devotional address delivered Tuesday, August 24, 1971.
15. Eyring, untitled address, July 5, 1971. From transcript included in 1971 Journal.
16. Journal, August 16, 1971.
17. Outline for remarks made to student orientation leaders, August 14, 1971.
18. Journal, Wednesday, August 18, 1971.

CHAPTER 11: PREPARE YE, PREPARE YE

1. Interview with Robert Todd, January 7, 2011.

2. Journal, October 22, 1971.

3. Henry B. Eyring, "A Charted Course," BYU Annual University Conference, August 26, 1996.

4. Henry B. Eyring, "Waiting Upon the Lord," BYU fireside, September 30, 1990.

5. Ibid.

6. Report of the Select Committee on Higher Education in the Church Education System, 2.

7. Ibid., 3.

8. Ibid., 4–5.

9. Ibid., 13–14, 16.

10. Interview with Dallin H. Oaks, July 21, 2012.

11. Charge to the Study Definition Committee for the Role of Ricks College in the Church Education System, November 22, 1971.

12. Stanford administrator Frank Newman was asked by U.S. Secretary of Health, Education, and Welfare Robert Finch to chair a national task force on higher education. Newman's task force published its findings in early 1971.

13. James 1:22.

14. Jacob Spori, founding principal of the elementary school Bannock Academy, which became Ricks College, predicted in 1888, "The seeds we are planting today will grow and become mighty oaks, and their branches will run all over the earth."

15. Journal, October 1, 1971.

16. Interview with Keith Sellars, December 27, 2010.

17. Henry B. Eyring, "Gifts of Love," BYU devotional, December 16, 1980.

18. Interview with Keith Sellars, December 27, 2010.

19. Henry B. Eyring, "To Know and to Love God," address to CES religious educators, February 26, 2010.

20. Interview with Henry B. Eyring, June 29, 2010.

21. Interview with Mack Shirley, December 6, 2010.

22. Journal, August 23, 1972.

23. Henry B. Eyring, "Letter from the President," *Viking Scroll*, April 17, 1973.

24. Journal, April 18, 1973.

CHAPTER 12: ORGANIZE YOURSELVES

1. Charge to the Study Definition Committee for the Role of Ricks College in the Church Education System, November 22, 1971.
2. Journal, January 10, 1974.
3. Interview with Richard G. Scott, December 11, 2012.
4. Joe J. Christensen was the Associate Commissioner responsible for seminaries and institutes; in 1985, he would become president of Ricks College.
5. Journal, August 12, 1972.
6. Journal, August 22, 1975.
7. *MIA* stands for Mutual Improvement Association, the forerunner of the Young Men and Young Women organizations of the Church.
8. Journal, March 30, 1977.
9. Dr. Lester Peterson was born on May 31, 1932, making him exactly one year older than Hal.

CHAPTER 13: FOLLOW THE BRETHREN

1. Boyd K. Packer, "Follow the Brethren," BYU devotional, March 23, 1965.
2. Henry B. Eyring, "The Charted Course," BYU Annual University Conference, August 26, 1996.
3. Ibid.
4. "News of the Church," *Ensign*, May 1977, 119.
5. Journal, June 6, 1972.
6. The Hyrum Manwaring Student Center, home to the college's cafeterias, bookstore, and ballrooms, is named for former Ricks College President Hyrum C. Manwaring.
7. J. Reuben Clark Jr., in Conference Report, April 1937, 26; quoted in Ezra Taft Benson, "Prepare Ye," *Ensign*, January 1974, 69.
8. Benson, "Prepare Ye," 69.
9. *M-Man* was the name given to single male Church members between the ages of 18 and 30 at the time.
10. Interview with Greg Palmer, April 19, 2012.
11. Journal, May 31, 1975.
12. Journal, June 8, 1975.

CHAPTER 14: LET THEM STAY

1. Henry B. Eyring, "Learning to Hear the Lord's Voice," talk given at Logan Institute of Religion, January 19, 1992; in Henry B. Eyring, *To Draw Closer to God: A Collection of Discourses* (1997), 28–29.
2. Journal, December 27, 1973.
3. Interview with Dallin H. Oaks, July 21, 2012.
4. Kathleen Johnson Eyring, Introduction to Ricks College devotional, September 7, 1976.
5. Journal, June 5, 1976.
6. *The Spirit of Ricks: A History of Ricks College* (1997), 324–25.
7. Interview with Robert E. Wells, January 1, 2013.
8. This discussion of disaster relief efforts draws heavily from, and with appreciation for, Bruce D. Blumell, "The LDS Response to the Teton Dam Disaster in Idaho," *Sunstone*, March-April 1980, 35–42.
9. Allan Clark was Ricks's budget officer.
10. Wilson Walker was a member of the Ricks College psychology faculty.
11. Gary Ball, a farmer whose farm and home were not affected by the flood, lived in Hal's ward.
12. Henry B. Eyring, "Always Faithful," Bountiful High School commencement, May 24, 1998.
13. Interview with Henry B. Eyring, May 24, 2011.

CHAPTER 15: PREPARE THE WAY

1. Journal, June 14, 1978.
2. See "News of the Church," *Ensign*, October 1977, 84.
3. Ibid., 85.
4. Henry B. Eyring, "Rise to Your Call," *Ensign*, November 2002, 76.
5. Interview with Jeffrey R. Holland, January 6, 2011.
6. Henry B. Eyring, "That We May Be One," *Ensign*, May 1998, 66.
7. Journal, April 12, 1979.
8. Interview with Stan Peterson, January 7, 2011.
9. The Executive Committee is a subgroup of the Church's Board of Education, comprising several members of the Quorum of the Twelve and other general Church officers but not any members of the First Presidency, all of whom sit on the Board.
10. Journal, November 11, 1977.

11. Henry B. Eyring, "A Priesthood Quorum," Ensign, November 2006, 44.

12. Journal, February 10, 1980, and July 23, 1982.

13. Mosiah 3:19 reads: "For the natural man is an enemy to God, and has been from the fall of Adam, and will be, forever and ever, unless he yields to the enticings of the Holy Spirit, and putteth off the natural man and becometh a saint through the atonement of Christ the Lord, and becometh as a child, submissive, meek, humble, patient, full of love, willing to submit to all things which the Lord seeth fit to inflict upon him, even as a child doth submit to his father."

CHAPTER 16: HEARKEN UNTO THE LORD'S SERVANT

1. Henry B. Eyring, untitled address, Area Directors Convention, April 6, 1981.

2. Henry B. Eyring, "Ears to Hear," Ensign, May 1985, 77.

3. The position of regional representative was a forerunner to Area Seventy.

4. Journal, August 31, 1978.

5. Henry B. Eyring, "Our Hearts Knit as One," Ensign, November 2008, 68.

6. Henry B. Eyring, "Faith of Our Fathers," BYU Campus Education Week, August 20, 1996.

CHAPTER 17: INCREASE LEARNING

1. Bruce R. McConkie, "Come: Let Israel Build Zion," Ensign, May 1977, 117, 118.

2. Henry B. Eyring, "A Steady, Upward Course," BYU–Idaho devotional, September 18, 2001.

3. Elders Charles A. Didier and James M. Paramore were members of the First Quorum of Seventy and, at the time, members of the Church's Audio Visual Committee. Elder M. Russell Ballard, of the Presidency of the Seventy, chaired the committee.

4. Henry B. Eyring, "Go Forth to Serve," BYU commencement, April 23, 1998.

CHAPTER 18: LABOR DILIGENTLY

1. Henry B. Eyring, "Going Home," BYU devotional, November 18, 1986.

2. Lowell Bennion, a distant cousin of Mildred, was director of the Salt Lake Institute, adjacent to the University of Utah.

3. Victor L. Brown served as Presiding Bishop of the Church from 1972 to 1985.

4. Neal A. Maxwell was at this time a member of the Quorum of the Twelve Apostles.

5. Gamaliel was a respected Pharisee who taught Paul and spoke eloquently in defense of Peter and John (see Acts 5:34).

6. See Henry B. Eyring, "Excellence in Education," in *Excellence* (1984), 19–25.

7. Seniors taking physics courses at Bountiful High School were required to build balsa-wood bridges to be stress tested in a classroom competition.

CHAPTER 19: THE BISHOP AND HIS COUNSELORS

1. Robert D. Hales, "The Mantle of a Bishop," *Ensign*, May 1985, 30.

2. Interview with Henry B. Eyring, November 26, 2012.

3. Journal entry of Kathleen Johnson Eyring, May 10, 1985.

4. Interview with Glenn L. Pace, January 7, 2011.

5. Interview with H. David Burton, November 23, 2010.

6. Interview with Robert D. Hales, November 23, 2010.

7. Matthew 5:25.

8. Interview with Robert D. Hales, November 23, 2010.

9. Interview with Henry B. Eyring, January 27, 2012.

10. Interview with Henry B. Eyring, January 27, 2012.

11. Elder William Grant Bangerter was a member of the Seventy and the father of future Relief Society General President Julie B. Beck.

12. Elder McConkie passed away two days later.

13. Henry B. Eyring, "The Temple and the College on the Hill," BYU–Idaho devotional, June 9, 2009.

CHAPTER 20: LET HIM HEAR

1. Interview with Robert D. Hales, November 23, 2010. Elder Hales's reference is to 1 Samuel 3:9.

2. Henry B. Eyring, "A Child of God," BYU devotional, October 21, 1997.

3. Interview with Richard G. Scott, April 13, 2011.

4. Elder Dean Larsen was a member of the Seventy.

5. Henry B. Eyring, "Teaching is a Moral Act," BYU Annual University Conference, August 27, 1991.

6. The Appropriations Committee of the Church approves all expenditures of tithing funds and includes, among others, the First Presidency and the Presiding Bishopric.

7. Marvin J. Ashton was at this time a senior member of the Quorum of the Twelve.

8. Elder Theodore Tuttle, of the Seventy, did pass away eight weeks later.

9. Elder F. Burton Howard was a member of the Seventy.

10. Henry B. Eyring, "Because of Your Steadiness," *Ensign,* May 1988, 39.

11. Henry B. Eyring, Mother's Day sacrament meeting talk, Bountiful 48th Ward, May 8, 1994.

12. At this point, Kathy read Joseph Smith History 1:15–16.

13. Here Kathy read Alma 22:17.

14. Kathleen Johnson Eyring, untitled sacrament meeting talk, Bountiful 48th Ward, July 17, 1988.

CHAPTER 21: A HOUSE OF FAITH, A HOUSE OF LEARNING

1. "News of the Church," *Ensign,* November 1991, 106.

2. Boyd K. Packer, "'To Be Learned Is Good If . . . ,'" *Ensign,* November 1992, 72–73.

3. Gordon B. Hinckley, "Trust and Accountability," BYU devotional, October 13, 1992.

4. Henry J. Eyring, *Mormon Scientist: The Life and Faith of Henry Eyring* (2007), 125, 173.

5. Henry B. Eyring, "Teaching Is a Moral Act," BYU Annual University Conference, August 27, 1991.

6. Interview with Alan L. Wilkins, November 2, 2012.

7. Ibid.

8. Henry B. Eyring, "A Charted Course," BYU Annual University Conference, August 26, 1996.

9. Interview with James D. Gordon, July 19, 2012.

10. Larry Lyon, Michael Beaty, and Stephanie Litizzette Mixon, "Making Sense of a 'Religious' University: Faculty Adaptations and Opinions at Brigham Young, Baylor, Notre Dame, and Boston College," *Review of Religious Research* 43, no. 4 (2002): 339, 344.

11. Henry B. Eyring, "A Consecrated Place," BYU Annual University Conference, August 27, 2001.

12. Ibid.

13. Doctrine and Covenants 112:4.

14. Henry B. Eyring, "'Always Remember Him,'" *Ensign,* May 1995, 25.

15. Universities typically distinguish faculty members as assistant professors, associate professors, and full professors.

16. Henry B. Eyring, "A Steady, Upward Course, BYU–Idaho devotional, September 18, 2001.

17. Ibid.

18. Ibid.

19. Keith F. Patterson, BYU–Idaho devotional, March 10, 2009.

CHAPTER 22: FEED MY SHEEP

1. Interview with Neil L. Andersen, December 11, 2012.

2. Ordination and setting apart of Elder Henry B. Eyring by President Gordon B. Hinckley, April 6, 1995.

3. Interview with Russell M. Nelson, December 11, 2012.

4. See Journal, March 17, 1990.

5. Interview with L. Tom Perry, December 11, 2012.

6. Interview with Neil L. Andersen, December 11, 2012.

7. Interview with David A. Bednar, April 13, 2011.

8. Ibid.

9. Henry B. Eyring, "Helping a Student in a Moment of Doubt," address to CES religious educators, February 5, 1993, citing Gordon B. Hinckley, "What Shall You Teach?" address to BYU faculty and staff, September 17, 1963, 5.

10. Interview with D. Todd Christofferson, December 11, 2012.

11. Henry B. Eyring, "The Power of Teaching Doctrine," *Ensign,* May 1999, 74.

12. Henry B. Eyring, "To Know and to Love God," address to CES religious educators, February 26, 2010.

13. Interview with Quentin L. Cook, December 12, 2012.

14. Henry B. Eyring, "A Child of God," BYU devotional, October 21, 1997.

15. Henry B. Eyring, "Come unto Christ," BYU fireside, October 29, 1989.

16. Henry B. Eyring, "Remembrance and Gratitude," *Ensign,* November 1989, 43.

17. Interview with Richard G. Scott, April 13, 2011.

18. Interview with M. Russell Ballard, December 12, 2012.

19. Interview with Dallin H. Oaks, July 19, 2012.

20. Interview with David A. Bednar, April 13, 2011.

21. Interview with Dieter F. Uchtdorf, December 11, 2012.

CHAPTER 23: STAND BY MY SERVANT

1. Henry B. Eyring, "Blessed Are the Peacemakers," Church Educational System Fireside, February 6, 1994.

2. "God Helps the Faithful Priesthood Holder," *Ensign*, November 2007, 55.

3. Ibid., 56.

4. The Public Broadcasting System is a nationwide network of not-for-profit television stations in the United States.

5. James E. Faust, Ricks College devotional, March 26, 1974.

6. "Faith and Keys," *Ensign*, November 2004, 27.

7. Henry B. Eyring, "You Are Never Alone in the Work," Seminar for new mission presidents, June 24, 2010.

8. *In Memoriam: President Gordon B. Hinckley, 1910–2001, A Supplement to the Ensign*, 26.

9. Ibid., 27.

10. Journal of President Thomas S. Monson, Sunday, February 3, 2008.

11. Gordon B. Hinckley, "Standing Strong and Immovable," Worldwide Leadership Training Meeting, January 10, 2004.

12. Leeds is a pioneer-founded community just north of St. George, on the road to Salt Lake City.

13. Henry B. Eyring, untitled talk delivered at Leeds, Utah, May 24, 2008.

14. Interview with Dieter F. Uchtdorf, December 11, 2012.

15. Ibid.

16. Journal of President Thomas S. Monson, April 6, 2008.

CHAPTER 24: CLEAVE UNTO HER

1. Kathleen J. Eyring to Henry J. Eyring, January 2, 1983.

2. Kathleen J. Eyring to John Eyring, Christmas 1991.

3. Kathleen J. Eyring to John Eyring, no date, circa 1990.

4. "Family Journal: The Small Plates," Wednesday, January 3, 2007.

5. "JCJ" are Sid's initials (Joseph Cyril Johnson).

6. Kathleen Johnson Eyring, tribute at La Prele Johnson's eightieth birthday celebration.

7. Mosiah 7:33 reads, "But if ye will turn to the Lord with full purpose of heart, and put your trust in him, and serve him with all diligence of mind, if ye do this, he will, according to his own will and pleasure, deliver you out of bondage."

8. Kathleen Johnson Eyring, "The Pursuit of Excellence Program," address to ward Relief Society sisters, circa 1990.

9. Kathleen Johnson Eyring, from an untitled talk.

10. Kathleen Johnson Eyring, untitled address to Bountiful High School seminary students, circa 1990.

11. Kathleen Johnson Eyring, untitled address given on Central and South American tour, circa 1996.

12. Kathleen Johnson Eyring, untitled talk given at Mueller Park Stake visiting teaching convention, January 22, 1987.

13. Ibid.

14. Kathleen Johnson Eyring, undated talk, circa 1992.

15. Henry J. Eyring, Journal, April 6, 2013.

16. Matthew 19:29.

17. Henry J. Eyring, "Always Faithful," Bountiful High School commencement, May 24, 1998.

INDEX